CAMBRIDGE STUDIES IN RUSSIAN LITERATURE

Marina Tsvetaeva

The Woman, her World and her Poetry

D1596513

CAMBRIDGE STUDIES IN RUSSIAN LITERATURE

General editor MALCOLM JONES

Marina Tsvetaeva

The Woman, her World and her Poetry

SIMON KARLINSKY

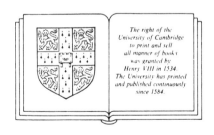

The right of the
University of Cambridge
to print and sell
all manner of books
was granted by
Henry VIII in 1534.
The University has printed
and published continuously
since 1584.

CAMBRIDGE UNIVERSITY PRESS

CAMBRIDGE

NEW YORK   NEW ROCHELLE

MELBOURNE   SYDNEY

Published by the Press Syndicate of the University of Cambridge
The Pitt Building, Trumpington Street, Cambridge CB2 1RP
32 East 57th Street, New York, NY 10022, USA
10 Stamford Road, Oakleigh, Melbourne 3166, Australia

First published 1986
Reprinted 1987, 1988

Printed by The Athenæum Press Ltd.,
Newcastle upon Tyne

British Library cataloguing in publication data
Karlinsky, Simon
Marina Tsvetaeva: the woman, her world and her poetry.
(Cambridge studies in Russian literature) 1. Tsvetaeva,
Marina — Biography 2. Poets, Russian — 20th century — Biography
I. Title
891.71′3 PG3476.T75z/

Library of Congress cataloguing in publication data
Marina Tsvetaeva: the woman, her world, and her poetry.
(Cambridge studies in Russian literature)
Bibliography: p
Includes index.
1. Tsvetaeva, Marina, 1892-1941. 2. Poets, Russian —
20th century — Biography. I. Title. II. Series.
PG3476.T75z743   1986   891.71′42 [B]   85-11309

ISBN 0 521 25582 1 hard cover
ISBN 0 521 27574 1 paperback

CE

Contents

Foreword

As a belated graduate student, after getting an M.A. in 1961, I decided I wanted to do a doctoral thesis on Marina Tsvetaeva. I had admired her verse and prose for a number of years. Since so little was known about her then, I thought it a good idea to investigate her biography and to establish the corpus of her writings. Few Slavicists in America would have agreed at that time that Tsvetaeva's poetry was worth a dissertation. Professor Gleb Struve of the University of California, Berkeley, was one of those few. With his encouragement and under his kind and patient direction, I completed the dissertation in 1964. A book based on it and bearing the same title, *Marina Tsvetaeva. Her Life and Art*, was published by the University of California Press in September 1966.

I had found so much information on Tsvetaeva, so many little pieces of fact that needed to be recorded, that I may have overdone comprehensiveness a bit and turned the results into something like a bouillabaisse. There was a biography, necessarily sketchy in some areas; a study of the poet's language and versification; a survey of all the genres that she practiced; and a great deal of annotations that recorded everything written about Tsvetaeva that I could find. My aim was to assert her reputation, record her circumstances and lay up the supplies for those who would study her after me.

Now, twenty years later, I have written a second, very different book about Marina Tsvetaeva. There is no need to assert Tsvetaeva's reputation today: she is an internationally famous poet, with figures of the stature of John Bayley, Susan Sontag and Joseph Brodsky writing about her in *The Times Literary Supplement* and *The New York Review of Books*. Her language and versification have been studied with great subtlety by G. S. Smith, Robin Kemball, Günther Wytrzens and a slew of linguists in the Soviet Union. Tsvetaeva's verse has been translated brilliantly into French by the late Eve Malleret; into English by Elaine Feinstein, Robin Kemball and Joseph Brodsky; her prose and verse into Italian by

Serena Vitale (who accompanies her translations by some of the most wonderful essays about Tsvetaeva ever written) and Pietro Zveteremich; into German by Ilma Rakusa, Felix Philipp Ingold and Marie-Luise Bott. In addition to these able scholars and poets, Tsvetaeva's recent reputation has also drawn to her a few translators into English and German who do not understand her elliptical style, miss her use of idioms and have nevertheless published their renditions of her prose and verse, often to considerable critical acclaim.

But fortunately the good outnumbers the bad. There have been imaginative studies of Tsvetaeva in Polish by Jerzy Faryno and Zbigniew Maciejewski. In the English-speaking countries, there are the doctoral dissertations of Ieva Vitins, Margaret Troupin Babby, Olga Peters Hasty and Michael Makin. There is also a detailed biography by Maria Razumovsky in German and in Russian and the as yet unpublished one by Irma Kudrova, which, judging from the one chapter I've seen and the overall quality of this critic's work, is sure to be superb. Lily Feiler is preparing a psycho-biography of Tsvetaeva, chapters of which I have cited in my book. All this and more has happened since my 1966 book.

The present study is not addressed primarily to a scholarly audience. My task this time round, therefore, was simply to introduce Tsvetaeva, rather than to amass every fact about her that can be found or to do an in-depth study of her poetry. I wanted to tell the story of her life, with the inclusion of all the factual materials that have come to light in the past twenty years, to place this life in its historical context, and to give an overview of her *œuvre* and of the criticism about it.

Many aspects of Tsvetaeva's biography were inaccessible or unknown when I was writing my dissertation in 1962–4. There were no bibliographies, no collections of critical articles, no minimally complete editions of her poetry. What she did and wrote in 1914–16 (the collection *Juvenilia*, the long poem 'The Enchanter' and the relationship with Sophia Parnok) was shrouded in a mist. The correspondence with Rilke and Pasternak was not available. The period after Tsvetaeva's return to the Soviet Union in 1939 was a near-total blank. These and many other lacunae have now been filled through publications that have appeared in the last two decades.

Marina Tsvetaeva often said that she did not belong in her time.

In her poem 'Homesickness' ('Toska po rodine'), she asserted that
while her fellow man may belong in the twentieth century, she
herself came from a time before there were centuries. And yet, it
would be hard to think of any other poet whose life was so
constantly affected by historical events. She was born during the
famine of 1892, which is the key to much in subsequent Russian
history. Tsvetaeva's views and sensibility were shaped by the revolutions of 1905 and 1917 and her art grew out of the creative ferment
of the period between those revolutions.

The October Revolution and the ensuing civil war are a major
theme in Tsvetaeva's life and her poetry. With a million other
Russians, she experienced the post-revolutionary exile in the 1920s.
She was repeatedly caught in the battles between various factions of
the emigration. She returned to the Soviet Union in the wake of the
Great Terror and she died, at the age of forty-eight, during World
War II. All these developments need to be understood if one is to
explain Marina Tsvetaeva's fate. I have made a particular effort to
outline in detail the historical and cultural background of her life
and writings. This is an area in which my 1966 book was particularly
deficient because at that time I myself did not know enough about
the February and October revolutions and the composition of the
post-revolutionary emigration. I am aware that some of the historical issues I felt compelled to emphasize (viz., the democratic
nature of the revolutions of 1905 and February 1917, as opposed to
the totalitarian October Revolution, or my insistence that the
Russian emigration of the 1920s and 30s was mostly liberal, rather
than monarchist or pro-fascist) are extremely unpopular with some
Western readers today. From past experience I know that making
such points can elicit disbelief or anger from critics. But this is what
decades of close study of the periods in question have shown me.
Everything about Marina Tsvetaeva's experiences further confirms
these conclusions.

This book could not have been written without the research and
publications of the scholars whose work is enumerated in the
Appendix on Sources at the end. I met many of them at the
memorable Tsvetaeva Symposium, organized by Robin Kemball
and held in Lausanne in the summer of 1982, and have admired the
depth of their dedication to Tsvetaeva. Those who helped me by
supplying unpublished materials or copies of their own publications
are thanked individually when the sources for each chapter are

listed. Serena Vitale and Viktoria Schweitzer have been especially kind in this respect and deserve additional gratitude. Closer to home, I want to thank Peter Carleton for help with editing and my colleague and neighbour Olga Raevsky Hughes for sharing her research with me. Robert P. Hughes, Hugh McLean and G. S. Smith read various portions of the manuscript and offered valuable suggestions.

Back in 1926, when Tsvetaeva was alive and at the peak of her genius, Dmitry Sviatopolk-Mirsky wrote that a book about her was needed and this book ought to be written with pride and rejoicing. Contemplating her fate four decades after her death, however, is likely to arouse humility and sadness. But if we consider her ultimate triumph, her 'victory over time and gravity,' as she once put it, we can indeed feel pride for her and rejoicing for all those who can now partake of the living waters of her imperishable poetry.

SIMON KARLINSKY

Fall of 1984

1

The house on Three Pond Lane

In the village of Talitsy near the city of Shuya in Vladimir Province of Central Russia, there lived in the middle of the nineteenth century a poor village priest named Vladimir Tsvetaev. The name Tsvetaev is derived from an odd imperative form of a verb which means 'to blossom' and it seems to have occurred only among hereditary provincial clergy. Marina Tsvetaeva once described her father's side of the family as an 'uninterrupted and uninterruptible clan: a primeval one,' and half-seriously suggested that its origins might be traced to the legendary epic hero Ilya of Murom, supposedly a native of the region around Vladimir.

Father Vladimir was one of those impoverished village clerics whose mode of life differed little from that of the surrounding peasantry to whose spiritual needs he ministered. He plowed his own land, threshed grain, and mowed hay until the end of his days. He enjoyed great esteem among his parishioners and his moral authority and prestige were so great that his advice was often sought by the city folk from the neighbouring towns. Not much is known of Father Vladimir's wife Ekaterina, who bore him four sons and who died when she was thirty-five. But we do have a handsome tribute in verse to her endurance and stamina, written by a granddaughter she never saw:

> My first grandmother had four sons.
> She had four sons, one wooden candle,
> A sheepskin blanket, a bag of hemp.
> She had four sons and her own two hands.

(The wooden candle, *luchina*, a splinter of wood dipped in slow-burning oil, was the cheapest form of indoor lighting in peasant huts, familiar from its evocations in Pushkin and other poets.)

The economic conditions under which Vladimir and Ekaterina Tsvetaev had to raise their sons can be further illustrated by the recollection of one of them, the poet's father, that he never had

I

shoes of his own until the age of twelve. If Marina Tsvetaeva valued Nikolai Leskov's novel *Cathedral Folk* (1874) higher than any of the acclaimed masterpieces by Tolstoy or Dostoevsky, it may well have been because she saw a parallel between that novel's protagonists, a provincial village priest and his wife, and her paternal grand-parents.

Of the four Tsvetaev sons, the eldest, Piotr, followed in his father's footsteps and inherited his parish in Talitsy. The other three became educators. Feodor, the third son, was a provincial school administrator, while the youngest one, Dmitry (1852–1920), was a professor of history. He taught at the University of Warsaw and was known for his reactionary politics and his anti-Semitism. Tsvetaeva's memoir about Andrei Bely, 'A Captive Spirit,' con-tains a dipped-in-acid portrait of her uncle Dmitry's wife, Elizaveta.

The second Tsvetaev brother, Ivan Vladimirovich (1847–1913), became passionately interested in Latin and in classical philology while attending the divinity school in Shuya. He eventually found his way to the University of St Petersburg, where he became the protégé of the famed philologist and ethnographer Izmail Srez-nevsky, under whose direction he specialized in the study of ancient Italic dialects. For his dissertation on the language of the Oscans, a pre-Roman Italic nationality, Ivan Tsvetaev made an extensive sojourn in Italy, which inspired him to branch out into his other field of study, ancient sculpture.

From 1877 on, Ivan Tsvetaev settled in Moscow, where he was appointed at the university, first as Professor of Roman Literature and later to the chair of the theory and history of the arts. At Moscow University he became close friends with the well-known and ultra-conservative historian Dmitry Ilovaisky (1832–1920), the author, among other works, of the history primer for children used in most Russian schools at the end of the nineteenth century. Ilovaisky's beautiful daughter Varvara (1858–1890) was a gifted singer who had studied voice in Italy. When she returned to Moscow, she formed a romantic attachment her family judged unsuitable.

Accordingly, her father resolved to marry Varvara to his collea-gue Professor Tsvetaev, an arrangement to which she consented even though she could not reciprocate her husband's love and went on loving the man she was forced to give up. In 1882 a daughter, Valeria, was born and in 1890 Varvara Tsvetaeva died while giving

birth to her son Andrei. One year after her death, Ivan Vladimirovich married her friend, the twenty-one year old Maria Alexandrovna Meyn (1868–1906), the half-Polish daughter of a wealthy
Baltic German businessman and publisher.

On her father's side of the family, apart from her grandmother
Ekaterina, Marina Tsvetaeva could trace her descent only through
the men. But on her mother's side, it was the matrilineal succession
that fascinated her. Her maternal grandmother was a Polish
noblewoman, Maria Bernacka, and *her* mother was Countess Maria
Leduchowska. The poet was thus descended, on her mother's side,
from three generations of Marias, all of whom were Polish and
aristocratic and all of whom died before the age of forty. This
circumstance gave rise, in her poetry, to the myth of her Polish
roots, 'Polish pride,' and a possible personal connection with one of
her favourite historical personages, Marina Mnishek (Maryna
Mniszchówna, ca. 1587–1614), whom most people remember from
either Pushkin's or Musorgsky's *Boris Godunov*.

The second marriage of Professor Tsvetaev followed the pattern
of his first one in an uncanny manner. Again the bride was a
musician – this time a pianist who, after one single concert appearance was not allowed by her father to play in public. Again the bride
was in love with another man. The man she loved was married and,
although divorce was possible, her father considered it a sin. 'When
my grandfather Alexander Meyn made her choose between the
loved one and himself,' wrote Tsvetaeva, who had access to some of
her mother's earlier diaries, 'she chose her father, and afterwards,
she chose what was the most difficult: a widower with two children,
still in love with his late wife.' Maria Meyn's own rationale for
accepting Ivan Tsvetaev's proposal was that she was a friend of his
first wife and that their children needed a mother.

This turned out to be a miscalculation. Her stepdaughter Valeria
never did forgive her father's second wife for what she saw as
usurpation of her mother's position and for becoming the mistress
of the Tsvetaev family home at Three Pond Lane (*Trekhprudnyi
pereulok*), No. 8. The house, which was a part of Varvara Ilovaiskaya's dowry, was technically the property not of Professor
Tsvetaev, but of Varvara's children, Valeria and Andrei. This was
where Marina Tsvetaeva was born on September 26 (or, according
to the Gregorian calendar now in use, October 9), 1892. Till the end
of her life, she continued to prefer the old Julian calendar, which

was in use in Russia when she came into the world. Two years later, in 1894, came the birth of her younger sister Anastasia, usually called Asya and still alive as these lines are being written.

The year Marina Tsvetaeva was born, 1892, was a fateful year in the history of Russia. Because of the disastrous crop failure in the previous year, there was a widespread famine in the provinces adjacent to the Volga. Though not as calamitous as the famine in the reign of Boris Godunov in 1601–3, and not to be compared to the starvation in the post-revolutionary period or during the collectivization of the early 1930s, it was the worst such instance within the memory of the people at the time. It shook Russian society from the stagnation and apathy that had come to typify it at the end of the 1880s.

The wide-ranging and by and large effective famine-relief work, in which a number of notable personalities took part, served notice of the extent to which the intelligentsia could engage in meaningful social action independently of the tsar's government. Vladimir Korolenko, the most politically engaged writer of the time, participated in famine fighting and published a book about it. Anton Chekhov dropped all literary activity and plunged into an organized campaign to prevent the farmers from slaughtering their horses for food, which would leave no draft power for next spring's plowing. When the famine was followed the next summer by a cholera epidemic, Chekhov volunteered his services as a medical inspector.

Leo Tolstoy, who no longer considered himself a writer at this time, but rather a leader of a religious sect, and his followers, the Tolstoyans, organized a string of soup kitchens and collected money for the famine victims. In February 1892, a young law student Sergei Diaghilev and his cousin Dmitry Filosofov (with whom in a few years Diaghilev would start the epochal journal *The World of Art*) came to Tolstoy's house in Moscow to offer their donation and to discuss ethical and moral problems. In a somewhat different vein, the young revolutionary Vladimir Ulianov, who as Lenin would become the founder of the Soviet system, launched a campaign to discredit and to sabotage the work of the famine-relief organizations, because his view was that the more peasants starved to death, the greater the likelihood of a revolution.

According to the historian Nicholas V. Riasanovsky, the shock of the 1892 famine was what led to the formation of the opposition political parties which were to bring about the revolutions of 1905 and 1917 (and were also to be important in Marina Tsvetaeva's personal and literary life): the liberal, middle-of-the-road Constitutional Democrats; the Socialist Revolutionaries, who continued the earlier populist tradition of Russian radicalism; and the Marxist party of Social Democrats, one of whose factions, the Bolsheviks, would eventually take over the country and exterminate all the other dissident parties and the libertarian outlook most of them represented.

In literature, too, 1892 was a watershed year. The great age of the Russian novel, which lasted from the 1860s to 1880s, was also a time of catastrophic decline of Russian poetry. A succession of utilitarian-minded positivist critics who dominated the literary scene after the 1860s tolerated poetry only if it contained social criticism or preached a simplistic moral. Language, style and craftsmanship were in a state of decay. Nineteenth-century poets who meant so much to Tsvetaeva and to those who came after her generation – Yevgeny Baratynsky, Afanasy Fet and Karolina Pavlova, for instance – were reviled and despised as empty-headed songbirds. The favourite poets of the 1880s were the maudlin poetaster Semion Nadson, hailed as the new incarnation of Pushkin merely because he wrote of the evils of exploitation and oppression; Alexei Apukhtin, author of flashy salon lyrics and a friend of Tchaikovsky, who set his poems to music; and Modest Musorgsky's friend Arseny Golenishchev-Kutuzov, whose verse wedded the most banal clichés to the most hackneyed rhymes that existed. The fact that Musorgsky could seriously consider Golenishchev-Kutuzov a poet of magnitude comparable to Pushkin's or Lermontov's testifies to the depths to which the understanding of poetry had plunged.

There were, it is true, two enormously attractive presences on the literary scene of the 1880s: Anton Chekhov and the philosopher-poet Vladimir Soloviov. Each one represented in his own sphere (Chekhov in the secular and realistic one and Soloviov in the spiritual and mystical) the breadth of outlook, universality and tolerance of other viewpoints that were not usual in Russian culture. But their impact would not be felt until the beginning of the twentieth century. In the first years of the 1890s, Chekhov had every reason to complain in his letters about the provinciality to which Russian literature and art had been reduced.

In 1892, Dmitry Merezhkovsky gave a public lecture 'On the

Causes of the Decline of Contemporary Russian Literature and on Its New Trends.' As spelled out in this lecture, later included in a collection of Merezhkovsky's essays, the causes were the compulsory adherence to radical utilitarian dogma, the ban on metaphysics and the disregard for artistic quality. One year later, Merezhkovsky's wife, the poet Zinaida Gippius, published in a major literary journal her poem 'Song,' the concluding line of which, 'What I need does not exist in this world,' created a considerable stir. This was the first of her authentically Symbolist poems, in which Gippius extended the boundaries of the usual nineteenth-century Russian meters and popularized accentual verse and assonance rhymes, later to be developed and perfected by such poets as Blok, Akhmatova and Mayakovsky.

Merezhkovsky's lecture and Gippius's poems were the early harbingers of the literary and artistic revival that came to be known as Russian Symbolism. Within two or three years, this trend was joined by such other important poets of the first Symbolist generation as Valery Briusov, Konstantin Balmont and Feodor Sologub (the second Symbolist generation, which included Viacheslav Ivanov, Alexander Blok and Andrei Bely, made its appearance in the early years of the twentieth century).

By the time Sergei Diaghilev, Dmitry Filosofov and the artists of their circle were ready to launch their journal *The World of Art* in 1898, there existed a group of major poets who had successfully revived the art of writing good verse and a group of important metaphysical philosophers, descended from Vladimir Soloviov's example. All of them were anxious to make common cause with Diaghilev in his efforts to liberate literature and the arts from the 'narrow prison of ideology and prejudice' (as Nikolai Gumiliov put it) to which they had been confined since the 1860s.

The spectacular explosion of artistic creativity that resulted from this alliance affected all aspects of cultural life in the early twentieth-century Russia. Its liberated and liberating influence was wide-ranging. Yet there were some areas where this influence did not penetrate. It was not felt, for example, in the academic families where Andrei Bely and, a decade later, Marina Tsvetaeva were growing up. Nor did it affect, as Tsvetaeva was to learn to her grief, the cultural attitudes of the leading figures of the liberal and radical opposition parties. But the world in which this poet was to develop, live, and create, began to take its political and artistic shape, as I have tried to show, the very year she was born.

We have at our disposal three primary sources on the childhood years of Marina Tsvetaeva: her early poetry, her sister's memoirs and her own autobiographical essays. All three are to be considered with caution as factual evidence. In the first category are the poems Tsvetaeva wrote between the ages of sixteen and nineteen and which were included in her first two published collections, *The Evening Album* and *The Magic Lantern*. Now, except for her plays and narrative poems written on subjects taken from folklore or historical sources and her philosophical and literary essays, all of Tsvetaeva's poetry and prose are personal confessions, where autobiographical elements are a basic component. But in the poems about her childhood in her first two collections, the reflections of actual experiences (and they are certainly numerous) are subordinated to the central myth that informs these two books: the myth of childhood as a magical region, an Eden from which one is expelled after growing up.

The resultant idealized depiction appears even more unreal when one remembers that the little child, who in some of these poems yearns for her mother and for the safety of the nursery, is at the same time a young woman of eighteen or nineteen who obstinately resists entering the world of adults. As biographical material, then, these early poems are of interest only as evidence of how the poet incorporated her actual experiences into the mythology of childhood that is expounded in those two early books.

Extreme idealization of the past is also a handicap with our second main source on the poet's childhood, the *Memoirs* (*Vospominaniia*) by her sister, Anastasia Tsvetaeva. Serialized in the 1960s in the journal *Novyi Mir* and published in book form in three different editions (1971, 1974 and 1983), these memoirs have become a great favourite with Soviet readers and a standard reference for Tsvetaeva scholars. Anastasia Tsvetaeva wrote her recollections during the seventh and eighth decades of her life, a life filled with hardship and privations, including an arrest on trumped-up charges and seventeen years spent in GULag camps and internal exile in remote regions of Siberia.

The rehabilitation and the eventual popularity of Marina Tsvetaeva's writings in the Soviet Union in recent decades propelled her surviving sister into a position of considerable literary eminence and gave her the access to publishing houses and the reading public that had been eluding her since she began her writing career at the age of twenty-two. In her gratitude, Anastasia Tsvetaeva has sought to minimize all conflict that was a part of her own and her sister's lives, either within the family or with the Soviet regime (Marina's conflicts with the émigré community in Paris are, of course, given extensive play). Therefore, while these memoirs are an inexhaustible storehouse of factual information on Tsvetaeva's life and an indispensable commentary on her early poetry, they need to be approached with wariness. Irma Kudrova and Viktoria Schweitzer, two devoted and knowledgeable Tsvetaeva scholars, were quite right to challenge in print the factual accuracy of these memoirs and to question Anastasia Tsvetaeva's depiction of her own and their mother's relationship with the young Marina. (See Appendix for the sources cited in this and subsequent chapters.)

There remains the remarkable series of the poet's own recollections about her earliest years, which she wrote during the 1930s, when, as Irma Kudrova put it, 'she distinctly understood the catastrophe that occurred in her interrelationship with the world' and 'insistently sought and found in the distant land of her childhood the seeds that later germinated and grew into the tragic realization [of being a] person who is disconnected from her time and her society.' Tsvetaeva's personal and literary memoirs are not always models of objectivity and reliability. We now know that she rearranged things, omitted some events she did not care to remember and was on occasion guilty of plain forgetfulness. But her memoirs are almost recklessly candid and, unlike her sister, she was incapable of falsifying her past experiences and attitudes in order to make them more acceptable within the notions of propriety or political correctness held by a later age.

Throughout the decade of the 1930s, Tsvetaeva felt compelled to return in her prose to the period between her earliest childhood memories and the departure of her family for Italy in 1902 because of her mother's illness, that is, to the first ten years of her life. Her memoiristic essays 'Women of the Flagellant Sect' ('Khlystovki'), 1934; 'The Devil' ('Chort'), 'My Mother's Fairy Tale' ('Skazka materi') and 'My Mother and Music' ('Mat' i muzyka'), all three published in 1935; and 'My Pushkin' ('Moi Pushkin'), 1937, are all devoted to that period. 'The Ivy-Clad Tower' ('Bashnia v pliush-che') of 1933 deals with a slightly later period when Marina was twelve and her younger sister ten. In addition, two other prose pieces from the same period, 'Natalia Goncharova,' 1929, and the memoir on Osip Mandelstam, 'Story of a Dedication' ('Istoriia odnogo posviashcheniia'), 1930, contain important episodes about little Marina's situation within her family (in fact, the writing of these two pieces might have suggested to the poet the memoir sequence enumerated above, which then followed).

Had Tsvetaeva been as popular and highly valued in her lifetime as she is now, her childhood memoirs would have been collected into a separate book soon after their publication in various period-icals, a book that would find its rightful place next to such earlier classics of the genre as Tolstoy's *Childhood* and *Adolescence* and Maxim Gorky's *Childhood*. The penetration into the psychology of a very young child is equal to the very finest fictional treatments of similar material to be found in Russian literature, such as Chek-hov's 'Grisha' and 'The Cook's Wedding' and Andrei Bely's auto-biographical novel *Kotik Letaev*. Anastasia Tsvetaeva has objected that little Marina could not have possibly felt about herself and other members of the family the way she described it in those memoirs. But neither Anastasia, nor anyone else can deny that this was how Tsvetaeva, the grown-up woman and the mature poet of the 1930s, *remembered* her childhood. Memoir after memoir, year after year, a consistent picture emerges, supported also by the poet's evocations of her childhood in letters to such friends as Vera Bunina and Boris Pasternak.

The picture presented in the memoirs is not entirely unhappy. We read of the leisurely life of the Tsvetaev family and their retainers in their house, with its dove-grey, dove-filled yard, the house of which the sixteen-year-old Marina was later to write:

> Our marvellous, our wonderful house in Three Pond Lane
> Which is now turning into verse.

We read of the summers at their *dacha* in the picturesque town of Tarusa on the river Oka. We meet the frequently changing governesses, among them the Baltic German Augusta Ivanovna and the somewhat flashy Parisienne named Alphonsine Dijon. Marina had no traditional Russian nanny (*niania*), but there was one for little Asya. This nanny was quite the opposite of Pushkin's folktale-reciting nurse, for in her case we find the six-year-old Marina ecstatically declaiming Pushkin's verse to the uncomprehending and disapproving *niania*.

The visits of her maternal grandfather Alexander Danilovich Meyn were particularly joyous occasions for Marina, or Musen'ka, as she was then known. He brought her presents and bananas (an exotic treat in those days), recited German poetry, and, above all, he showed a partiality for her and an affection she so desperately wanted and did not get from the members of her immediate family. The cheerful visits of her grandfather are contrasted with the infrequent visits of the dour, forbidding Professor Ilovaisky, the grandfather of Marina's half-sister Valeria and half-brother Andrei. Instead of presents, Ilovaisky brought copies of the anti-Semitic newspaper *The Kremlin*, of which he was reputedly the publisher, the circulation manager and the sole regular subscriber; otherwise, he showed little interest in the two little girls who were not directly related to him.

The siblings are clearly delineated through numerous references to them in the memoirs. Valeria Tsvetaeva, twelve years older than Marina, was kind to her as a child, though as adults they were hostile to each other and became permanently estranged. Musically, the Tsvetaev household was divided into two spheres: the vocal, which belonged to Valeria and her late mother, and the piano-playing one which was the realm of Maria Alexandrovna and her unwilling daughters. The feud between the stepmother and the stepdaughter, while under reasonable control most of the time, was present throughout Marina's childhood. Music, however, provided the ground for an occasional armistice, when Maria Alexandrovna would accompany at the piano Valeria's singing of the traditional Russian popular songs, the *romansy*.

Valeria's brother Andrei took no part in the Ilovaisky–Meyn division. He was his stepmother's particular favourite. Little Asya, who later, at the time of Marina's adolescence, would become her closest and dearest friend, emerges in the childhood reminiscences as the pampered baby of the family, selfish, spoiled and envious. Professor Tsvetaev is described as a kindly and considerate man, who on occasion would take Marina's side and defend her from her mother's whims and excessive demands. But his main interests clearly lay outside of his family and at home he could be absent-minded to the point of absurdity: 'my attentively incomprehending father.'

There was clearly no love between the parents, only civilized mutual accommodation. Eventually, they also found a common cause to which they could jointly devote their lives. This was Ivan Tsvetaev's project of organizing and building a museum capable of housing Moscow University's collection of replicas of ancient sculptures. Conceived in the 1870s, the project could not get off the ground until Professor Tsvetaev managed to secure the backing of the important financier, Yury Nechaev-Maltsev. His father-in-law, Alexander Meyn, was also a major donor. Deprived of a meaningful outlet for her energies by the termination of her musical career, Maria Tsvetaeva found fulfillment in helping her husband realize his dream.

Throughout their childhood Marina and Asya kept hearing of the museum as their 'gigantic younger brother.' Their mother was in charge of the extensive correspondence in French and German pertaining to the museum affairs. The parents jointly devised fund-raising schemes and travelled to the Urals to select the marble for the building. In 1904, while the family was staying in Germany, catastrophe struck. 'The last year ended for me with a great misfortune,' Professor Tsvetaev wrote on January 23, 1905 to his Athens correspondent, Countess Ina Kapnist, a Greek-Russian lady who helped him with museum affairs. 'While I was away, someone set fire to a storeroom in the new museum which contained sculptures. Everything from Capri perished and also many things from Athens, Naples, Rome and Paris. I wept in Freiburg for weeks. Now I am here, sorting out the fire debris. I am heartsick and have to start my Sisyphean task all over again.'

Other parts of this letter, which is now in the collection of the Museum of Russian Culture in San Francisco, show the father's possible affinities to his daughter's future politics and her verbal inventiveness, as in a passage where he says that he finds the progressive and the reactionary Russian journals equally odious and qualifies them in neologistic terms as *naprednianskie* and *nazadnianskie* (something like 'frontwarders' and 'rearwarders,' respectively).

The 'Sisyphean task' was indeed started all over. Maria Alexandrovna did not live to see the completion of the museum in which she had invested so much labor. But her two daughters, aged twenty and eighteen, both of them married (and Marina already an expectant mother) were present at the grand opening of the

Alexander III Museum of Fine Arts in Moscow. The unveiling
took place on May 18, 1912 in the presence of Tsar Nicholas II
and the imperial family. The museum was renamed the Pushkin
Museum after the revolution but the facade of the building still
bears the memorial plaque honoring Ivan Vladimirovich Tsvetaev. An even greater homage is paid to him in the passages
devoted to his museum in the memoirs of his two younger
daughters.

The family relationship which was undoubtedly central in Marina
Tsvetaeva's childhood and which, in her opinion, contributed
more than any other to her subsequent formation and development was the one with her mother. In a telling letter to the writer
Vasily Rozanov, Tsvetaeva wrote: 'My mother's youth, like her
childhood, was solitary, morbid, mutinous and deeply secretive.
Her heroes were Wallenstein, [the actor Ernst] Possart and King
Ludwig of Bavaria. An outing on a moonlit night on the lake
where he perished. [The two published versions of this letter have
po Oderu, "on the Oder," which must be a misreading for *po
ozeru*, "on the lake," since Ludwig II drowned in a lake in
Bavaria while wrestling with his physician.] A ring slips from her
finger, the water accepts it. An engagement to the dead king.'
   Her mother's girlish infatuation with the homosexual king of
Bavaria who was not interested in women seems to presage
Tsvetaeva's own later penchant for selecting unavailable or unin-
terested love objects. 'When [Anton] Rubinstein shook her hand,'
the cited letter to Rozanov continues, 'she wouldn't remove her
glove for two days. Her poets were Heine, Goethe, Schiller and
Shakespeare. More foreign books than Russian ones.' 'The entire
spirit in which she was educated was German.'
   A resolute, strongwilled woman, the poet's mother never quite
reconciled herself to the loss of the concert career she could not
have. The birth of her two daughters was a disappointment to her,
for she had expected them to be sons whom she had in advance
named Alexander and Kirill. The little girls were told about this,
repeatedly. To make sure her daughters had the things she
missed, their mother decided to turn them into musicians. Little
Asya played poorly and unwillingly, so the entire hope for a
musician in the family was vested in Marina. The memoir 'My
Mother and Music' is both Tsvetaeva's tribute to her mother's

culture, which she generously shared with her daughters, and the record of her own musical martyrdom.

The bitterness of the poet's childhood memories comes not only (or not so much) from the long and boring hours of forced piano practice, or from her mother's steady ridicule of her early and childish verse, strange from a woman who liked and understood poetry, nor even from the mother's general policy prohibiting anything the little girls might enjoy: 'There was no right to request anything in our home. Not even with one's eyes.' The worst part was the open preference which the mother accorded to her stepson and her youngest daughter at the expense of her firstborn child.

When she was a grown woman, Tsvetaeva rationalized her mother's coldness by describing a chance encounter her mother had with the man she loved and lost, an encounter of which she learned by reading her mother's diaries: '. . . having married a widower with two children to the misfortune of those children and of others, while loving and continuing to love the other one, whom she never afterwards sought to meet, and to whose question about her life, happiness, etc., asked when she met him by chance at her husband's lecture, she replied: My daughter is one year old, she is very husky and intelligent, I am entirely happy . . . (Lord, how at that moment she must have hated me, husky and intelligent, for not being his daughter!).'

The feeling of being unwanted came early. At the age of three, Marina 'had a frenzied wish to become lost' in the city of Moscow. At a very young age, she devised a daydream of being adopted by an imaginary devil, whose 'own little orphan' she would then be. When a group of Old Believer nuns jokingly offered to adopt her during a summer vacation in Tarusa, the child's reaction was unmistakable: 'Within me there lights up a wild, burning, unrealizable, hopeless hope: what if they could?' At the age of ten she dreamed of going to live with her grandfather Meyn's second wife in Switzerland, 'where I would be alone without Asya and be the very favourite daughter and perhaps even the son Alexander.' The memoir 'My Mother's Fairy Tale' suggests that the mother's constant favouritism could lead not only to fierce rivalry between her daughters, but at times even to genuine mutual hatred between them.

Punishment, disapproval or mockery could result from many things: failure to understand a story or a poem the mother read aloud; telling of a dream one had which the mother didn't think proper; or being subject to motion sickness, something from which Tsvetaeva suffered all her life. She had to learn to be secretive: 'Up to the age of four, as my mother testified, I told only the truth, but after that I must have come to my senses.' Still, despite all the pitfalls entailed, the little Marina was always happy when her mother shared the pleasures of reading with the children. The literature to which she introduced them was in German or in French and it was for the most part juvenile. The children were encouraged to read French novels for adolescents by Hector Malot and Zénaide Fleuriot, *Lichtenstein* by Wilhelm Hauff and Joseph Victor von Scheffel's sentimental romance in verse *Der Trompeter von Säkkingen*. From the latter came the words of the heartbreaking aria from the opera of the same title based by the composer Victor E. Nessler on Scheffel's poem, words which her mother was especially fond of singing at the piano and which Tsvetaeva was later to cite in several of her works as a motto to her entire life:

> Behüt' dich Gott! Es wär zu schön gewesen,
> Behüt' dich Gott, es hat nicht sollen sein!

> (May God protect you! It would have been too lovely;
> May God protect you, it was not meant to be!)

Curiously absent from the reading diet of the younger Tsvetaev children were Russian nineteenth-century classics and especially poetry, which was usually the first thing the children in intellectual families learned. To get her first introduction to her native literature, little Marina had to go into what she must have secretly realized was enemy territory: the room of her half-sister Valeria. It was there that Valeria read to her passages from Gogol's *Dead Souls*, which Marina, the future romantic poet, was disappointed to find out was *not* about corpses or ghosts. It was there, somewhat later, that the six-year-old Marina read Pushkin's 'The Gypsies' and, still later, *Eugene Onegin* and *The Captain's Daughter*.

Valeria's room was a magnet for Marina in some other ways as well. On several occasions she caught her older half-sister swallowing what looked like large silver beads. They were actually pills taken to ease menstrual pains, but Marina assumed they were some kind of poison and began to suspect that Valeria, with her 'gemlike eyes of a snake,' might be a witch. Above all, it was in Valeria's room, either in the Moscow home or in the summer residence in Tarusa, that Marina had visions of a strange being, part Great

Dane, part athlete and part lioness described in the memoir 'The Devil.'

The richly symbolic figure of the devil in this memoir stands for many attractive and prohibited things: love, uniqueness, danger and, for good measure, Russian literature. Her initial exposure to the devil occurred in the very same place as her first exposure to Pushkin, who was thus firmly connected with the idea of rebellion, first of all against her mother. 'In that bookcase [i.e., in Valeria's room] there lived the Guide (*Vozhatyi*),' Tsvetaeva wrote in 'My Pushkin,' the Guide being the rebel Emelian Pugachov as depicted in *The Captain's Daughter*. Love for this great rebel, criminal and impostor was clearly equated by the little girl with the love for her own private Lucifer, a connection which she later elaborated in her essay 'Pushkin and Pugachov.'

In a wonderfully perceptive paper read at the Tsvetaeva Symposium in Lausanne in 1982 (it is a part of a psychological biography in progress), Lily Feiler argued that the devil was conjured by little Marina's imagination as a counter-figure to her mother: 'the Devil serves as an opposing force to Mother. He is a force from "down-under" while Mother rules far above. He personifies the truth of instincts, while Mother stands for false emotions. The Devil, of course, symbolizes sin while Mother represents martyrdom.' Schematic though this may sound, it does cover the essential oppositions in Tsvetaeva's memoir.

Lily Feiler also emphasized the 'erotic overtones of Marina's description of the devil,' especially the ambiguity of the devil's physical gender. 'This passage seems to foreshadow Marina's later sexual confusion: the body of the devil is *female*, his cold, *merciless* eyes and his *boastful manhood* excite Marina,' Feiler wrote (the added italics are hers). Later on in her paper this ambivalence is convincingly connected with the adult Tsvetaeva's attraction to androgynous women and men.

Between the ages of six and ten, to judge from her memoirs, Marina Tsvetaeva lived a life rich in intellectual and emotional experiences. All by herself she discovered and came to appreciate Pushkin, establishing an understanding of his work that was to remain unchanged for the rest of her life. Her liberating and highly satisfying communion with her private devil gave her the sense of being a unique, chosen individual. She well realized, she wrote, that although her devil always appeared in Valeria's room, it was not to

Valeria that he came because Valeria was a lifelong joiner in social causes, whereas *his* favourites are always exclusive and excluded. One can well understand the horror of the aged Valeria Shevliagina, née Tsvetaeva, when after decades of studiously ignoring Marina's writings, she finally read 'The Devil' shortly before her death in 1966 and reportedly exclaimed: 'Where did she *get* those ideas? What is this devil nonsense and why did he have to live in *my* room?'

During this period of their lives, the younger Tsvetaev girls were taught at home by governesses. For Andrei, university students were hired as tutors. The major Russian universities were radicalized in the 1860s and they more or less stayed that way until 1917. A revolutionary student as private tutor was very much a part of the cultural scene, as a glance at the school years of Osip Mandelstam or Vladimir Nabokov will show. These idealistic young men were highly admired and it took considerable civic courage for Anton Chekhov to portray his student Trofimov in *The Cherry Orchard* as muddle-headed and faintly ridiculous. Marina Tsvetaeva in an unpublished memoir 'That Which Was' ('To, chto bylo') and Anastasia in her memoirs both remembered the awe and admiration in which they held Andrei's tutors.

Asya actually managed to fall in love with one of them, Arkady Lastochkin, when she was four. It was under the influence of this same Lastochkin that Marina composed one of her earliest poems at the age of six. The poem was about a political rally at the university. It read in its entirety:

> Everyone is running to the rally.
> Where's the rally? Where's the rally?
> In the courtyard over there.

Under the impact of the garden scene from Tchaikovsky's *Eugene Onegin* which she saw during a matinée at the music school where she was studying piano and of her secret readings of Pushkin's novel, Marina imagined that she was in love with another of Andrei's tutors and wrote him a passionate letter in imitation of Pushkin's and Tchaikovsky's Tatiana. The tutor took it with good humor and returned her letter after correcting her mistakes in grammar and spelling, which cooled her ardor.

From the age of six on, Marina persisted in writing poetry. Attempts to read her poems to the members of her family were met with her mother's ridicule and with incomprehension from the rest. Samples of those early poems – a mixture of echoes of Pushkin with newspaper clichés – which are quoted in 'Story of a Dedication' are indeed childish and inept. But the cruelty of her mother's mockery, Tsvetaeva was convinced as an adult, was motivated by a desire to have her daughter devote herself to the art of music and none other. In this the mother failed, for as Tsvetaeva later expressed it, 'music was a possibility, but poetry was inherent.' Unappreciated by her family, Tsvetaeva's earliest poetry found a champion in Sergei Ilovaisky, Professor Ilovaisky's young son from his second marriage. Sergei was the first in the long line of such champions – a line that would eventually include Voloshin, Bely and Pasternak – who believed in her poetry and urged her to go on writing and ignore the verdict of supposedly competent authorities who were sure that she had taken the wrong path.

In 1901, when she was nine, Marina had her first taste of public education when she was enrolled in the first grade of a classical *gimnasia*, the traditional school that offered a comprehensive curriculum with emphasis on languages, classics and sciences. Anastasia, with her yen for conventional respectability, wrote in her memoirs that Marina was a brilliant and popular student. Marina, more honest, confessed: 'The first school year was like all the rest: I changed schools the way I changed grades and cities – without friends, with a love for one particular girl, unattainable because she was older, with invariable sympathy from the same three teachers, those of Russian, German and French, with invariable contempt from all the rest.'

After one year at the school she had to withdraw. In November of 1902, her mother was told by doctors that she had tuberculosis and that her only chance of survival was to move to Italy. Thus began three years of life and schooling abroad for Marina and Asya. Leaving Andrei in Moscow in the care of his grandfather, the family travelled to Nervi near Genoa, where they settled at a boarding house for tubercular patients run by a Russian named Alexander Miller. Miller's daredevil young son Vladimir (or Volodya) became the idol and the playmate of Marina and Asya and was immortalized in several of the poems of Tsvetaeva's first collection of verse.

Several other denizens of Miller's boarding house in Nervi (where the two younger girls stayed with their mother after Pro-

fessor Tsvetaev and Valeria returned to Russia) were to haunt
Marina's memories in years to come and to appear in her poems and
essays. A young German, Reinhard Roever, soon to die of tuberculosis, introduced the Tsvetaev girls to the notion of immortality by
burning a piece of cigarette paper and exclaiming, as the ashes flew
upward, 'Die Seele fliegt!' In the middle of the winter, the Tsvetaevs were joined by the second wife of Professor Ilovaisky, Alexandra, accompanied by her beautiful son and daughter, Sergei and
Nadia, both of whom were mortally ill with tuberculosis. In 'The
House Near Old St Pimen's Church,' 1934, Tsvetaeva would describe the damp and drafty quarters in which Ilovaisky's children
from his two marriages were raised and which caused all but two of
them to die of tuberculosis by the age of twenty.

Nadia Ilovaiskaya was involved in a secret love affair with a
Russian young man of whom her mother did not approve. Marina
and Asya carried messages between the two lovers. Two years later
Marina learned from her father of Nadia's death and for the first
time understood the magnitude of her own attachment to this young
woman. As the adult Tsvetaeva was to write to Vera Bunina on May
23, 1928, it was only after Nadia's death that she could give her
feelings free rein. The memory of Nadia haunted Marina's imagination and dreams from the summer of 1904 to the end of 1905. 'The
House Near Old St Pimen's Church,' which Tsvetaeva began in 1928
and completed five years later, was the mature poet's reconstruction
of the world of the Ilovaiskys and Tsvetaevs as well as her monument
to that youthful infatuation with the lovely Nadia.

Also staying at the *Pension Russe* in Nervi in 1902 was a group of
revolutionary anarchists headed by Vladislav Kobyliansky, nicknamed 'The Tiger,' with whom the Tsvetaevs became friendly. The
anarchists taught Marina and Asya revolutionary songs and conducted with each other and with Russian revolutionaries of other
persuasions heated debates on proper revolutionary mentality and
the correctness of various party lines. Disagreement on such matters
in those days did not prevent members of different parties hostile to
the tsar from remaining on cordial terms with each other. Under the
impact of these new friends, the ten-year old Marina produced a few
revolutionary poems of her own, some of which she was to recite
exactly thirty years later during a poetry reading in Paris devoted to
her 'childhood poems about children, childhood revolutionary
poems and poems written at school and in early youth.'

During the next two years, Maria Alexandrovna sought medical help in sanatoriums in Switzerland and Germany and her daughters were placed in nearby boarding schools. 1903–4 was spent by Marina and Asya in Lausanne, at the *pensionnat* of the Lacaze sisters, Mlle Lucille and Mlle Marguerite. It was a warm, congenial environment, despite the unfamiliar atmosphere of Roman Catholic piety and even attempts at proselytizing. It was there that Marina had the memorable experience of going to confession in a Catholic church and hearing the priest dismiss her fascination with the Devil as childish and trivial.

Far worse was the boarding school in Freiburg in the Black Forest, owned and operated by the Brink sisters, Fräulein Pauline and Fräulein Annie. Here, there was regimentation, discipline, uncomfortable quarters and miserable food. Contrasting with the school was the nearby hotel, the Gasthaus zum Engel, run by the kindly Meyer family, with whose children Karl and Marile the Tsvetaev girls became great friends. One unforgettable day, Marina and Asya were taken by the Brink sisters to have tea with a real princess, the Fürstin von Thurn und Taxis. Marina confused the name Thurn with the German word for tower, 'Turm,' and she mistook Taxis for 'Taxus,' which means yew, but which she thought meant ivy – hence the title of the memoir she wrote about this visit, 'The Ivy-Clad Tower.'

Although there was no such tower topping the princely castle, the outing provided the girls with a welcome escape from the dreariness of the school they detested. Marina tried not to appear too awed by the surroundings and made a spirited case for the Russian side of the Russo-Japanese war which was then in the news. Asked by the princess to express a wish, she admitted her desire for her own copy of the book *Heidi* by Johanna Spyri. Many years later, when she read Rainer Maria Rilke's 'Duino Elegies' and his posthumously published letters, Tsvetaeva realized that her hostess on that festive occasion was also a friend and correspondent of the poet she revered.

For many years, Tsvetaeva would fondly remember the effigy of St George on the Schwabentor in Freiburg. She had been exposed to German language and literature since her earliest childhood, but her lifelong love affair with Germany dates from her stay in the Black Forest. In her 1919 essay 'On Germany' ('O Germanii'), she pointed out that her affinity with German literature, music and landscape was the exterior expression of two psychological qualities which she felt were part of her innermost core and which could be expressed or described only in German. These are *Übermass*, which denotes excess and extravagance, and *Schwärmerei*, a state of being either ecstatic or gushing. Tsvetaeva well realized that outside of their German context the states these words convey are undesirable and possibly ridiculous. Her Germanophilia was expressed by Tsvetaeva in the defiantly pro-German poems she wrote and read in public during World War I and in the essay 'On Germany' which she wrote after the war ended.

In 1905, the condition of Maria Alexandrovna's health, which had briefly improved during her stay abroad, became worse. Her doctors saw no further point in keeping her in foreign sanatoriums and she decided to return to Russia. The three years abroad altered significantly the relationships of Marina and Asya with their mother and with each other. Her illness made Maria Alexandrovna less harsh and demanding. The two girls, finding themselves removed from their mother's dominance and alone in a foreign environment, turned to each other for company and support. Their earlier rivalry and mutual resentment receded into the past. Their contact with each other and with their mother became far warmer than it had been earlier. It was this warmth that Anastasia later projected in her memoirs and Marina reflected in the poetry of her late teens. But she never forgot what things were like in the earlier period and she was to convey the earlier situation in her mature writings with a vehemence which her sister's recent denials cannot blot out.

Since a warm climate was indicated, Maria Alexandrovna chose the city of Yalta in the Crimea. She and her daughters settled there just when the whole of Russia was being engulfed in the revolutionary wave of the summer of 1905. The humiliating defeats of the Russian forces in the unpopular Russo-Japanese war, begun in 1904, had turned much of the public opinion against the government of Tsar Nicholas II. On January 22, 1905, the day that went down in history as 'Bloody Sunday,' a huge demonstration of workers carrying sacred icons and portraits of the tsar marched peacefully on the Winter Palace in St Petersburg to present their grievances. They were met with gunfire. Hundreds were killed or wounded. Indignation and revulsion swept the country. There followed strikes, peasant uprisings and massive revolutionary agitation by both liberal and radical parties.

Like many of the young people of the time, the thirteen-year-old Marina was affected by the revolutionary groundswell. This mood was further enhanced by her contacts with some of their Yalta neighbours, among whom was Ekaterina Peshkova, the wife of the most admired revolutionary writer in Russia, Maxim Gorky. Asya became the playmate of Peshkova's children, her son Max and her soon-to-die little daughter Katia. The Tsvetaev girls knew that Gorky had become estranged from his wife because of his much-publicized affair with Maria Andreyeva, an actress with the Moscow Art Theater. As Anastasia recalled it, she and Marina hated Andreyeva for taking away their friends' father. Tsvetaeva's first collection of verse contains the poem 'At the Child's Coffin,' which is a requiem for little Katia Peshkova and which is dedicated to Ekaterina Peshkova.

In 1926, when she was in her early thirties, Tsvetaeva filled out at Boris Pasternak's request a questionnaire circulated by the Study Group of Revolutionary Literature organized by the Revolutionary Art Section of the Soviet Academy of Arts and Sciences. Aware of the incongruity of the response by the leading anti-Soviet poet of the Russian emigration to such a questionnaire, Tsvetaeva described her adolescent revolutionary sympathies in a deliberately defiant and provocative manner. Between the ages of thirteen and fifteen, she wrote, she was enthusiastic about the People's Freedom Party (a terrorist revolutionary organization), read books on economics, the literary miscellanies published by the neo-realist and radical literary group Znanie (headed by Maxim Gorky) and the poetry of Yevgeny Tarasov (a writer of propagandistic doggerel, who enjoyed a brief popularity during the 1905 revolution). She admired such revolutionary figures as Lieutenant Piotr Schmidt (executed in 1906; he was later the protagonist of Pasternak's narrative poem) and the Socialist Revolutionary heroine Maria Spiridonova (who was sentenced to prison for shooting a policeman in 1906 and who later died in a Soviet concentration camp).

'But I broke with all ideology at sixteen,' Tsvetaeva went on. Later on in the same questionnaire she wrote: 'My first encounter with the Revolution was in 1902–3, through the émigrés [i.e., the anarchist revolutionaries at Nervi], my second one in 1905–6 (Yalta, the Socialist Revolutionaries). There was no third encounter.' After the October Revolution, both the anarchists and the

Socialist Revolutionaries came to be regarded as traitors and enemies of the revolution. Tsvetaeva's uncompromising honesty in filling out this questionnaire precluded any possibility of its being used in the projected bio-bibliographical dictionary of twentieth-century writers, for which the questionnaire was intended.

Maria Alexandrovna may have had some sympathy for the revolutionary program of the Constitutional Democrats: turning Russia into a constitutional monarchy, with civil rights and universal suffrage in the manner of Western European countries. But her daughters had picked up far more radical notions than that from their Yalta friends. Because of the state of her health, the mother realized the need to make a last will and testament so as to arrange for the disposal of the inheritance she herself had received upon the death of her father. As Tsvetaeva described it in her letter to Raisa Lomonosova, dated April 3, 1930: 'My mother was dying in 1905. My sister and I were small children but already precocious, especially I, the older. So there was a fear: what if, when they grow up, they will "join a party" and donate it all for the destruction of the country.'

The mother decided to leave the money to her two daughters, but she made a proviso that they could not touch it until they reached the age of forty. Since neither Marina nor Asya had reached forty at the time of the October Revolution, the outcome of their mother's will was that the money she left them was confiscated. But the form her last will took testifies to the intensity of Tsvetaeva's involvement with revolutionary ideas during her early adolescence. This is further confirmed in her confessional letter to Vasily Rozanov of April 8, 1914, where she wrote: 'From the age of fourteen to sixteen I raved of nothing but revolution . . . ' But this enthusiasm faded by the time she came to write her earliest published poetry, where it left no trace.

In March 1906, Maria Alexandrovna's coughing became unbearable and she suffered periodic hemorrhages. By June it was clear that she was about to die. She preferred to die at the Tsvetaev home on the Three Pond Lane in Moscow, but in the middle of the trip to Moscow she was judged too weak to travel farther and she was taken to Tarusa instead. As her last show of strong will, Maria Alexandrovna declined all help while entering the family's Tarusa house and insisted on playing the piano there for the last time. She died on July 5, 1906. The last thing she said to her daughters was: 'I shall miss only the music and the sun!'

Marina Tsvetaeva may well have resented what her mother had done to her childhood, but she also repeatedly stressed how much she owed to her. She felt that her mother had given her the love of culture, a contempt for materialistic values, her pride and independence. She saw her mother's life as a tragedy of unfulfilled longings and wasted potential. A decade after her mother's death, Tsvetaeva felt that the aim of her own and her sister's life was to make that tragedy explicit. As she wrote to Rozanov: 'Her tormented soul lives on in us, but we reveal what she concealed. Her rebellion, her madness, her longing have grown in us to the level of a scream.'

2

The prolonged adolescence

Alarmed by the revolutionary fury of the summer of 1905 and the successful general strike in the fall of that year, Nicholas II issued the October Manifesto which guaranteed civil liberties and established a legislative parliament, the Duma. Labor unions and political parties of every stripe became legal. Preliminary governmental censorship of books and periodicals, which in any case had been slowly atrophying since the end of the nineteenth century, had now virtually disappeared. Those in the moderate-to-liberal range of the political spectrum were satisfied with the tsar's concessions. But many radicals saw the October Manifesto as opening the way toward the pluralistic parliamentary system they despised and they redoubled their resistance. The revolution of 1905 was suppressed early in 1906 and the country, instead of rejoicing in the very real new freedoms it had won, was plunged into uncertainty and despair.

In the fall of 1906, Marina Tsvetaeva, aged fourteen, and her sister Asya, aged twelve, returned to their father's Moscow house on Three Pond Lane. The forced musical education of Marina was gradually discontinued, leaving as its residue the astounding rhythmic variety of her later poetry and prose and the occasional musical imagery found in them. For a few years Marina took over her late mother's function of helping Professor Tsvetaev with the French and German correspondence related to his museum. Valeria, now twenty six, was pursuing her varied interests and careers as professional dancer, schoolmistress, and political organizer for the Social Democratic Party. Though nominally living at Three Pond Lane, she was rarely at home. Tsvetaeva's poem 'The Dining Room' ('Stolovaia') in *The Evening Album* reflects the cheerless atmosphere of the Tsvetaev home during the years that followed her mother's death.

The two younger Tsvetaev daughters were enrolled in the kind of school which Marina had already briefly experienced in 1901, the *gimnasia*. Study at the *gimnasia* seems to have been one of

Tsvetaeva's least agreeable experiences. In later years, she on two occasions listed as the three greatest joys of her life (all three privative in nature) *not* having to go to the *gimnasia*, to awaken *not* in the Bolshevik-controlled, starving Moscow of 1919 and, a souvenir of her musical martyrdom, *not* to hear a metronome. She was constantly changing schools and taking entrance examinations. Anastasia, for understandable reasons, attributes those peregrinations to Marina's revolutionary fervor, which she says antagonized teachers and awed other students. Tsvetaeva's own recollections and the memoir of Alexandra Zhernakova-Nikolaeva (published in Paris in 1963) suggest more prosaic reasons: Marina's incapacity for mathematics, her aversion to natural sciences and her insurmountable boredom with all the compulsory subjects taught at the *gimnasia*, with the exception of literature and languages. The outcome was failing grades and expulsions.

One subject she did learn to appreciate during her school years was history. She initially found the liberal-minded history texts that came into use after the 1905 revolution to be on the dull side, with their, as she put it, 'unending class struggle' – 'no eyes, no faces, only heaps of people and all they ever do is fight.' But after reading at home Dmitry Ilovaisky's ultra-conservative and supposedly obsolete history primer, the young Tsvetaeva became aware of the possibilities of history writing as an art. 'Here, there were *living* people, living kings and queens. And not only kings, but also monks and scamps and robbers.' She especially appreciated a footnote in the primer that read: 'In the Pontic swamps, Mithridates lost seven elephants and one eye.' 'I liked that eye,' Tsvetaeva later commented. 'It was lost and yet it remains. I maintain that this eye is art.' Thereafter, reading books on history became a life-long habit with Tsvetaeva.

She made no friends among her classmates at any of the schools she attended between 1906 and 1910. She did find a confidante in Dr Lydia Tamburer, a dentist to whom Professor Tsvetaev brought Marina and Asya to have their teeth examined and who unexpectedly became their close friend. Some twenty years older than Marina, Dr Tamburer was the earliest of Tsvetaeva's substitute mother figures, older women friends of Maria Alexandrovna's or Valeria's generation, who gave her the warmth and support that her mother and half-sister were unable to provide. Lydia Tamburer is a prominent presence in *The Evening Album*, where some of the poems are addressed to her while others describe her or members of her family.

Also represented in that first collection are two classmates of Asya's, whom she brought to the house on Three Pond Lane and to whom Marina took a liking. They were Anna Kalina and Galia Diakonova. Each one had a poem dedicated to her in *The Evening Album*. Anna Kalina's family left Russia in 1912 and she did not see Tsvetaeva after that, except for a brief encounter in Paris during the 1930s. Galia Diakonova (1893–1982) went abroad after the revolution, where she became first the wife of the French surrealist poet Paul Eluard and then gained fame as the fabled Gala Dali, the model of many an apocalyptic vision painted by her second husband, Salvador Dali.

Asked about her early friendship with Tsvetaeva, Anna Kalina, who had changed the spelling of her name to Kallin, wrote to me in 1965 from London (where she was sharing a residence with Tsvetaeva's friend and patroness from the Paris days, Salomea Halpern) that a copy of the poem dedicated to her, 'The Elfin Girl in the Hall' ('El'fochka v zale'), was sent to her by mail before its publication in *The Evening Album*. There was also one more poem dedicated to her, 'Remember the Princess' ('Printsessu pomnite'), which was not included in the collection and was apparently never published. Her encounters with Marina and Asya dated from 1908 to 1910.

'For about two years, I came to see them almost daily, in the twilight after school,' Miss Kallin wrote. 'They lived in a typical Moscow private home of no particular architecture, rather somber, with large rooms [...], both cozy and a bit terrifying. In the large hall there stood a grand piano which belonged to Marina's mother, and I (being something of a Wunderkind) used to play it, mostly Chopin and Scriabin. Marina liked this very much. Marina and I were unbelievably romantic, Asya somewhat less so. Marina assured us that if we were to sit in a dark room and stare at a wall for a sufficiently long time, there would materialize out of it (but only half-way) a vampire.'

Anna Kallin recalled that in those years Marina had in part withdrawn into a poetic and fantastic world of her own making. 'Marina must have simultaneously had several such worlds.' The withdrawal was a form of rebellion against the world of the adults. 'It is a pity I cannot answer all your questions,' Miss Kallin wrote,

'– all that remains with me is a memory of the dark house in the evening, a dark hall, and an inspired young girl who turned everything into a fairy tale and who forced me to dream (*je ne demandais pas mieux*). Both Marina and Asya were very plain. I saw neither of them later, but judging from photographs, Marina must have become more attractive later.'

As to Galia Diakonova, Miss Kallin remembered her as a 'nice, merry and simple girl, not especially interesting.' Informed about the Salvador Dali exhibition held at the Huntington Hartford Museum in New York, where a three-story high painting of the Virgin Mary for which Gala Dali had posed was shown, Anna Kallin wrote to me: 'I still cannot grasp the metamorphosis of Galia Diakonova! We were all very fond of her but we also treated her a bit patronizingly. She would withdraw into a corner in the main hall of the Tsvetaev home – quiet, *modest* (which could not be said about the three of us, Marina, Asya and me), with her long eyelashes. And now, there she is, a Blessed Virgin several stories high.'

To counter the boredom of studying at the *gimnasia*, Marina wrote poetry, which she showed to only a few close friends. She did not seem to be aware at first of the great burst of creativity and innovation that was occurring in Russian poetry in those years. Her favourite poets were the German ones, especially Goethe and Heine. A particularly strong impression was made on her by Friederich de Lamotte-Fouqué's German prose romance *Undine*, about the love of a water-sprite for an undeserving man, which she must also have known in the popular Russian version in verse by Vasily Zhukovsky. The models for her Russian verse, which by 1908 had become remarkably proficient and elegant, were at this stage Russian romantic poets – not the great figures of the Romantic Age, such as Zhukovsky or Lermontov, but their followers in the second half of the nineteenth century: Fet, Yakov Polonsky, and possibly even Apukhtin.

Juvenile romances remained her preferred reading, among them the lachrymose and hugely popular novels by Lydia Charskaya (pen name of Lydia Churilova, 1875–1937) which described sentimental attachments between teenaged girls in boarding schools. In the fall of 1908, Tsvetaeva made what seemed to her a momentous literary discovery. She read Edmond Rostand's verse drama *L'Aiglon*, which is about the young Duke of Reichstadt, Napoleon's son by Marie Louise of Austria. It so overwhelmed her that for the next

two years she became a worshipper of a triple cult: of Napoleon, of
his son and of Rostand. The revolutionary enthusiasm of a few years
ago was forgotten and she was now a Bonapartist monarchist.

She decorated her room with Napoleonic memorabilia, she read
everything she could find about him and she undertook a Russian
translation of *L'Aiglon*. She even covered up the image of Christ in
the icon in her room with Napoleon's picture, something which
deeply hurt her father when he discovered it. Nonetheless, she
obtained her father's permission to travel all alone to Paris that
summer. The official reason for the trip was to sit in on a course on
Old French Literature at the Sorbonne, but the true reason was to
be in Napoleon's city and to see Sarah Bernhardt in *L'Aiglon*.

'I was in Paris for the first time at sixteen: alone, adult, independent, severe,' she later wrote. 'I settled on the Rue Bonaparte out of
love for the Emperor and apart from N (my triumphant *Non* to
everything that was not he) in Paris I saw nothing. That was
enough.' Sarah Bernhardt was not performing just then, but Marina
was tremendously impressed with her Carmen-like French teacher,
Mlle James (with whom she studied at the Alliance Française rather
than at the Sorbonne), who however had no use for Rostand. When
Marina could not restrain herself from impulsively kissing the hands
of Mlle James, the latter remarked: 'How strange those Russian
girls are! Are you perhaps a poet in your language?'

In the winter of 1909, a new and important literary influence
entered her life. Lev Kobylinsky, a minor Symbolist poet and
literary critic better known under his pen name Ellis, was thirty five
and a graduate student at Moscow University when Marina and
Asya met him at Lydia Tamburer's. Ellis published his essays in
Libra (*Vesy*), the most important Symbolist journal of the time,
which was edited by Valery Briusov. He was a member of the
literary group of the Argonauts, centered around Andrei Bely.'A
disorganized poet, but a human being of genius,' as Tsvetaeva later
described him, Ellis soon gained complete sway over the minds and
hearts of both Marina and Asya.

In a witty and humorous narrative poem, 'The Enchanter'
('Charodei'), written five years later, Tsvetaeva reminisced about
the intense emotional triangle between herself, her sister and the
man whose age was more than the sum of theirs. This was also,
clearly, the period of her maximal closeness with Asya, who was
becoming, as Alexandra Zhernakova-Nikolaeva remembered, 'a

second copy of Marina, but without her sister's talent, intelligence or depth.' Ellis, closely involved with the poetry of Dante and Baudelaire, who for him represented the equally attractive polarities of good and evil, opened new literary horizons for the Tsvetaev sisters. At his lodgings at the Hotel Don, which the volatile Ellis shared with a more sedate member of the Argonaut circle, the literary translator Vladimir Nilender, Marina and Asya heard discussions of the latest literary theories and became acquainted with the poetry of Briusov, Blok, Bely and Kuzmin.

There was, Marina learned, a whole vibrant world of French and Russian Symbolist poetry, which went beyond the nineteenth-century romantics, novels for juveniles, and Rostand's tinselled dramas that had until now been her chosen literary fare. This realization enriched her but it did not cause her to give up her earlier favourites all at once. Even after the publication of her first book, the eighteen-year-old Tsvetaeva assured Maximilian Voloshin that although she had read Baudelaire, Rimbaud and Claudel, she did not really care for them because she loved only Napoleon 'and Rostand, Rostand, Rostand.'

A jealous literary mentor, Ellis never offered to introduce the Tsvetaev sisters to any of the famous poets, such as Briusov or Bely, with whom he associated. One spring day in 1909, Asya recognized Valery Briusov on a Moscow streetcar. She accosted him, shouting lines from his poems and creating a scene. The usually decorous Briusov tried to escape by leaving the streetcar, but Asya barred his way and, identifying herself, concluded the assault with: 'Give my regards to Ellis!' Marina commemorated the incident in a poem in her first collection:

> How shameful! You, so far from timid,
> You, who in your verse sing the new moon
> And dryads and overgrown paths, –
> You were frightened by a little sorceress.
> . . . . . .
> Were you frightened by the ardent poison
> Of her bright eyes, where only sparks can be seen?
> Were you afraid of a curly-haired girl?
> Poet, you ought to be ashamed!

This poem was the first salvo of Tsvetaeva's periodic clashes with Briusov which went on until his death and culminated in her 1925 essay on him, 'A Hero of Labour.'

Between October 1909 and January 1910, a complex emotional

imbroglio was created which involved Marina, Ellis, Vladimir
Nilender and, possibly, Asya as well. In her memoirs, Anastasia
Tsvetaeva outlined a straightforward and, most likely, laundered
version of the events of that winter. As she tells it, Ellis fell in love
with Marina and wrote her a letter with a marriage proposal, which
he asked his roommate Nilender to deliver. Marina saw the proposal as a betrayal of her friendship for Ellis. When she discussed
this with Nilender, they realized their mutual attraction. From
being a go-between, Nilender turned into a suitor and proposed
marriage in his turn. After searching conversations and a great deal
of nocturnal strolling through the cold streets of Moscow, Marina
decided to give up both men.

Marina Tsvetaeva's own account of these relationships in 'The
Enchanter' and in a sequence of poems in the section 'Love' of *The
Evening Album* implies that the situation was far more complicated
and less conventional than Anastasia, writing in the Soviet Union,
was willing to reveal. In 'The Enchanter,' the two sisters vow never
to marry anyone but to live out their lives in chaste friendship with
their 'angel, demon, tutor and knight' – Ellis. Individual poems
dating from December show Marina embroiled in two contiguous
triangles: one with Ellis and Nilender and another one with Nilender and Asya. The two sisters form an indissoluble unit and they can
offer themselves in love only as a pair. They long for love: 'Your
love may have been a mistake/But without love we perish, O
Enchanter!'

Two poems of December 1909, 'The Sisters' ('Sestry') and 'A
Threesome' ('Vtroem'), graphically tell of ecstatic moments of
passion Marina and Asya shared with Nilender. What frightened
and repelled them was the physical consummation of this passion:

> Ah, you're not our brothers, no you're not!
> You came out of darkness, you went into a mist.
> Your insane embraces are for us
> An unfamiliar intoxicant.
>
> While you're still here, it's laughter and jokes,
> But as soon as your footsteps recede
> What you've said becomes oddly terrifying
> And my heart senses that you're our enemies.

The intricacy of the relationships is spelled out in the brief poem
'Two Squared' ('Dva v kvadrate'):

For a long time, your glances couldn't tell
Which of the sisters was the one.
There is no point in reproaches.
We are, after all, two. Is it your fault?

'He left!' 'Which one of them?'
Each one of us is affectionate with both.
There is no point in reproaches.
You are, after all, two. Is it our fault?

The quadrangle was dissolved by January 1910, but Marina kept addressing poems of love and farewell to Nilender for the greater part of that year.

In March of 1910 a scandal broke out in the press which involved Ellis and Professor Tsvetaev. Three months earlier, some valuable etchings were stolen from the collection of the Rumiantsev Museum, of which Tsvetaeva's father was the curator. The thief was a museum employee. The etchings were recovered, but it was charged at the time that the thefts took place due to Professor Tsvetaev's negligence. While the investigation was still going on, Ellis, who was known to be a friend of Tsvetaev's daughters and a frequent visitor at his home, was caught cutting pages out of non-circulating books at the Rumiantsev Museum. Criminal charges were lodged. The yellow press had a field day denouncing the immorality of the 'decadents' (as anyone connected with Symbolism and other modernist trends was often called in those days). A high level investigation eventually cleared Professor Tsvetaev, but he was nevertheless relieved of his duties at the Rumiantsev Museum.

The doors of many homes were now closed to Ellis. Marina was no longer allowed to see him or Nilender. But she sent Ellis a consolatory poem 'To the Former Enchanter' ('Byvshemu char-odeiu') in which she refused to pass judgment on him or to join the pack that was hounding him. (Three years later, Ellis went abroad, where he lived in great obscurity. He had no further contact with Tsvetaeva or with any of his other literary friends. He died in Switzerland in 1947.)

By this time, not only the literary horizons but also the personal appearance and habits of Marina Tsvetaeva had begun to change under the impact of her new associates. At the age of seventeen, she bobbed her hair, started wearing high heels and took up smoking.

This may have alarmed her father, because in the summer of 1910, when he went to Germany to look for sculpture reproductions for his museum, he boarded Marina and Asya with the family of a pastor in the suburbs of Dresden. The aim was to teach them some good habits in home economics. This training was not a success, for at the end of the summer Marina, by her own confession, still couldn't tell a beet from a carrot. But her admiration for Germany and Germans was only enhanced by her stay at the Saxon capital.

The year 1910 also marked the high point of Tsvetaeva's infatuation with the legend of the Russian painter and diarist Maria Bashkirtseva (1860–1884). The French diary of Bashkirtseva, who died young of tuberculosis, was published after her death by her mother. *Le Journal de Marie Baschkirtseff* became an international best seller, translated into many languages and much read at the turn of the century. The candour of the diary and Bashkirtseva's astute self-analysis were especially appreciated. In a later age, Simone de Beauvoir in *The Second Sex* cited Bashkirtseva as a casebook study of self-centered female narcissism. Tsvetaeva entered into correspondence with Bashkirtseva's mother. She later planned to write a book in verse to be called *Maria Bashkirtseva* and she dedicated *The Evening Album* to Bashkirtseva's memory.

Returning to Moscow in the fall, the now eighteen-year-old Marina found herself enrolled in still another *gimnasia* (the usual graduation age was sixteen or seventeen). Bored with her studies and deprived of contact with Nilender, whom she apparently still loved, she resorted to a stratagem which spelled the beginning of her literary career. She selected a number of poems she had written to and about Nilender, added to them a number of other poems she had written between 1907 and 1910 and had them printed as a book at her own expense. She called the book *The Evening Album* after a small album bound in blue leather which she and Asya had given Nilender the previous Christmas.

'I published it,' Tsvetaeva later wrote, 'for reasons alien to literature, but related to poetry: as a substitute for a letter to a man with whom I was denied the possibility of communicating in any other way.' Describing the process of the book's publication in 'A Hero of Labour' in 1925, by which time Lenin's government had imposed the most stringent press controls and censorship in Russian history, Tsvetaeva made it a point to remind her readers how easy things were in the period between the revolutions of 1905 and 1917.

'It was simple to publish a book in those days. You gathered the poems, took them to a print shop, selected the design, paid the bill and that was all. This was what I did, without telling anyone, while I was still a high school student.'

The book appeared at the end of October 1910. In 'A Hero of Labour,' Tsvetaeva wrote that after the book was printed, she took all five hundred copies to one obscure book store and considered the affair closed. As she remembered it, she didn't send out any review copies and did not even know at the time that such a practice existed. But recently, the indefatigable Tsvetaeva bibliographer Lev Mnukhin discovered several inscribed copies she did send out at the time of the book's publication, including one addressed to Briusov and another one to the Musaget publishing house. On December 1, 1910, she sent an inscribed copy to the poet and art critic Maximilian Voloshin, whom she had not yet met at the time. But it *is* true that the book was not announced or advertised anywhere and that it was something of a surprise when four prominent literary personalities reviewed this production of an unknown schoolgirl.

The four were, in order of appearance, Voloshin, Gumiliov, Briusov and Marietta Shaginian. Voloshin's review came ten days after he received the book. He perceptively pointed out that this book had to be read as a unit, as if it were one continuous diary, an observation that applies to all of Tsvetaeva's subsequent collections. The poet's voice, he wrote, is on the border between the final days of childhood and early youth. Although this voice at times breaks, like a child's voice, it can convey nuances 'of which we adults couldn't even dream.'

Nikolai Gumiliov was the leader and, with Anna Akhmatova (his wife at the time) and Osip Mandelstam, a principal practitioner of the Acmeist school in Russian poetry. In the prestigious art journal *Apollon*, he published a brief review which showed enviable critical foresight. 'Marina Tsvetaeva,' he wrote, 'is inherently talented, inherently original. It does not matter that her book is dedicated "to the radiant memory of Maria Bashkirtseva," the epigraph is taken from Rostand, and the word "mama" is almost never absent from its pages. All this only suggests the young age of the poetess, which is soon confirmed by her own lines of confession. There is much in this book that is new: the audacious, at times excessive, intimacy of tone; the new themes, such as childhood infatuation; the spontaneous, unthinking delight in the trivia of everyday life. And, as one would have thought, all the principal laws of poetry have been instinctively guessed, so that this book is not only a charming book of a young girl's confessions, but also a book of excellent verse.'

Valery Briusov, one of the pillars of Russian Symbolism and then at the height of his renown, took a more guarded approach. Since his incident with Asya on the streetcar in the spring of 1909, he had had an encounter with Marina at a Moscow book store, where she overheard Briusov tell a salesman: '... I am no admirer of Rostand.' The same day she wrote Briusov a hurt and indignant letter, accusing him of insensitivity for failing to see that Rostand was a poet of the caliber of Heine, Victor Hugo and Lermontov. On the last page of the inscribed copy Tsvetaeva sent him, Briusov noted: 'Well-schooled. But it is all a bit insipid. Too much saccharine emotionality.' In his review, Briusov took exception to the very things that charmed Gumiliov. The excessive intimacy of tone frightened him, the spontaneity of the book seemed to him to spill into indecorous slovenliness (*domashnost'*). Briusov urged Tsvetaeva to broaden her poetic horizon and not waste her undoubted talent on 'unnecessary, albeit elegant trifles.'

The Russian-Armenian poet and, later, novelist Marietta Shaginian, writing in a newspaper published in the southern town of Taganrog (Anton Chekhov's birthplace), pointed out the young poet's independence from current literary fashions and the authenticity of the child's mentality which her poems conveyed. Tsvetaeva wrote that she had found Shaginian's review especially valuable. An orthodox Stalinist in the later decades of her life, Marietta Shaginian subsequently managed to edit her pre-revolutionary favourable reviews of Tsvetaeva not only out of her biography but apparently even out of her memory. In her memoirs published in 1977, Shaginian claimed that she first heard of Tsvetaeva only after the latter's return from emigration in 1939.

After the publication of her book, the young poet went on attending the *gimnasia*. Shortly before sending her book to Voloshin, she heard him give a lecture on Villiers de l'Isle Adam, for whose Faustian drama *Axël* (later considered the quintessential work of Symbolist literature by Edmund Wilson) she then conceived a profound admiration. At her invitation, Voloshin called on her at Three Pond Lane. Their encounter on that occasion and the impact that her friendship with Voloshin had on her further literary

development were lovingly described by Tsvetaeva in her memoir
'The Living About the Living' ('Zhivoe o zhivom'), 1933.

Maximilian Voloshin (1877–1932) was not a first-rate poet, but
his verse was colorful and often eloquent. As a person he was larger
than life. A burly, blond-bearded giant ('three hundred pounds of
masculine beauty' was his modest self-description), he possessed
huge stores of enthusiasm and altruism. A man of uncertain or
underdeveloped sexuality, both of whose marriages were of the
mariage blanc variety, Voloshin cultivated the friendship of women
and poets. 'When a woman turned out to be a poet or, more exactly,
the poet was a woman,' Tsvetaeva wrote, 'there were no bounds to
his friendship, protectiveness, attention, admiration and creative
cooperation.'

Voloshin quickly replaced Ellis as Tsvetaeva's literary guide.
Awed by her poetic talent, he soon saw that her taste needed
developing. She still preferred Rostand to Mallarmé, and in her
letter to Voloshin of January 5, 1911 she expressed her contempt for
Chekhov (whom she apparently never did read), while raving over
The Goddesses, a trilogy of quasi-Nietzschean early potboilers by
Heinrich Mann. Unable to interest her in some of his favourite
French Symbolists or eighteenth-century writers all at once, Vol-
oshin resorted to a gradual approach, offering Tsvetaeva novels by
George Sand and Alexandre Dumas père first and then moving on
to more sophisticated literary fare.

It was Voloshin who first brought Tsvetaeva to Musaget, some-
thing that Ellis had earlier avoided doing, despite her interest.
Musaget was both the editorial offices of the Argonauts' publishing
house and a literary café. At the discussions there, the young
Tsvetaeva met the leading Symbolist poet Viacheslav Ivanov, the
literary historian Mikhail Gershenzon, the young philosopher
Feodor Stepun, Anna (Asya) Turgeneva, who was soon to marry
Andrei Bely, and other members of Moscow's literary community.
When Musaget brought out an anthology of contemporary Russian
poetry early in 1911, the two latest poems by Marina Tsvetaeva
appeared in it next to the work of some of the best-known poets of
the day, such as Blok, Bely, Gumiliov, Kuzmin, Voloshin and
Viacheslav Ivanov. Also featured in the anthology were several
other promising beginners, among them Vladislav Khodasevich.

Tsvetaeva spent most of April of 1911 all alone in the ruins of a
Genovese fortress at Gurzuf, in the Crimea, reading French novels

and trying to come to terms with the reasons for the failure of her relationship with Nilender. She wrote a letter to Voloshin about her fear that she had become too bookish and too withdrawn from life: 'It is the fault of books and also of my deep mistrust of real, genuine life. A book and life, a poem and what had brought it forth: – what incommensurable quantities! And I am so infected with this mistrust that I see (I am beginning to see) only the material, natural side of everything. But this is a direct path to skepticism which is hateful to me, which is my enemy.' Later in the same letter she wrote: 'There remains a sense of utter solitude for which there is no cure. The body of another person is a wall, it prevents me from seeing his soul. Oh, how I hate this wall! But I do not want a paradise where everything is blissful and airy – I so much love faces, gestures, the everyday life. Nor do I want a life where everything is clear, simple and coarsely crude.'

At the end of that month she went to join Voloshin (with whom she was now on first-name terms, something that happened very rarely in her life) and his mother at their now famous Crimean retreat. The boarding house for poets and artists which the Voloshins operated at the remote village of Koktebel, not far from Feodosia, has become a favourite topic with writers of memoirs. The memoirists have made the most of the literary luminaries who visited Koktebel and of the eccentric manners of Voloshin's half-German mother Elena Ottobaldovna. Nicknamed Pra (a contraction of the word meaning 'ancestress') by her son, she usually wore Near Eastern male garb, which, combined with her close-cropped grey hair, often resulted in her being mistaken for a man. Marina and Pra soon developed a lasting mutual attachment and Pra replaced Lydia Tamburer as her confidante and mother figure.

Also staying with the Voloshins at Koktebel were two Efron sisters, Vera and Elizaveta (usually called Lilia), and their seventeen-year-old younger brother Sergei, who had just recovered from a bout of tuberculosis. The Efrons had an unusual family background. Their Jewish father came from a clan of noted rabbis. Their mother was born Elizaveta Durnovo, the beautiful daughter of an aide-de-camp to Tsar Nicholas I. Under the influence of the famed anarchist Peter Kropotkin, this aristocratic young woman became a revolutionary and joined the terrorist group People's Freedom. She met her future husband at one of this group's conspiratorial meetings. In 1880 she was arrested and incarcerated at the St Peter and Paul Fortress.

Through her father's intercession she was allowed to go abroad, where she married Yakov Efron and where the first three of their nine children were born. The family was later allowed to come back to Russia, but Elizaveta Durnovo-Efron kept returning periodically to revolutionary activities (at least in the account of her granddaughter, Marina Tsvetaeva's daughter Ariadna Efron), right up to the revolution of 1905.

Sergei Efron was introduced to Tsvetaeva on the beach in front of the Voloshins' villa on May 5, 1911. In her memoirs and letters she several times told the story of how she challenged him to find her favourite pebble on the seashore, having decided secretly that if he did, she would marry him. Sergei immediately brought her the cornelian bead she had in mind. From that moment on, they became inseparable. Sergei, it turned out, had literary ambitions and was hoping to become a fiction writer. His sisters were alarmed about his growing closeness with Marina. They felt that at seventeen he was too young for a full-fledged romance and they were worried about how this might affect his health, since he had not yet fully recovered from the tuberculosis.

In July, Marina Tsvetaeva accompanied Sergei Efron to a health resort in the Ural Mountains, where he had been scheduled to take a koumiss (fermented mares' milk) cure as a precaution against a relapse. In the fall she brought him to Moscow and, since her father happened to be abroad, asked him to move in with her at the family home in Three Pond Lane. By the time her father returned, Sergei and Marina took an apartment in Moscow together with Vera and Lilia Efron. That same fall they submitted to a publisher two manuscripts – she of her second collection of verse, *The Magic Lantern*, dedicated to him, he of his book of short stories, dedicated to her.

Marina Tsvetaeva and Sergei Efron were married in a quiet ceremony in Moscow in January of 1912, when she was nineteen and he eighteen. Anastasia Tsvetaeva, her sister's imitator in everything, was married shortly thereafter to a young man she had met at a skating rink. *The Magic Lantern* (*Volshebnyi fonar'*) was published early in 1912 and at the beginning of 1913 Tsvetaeva published her third collection of verse, *From Two Books*, which was indeed a selection of poems from her first two books with an added

new preface. The critical reception of the second and third collections was not anywhere as impressive as the one that greeted *The
Evening Album*.

'... I was never under anyone's influence,' Tsvetaeva wrote to
George Ivask on April 4, 1933. 'I began with writing, not with
reading poets.' In 'Story of a Dedication,' however, she recalled
writing bad and imitative poetry as a child: 'Bad poetry? Why, it
is like measles. It is something that is best gotten over in childhood.' A few excerpts from her immature poetry are cited in her
memoirs and those of her sister, but there are not enough of them
to form a considered opinion. The earliest poems that found their
way into her first two collections date from the winter of 1907–8.
Their themes and ideas may be adolescent and occasionally naive,
but technically they are the work of a master.

Her first two collections, *The Evening Album* and *The Magic
Lantern*, may be best considered as one unit, not only themati-
cally and stylistically, but chronologically as well. Many of the
poems in the second collection bear the date 1911, which means
that they were written after the publication of *The Evening
Album*. But *The Magic Lantern* also contains a number of
undated poems which, as internal evidence shows, were written
concurrently with the ones included in *The Evening Album* and
possibly even before them. Tsvetaeva herself once referred to
these two collections as 'the same book in spirit.' These two collections, therefore, represent a definite stage in her poetic evolution, a stage that encompasses the period from the autumn of
1907 to the beginning of 1912.

In his not entirely favourable review of *The Evening Album*,
Valery Briusov astutely observed that Tsvetaeva's poems always
have their point of departure in concrete facts, 'in something that
she had actually experienced.' Like all of her lyric poetry, those
first two books are a diary of her life, encounters, interests and
current reading, all of it transfigured by the alchemy of poetry
into a higher reality. Thus, of the three sections into which *The
Evening Album* is divided, the first one, 'Childhood,' reflects the
author's travels to Nervi, Lausanne and the Black Forest, the
details of her schooling and her relationships with family and
friends. Much of the book's second section, 'Love,' outlines her
involvement with Ellis and Nilender, while the third section,

'Only Shadows,' gives expression to her Bonapartist sympathies, her love for juvenile romances and her hopes for the future.

Real experience, however, is filtered in these two books through an emotional outlook that can be best understood within the context of the romantic and idealistic revival that took place in French literature at the end of the nineteenth century. This was the revival exemplified in the novel *Les Pléiades* by Joseph-Arthur de Gobineau and the already mentioned *Axël* by Villiers de l'Isle Adam. Tsvetaeva encountered the outlook embodied in these works in a vulgarized and diluted form in Rostand's *L'Aiglon* and in his *La Princesse lointaine*, which she also highly valued at the time.

This is a view that leads the poet to expect from life more than it can possibly give. A concomitant tendency is to admire everything exceptional and heroic and to reject the average, the humdrum, the prosaic. A very precise expression of this attitude is found in the poem 'A Prayer' ('*Molitva*') which Tsvetaeva wrote in Tarusa on her seventeenth birthday. It begins:

> Christ and God! I long for a miracle
> Right now, immediately, at break of day!
> O let me die, while still
> All life is like a book to me.
>
> Thou art wise, Thou wouldst not sternly say:
> 'Endure, the time is not yet come.'
> Thou Thyself gavest me so much!
> I long for all the roads at once.

The poet then outlines various mutually conflicting 'roads' which she longs to follow

> So that yesterday would be legend,
> So that every day would be madness

and then concludes the poem with the words

> Thou gavest me a childhood better than a fairy tale
> So give me a death at seventeen!

In 1976, the fine American poet Alfred Corn found in the eighth line of this poem the epigraph and the title of his book *All Roads at Once.*

A heroic, miraculous death is preferable to the disappointment and frustration inherent in attaining maturity. Hence the indiscriminate fascination with any gifted or sensitive person who died young, be it the Duke of Reichstadt, Maria Bashkirtseva, Lydia Tamburer's son Sergei or the Georgian princess Nina Dzhavakha, the title character of Charskaya's cloyingly sentimental novel, beloved by generations of Russian teenaged girls. The spirit of Rostand presided over much in the world of Tsvetaeva's first two collections, both of which contain epigraphs from Napoleon, his son and Rostand and poems about characters and situations from *L'Aiglon*. This series reaches its slightly absurd climax in the poem 'Separation' ('Rasstavanie'), where the fate of the Duke of Reichstadt is likened to that of Christ and his place of exile, the palace of Schönbrunn, is equated with Golgotha.

The only alternative to an early, glorious death is a permanent stay in the nursery. Children inhabit a magical region and they are superior in every way to adults:

> Over the world of crepuscular visions
> We children reign today.
> . . . . . .
> We are links in a mysterious chain.
> We will not be discouraged in this struggle.
> The ultimate battle is nearing
> And the power of those dim ones will be over.
>
> We despise adults because
> Their days are simple and dull.
> We know, we know much
> Of what they do not know.

The atmosphere of the nursery is ever-present in both books. It is expressed in the abundance of diminutives, in the frequent rhyme *mal'chik – pal'chik* ('little boy,' 'little finger'), in recurrent catchwords, such as 'baby,' 'mummy' and 'fairy tale.' There are dirges for departing childhood, poems about the childhood of Sarah Bernhardt, Sergei Efron and even Maximilian Voloshin.

In several poems placed at the end of *The Magic Lantern*, the nineteen-year-old poet is desperately fighting the impending eviction into the prosaic adult world. A tentative solution to this problem is suggested in two interconnected poems in the second collection. 'From a Fairy Tale Into Life' ('Iz skazki v zhizn'') is a farewell lament for Asya Turgeneva, newly married to the adult and famous Andrei Bely. 'From One Fairy Tale Into Another' ('Iz skazki v skazku') was addressed by Tsvetaeva to Sergei Efron at the time of their marriage. In it, she asserted her intention to remain a little girl for the rest of her days and promised to teach her husband how to remain forever a child.

At seventeen and eighteen Tsvetaeva may have been only a promising, at times immature poet, but she was already an amazingly skillful versifier. She did not seem aware at the time of the possibilities of Russian accentual verse (*dol'nik*), which was widely practiced among her senior contemporaries and restricted herself to the five canonic meters of Russian nineteenth-century versification. Any possible metrical monotony was easily overcome by young Tsvetaeva's amazing strophic inventiveness. From the very beginning Tsvetaeva shows a mastery in this area that gives her a place alongside Zhukovsky and Fet, the two poets particularly noted for their originality in inventing new types of stanzas. Structural resourcefulness typical of the mature Tsvetaeva is also manifest at this early period. She likes segmenting her poems into three sections, each of which is a syntactic and thematic variation on the poem's central idea. Thus, 'Rouge et bleue' in *The Evening Album* consists of three long stanzas which show the poem's two protagonists successively as little children, as young girls and as grown-up women in frustrating situations appropriate to each age. The structural parallelism brings out the parallelism in these two women's fate.

In a highly interesting study of role conflict in Tsvetaeva's poetics, Antonina Filonov Gove found that 'Rouge et bleue' is one of several poems in the first two collections in which the poet explicitly rejects the standard role allocated to women in human society. One of the reasons the persona clings so desperately to childhood is that some of the 'roads' she mentioned in 'A Prayer' are barred to her: the roles of a warrior, a bard or a drummer marching at the head of a platoon. The most attractive role of all for Tsvetaeva, then and later, was that of an independent Amazon, a role she had in her grasp and voluntarily relinquished. Voloshin was nothing less than prophetic when he wrote in his review of *The Evening Album* that the essence of Tsvetaeva's poetry was encompassed in the following quatrain:

> I love women who knew no fear in battle,
> Who were able to handle a sword and a spear.
> But I know that only in the cradle's prison
> Is my ordinary feminine happiness.

And indeed, the maternal instinct, which in Tsvetaeva's case most definitely extended to her husband as well as to her children, imprisoned this rebellious poet more securely and guided the tragic turns of her fate more imperiously than any government or revolution ever could.

3

Two rival suns

Marina Tsvetaeva's marriage to Sergei Efron inaugurated the period of greatest material affluence she was ever to experience and temporarily blunted her literary ambitions. She could now, at last, forget the hateful *gimnasia*, from which she never did graduate. Throughout her childhood and adolescence, Tsvetaeva was tormented by her plump and rosy-cheeked appearance. She felt it clashed with the poetic image she had of herself, making her resemble not her favourite Pushkin heroine, Tatiana, but rather Tatiana's chubby sister Olga.

After her marriage, she slimmed down, began to pay attention to her clothes and did interesting things to her hair. Photographs dating from ca. 1911–16, the stylish portrait of her painted by Magda Nachmann in 1913 and memoirs of contemporaries show us a new Marina Tsvetaeva: sociable, self-assured and elegant. She was at peace with herself, knew she was attractive and was secure about her place in the human community. This is the only period in her life of which this can be said.

Thanks to the generosity of Suzanne Meyn (the Swiss second wife of Tsvetaeva's maternal grandfather, who after his death treated Marina and Asya as if they were her own grandchildren), Marina and Sergei were able to purchase in 1912 their own house in Zamoskvorechie, the old quarter in Moscow that was traditionally populated by merchant-class families. In this house their daughter Ariadna was born on September 5, 1912. Two years later they gave up the house to move to a more centrally located apartment at No. 6 Boris and Gleb Lane in Moscow (*Borisoglebsky pereulok*), which was to remain Tsvetaeva's home until her departure from Russia in 1922. But they had a second home with the Voloshins in the Crimea where they frequently stayed in summer. During the winter, Voloshin's mother, Pra, usually shared a residence in Moscow with Sergei Efron's sisters Vera and Lilia. In addition to her sister Asya, these women were Marina

Tsvetaeva's closest companions in the years immediately after her marriage.

Some time during the winter 1913–14, Anastasia Tsvetaeva formed a friendship with one of the best-known writers of the time, Vasily Rozanov (1856–1919), and began a correspondence with him. Learning with delight from her sister that Rozanov had a great interest in their father (who had died a year earlier and with whose conservative politics Rozanov had an affinity), Tsvetaeva wrote Rozanov three long confessional letters about her family's history and her own life and situation. Chock-full of previously unavailable information, these letters have become, since their publication in excerpts in the Soviet Union in 1969 and in complete form in Paris in 1972, an indispensable source for studying Tsvetaeva's biography and psychology.

In her letter to Rozanov of March 7, 1914, Tsvetaeva wrote: 'To tell you about myself: I am married and have a one-year-old daughter Ariadna (Alya). My husband is twenty. He is extraordinarily and nobly handsome, he is beautiful outwardly and inwardly.' Mindful of Rozanov's well-known aversion toward Jews, she added: 'Within Sergei there are united, dazzlingly, two bloods, Jewish and Russian. He is dazzlingly gifted, intelligent and chivalrous.' And later in the same letter: 'I love Sergei boundlessly and forever. My daughter I adore.'

Marina Tsvetaeva's situation during this period paralleled in a curious way the situation of her native country and its culture. The last few years before the outbreak of World War I were the years of unprecedented economic prosperity in Russia. This was due to the success of the land reform carried out by Prime Minister Piotr Stolypin, the remarkable spread of the agricultural and consumers' cooperatives and a series of bountiful harvests that came year after year. For the first (and only) time in its history, Russia became a major food exporter.

In literature, philosophy and the arts, the beginning of the second decade of the twentieth century was a time of staggering brilliance. Either by earlier or by later standards, the cultural atmosphere was unbelievably free. The revolution of 1905 had made possible the kind of advocacy in political, religious and sexual areas that had been unthinkable earlier: the Bolshevik newspaper *Pravda*, still extant and thriving, first went legally on sale in 1912. On the other hand, Diaghilev's journal *The World of Art* and several other fine literary and art journals that patterned themselves on its example succeeded in liberating Russian culture from the dictatorship of the nineteenth-century radical utilitarian tradition, with its ceaseless demands for photographic realism and social relevance to the exclusion of everything else.

This double liberation made possible the explosion of creativity and innovation that is often credited in the West to the post-revolutionary period, though it took place in the decade between the revolutions of 1905 and 1917. In painting, the various modernist schools, which have been getting so much attention recently, were all fully formed by 1912. In music, Scriabin, Stravinsky and the young Sergei Prokofiev were ushering in the twentieth century. In the theater, a pleiad of inspired stage directors, which included Vsevolod Meyerhold and Yevgeny Vakhtangov, nurtured by Stanislavsky's example, moved away from his realistic and psychological concept of drama and began to map out the forms that theater was later to assume in Western countries. In all cultural areas, there was a rediscovery of the Russian and Western past and a receptivity to new ideas and styles that originated in other cultures.

In literature, poets of the senior and junior Symbolist generations were still at the peak of their powers in 1910, when their supremacy was challenged by several new poetic movements, which ostensibly revolted against Symbolism, but which in fact built on its achievements and were its true heirs. There was Acmeism, whose sane and sensible poetics insisted on the primacy of reality and everyday life in preference to the mysticism of the Symbolists. Mikhail Kuzmin was the model and the inspiration for this movement, though he never joined it. For a few years, Acmeism united Gumiliov, Akhmatova and Mandelstam, after which all three outgrew it and went their separate ways.

There were several varieties of Futurism in Russian poetry, all of which combined an enthusiasm for modernity with an emphasis on the verbal aspects of poetic expression. The most important of the Futurists, Velimir Khlebnikov and Vladimir Mayakovsky, developed styles patterned on current trends in the visual arts, such as Cubism, with unexpected shiftings of planes and use of primary shapes and colors. The young Boris Pasternak began his literary career as an adherent of one of the minor trends within Russian Futurism. Adding further to the variety, there was a group of peasant poets, led by Nikolai Kliuev and the most notable of his disciples, Sergei Esenin. These poets were called 'peasant' not so much because of their origin, but because they advocated a kind of peasant separatism from the rest of Russian culture and because the fate of Russian village life in the twentieth century was their obsessive theme. In their verse, they combined the poetic manner of the Symbolists with the folklore of the Old Believer sects of Northern Russia.

Yet, despite all this economic and artistic progress, the political situation in the country was in many ways bleak. Alexander Solzhenitsyn has compared the relationship between the imperial government and Russian society in the pre-revolutionary decade to that of two horses harnessed to the same vehicle but determined to pull it in opposite directions. After authorizing the legislative Duma, Nicholas II kept disbanding it and interfering with its projects. His hysterical, German-born consort, Alexandra, did everything she could to deprive the people of the rights they had won after the 1905 revolution. By insisting that her adviser, the corrupt and illiterate faith healer Grigory Rasputin, be given the power to decide matters of state, Alexandra damaged the prestige of the Romanovs beyond repair.

As was observable later in the Weimar Republic in Germany and in post-Vietnam America, epochs when new rights and freedoms are being gained are often perceived by contemporaries as periods of decline and oppression. Speeches by Constitutional Democratic and Socialist Revolutionary representatives in the Duma and the poetry of Blok and Bely dating from the interim between the revolutions of 1905 and 1917 depict that time as the harshest, most repressive age that the country had ever seen. In 1909, on the eighty-fourth anniversary of the Decembrist rebellion of 1825, Zinaida Gippius addressed an impassioned poem to the ghosts of the Decembrists, where she assured them that nothing had changed in Russian society since their time (she was writing half a century after the liberation of the serfs and other momentous reforms of Alexander II, to say nothing of 1905). This is but one example out of hundreds one could cite to show that nothing short of the abolition of the monarchy could have satisfied society at that stage.

Within the rich and highly sophisticated literary environment of the time, the poetry that Marina Tsvetaeva published in *The Evening*

Album in 1910, for all its individuality and technical polish, could not help appearing limited in scope and somewhat provincial in outlook. After *The Magic Lantern* and *From Two Books*, even critics who had welcomed her first book, such as Gumiliov and Shaginian, made clear in their reviews that they were not willing to stay with her indefinitely in the same corner of the nursery and that they could not see why she would want to do so, either.

It is not likely that Tsvetaeva was impressed or convinced by these critics' advice. But, without ceasing to write poetry, she stopped publishing it and devoted herself entirely to her husband and daughter. In her relationship with the little Ariadna, Tsvetaeva was every bit as arbitrary and demanding as her mother had been during her own childhood. This can be seen in her journal of her daughter's infancy, 'Alya. Notations on My First Daughter,' which Véronique Lossky published in 1981, and in three poems addressed to Ariadna, all called 'To Alya,' which Tsvetaeva wrote in 1913 and 1914. Written before the child was two, these texts saddle her with expectations of future greatness and astounding accomplishments. She is to have a fabulous love life when she grows up. She is to be a great beauty and a greater poet than her mother. Tsvetaeva's love for her daughter was frankly jealous and possessive. The child is not to be involved with anyone except her mother and to live only for her:

> I am a serpent abducting a princess.
> A dragon! A bridegroom to end all bridegrooms!
> O light of my eyes! O jealousy
> Of my nights!

The same maternal solicitude, but of a far more indulgent variety, is discernible in Tsvetaeva's relationship with her husband. In it she took the lead from the very start. She was the one who decided they were to marry and she instilled in him a romantic outlook and the exalted notions of honor and old-fashioned courtesy that she admired in men. In two poems she addressed to her husband in the summer of 1913, he is depicted as frail, passive, jewel-like and harboring mysterious hidden powers. Here is her portrait of Sergei on the beach at Koktebel:

> Your limbs are like aquatic plants,
> Like willow branches at Malmaison ...
> Thus you lay there in the seafoam spray
> Absent-mindedly resting

The aquamarine and chrysoprase
Of your blue-green, blue-gray,
Always half-closed eyes
On some light-golden melons.
. . . . . .
Thus, gemlike and calm, you are stretched,
Not even deigning to look.
But should you look, wars will flare up
And mountains will slide into the sea

And new moons will light up
And joyful lions will lie down
At the mere inclination of your youthful,
Of your magnificent head.

In a postscript to the already cited letter to Rozanov of March 7, 1914, we read: 'I want to tell you a few more words about Sergei. He is very sickly. When he was sixteen, he had incipient tuberculosis. Now it has stopped, but the general state of his health is much worse than it should be. If you only knew what an ardent, generous and profound young man he is! I constantly tremble over him. His temperature goes up from the slightest excitement [. . .]' 'He is the person closest to me for the rest of my life. I could never love anyone else, there is too much longing and protest within me for that. Only in his presence can I live as I do – utterly free. No one, not a single one of my friends understands my choice. Choice! God, as if there were anything to choose.'

Less than a month later, her solicitude for Sergei, as expressed in her letter to Rozanov of April 18, 1914, took an embarrassing turn. At twenty-one, Sergei still did not have his high school diploma (*attestat zrelosti*). He was trying to obtain it by taking examinations at the Feodosia *gimnasia*, since without the diploma he could not enroll in a university and ran the risk of being drafted into the army. The principal of the school where Sergei was to take his examinations was known to be a great admirer of Rozanov's writings. Marina's idea of helping her husband was to ask Rozanov to write the principal 'an affectionate letter' accompanied by an inscribed copy of one of his books, which she believed would result in the principal arranging for Sergei to pass whether he deserved to or not. We do not know what action Rozanov took, but it is not too surprising that his correspondence with Tsvetaeva stopped after this letter.

Sergei Efron's efforts to obtain a high school diploma at twenty-one was symptomatic of his later fate. A man of great delicacy and personal charm, he was to remain a student for much of his life, enrolling in various schools and courses well into his forties. Except for the time he was away during the Civil War and apart from the grants and stipends he obtained for university studies in the 1920s and for far less attractive activities in the 1930s, he remained a lifelong financial dependent of his wife.

1913 was the year when Tsvetaeva's poetry began to mature and to evolve away from the adolescent tone of her first two collections. This can be observed in several poems on the subject of death which she wrote that year. They show a turn toward sobriety of tone and a simplicity that borders on austerity, especially when compared to the ostentatiously romantic manner of her earlier poetry. Her understanding of death in these poems is fundamentally different from the youthful desire for an early, glorious death which she had voiced only a few years earlier. Now the attitude is a calm acceptance of death as an ever-present fact in our lives. In one mature and precisely worded poem after another, the young wife and recent mother writes of her own funeral, addresses a passer-by at her future tomb and speaks from her grave to a remote descendant. There is no fear of death in these poems, nor are they tragic. Ultimately, the tone is affirmative and almost optimistic.

These poems form a part of Tsvetaeva's next collection of verse which she called *Juvenilia* (*Yunosheskie stikhi*) and which comprises the poetry she wrote between the beginning of 1913 and the last day of 1915. The title is not very appropriate, since the term *juvenilia* describes her first two books much better than the book she thus named. Never published in its complete form during the poet's lifetime, the collection has appeared in two editions in the West since 1976. Only a few individual poems from it were included in Soviet editions.

Juvenilia is clearly a transitional collection, the only such instance in Tsvetaeva's output. Much of its poetry is still in her early romantic manner. Such is the case with a cycle of poems addressed to her sister Asya and a set of memorial poems occasioned by the death of Sergei Efron's older brother Piotr. Such is also the case with several poems about literary figures, though by now Tsvetaeva had graduated from Rostand and Bashkirtseva to Pushkin and

Byron. But the poems about death, discussed above, were a new departure and so was the ambitious project she undertook in the first half of 1914. This was the long narrative poem 'The Enchanter,' which she dedicated to Asya and subtitled *poèma*.

In the eighteenth century, the term *poèma* designated in Russian literary terminology an epic poem written in imitation of Homer or Virgil. In Pushkin's time, this term was applied to the Byronic tale in verse. In the eighteenth and nineteenth centuries the genre of *poèma* presupposed a developed fictional or historical plot. Twentieth-century Russian poets, however, replaced the traditionally well-constructed plot of the earlier *poèma* with a fragmentary autobiographical narrative, usually centered on the poet's own psychological experiences rather than on external events. Had Tsvetaeva's 'The Enchanter' been published shortly after it was written instead of having to wait six decades, it would have taken its rightful place as a pioneering example of this new twentieth-century form of autobiographical narrative poem. It predates such major instances of this genre as Viacheslav Ivanov's 'Infancy' (1918), Andrei Bely's 'The First Encounter' (1921), and Mayakovsky's 'About This' (1923).

Written in a special stanza devised for the occasion and consisting of three lines of iambic tetrameter followed by a two-foot iambic line, 'The Enchanter' traces and celebrates the impact that their friendship with Ellis had on the two Tsvetaev sisters. The model for this poem may have been 'Three Meetings' by Vladimir Soloviov (1898), a verse narrative that tells, in humorous and self-deprecating tones, of the poet-philosopher's innermost mystical experience of being in contact with St Sophia, the feminine personification of Divine Wisdom. Tsvetaeva, similarly, pokes puckish fun at her own and her sister's childishness and naiveté and at the scatterbrained ways of Ellis, while recounting, with love and gratitude, Ellis's lectures on the Symbolist and mystical theories of Soloviov, Merezhkovsky and Blok, and the festive and enchanted evenings the sisters spent with him. The poem is the maturing poet's farewell to her younger self, which she leaves behind but does not renounce.

In addition to 'The Enchanter' and the poems about death, there is one more important work in *Juvenilia* which shows Tsvetaeva's growing poetic power. This is the seventeen-poem cycle 'Woman Friend' ('Podruga'), written between October 16, 1914 and May 6, 1915. The cycle arose out of a wrenching personal involvement which was one of the major episodes of Tsvetaeva's biography. Like 'The Enchanter,' it remained unknown to Tsvetaeva scholars until the 1970s, leaving a big lacuna which it is now possible to fill.

'We shall never part. Our finding each other was a miracle,' Tsvetaeva wrote to Rozanov in March of 1914, referring to her husband. There is no reason to doubt her sincerity. Yet, six months later an event occurred that gives these words an ironic ring. In October of that same year, in a Moscow literary salon, Marina Tsvetaeva met Sophia Parnok, whom she later described as: 'Not a woman and not a boy / But something stronger than me.' Sophia Parnok (1885–1933) came from an affluent Jewish family in Southern Russia and she was known at the time as a translator of poetry and a literary critic who signed her work with the male pseudonym Andrei Polianin. Many years later, long after the contacts between her and Tsvetaeva ceased, she was to develop into a remarkable and powerful poet in her own right. Throughout her life, she was openly and aggressively lesbian.

The very first impression made by Parnok must have affected Tsvetaeva in a manner best described by the French expression *un coup de foudre*:

> My heart told me instantly: 'There she is!'
> I forgave you everything in advance
> Not yet knowing your name, knowing nothing . . .
> Oh love me, I must have you love me!
>
> I can see by the curve of your lips,
> By their deliberate arrogance,
> By the heavy ridge of your eyebrows
> That your heart must be taken by storm.
> . . . . . .
> Refuting all mockery with my verse
> I reveal here to you and the world
> All that's in store for us two within you,
> My fair stranger with Beethoven's face.

The relationship between the two women, inaugurated immediately after they were introduced in October of 1914, remained the central fact of both of their lives until February 1916, leaving some lingering traces in Tsvetaeva's poetry till April of that year. This relationship and its record in the poetry of Tsvetaeva remained unnoticed by scholars and biographers (the present writer included) until the end of the 1970s. Then Sophia Poliakova, the Soviet scholar who had spent decades studying the biography and writings of Sophia Parnok and her relationship with Tsvetaeva, realized that she could not publish any of her findings in the Soviet Union and sent them abroad. Poliakova's book *The Sunset Days of Yore: Tsvetaeva and Parnok*, brought out in Russian by Ardis Press, her textual study of the cycle 'Woman Friend,' and her introductory essay to the Ardis edition of Parnok's collected poetry have brought important new dimensions to Tsvetaeva studies, dimensions which no responsible scholar has the right to ignore.

Tsvetaeva's bisexuality, revealed by Poliakova, should not come as a surprise because the poet herself shows in her memoirs and letters that it was a part of her psychological profile since early childhood. In 'My Pushkin,' Tsvetaeva reminisced about how her mother mocked and berated her when she was six for claiming to appreciate a scene from Tchaikovsky's *Eugene Onegin* which the mother thought she was too young to understand. The mother assumed that the little girl had fallen in love with the singer who portrayed Onegin. 'My mother was mistaken,' the adult Tsvetaeva wrote. 'I did not fall in love with Onegin, but with Onegin and Tatiana (and perhaps with Tatiana a little bit more), with both of them jointly and with love.'

Infatuation was to remain Tsvetaeva's most characteristic form of emotional contact with another person. In love, she sought romance and the acknowledgement of an intense mutual need. She always mistrusted the physical, carnal aspect of love. Her affair with Sophia Parnok awakened her sensuality and gave her the kind of erotic fulfillment that she did not get from her passionate but chaste involvement with Nilender, nor, apparently, from her marriage with Sergei Efron. Hence the combination of amorous frenzy and unconcealed resentment powerfully expressed in certain poems of 'Woman Friend,' especially poems 13 and 14 of the cycle. The inner conflict of these poems has nothing to do with rejection of lesbian love or fear of social sanctions.

Unlike the post-revolutionary Soviet Union, Russian society of the last pre-revolutionary decades was remarkably open on the subject of love between members of the same sex. While the press in English-speaking countries wrote of Oscar Wilde with horror and revulsion at the time of his trial and conviction in 1895, most Russian writers, Vasily Rozanov included, saw in his trial the persecution of a gifted man by the hypocritical British authorities.

The suspension of censorship after 1905 enabled Mikhail Kuzmin to publish in 1906 his autobiographical *roman à thèse*, *Wings*, an eloquent defense of homosexuality, which enjoyed a tremendous popular success and had to be reprinted every few years until the October Revolution, after which it was banned.

Among the well-known writers of the period who wrote openly and favourably of the same-sex love were Viacheslav Ivanov; his wife Lydia Zinovieva-Annibal (who specialized in the theme of lesbian love and whose book of short stories, *The Tragic Zoo*, given to her by Voloshin, Tsvetaeva particularly admired); the novelist Yevdokia Nagrodskaya; the leading poet of the peasant group, Nikolai Kliuev; and a few years later, Sophia Parnok herself. Among the neighbours of the Voloshins in Koktebel, there was Vladimir Soloviov's younger sister Polyxena, a minor Symbolist poet and the translator of *Alice in Wonderland* into Russian, who appeared everywhere with a woman who was her lifelong lover and companion. Tsvetaeva later mentioned them in 'Letter to an Amazon,' her 1933 essay on lesbian love.

Tsvetaeva's affair with Parnok soon became known to everyone in her immediate circle. Poliakova's book cites letters from Pra (Elena Voloshina) to her friend, the painter Yulia Obolenskaya, dating from the fall of 1914, in which the main concern is with Sergei Efron's hurt feelings. 'What did Sergei tell you and why do you fear for him?' Pra wrote Obolenskaya on December 30. 'Now, with Marina it *is* a bit frightening. Things are getting really serious. She went on a trip with Sonia [i.e. Parnok] somewhere or other for several days, telling no one where they went. Sonia has already broken with the girl friend with whom she used to live and has rented a separate apartment on the Arbat [Street]. All this worries and alarms Lilia [Sergei's sister] and me, but we do not have the power to break this spell.' The madcap trip taken by Tsvetaeva and Parnok at the end of December 1914 to the ancient city of Rostov the Great, where they visited a Christmas fair and made love in a monastery hostel, is described in vivid detail in the seventh poem of 'Woman Friend.'

Parnok was a regular contributor to *Northern Annals*, a liberal literary journal published in St Petersburg by a wealthy Russian-Jewish couple, Sophia Chatskina and her husband Yakov Saker. Tsvetaeva met them through Parnok. From January 1915 until it was closed after the October Revolution, *Northern Annals* was the principal publishing outlet for her lyric poetry. The journal also serialized her translation into Russian of the novel *La Nouvelle Espérance* by Countess Anna de Noailles. Since Tsvetaeva did not like to receive fees for her work, the publishers paid her with presents and entertainment which, as it turned out, enriched her poetic and thematic scope.

When Chatskina and Saker visited Moscow, they took Tsvetaeva to hear a Gypsy chorus and presented her with the three-volume edition of Russian folk tales collected by the well-known folklorist Alexander Afanasiev. Shortly thereafter, Gypsy music and motifs from Russian folklore made their appearance in Tsvetaeva's poetry. They are particularly prominent in the lyrics written in 1916 and included in her next collection, *Mileposts I*. In devising a new lexicon and diction to accommodate these new themes, she was to complete her escape from the closed world of the salon and the nursery, to which her earlier poetry had been confined.

The affair with Sophia Parnok was a stormy one from the very beginning. Parnok was something of a female Don Juan. Her attentions to other women, if we may take poem 5 of 'Woman Friend' literally, must have begun less than a month after the relationship was initiated. Throughout the cycle, poems that express closeness and intimacy alternate with poems about jealousy and resentment. World War I, which Russia entered in August 1914 and which Tsvetaeva all but overlooked at first, gave Sergei the opportunity to escape from the untenable situation in which he found himself. In March 1915, he enlisted as a civilian male nurse and went to the front.

That spring and summer, Tsvetaeva and Parnok lived together as a couple. Tsvetaeva's daughter and sister Asya accompanied them when they went to the Ukraine for a vacation at an estate belonging to some friends of Parnok's. From there Tsvetaeva wrote her sister-in-law, Lilia Efron, an affectionate and meditative letter, in which she told her: 'I love Sergei for life, he is my very own and I will never leave him for anyone. I write him at least every other day, he knows all about my life, though I try to write less about what is most sad. There is a burden in my heart always. I go to sleep with it and I wake up with it.'

'Sonia loves me,' the letter continues, 'and I love her and this is forever and I shall never be able to leave her. The rift comes from the fact that I must divide my days. My heart knows how to combine it all.' A few lines later: 'I can't stand causing pain and I can't help causing it.' Her own pain from having to decide between her two great loves was also expressed by Tsvetaeva in a brief poem written in October 1915. In a rare instance of building an entire lyric on a borrowed theme and imagery, she paraphrased the despairing song 'Die Nebensonnen' from Franz Schubert's cycle *Die Winterreise*:

> Two suns are growing cool, O God have mercy!
> One in heaven, the other in my breast.
> How these suns – will I ever forgive myself? –
> How these suns used to drive me wild [with love]!
> And both are growing cool, their rays no longer hurt.
> And the more ardent one will be the first to cool.

The high emotional cost the poet had to pay for her love for Parnok also found its expression in the conclusion of the last poem in *Juvenilia*, where we read: 'But as I ran, Fate herself / Grabbed me by the hair with her heavy hand,' and in the poem about lawless women who do not live by the customs of society written in November 1915, which begins: 'We are sure to end up in hell, O my ardent sisters.'

At the end of December 1915, Tsvetaeva, accompanied by Parnok, went to St Petersburg (by now renamed Petrograd because of the war with Germany) for an extended visit. In the account of the trip in the memoir about Kuzmin, she edited out the presence of Parnok, but her letter to Kuzmin published in Sophia Poliakova's book reestablishes the true facts. As remembered in this letter, their stay with Chatskina and Saker in Petrograd was one continuous round of mutual recriminations and tearful scenes between Tsvetaeva and Parnok. What Tsvetaeva preferred to remember in her Kuzmin memoir, 'An Otherworldly Evening,' written twenty years after the events, was her own appearance at a literary soirée in the home of the noted naval architect Akim Kannegiser, where she recited her verse to a brilliant gathering and met several important poets.

The Kannegiser home was a major artistic and literary center of the northern capital. Numerous writers of the Russian emigration were to remember it in their memoirs. Tsvetaeva saw a great deal of the Kannegiser family during that visit and became especially friendly with the elder son, Sergei. But she also got to meet the younger son, Leonid, a budding poet and a close friend of the celebrated peasant poet Sergei Esenin. (Tsvetaeva strongly intimates in 'An Otherworldly Evening' that Esenin and Leonid Kannegiser were lovers at the time of her visit, a supposition supported by a close reading of some of their respective poems of the summer of 1916.) After the October Revolution, Leonid Kannegiser went down in history as the assassin of the dreaded secret police chieftain, Moisei Uritsky.

Anna Akhmatova, then already the most popular woman poet in Russia, was not present at the Kannegiser literary soirée, to Tsvetaeva's great disappointment. But two major poets with whom she was to establish lasting literary and personal ties were there: Mikhail Kuzmin and Osip Mandelstam. Tsvetaeva had briefly met Mandelstam at the Voloshins' in Koktebel the previous summer, but it was only after hearing each other recite at the Kannegisers' that the two poets realized each other's literary importance. That January they had a conversation in Petrograd, which was interrupted and which Mandelstam felt was so significant that he travelled to Moscow in February in order to continue it. In the following months he became something of a commuter between Petrograd and Moscow.

Kuzmin was, together with Balmont and Blok, one of the three poets whose influence on Tsvetaeva is most clearly discernible during the period of her evolution from *The Evening Album* to *Mileposts I*. The Kannegiser soirée was the only time the two of them ever met in person. But Tsvetaeva felt a deep personal and literary affinity with Kuzmin throughout her life. She wrote to him with great frankness about her involvement with Sophia Parnok and she left two unforgettable literary portraits of Kuzmin, one in verse, in the poem 'Two Conflagrations' ('Dva zareva'), 1921, and the other in prose, in 'An Otherworldly Evening,' 1936. The title of the latter refers to Kuzmin's 1921 collection of verse, *Otherworldly Evenings* (*Nezdeshnie vechera*).

Tsvetaeva recited her pacifist and pro-German poetry at the Kannegisers' marvelling that no one made objections to her themes at the height of the war against Germany. She heard Esenin, Mandelstam and Kuzmin read their latest work. Kuzmin, who was a composer as well as a poet, had promised to sing some *chansons* to his own piano accompaniment, a speciality for which he was admired. Tsvetaeva was intensely curious about this, but she had promised Parnok, who had stayed at Chatskina's with a migraine headache, that she would get home early and tell her all about the soirée. Despite the entreaties of the Kannegisers and of Kuzmin, Tsvetaeva did not stay for Kuzmin's singing. When she returned to Chatskina's, Parnok had already gone to bed. As Tsvetaeva later wrote to Kuzmin: 'I shall never forgive her that I did not stay then.' In 'An Otherworldly Evening,' Tsvetaeva dissembled and wrote that it was Sophia Chatskina who promised to wait for her and then went to sleep, rather than Sophia Parnok.

Returning to Moscow in the middle of January 1916, Tsvetaeva still had hopes of salvaging her relationship with Parnok. When Osip Mandelstam left Moscow on February 5 after the first of his brief visits, she rushed over to see Parnok only to find another woman seated on Parnok's bed and to be told that their affair was over. It was a blow to Tsvetaeva's pride from which she never quite recovered. At first she wrote of her lost love in a tone of wistful regret. Later came unforgiving resentment and hatred. In April 1916, she wrote a valedictory poem addressed to Parnok, which was also a requiem for their relationship. Building the entire poem on the archaic and traditional phrase *vo vremia ono*, 'in time of yore,' Tsvetaeva employed diction reminiscent both of a prayer and a funeral lament:

> In nights of yore you were unto me like a mother,
> In the night I could call upon you,
> Feverish light, sleepless light,
> Light of my eyes in nights of yore.
>
> O beneficent one, recollect
> Those days of yore that had no sunset,
> Maternal and filial,
> Sunsetless and eveningless.
>
> I did not come to disturb you. Farewell.
> I will only kiss the hem of your dress
> And look with my eyes into your eyes
> Which I covered with kisses in those nights of yore.
>
> The day will come when I die and the day when you die.
> The day will come when I'll understand and
> the day when you'll understand.
> And on that day of forgiveness, there will return
> That irretrievable time of yore.

Her affair with Sophia Parnok brought Tsvetaeva a great deal of pain. Recalling their closeness in her diary in 1920, Tsvetaeva

wrote: ' . . . she would reject me, turn to stone, trample me under
her feet – but she did love me.' She once described her breakup with
Parnok as 'the first catastrophe' of her life. But this pain and this
catastrophe gave her something without which she could not have
become the great poet she was: maturity. This is the maturity that
first appeared in 1915 in 'Woman Friend.' The poems written early
in 1916, especially the group addressed to Mandelstam, show the
versatility and the inspired virtuosity of a poet who was now
reaching the peak of her powers.

With Parnok out of her life, Tsvetaeva had time for the infatuated
Osip Mandelstam who kept returning to Moscow for brief stays that
spring and early summer. Much has been written about a romance
between these two poets. But 'romance' is certainly the wrong word
to describe something so onesided. Tsvetaeva loved Mandelstam
very much that spring, but only as a poet, not as a man. As she later
wrote to Alexander Bakhrakh, her response to Mandelstam was:
'Why do you want Marina when there's Moscow? Why Marina
when there's the springtime?'

Osip Mandelstam was born in Warsaw and raised in St Petersburg. His poetry that appeared in *Apollon* from 1910 on and his first
collection of verse, *Stone*, 1913, brought him rapid recognition as a
major new poet. But prior to his 1916 travels to Moscow, he could
only write – brilliantly – of Western culture, Western history,
Western classics. Tsvetaeva's offering to him of the city of Moscow
(instead of her own self, to which he was drawn) was also a gift of the
Russian past and of Russian cultural heritage, a heritage to which
the cosmopolitan Jewish poet had, he felt, only a dubious right.
During their tours of Moscow churches and cemeteries, Tsvetaeva
convinced Mandelstam that he had a claim to Russian history and
tradition that was as valid as his right to feel at home in the cultures
of ancient Greece or medieval France.

'His friendship with Tsvetaeva, in my opinion, played a tremendous role in Mandelstam's life and work,' wrote Nadezhda
Mandelstam in her second volume of memoirs. 'It was a bridge over
which he passed from one period to the next. [. . .] Bestowing on
him the gift of her friendship and of Moscow, she somehow released
him from the spell [of St Petersburg]. It was a miraculous gift,
because with only Petersburg and without Moscow, there is no
possibility of breathing freely, no real sense of Russia and no moral

freedom of which Mandelstam wrote in his essay on [the philosopher Piotr] Chaadaev.'

Near the beginning of Mandelstam's next collection of verse, *Tristia*, we find three poems addressed to Tsvetaeva, which are indeed a new departure in his work. All three date from the first half of 1916. The lovely poem on the churches of the Moscow Kremlin and their Italian antecedents, 'In the Discordant Polyphony' ('V raznogolositse'), contains a handsome compliment to Tsvetaeva, who appears at the end of the poem in the guise of the goddess of dawn, Aurora, 'but with a Russian name and in a pretty fur coat.' The morbid 'In a Straw-Lined Sledge' ('Na rozval'niakh, ulozhen-nykh solomoi') is a veritable kaleidoscope of complex allusions to historical events that took place in Moscow from the seventeenth to the nineteenth centuries.

It is from this point on that the theme of Russia's fate and history permanently enters Mandelstam's poetry, greatly enriching and broadening its scope. The third poem Mandelstam addressed to Tsvetaeva that spring, 'Not Believing in the Miracle of Resurrection' ('Ne veria voskresen'ia chudu'), commemorated his visit in early June to the city of Alexandrov in Vladimir Province, where Tsvetaeva was visiting her sister Asya. Many years later, in 1929, Tsvetaeva, irritated by the poet Georgy Ivanov's distorted memoir about his friendship with Mandelstam (where the poem addressed to Tsvetaeva about Mandelstam's stay in Alexandrov was said to have been inspired by a nonexistent 'vulgar lady doctor'), wrote her own memoir about that visit and that poem, 'Story of a Dedication.' More recently, Anna Saakiants published an interesting letter from Tsvetaeva to Lilia Efron which supplies further details about Mandelstam's stay in Alexandrov.

After June 1916, there were only cursory contacts between the two poets, one of which took place a few days before Tsvetaeva's departure from Russia in 1922 and was described in Nadezhda Mandelstam's memoirs. Tsvetaeva continued to maintain her high regard for Mandelstam's poetry, mentioning him with respect and admiration in subsequent years. She did, however, take a strong dislike to his volume of prose, *The Noise of Time*. Mandelstam turned against her in the 1920s, motivated, possibly, by her uncivil treatment of his wife during the encounter Nadezhda Mandelstam mentioned, and had some harsh and unfair things to say about her poetry in one of his essays.

But if Tsvetaeva opened up new horizons for Mandelstam through her 'gift of Moscow,' she also received from him at the same time a reciprocal gift: a new awareness of the heritage she was sharing with him. As discussed, imaginatively and in great detail, by Gregory Freidin in his book *A Coat of Many Colors: Osip Mandelstam and His Mythologies of Self-Presentation*, the poetic exchange between Tsvetaeva and Mandelstam emerges as both redolent of mythic associations and slightly sinister. 'The traditional "epistolary" exchanges between poets,' Freidin writes, 'took the form of a fundamentally more archaic, and therefore supremely modern, poetic ceremonial of the exchange of gifts, a Russian *potlatch* of sorts.' (A potlatch, for those who need to have it explained, was a ceremony of exchanging gifts among the American Indians of the Pacific Northwest, the object of which was to defeat an opponent by a reckless show of generosity.) Claiming ownership of the city of Moscow and of its past and offering to share this ownership with another imposes a momentous responsibility. Both Tsvetaeva and Mandelstam proved that they could live up to it.

Besides her conversations with Mandelstam and the poems they addressed to each other, there were several other factors that could have been responsible for Tsvetaeva's turn to her native roots in her poetry. There was the trip to Petrograd, where, as she makes clear in 'An Otherworldly Evening,' she felt that she was an ambassador from Moscow to the poets of the St Petersburg school of poetry. There was her wrenching estrangement from Sophia Parnok, who was cosmopolitan and Jewish, as were, incidentally, most of the people close to Tsvetaeva in 1915, such as Chatskina and Saker and the Kannegisers, to say nothing of Sergei Efron and his family. There was, in the first months of 1916, her intense if transient enthusiasm for the poetry of Tikhon Churilin (1885–1946). Churilin was an authentic surrealist before such a category was invented. After several years in a mental institution, he published in 1915 *Springtime After Death*, a book of visionary poems that described states of mind on the verge of insanity.

In a poem addressed to him, Tsvetaeva called Churilin a cygnet (*lebedionok*; he was associated for her with swans because the name of his native town, Lebedian', comes from the stem meaning 'swan'). Mandelstam was symbolized by a young male bird of another species, an eaglet. In her poetry, Tsvetaeva depicted both of them as her fledglings, to whom she gave her blessings for their impending soaring flight into the glory of immortality. Then, on March 23, two days before the Feast of the Annunciation, she announced that she'd had enough of them:

> On the day of Annunciation
> I solemnly affirm:
> I have no need of tame doves, swans or eaglets!
> – Fly anywhere you like
> At Annunciation, my holiday.

In three poems, written on three consecutive days in April, she took stock of her situation. On the 26th, she wrote the already quoted valedictory poem to Sophia Parnok (p. 57). The next day, she addressed a penitent poem to Sergei Efron in which she desperately pleaded for his help and understanding, complained of being cheated by 'impostors and rapacious dogs,' and compared herself to a sinking ship and a homeless tramp. 'At your palace, my lawful Tsar / I stand – a beggar,' the poem concluded. And one day after that, in a bitterly self-deprecating poem couched in diction and meter (or rather, the absence of meter) reminiscent of *raëshnik*, a kind of doggerel used by itinerant vendors and carnival barkers, Tsvetaeva proclaimed a rummage sale of her emotional castoffs.

We do not know what solace Sergei had to offer. In any case, that spring he managed after numerous tries to enroll in a military school for ensigns, so that his wife could not have seen much of him. In the early summer months of 1916, there began Tsvetaeva's still-mysterious romance with Nikodim Plutser-Sarna, an economist whom she went on seeing throughout 1917 and whom she described on a copy of *Mileposts I* which belonged to the poet Alexei Kruchionykh as 'the only man who knew how to love me.' But, as always with Tsvetaeva, it was poetry that provided a never-failing retreat. That spring and summer, she immersed herself in the writings of two poets who now became for her the two central and most beloved figures in Russian literature, Alexander Blok and Anna Akhmatova. Both of them were poets of the St Petersburg tradition and neither of them had any problems with their Russian identity – as Mandelstam did and as, for that matter, Tsvetaeva also did in her poems of early 1916, where she assumed the identity of a Pole and of a noblewoman of ancient lineage (*boliarynia*), to neither of which she really had any right.

In writing her extended cycles addressed in homage to Blok and

Akhmatova, in her exchanges of poems with Mandelstam and in the cycle of nine poems 'Verses About Moscow,' which she began in March 1916 and completed in August of that year, Tsvetaeva constantly confronted the question of her reciprocal connection to various aspects of her native culture: its language, its architecture and its mystical traditions, whether those of the Orthodox Church or of ancient necromancy. Her assertion of her inalienable right to this Muscovite patrimony is what forms the core of her collection *Mileposts I* and gives the poems of that collection their particular flavour.

The poems included in *Mileposts I* (*Versty I*) were written between January and December 1916 and the book thus constitutes an uninterrupted lyrical diary for that year. Initially, Tsvetaeva contemplated a larger collection which would comprise her poetry for 1916 and 1917 and would be called, somewhat enigmatically, *Mother Milepost* (*Mater'-Versta*). But when she was sorting out her poetry in 1921, she must have realized that her verse of the last pre-revolutionary year formed a well-defined unit, while the poetry she wrote from 1917 on broke into two distinct strains, the lyrical and the political. Thus came the division into volumes which is appropriate both chronologically and stylistically: the poetry of 1916 went into *Mileposts I*, while the poems written between 1917 and 1920 were subdivided into several other collections in accordance with their thematic content.

In her first two collections, published in 1910 and 1912, Tsvetaeva used a late-Victorian, upper-class diction that was not always free of self-conscious artificiality. In the better poems of *Juvenilia*, her style moved toward greater clarity. Her poems about death, the cycle about her affair with Sophia Parnok and some of the poems of early 1916 addressed to Mandelstam have the kind of magical simplicity of tone and style that we find in the earliest poems by Mandelstam and the last poems Boris Pasternak wrote before his death. This is a simplicity that is very hard for a poet to achieve or for a critic to define. There is an almost Mozartian purity of language. Every word is direct and seemingly inevitable.

In *Mileposts I* this simplicity remains in certain poems. But elsewhere in the book we find a colorful explosion of styles and manners. Until now, Tsvetaeva's verse used only the traditional Russian binary (iambic and trochaic) and ternary (the dactyl, the amphibrach and the anapest) meters. Her poems were always rhymed and their rhymes were conventional nineteenth-century ones, typical for Russian poetry from Pushkin to Vladimir Soloviov. Much of *Mileposts I* is in accentual verse, the rhymes are often assonances or half-rhymes, and there is blank verse, free verse without meter or rhyme, and imitation of folk poetry, such as *raëshnik*.

The limpid diction of *Juvenilia* is now overlaid by other stylistic strains, which will eventually become incorporated into Tsvetaeva's mature later style. The two most important of these can be described, somewhat schematically, as her use of archaisms and of colloquial or vulgar diction. Tsvetaeva was not a linguist and her use of these two language strata was intuitive, creative and, occasionally, indiscriminate. Her archaist manner comprised Church Slavic and Old Russian vocabulary and grammar of the Russian Bible and of Orthodox prayers; also, the remnants of chancery language of pre-Petrine Russia, as well as her later deliberate imitation of the style of eighteenth-century Russian poets. Her colloquial manner likewise absorbed a number of linguistic phenomena of various origins: uneducated and peasant speech, regional expressions, formulae from folklore and, where appropriate, deliberately coarse language.

Tsvetaeva was not a pioneer in any of these areas. Archaic and ecclesiastic diction was typical of Symbolist poets such as Viacheslav Ivanov and Alexander Blok. Colloquialisms and peasant speech were a feature of Alexei Remizov's prose and an uncontested specialty of the peasant group of poets. Accentual verse and assonance rhymes were launched, as already mentioned, by Zinaida Gippius in the early 1890s. By about 1910, they had become standard in the work of junior Symbolists and Acmeists. But Tsvetaeva assimilated all these diverse strains into her poetry with considerable skill and made them a part of her personal mode of expression. By 1916, she mastered the entire range of innovations introduced by the Symbolists, the peasant poets, the Acmeists and, to a minor extent, even the Futurists and in doing so achieved a striking originality of her own.

It may be paradoxical, but in the collection in which Tsvetaeva's originality became so strongly manifest, we can discern more clearly than in any other the influence on her of other contemporary Russian poets. This is particularly obvious in some of the poems of the cycles addressed to Akhmatova and Blok, where Tsvetaeva sometimes chose to speak to those poets in approximations of their own voices. Here, for example is a brief poem from the Akhmatova cycle, which reproduces some of Akhmatova's stylistic mannerisms, including the assonance rhymes and accentual meter (not conveyed, obviously, in the English version) and the typical Akhmatovan final *concetto* that involves religion and hints at some undisclosed, possibly tragic, relationship between the poet and the person described:

> At the market place people were shouting.
> Clouds of steam floated out of a bakery.
> I retain in memory the crimson mouth
> Of a gaunt-faced street songstress.
>
> In a dark tiny-flowered kerchief
> – May the grace be granted –
> You, standing with eyes downcast in a crowd
> Of praying women in St Sergius-Trinity [Monastery].
>
> Pray for me, my beauty,
> Melancholy and diabolical,
> When the [dissenter sects of the] forests
> Elect you Our Lady of the Flagellants.

To express the personal drama which is the subject of many poems in *Mileposts I*, Tsvetaeva resorted to wide use of personae or stylistic masks. Her new mastery of unlettered, colloquial speech stands her in good stead when she addresses the reader through the mask of a Moscow woman of the lower classes, a 'tavern queen' (*kabatskaia tsaritsa*) or a religious pilgrim, sinful, proud, passionate, occasionally a criminal, occasionally dabbling in magic. Tsvetaeva's daughter, Ariadna Efron, tried in her memoirs to attribute this strain to Tsvetaeva's exposure to large masses of common Russian people during her travels after the October Revolution. But since this manner is very much in evidence almost two years before that revolution, the travels in question must have been the wide-ranging ones in the company of Sophia Parnok during their closeness in 1915.

Stylistically and technically, *Mileposts I* was the most daringly experimental of Tsvetaeva's collections and it constituted a watershed in her poetic evolution. In it, she not only learned whatever the great age of Russian poetry in which she lived had to teach her, but she also became a major innovator in her own right. Some of the innovations launched in this book were to be developed and consolidated in her later volumes.

One that is already fully formed in *Mileposts I* is her introduction into Russian poetry of special meters which George Ivask in the 1930s and G. S. Smith in the 1970s have termed *logaoedic*. These meters are built on the already existing meters. But they combine, on a regular basis, more than one kind of foot in a line – a practice that simply did not exist in Russian poetry until that time. Khlebnikov experimented with mixing several meters in one poem somewhat earlier, and Mandelstam has a few early poems which add an extra stressed syllable where the meter does not call for it. What Tsvetaeva does, however, is to invent a new, *ad hoc* metrical pattern, which she then sustains throughout a particular poem. Here is a stanza from a much-anthologized poem from *Mileposts I* in which this is done, quoted first in the original, then in translation:

> V ogromnom gorode moiom – noch'.
> Iz doma sonnogo idu – proch'.
> I liudi dumaiut: zhena, doch'.
> A ia zapomnila odno: noch'.
>
> In my immense city it is night.
> From the sleeping house I walk – away.
> And people think: she's a wife, she's a daughter.
> But I remembered one thing only: the night.

Here, one stressed monosyllabic word is regularly added to what would otherwise have been a line of very usual Russian iambic tetrameter, turning it into something quite unique. Repeated for four quatrains, with only one rhyme per quatrain, the metrical pattern creates a hypnotic effect, in keeping with the sense of alienation and unreality experienced by the persona of the poem.

For all the thematic and technical variety of its poetry, the collection *Mileposts I* is unified by its forcefully sounded central theme: the city of Moscow and the poet's involvement with its topography and history. As Tsvetaeva wrote much later to George Ivask: 'Yes, it was I who in 1916 was the first to speak thus of Moscow [...]. And I am happy and proud of this, for it was the Moscow of the last hour and last time.'

The choir practice and the mass

World War I began for Russia with the shattering defeats of August 1914, so graphically described by Barbara W. Tuchman in *The Guns of August* and by Alexander Solzhenitsyn in *August 1914*. Two and a half years later, casualties were counted in millions, food and fuel were becoming scarce and the pre-war prosperity was replaced by mounting inflation. At the end of February 1917 (early March by the Western calendar), there were protest demonstrations in Petrograd. Troops sent out to suppress them joined the rioters and the government's authority simply collapsed. Nicholas II was forced to abdicate, a provisional government was formed by a coalition of the majority parties in the Duma and both capitals were ablossom with red flags and jubilant crowds.

Vladimir Nabokov, Sr, the father of the future novelist and one of the founders of the Constitutional Democratic (CD) Party, remembered the exultation of the first days of the February Revolution in his memoir on the Provisional Government: 'I experienced a sense of spiritual elation such as I have not since known. It seemed to me that something great and sacred had occurred, that the people had cast off their chains, that despotism had collapsed.' Andrei Bely, who was in Petrograd staying with Zinaida Gippius and her husband Merezhkovsky, watched the revolutionary victory parade on March 1 and shouted through the window to the soldiers carrying huge red banners: 'This is a sacred round dance!'

His hostess watched the parade with him. As she noted in her diary, she was experiencing both joy and misgivings: 'This morning's radiance,' Zinaida Gippius wrote, 'is the intoxication with the truth of the revolution, infatuation with liberty that was wrested, not granted. It is there in the regiments with their music, in the serene faces of the street and of the people. But this radiance is not shared or even understood by those who ought to be playing the leading roles right now. They ought to – but they can't and they won't and they'll let us down.'

Marina Tsvetaeva was in Moscow at the time of the February Revolution, expecting the birth of her second child. On March 2, one day after the Petrograd parade that was seen by Bely and Gippius, there was a similar one in Moscow. Tsvetaeva described it in what was possibly her first poem of a political theme. It began:

> Over a little church, pale blue clouds.
> Cries of crows.
> And they pass – the color of ashes and sand –
> Those revolutionary troops.
> Oh, my lordly, oh my royal sadness!

Two concepts basic to Tsvetaeva's thinking will help explain this reaction. Her youthful revolutionary sympathies were directed towards an anarchist revolution, not a Liberal Democratic one, let alone Marxist. While she had left those sympathies behind by the time she turned sixteen, the ideal of rebellion remained. But it was an individualistic and heroic rebellion. Her favourite heroes were always those who raised themselves high above the crowd by their own efforts, only to be vanquished by mediocrities: Joan of Arc, Napoleon, Byron, Pushkin, the False Dmitry and his Polish wife Marina, the Pugachov of *The Captain's Daughter*.

There was no one like this among the parliamentary politicians and the dusty troops of the early days of the February regime. A few months later, however, when she briefly mistook Alexander Kerensky for the Russian Bonaparte, Tsvetaeva came close to accepting the February Government. The second concept basic to Tsvetaeva's politics is that for her *any* kind of politics was incompatible with ethics. 'Politics is a self-evident abomination,' she wrote in 'On Germany,' 'from which nothing but further abominations should be expected. The very idea of trying to bring ethics into politics!'

Her basic humanity invariably led Tsvetaeva to take the side of the underdog, which for her meant any individual of whatever station who was threatened by a dehumanized collective, be it a mob, a political party or the state. Listening as a child to a fairy tale about a cruel ogre, Tsvetaeva felt an instant sympathy for the villain once he had been captured and punished. Now her underdog was the tsar. Tsvetaeva had no interest or sympathy for Nicholas II before the revolution, but after his deposition he and his son became the object of her solicitude, which turned to veneration after he and his family were assassinated. In April, she wrote three poems expressing her concern for the fate of the tsar. The publication of one of them, describing thieves and derelicts of Moscow's skid row praying for 'God's servant Nicholas,' brought down on Tsvetaeva the censure of Vladimir Mayakovsky.

An expressive poem written in May indicates that Tsvetaeva's rejection of the February Revolution also had aesthetic causes. Evoking the goddess of liberty, once worshipped by noble Frenchmen, such as the Duc de Lauzun (about whom she would shortly write a play) and the Marquis de Lafayette, as well as by Russian aristocrats who had joined the Decembrist Rebellion of 1825, Tsvetaeva then fused this goddess with the Most Beautiful Lady of Blok's mystical vision. But the image she found for the Russian revolution was nothing like these exalted personifications:

> Out of your severe, well-proportioned temple
> You went into the screech of city squares.
> O Liberty! The Most Beautiful Lady
> Of [the French] marquis and of Russian princes.
>
> The terrifying choir practice is now.
> The mass is still ahead.
> O Liberty! You're a wanton harlot
> [Leaning] on a crazed soldier's chest!

The central idea of this poem, which is that the February Revolution is not the main event, but only a rehearsal for something far more fearful, was shared – though from a different political perspective – by both Blok and Mayakovsky who saw the Liberal-Democratic revolution as only the first step toward a more fundamental change.

A number of Constitutional Democrats (CDs) and Socialist Revolutionaries (SRs), with whom Tsvetaeva would later associate or work during her years of emigration, were having their moments in the limelight during the February regime. The historian and the founder of CD Party Pavel Miliukov was the Minister of Foreign Affairs in the first provisional government. The SR Ilya Fondaminsky was the Commissar of the Black Sea Fleet. Another SR, Vadim Rudnev, became the first (and only) freely elected mayor of Moscow in history. Two decades later, these three men had become editors of Russian publications in Paris with whom Tsvetaeva had to deal in order to publish her work.

The leader of the SR Party, Victor Chernov, returned from many years of exile abroad and assumed the post of Minister of Agriculture in the new government. In this capacity he proceeded to draft a sweeping land-reform project that would have assured for Russian peasants the most equitable distribution of arable land in history. (The popularity of the SRs and of Chernov personally was so great that even after the October Revolution he was elected president of the Constituent Assembly by the vast majority of the deputies, i.e., became the head of the new Russian Government, which would thus be Socialist. But Lenin declared the election invalid and had the deputies dispersed by armed troops.) Chernov's wife Olga Kolbasina and her three daughters (two from an earlier marriage and one by Chernov) had returned with him from exile. They were all about to embark on their amazing adventures during the February and October Revolutions which are described in *Cold Spring in Russia*, a book written many years later by one of the daughters, Olga Chernov Andreyev. This family was to be Tsvetaeva's neighbours and close friends during her stay in Czechoslovakia and the early days of her Paris emigration.

The Marxists were also returning from exile. The grand old man of Russian Marxism, the aristocratic Georgy Plekhanov, and the fabled revolutionary heroine Vera Zasulich came back to triumphant welcomes. On April 16, Vladimir Lenin emerged from the famous sealed railroad car at the Finland Station in Petrograd. He came financed and backed by the German General Staff (which hoped that the takeover of Russia by the extreme left would also take it out of the war) for the express purpose of subverting the nascent Russian democracy. As their lever for attaining power, Lenin and his able associate Leon Trotsky planned to use the Petrograd Soviet, a council of radicalized workers' and soldiers' deputies, patterned after the similarly named organization which had proved to be effective during the revolution of 1905.

Three days before Lenin's arrival at the Finland Station, Marina Tsvetaeva's second daughter Irina was born. Sergei Efron had been studying at his military school since the spring of 1916. Early in August, Tsvetaeva wrote Max Voloshin one of her maternally solicitous letters on behalf of her husband, asking Voloshin to arrange, through an artillery general he knew, a comfortable assignment for Sergei in the south of Russia. On August 24 she wrote to Voloshin: 'Dear Max, I'm coming to Feodosia with the children. In

Moscow there is hunger and soon there will be cold. Everyone is telling me to leave. So we will see each other soon.' She also wrote that she had asked her sister Asya, who lived in Feodosia, to find her an apartment.

That fall, however, Tsvetaeva travelled to the Crimea all alone. In Maria Razumovsky's plausible surmise, she went not only to look for lodgings, but also on an errand of mercy in order to console her bereaved sister. Anastasia Tsvetaeva's early marriage, entered into when she was sixteen, had soon collapsed. She eventually married a man much older than herself, Mavriky Mintz, but in the summer of 1917 she lost to illness both Mintz and the son she had borne him. It thus happened that Marina Tsvetaeva was in the Crimea on October 25 (November 7), 1917, the day Lenin's troops stormed the Winter Palace and overthrew the Provisional Government. In Feodosia, she witnessed and described in a striking poem the event that became for her the very image, both symbolic and concrete, of the October Revolution: the sacking of wine cellars and the ensuing orgy of drunken pillaging.

> Night. North-Easter. Roar of soldiers. Roar of waves.
> A wine cellar has been pillaged. By the walls,
> Down the gutters, it goes pouring – precious flood,
> And a blood-red moon is dancing in the wash.
> . . . . . .
> Barracks, dockside – drinking all. The world is ours!
> Ours the cellars and their princely stocks of wine!
> The whole town is there, stampeding like a bull,
> Crowding round a turbid puddle for a drink.
>
> In the cloud of wine, the moon. Who's there?
> Be a comrade, now, my beauty: 'ave a drink!
> And around the town a jolly rumor runs:
> There's a couple somewhere's drowned 'emselves in wine.

This poem is a part of Tsvetaeva's *The Demesne of the Swans (Lebedinyi stan)*, her collection of poems about the February and October Revolutions and the ensuing civil war – the period known as the epoch of War Communism. Like the diaries she began keeping in November 1917, this collection shows Tsvetaeva in a new literary role which she deliberately chose at that time, that of chronicler of the momentous period in which she was living. *The Demesne of the Swans* could not be published in its entirety until 1957, when Gleb Struve brought out the first edition in Munich. It is also the only one of Tsvetaeva's collections which exists in a complete English translation, a fine one by Robin Kemball. The unrhymed poem cited above is in Kemball's translation, though other texts from *The Demesne of the Swans* in the present chapter are given in my own prose versions for the purpose of total exactitude which no rhymed translation, no matter how excellent, can achieve.

On November 2, Tsvetaeva started back for Moscow. For three days and two nights she travelled in an overcrowded train, a trip she later described in 'October Revolution in a Railroad Car.' When the train stopped in the cities of Kharkov and Oriol, she bought local newspapers. The news was confusing and ominous: 'The Kremlin and all monuments have been demolished. [This turned out not to be true.] Buildings harboring cadets and officers who refused to surrender were blown up. 16 000 killed. At the next station it goes up to 25 000.' Many other passengers, on reading the news, left the train to return to the south. In an agony of apprehension about the fate of her husband and children, Tsvetaeva made a diary entry addressed to Sergei Efron: 'If God performs this miracle and leaves you among the living, I will follow you like a dog.'

Moscow was militarized when she arrived, with road blocks and patrols in the streets. Sergei had just graduated from the military school and, quite amazingly, obtained from the newly victorious Communist authorities his graduation pay and permission to depart for southern Russia for the transparent purpose of joining one of the anti-Bolshevik groups that were being formed there. On the very day of her arrival, Tsvetaeva again left Moscow to accompany Sergei and a fellow-officer to the Crimea, again leaving her daughters in the care of Sergei's relatives. Many people were still confused about the significance of the October Revolution, but not Maximilian Voloshin, whose advice Marina and Sergei sought out in Koktebel: 'And ingratiatingly, almost happily, like a kindly wizard talking to children, [he drew for us] picture after picture – the entire Russian revolution for the next five years: the terror, the civil war, executions, roadblocks, the Vendée [i.e., the peasant resistance during the French Revolution], bestialization, loss of human face, unleashed elemental spirits, blood, blood, blood . . .'

In the Crimea, plans for the immediate future were made. Sergei was to join the White Army, while Marina was to bring the children to the Crimea and live for the duration with the Voloshins. In their memoirs published decades later in the Soviet Union, Tsvetaeva's sister and daughter both feigned perplexity about how Sergei Efron, the son of People's Freedom revolutionaries, could have joined the anti-Bolshevik resistance. Ariadna Efron cited the bad influence of the monarchist milieu at the military school and 'perversely understood notions of comradeship' as the things that supposedly led her father to join the wrong camp. But as Vladimir Varshavsky has argued in his book *The Unnoticed Generation*, after the October Revolution the political right wing 'had ceased being the symbol of evil, reaction and despotism. Compared to the Bolshevik terror, the old regime began to look like the realm of freedom, legality and humanitarianism.' It was for exactly the same reasons that their parents had joined the Populist and Marxist parties at the end of the nineteenth century that many idealistic young Russians rushed to the anti-Bolshevik resistance groups, whether those led by the Socialist Revolutionaries on the Volga, by the Mensheviks in Georgia, by the anarchists in the Ukraine ('the Greens') or the monarchist White Army in which Sergei Efron enlisted in the Crimea.

On November 25, Tsvetaeva went to Moscow to get her children. By the time she arrived the civil war was on. The way back to the Crimea was cut off. Tsvetaeva was separated from her husband and her sister (who remained in the Crimea) for the next five years. At the most difficult time imaginable, she was trapped in Moscow with two small children, with no income and entirely on her own for the first time in her life. She was twenty-five years old, very near-sighted and utterly impractical. She was terrified of automobiles and elevators and she easily lost her way in the streets and even inside buildings. She survived the harrowing five years of cold, starvation and terror because of her tremendous human vitality and with the help of kindly friends and neighbours. The diaries she kept during the years 1917–21 were later reworked into the book *Omens of the Earth* (this seems closer to the Russian title, *Zemnye primety*, than *Terrestrial Indicia*, another possible rendition). The book has been published only in excerpts. Marina Tsvetaeva as both person and poet is outlined in these excerpts with all her ineptitude, stamina, independence of spirit and occasional moments of reckless heroism.

The provisional liberal-democratic government established in February lasted for only eight months. Continually sabotaged by both

the monarchist right and the Bolsheviks and working in an atmosphere of squabbles and divisiveness, it still managed to promote
human rights and freedoms on a scale not experienced in Russian
history before or since. All citizens became equal before the law.
Women and minorities were given full civil and political rights,
including the vote. A woman, the prominent feminist Sophia
Panina, was given a cabinet-level post, the first such instance in
Russia. Freedom of religion, speech, press, assembly, unions and
strikes became a reality. Not even a vestige of censorship in any area
remained. Poland and Finland were given their independence. An
eight-hour working day was introduced.

The February Revolution was the culmination of six decades of
democratization of Russian society which began with the liberal
reforms of Alexander II in the 1860s. Both the post-reform decades
and the parliamentary period after 1905 brought Russia closer to
the ideals of personal liberty, guaranteed human rights and
economic equality which had inspired the American and French
revolutions at the end of the eighteenth century and the European
revolutionary ferment of 1848. The pedigree of the October Revolution which succeeded the February one was quite different.
Independently of each other but with striking unanimity, two
thoughtful Russian investigators of the origins of Bolshevism, Igor
Shafarevich working in the Soviet Union and Vladimir Varshavsky
in emigration, have traced the genealogy of Lenin's revolution to
the chiliastic Christian sects of the Middle Ages led by Dolcino,
Thomas Münzer and John of Leyden and, in a later manifestation,
the Jacobin phase of the French Revolution as represented by
Marat and Robespierre, whom Lenin vastly admired.

In all of these cases, the aim of the revolution was not equality or
justice or prosperity. It was instead the total control of society by a
small elite dedicated primarily to disseminating a fanatically held
dogma with which the population had to be indoctrinated by means
of intimidation and terror. In each case, there was a stratum of the
population officially held responsible for everything that was wrong
with society and with human nature in general and whose extermination en masse, it was claimed, would solve for good all remaining
problems and usher in a Golden Age. For the medieval chiliasts, the
demons to be expunged were the Catholic clergy; for Marat and
Robespierre, aristocrats and royalists; and for Lenin and Trotsky, a
vague category called the bourgeoisie: supposedly the former prop-

ertied class, but in actual practice any person possessing culture or education, regardless of economic level, who did not totally subscribe to Bolshevik orthodoxy.

Both before and after the October Revolution, Lenin described the state model he favoured, the dictatorship of the proletariat, as 'completely unlimited power, restrained by no laws or rules whatsoever and relying directly on violence.' Furthermore, in Lenin's view, this unlimited power was best wielded by a dictator armed with the correct dialectical analysis and brooking no interference from any group, his own party included. Given the fact of human fallibility and our mammalian genetic heritage, such an approach could only lead to autocracy, subjugation and slavery. But because Bolshevik rhetoric drew heavily on the vocabulary of democracy, many people, then and now, have chosen to see the October Revolution as the enhancement and continuation of the 1905 and February revolutions rather than their negation and reversal. Still others read into it whatever utopian dream their imagination is able to conjure. Here, for example, is how three major Russian poets, one nobleman and two peasants, perceived the significance of the October Revolution.

Alexander Blok, who in his poetry of 1906–16 longed for a spiritual transformation of the world that would sweep away all materialistic values, saw in Lenin and Trotsky's seizure of power not a change of government in Russia but the advent of a new, transcendent form of existence. Nikolai Kliuev hailed Lenin as a peasant tsar who would restore the patriarchal ways and religious piety of the Russian countryside and protect village life from modernization and Westernization. Sergei Esenin welcomed the October Revolution with a series of visionary poems in which he equated Russia giving birth to world revolution with nature yielding a harvest, a cow producing a calf and the Virgin Mary giving birth to Christ. All three eventually understood the futility of their illusions. Blok died in 1921, dejected and depressed, ceaselessly muttering 'May God forgive me.' Esenin, denounced and reviled in the Soviet press, killed himself in 1925. Kliuev, ostracized by the mid-1920s, was sent to a labour camp where he died.

On the whole, women – whether poets or political figures – saw the situation with greater clarity than did the men. Vera Zasulich, a revered figure in Russian Marxism, regarded the Soviet regime as the betrayal of everything she had fought for and believed. Rosa

Luxemburg, another famed Marxist, had the time to denounce Lenin's course of action before she was murdered in Germany. The anarchist Emma Goldman, deported to the Soviet Union from America, quickly realized that Lenin and Trotsky were dismantling every organization and institution that could further the democratization of Russian society: the cooperatives, the trade unions and the vaunted Soviets (the councils of workers and soldiers), which gave the Soviet Union its name but which were quietly discarded once the Bolshcviks had used them to gain power. Unlike many male poets, the three most important women poets in Russia at the time of the October Revolution – Gippius, Akhmatova and Tsvetaeva – who differed from each other in almost every aspect one can think of, were united in their rejection of Bolshevism.

The early days of the Soviet regime and the time of War Communism are a subject of never-ending study in the Soviet Union as well as in the West. The principal events and the leading personalities of those years are often examined on the basis of sources published in the Soviet Union only. Or else historians are likely to turn to the testimony of foreign visitors, such as Lincoln Steffens, John Reed or Bessie Beatty, who were in Russia as guests of the Bolshevik authorities, didn't know the language and knew nothing about the country's past. Western historians often disregard as a source the diaries and memoirs of Russian writers and poets which were published abroad and thus escaped both the retroactive censorship and the rewriting of history that began within days after the Bolshevik takeover.

There are many such documents and they differ in their literary quality and tone. Among them, we find Ivan Bunin's bitterly uncomprehending *Accursed Days*; the passionate political engagement of the diaries of Zinaida Gippius; the objective detachment of Vladislav Khodasevich's memoirs about his contacts with the Bolshevik elite and rank-and-file; and Alexei Remizov's poetic diaries, *Russia in a Whirlwind*, where he recorded both the reality of those days and his dreams and found that the dreams were often more realistic and made more sense. A place of honor in this series belongs by right to Marina Tsvetaeva's fragmentary *Omens of the Earth*, 'The Tale of Sonechka,' and several episodes dealing with those days in her various literary memoirs. These texts are valuable both as a record of their time and as a lyrical portrait of the poet herself. They also make fascinating reading when juxtaposed with the astute economic and political analysis in Emma Goldman's book *My Disillusionment in Russia* and her 1935 essay 'There Is No Communism in Russia,' observations made at the same time and place by a woman of a vastly different mentality.

'October Revolution in a Railroad Car' ('Oktiabr' v vagone') was the earliest of the *Omens of the Earth* pieces. It traces Tsvetaeva's peregrinations between Moscow and Crimea in October and November 1917. The atmosphere is ominous and the air in the trains is thick with hatred for the educated classes, showing that the Bolshevik campaign of vilification of the intellectuals, which Emma Goldman had found so distasteful, was bearing fruit. In Marxist terminology, 'bourgeois' was a sociological term, but its colloquial Russian equivalent popularized by the Bolsheviks, *burzhui* (fem. *burzhuika*), rapidly came to mean something like a human weed needing prophylactic eradication, corresponding to the later use of 'rotten egg' in China and *gusano* (a worm) in Cuba. Marina Tsvetaeva was often to hear herself called *burzhuika* in the next few years.

Three other prose pieces intended for *Omens of the Earth*, 'Free Passage' ('Vol'nyi proezd'), 'My Jobs' ('Moi sluzhby') and 'Garret Life' ('Cherdachnoe'), record Tsvetaeva's day-to-day life in 1918 and 1919. As a mother of two small children, she was freed from the forcible labor conscription, a practice initiated by Trotsky and compared by some of his fellow Bolsheviks to a new form of serfdom. But since she did not hold a regular job, she was not entitled to any kind of ration card, even of the lowest category. This was the time when Lenin's government was wooing many prominent writers by issuing them special food rations. But Tsvetaeva was not well-known enough to merit such treatment. To save fuel, she and her daughters lived in one small room in the garret which was formerly Sergei's den. Most of her material possessions were gradually bartered for food. Soon, she had only one dress left and it was also used for sleeping. Most waking hours were devoted to searching for the barest necessities: food, fuel and, because Tsvetaeva was an addicted smoker, tobacco. There was no running water anymore and the disposal of garbage was a never-ending headache.

People with apartments of more than one room were required to take in tenants. Tsvetaeva at first got several cheerful young anarchists who made free not only with her own valuables, but with the belongings of her sisters-in-law as well. Then the anarchists were replaced by a modest young Pole named Henryk Sachs (or Zaks), whom Tsvetaeva described as 'the meekest and most ardent of Communists.' Sachs happened to work as the personal assistant to Felix Dzerzhinsky, the aristocratic Pole who headed the Cheka (an acronym for 'Extraordinary Commission'), Lenin's political police. Organized early in 1918, the Cheka soon became the most dreaded institution ever known in Russian history. The very address of its headquarters, Gorokhovaya 2 in Petrograd and Lubianka Square in Moscow, struck terror in the hearts of everyone in Russia. Hundreds of innocent hostages were shot simply to discourage any resistance to the Bolshevik rule. After August 30, 1918, when Tsvetaeva's one-time host Leonid Kannegiser assassinated Uritsky, the head of the Petrograd Cheka, while in Moscow on the same day the Socialist Revolutionary Fanny Kaplan took a shot at Lenin, the Cheka plunged the country into a monstrous bloodbath. Hostages selected at random for having belonged to the gentry or to pre-revolutionary socialist or liberal parties were executed by the thousands without investigation or trial. Remizov reported that in one small town where no noblemen or Socialists could be found, schoolteachers were shot by the local Cheka instead. Yet, in Tsvetaeva's apartment, one of the top officials of the Lubianka acted not as an executioner but as something of a guardian angel.

As described by Tsvetaeva, Henryk Sachs resembles one of the ascetic knights errant of Communism who appear in Andrei Platonov's great phantasmagoric novel about the October Revolution, *Chevengur*. Marina Tsvetaeva did not hide the fact that her husband was fighting against the Bolsheviks with the White Army. She went to the extent of advertising that fact by wearing a leather belt and carrying a field pouch which were a part of a tsarist officer's uniform (in her memoirs, Anastasia Tsvetaeva defused the meaning of the field pouch by calling it a mailman's pouch). In conversations with Sachs, Tsvetaeva did not conceal her hatred of the Soviet system and her hope for its defeat. Yet he treated her with friendly deference and constantly shared his rations with her and her children. Unlike the Bolshevik elite described in Khodasevich's *The White Corridor*, who lived in luxury, Sachs insisted on being issued the same rations as the rest of the working population.

In the spring of 1918, Tsvetaeva's half-brother Andrei, whom she hardly ever saw, came to ask her to intercede with Sachs on behalf of Andrei's grandfather Ilovaisky, arrested by the Cheka for having 'the wrong political views.' Tsvetaeva assured Sachs that Ilovaisky was one hundred years old (he was actually eighty five), that he once knew Pushkin (Ilovaisky was five when Pushkin died), and she pointed out that arresting people of such advanced age for their views was 'unseemly.' It took Sachs almost a week to convince Felix Dzerzhinsky (the sole friend Sachs had, she noted) to release Ilovaisky. Tsvetaeva later heard that Ilovaisky's interrogators decided he must be senile when to their questions about his attitude to Lenin and Trotsky, he replied that he had never heard of either. Henryk Sachs liked and understood Tsvetaeva's poetry and he visited her after he moved away. His was the kind of friendship that she especially valued: good will between people belonging to two hostile camps, whether political or literary. As in several other instances of her friendly contacts with Bolshevik party members (e.g., Piotr Kogan, Anatoly Lunacharsky and Boris Bessarabov), Tsvetaeva saw in Sachs's amity the overcoming of *partiinost'*, the untranslatable Russian term for 'party-mindedness' or 'party spirit.' In 'The Living About the Living,' she described *partiinost'* as 'something that is self-evidently not human, not animal, and not divine, which destroys in a person the human being, the animal and the divinity.'

It was Sachs who got Tsvetaeva a job as a filing clerk at the People's Commissariat of Nationalities, which she took with considerable reluctance in November 1918. In 'My Jobs' she described, with humor and revulsion, her ordeal by office work: 'I enter, timid and incongruous, in a man's mouse-colored sweater, feeling like a mouse.' She was depressed by the senseless tasks she was given (writing summaries of news stories and pasting clippings on sheets that were filed and forgotten); it was distasteful for her to work in the office that was concerned with recording the defeats of the White Army (which had all of her sympathy); and she keenly felt the absurdity of taking time from her intense creative work to engage in hours of mechanical drudgery. But there was no other way of obtaining food rations for her daughters under the existing conditions.

After a while, she began bringing her notebook to work and to do her own writing when there were no clippings to process. *The Phoenix*, her verse play about Casanova, was written at her office desk. A pretty blonde girl at one of the other desks, nicknamed the

White Negro by Tsvetaeva, confessed one day that she was dreaming of assassinating Lenin for 'robbing churches' and persecuting religious believers. She was held back by the knowledge that if she carried out her plan, her father would be immediately shot – a consideration that no pre-revolutionary terrorist had to face. Tsvetaeva lasted at the People's Commissariat of Nationalities for five and a half months, after which she left, unable to produce a required report of insurmountable complexity. She was so little interested in the organization for which she worked that she never did learn that the head of the commissariat during her employment was Joseph Stalin. Her second attempt at working in a government office was such a nightmare of alien and incomprehensible activity that she herself quit, in tears, after a single unbearable day.

The economic devastation and food scarcity of the first post-revolutionary years were not due only to the consequences of World War I and the civil war. Striving to wipe out all vestiges of capitalism and private enterprise, the Bolshevik government prohibited all commerce and all trading between the cities and the countryside. This led to acute shortages of agricultural products in the cities. A black market arose which in a modified form has remained a fixed part of Soviet reality to this day. At the same time, a program of forcible requisitioning of produce, the *prodrazverstka*, was imposed, which in many localities meant the confiscation of the peasants' entire crop and livestock by the government, leaving them no draft power for plowing and no grain for spring sowing. This in turn led to famine and to peasant rebellions, such as the one in the Tambov area which lasted from 1920 to 1922.

Marina Tsvetaeva's 'Free Passage' is her eyewitness account of a trip to a requisitioning point in the Tambov Province and of the conditions there that were to lead to the so-called Antonov Rebellion a year and a half later. Since travel for personal reasons had been outlawed, a fellow employee suggested that Tsvetaeva travel under the bogus pretext of 'studying peasant embroideries.' But her real purpose was to barter for food. The 'free passage' of the title refers to the permit to bring back 1½ poods (60 lbs.) of grain, a permit that came with the travel authorization. The people in charge of the requisitioning point were, to Tsvetaeva's surprise, not proletarians or long-time revolutionaries, but representatives of the pre-revolutionary propertied class. One of the men in charge of the requisitions was the son of a formerly affluent dressmaker, who used to count the wife of Tsvetaeva's Uncle Dmitry among her customers. Another, Iosif Kaplan, was the husband of a woman who owned a prosperous knitwear factory in St Petersburg. These members of the bourgeoisie had joined the Bolsheviks and were now lording it over the peasants, confiscating their produce at will.

Profiteering was the undisguised motive of these Communist officials. Kaplan's wife dealt in gold and ran a black market restaurant on the side. Tsvetaeva witnessed a nasty row between the Jewish and Russian-Orthodox Communists, with the Jews insensitively mocking the Orthodox religion and the non-Jews responding with the stalest anti-Semitic verbiage. The impractical poet proved no match at the bargaining with the sullen, hoarding peasants, who forced her to accept amber beads and dolls for her children instead of the vitally needed grain, eggs and other foodstuffs in exchange for the soap and chintz she had brought for barter. Her bartering would have been a total failure had not her travelling companions given her a hand with it. Disgusted with the life at the requisitioning point, which she saw as a den of thieves out of an old fairy tale, Tsvetaeva struck up a friendship with a huge and handsome Bolshevik soldier, who was a former bank robber and a decorated military hero during World War I. She nicknamed him Stenka Razin after the famed seventeenth-century rebel, read her poetry to him, listened to his telling of a folklore version of the legend of the Invisible City of Kitezh (which she would later use in her poem 'The Pied Piper') and presented him with her favourite silver ring. This encounter made up for the ugliness and mendacity which she had to endure in order to obtain food for her children.

In the winter of 1919–20, starvation, the violence of the Cheka and lack of fuel reached levels that would be hard to credit if we did not have so many eyewitness accounts recorded by articulate and eloquent people. Tsvetaeva's journal of her life during that winter, 'Garret Life,' is further fleshed out by Konstantin Balmont's memoir 'Where Is My Home?' and Prince Sergei Volkonsky's dedicatory piece from his book *Existence and Being*, which describe Tsvetaeva's life at that time (these two essays are appended to the 1979 edition of Tsvetaeva's *Selected Prose*). 'It was in those horrible, those vile Moscow years,' Volkonsky wrote. 'Do you remember how we lived? In what filth, in what disorder, in what homelessness? Ah, but that's nothing! Do you remember insolence personified, wearing a sheepskin cap, barging into your apartment? Do you remember the insulting demands, the taunting questions? The terror of hearing a doorbell ring, the repulsive searches, the offensiveness of the "comradely" treatment? Do you recall the meaning of hearing an automobile driving past your windows: will it stop or won't it? Oh, those nights!' (All the automobiles in Russia had been requisitioned by the Bolshevik authorities and were often used for nocturnal raids and searches.)

Addressing Tsvetaeva after they had both emigrated, Volkonsky commented on the inability of those who had not experienced such conditions to imagine them or to believe that they did occur: 'There is no point in being angry with them: how can the human imagination visualize what is unimaginable? But one thing surprises me: why can't people apply to themselves what others have experienced? To connect the reality of other people's suffering with the possibility of one's own suffering – how very few are capable of taking this step!' As Tsvetaeva's 'Garret Life' testifies, conditions of such extreme adversity bring out not only the worst human instincts, but some of the best ones as well. Her survival in 1919–20 depended almost entirely on others, mostly women neighbours. A Jewish woman who lived downstairs kept lending her money, sending her food and providing her with water for washing dishes and doing laundry. This woman's domineering husband, who detested Tsvetaeva, managed to maintain his family in pre-revolutionary conditions of affluence, which meant that he was either a Communist party bigwig or a successful black marketeer.

Next door, there lived the family of a cobbler named Gransky, one of whose daughters was selected to live in one of the model homes for Soviet children sponsored by Alexandra Kollontai, the incongruously elegant People's Commissar of Social Welfare. Rather than turning in her daughter's ration card to the authorities, Gransky's wife passed it on to Tsvetaeva, thus enabling her to get one hot take-out meal a day at a communal soup kitchen. Tsvetaeva was also helped out with food and fuel by her friend, the actress and poet Vera Zviagintseva, and she tried, whenever possible, to eat at the homes of friends and admirers. Still, as the terrible winter progressed, she found herself unable to provide for the children and she yielded to the advice of friends to place her younger girl, Irina, in a state-operated orphanage.

Tsvetaeva's elder daughter Ariadna, who was five at the time of the October Revolution, was growing into a precociously bright and

witty child. During the particularly hungry post-revolutionary
years, a kindly milkmaid named Dunia would obligingly take
Ariadna to the countryside for repeated visits, so as to build up her
strength with the better nourishment available there. But little
Irina's infancy coincided with the years of privation. She was an
undernourished child, small for her age and having trouble learning
to walk and speak. While Irina was at the orphanage, Ariadna came
down with malaria, which kept Tsvetaeva by her bedside for two
months. At the end of that period, she learned that her younger
daughter had died of starvation on February 2, 1920. Her despair at
the news was expressed in two frenzied letters she wrote to Vera
Zviagintseva during the next week: 'Dear Vera, I have no future, no
will power, I'm afraid of everything. If S[ergei] is not among the
living, I won't be able to go on in any case.[. .] Why drag on this
torment if it is possible not to suffer?' In April, she wrote a brief,
moving poem about how she once had two children's heads on
which to rest each one of her hands, until

> With both clenched hands
> As desperately as I could
> Rescuing the older one from the darkness
> I could not protect the younger.
> . . . . . .
> Radiant, with her thin little neck,
> Like a dandelion on its stem.
> I have not yet fully grasped
> That my child [lies buried] in the ground.

In describing Marina Tsvetaeva's life in Moscow after the
October Revolution, Prince Sergei Volkonsky carefully distinguished between *byt* (everyday material existence) and *bytie* (a
higher, spiritualized state of being). This very Tsvetaevan distinc-
tion, with its semantic dependence on a variation of the same verbal
stem, has great validity not only for her life in the period in question
but for the rest of her life as well. The years of oppression and
material hardship were also the years of great productivity and
creative development for Tsvetaeva the poet. The poetry that was
included in *The Demesne of the Swans* and the prose pieces about
the conditions of her life intended for *Omens of the Earth* reflected
her and Russia's *byt* of that period. *Bytie* was expressed in two other
collections written in those same years, *Mileposts II* (*Versty II*,

1917–21) and *Craft* (*Remeslo*, 1921–22), as well as in the lyrics on romantic themes that appeared in the collection *Psyche* (*Psikheia*, 1923), which also contained poems from several of her other collections. In Volume Two of the New York 1982 edition of her complete poetry there is also an additional large body of lyrics dating from that period which Tsvetaeva did not include in any of her collections but published later in periodicals.

During the years of War Communism, Tsvetaeva extended her range and, in addition to lyric poetry, turned to larger epic forms (her earliest epic poem, 'The Tsar-Maiden' ('Tsar'-devitsa') was written in 1920), to drama and to prose. The period was also rich in important literary contacts and rewarding personal friendships. Travelling by train from Moscow to the Crimea in November 1917, Tsvetaeva heard a young officer in the upper berth recite a poem about the February Revolution written by a friend of his. The poem was so impressive that upon returning to Moscow she immediately looked up its author. He was the young poet Pavel Antokolsky. The encounter was an instant meeting of the minds, 'something of an earthquake,' as Tsvetaeva later put it. Antokolsky was not only a poet, but also an actor at an experimental offshoot of the Moscow Art Theater called the Third Studio, which was under the direction of Yevgeny Vakhtangov.

Through Antokolsky and the Third Studio, Tsvetaeva came into contact with a group of theatrical folk, several of whom became quite important in her life and poetry during the next two years or so. There was the elderly and courtly Alexei Stakhovich, who was once an officer in the guards, then held the position of aide-de-camp at the imperial court, and still later became an actor at the Moscow Art Theater. After the revolution, when Tsvetaeva met him, he was a much admired teacher of deportment and etiquette at a theatrical school attended by the members of the Third Studio. Tsvetaeva had heard a great deal about Stakhovich from her actor friends before she actually got to meet him. His suicide in February 1919 was perceived by her as a momentous and symbolic event, marking the proximate disappearance of the cultural values which she associated with the eighteenth and early nineteenth centuries and with which she was identifying more and more in poems that were later included in *Mileposts II* and *Psyche*. She dedicated several poems to the memory of Stakhovich, one of which she was scheduled to read at a commemorative ceremony at the Moscow Art Theater. Her 84   Marina Tsvetaeva

reading was vetoed by Vladimir Nemirovich-Danchenko, one of the theater's two founders (with Stanislavsky), who felt that the poem was dangerously outspoken. There is also a section on Stakhovich in *Omens of the Earth*.

Three other memorable people were brought into Tsvetaeva's life by Antokolsky and the Third Studio. They were the actor Yury Zavadsky (Yura), who was to become one of the best-known Soviet stage directors in subsequent decades; the actor Vladimir Alexeiev (rhymes with 'Nureyev'); and the half-English actress Sophia Holliday, usually called Sonechka (pronounced SO-nechka, with a stress on the first syllable). Both Zavadsky and Alexeiev were spectacularly handsome. Zavadsky resembled a languid angel, while Alexeiev's manly and athletic looks made Tsvetaeva think of a sea captain. Sonechka Holliday was a tiny, childlike woman who had scored a great success in her debut role as the heroine of a dramatization of Dostoevsky's story 'White Nights.' Tsvetaeva became emotionally involved with all three actors in one way or another. She described these involvements first in cycles of poems written while she was still seeing them ('The Brothers,' 'The Cloak,' 'The Comedian' and 'Verses to Sonechka') and much later in a long, rambling memoir 'The Tale of Sonechka,' 1937.

The polygonal entanglement outlined in the memoir and the poems far exceeded in complexity the 1909–10 one that was reflected in *The Evening Album*. To begin with, although Antokolsky and Zavadsky were both later married, at the time Tsvetaeva met them they were in the midst of a love affair with each other. She was charmed by their love and refused to censure it:

> They sleep, their hands interlaced,
> A brother with brother,
> A friend with friend,
> Together on the same bed.
> . . . . . .
> Their hands I will not sunder.
> I would rather,
> I would rather
> Blaze in scorching flames in hell!

These lines from 'The Brothers' take up the theme of male homosexual love which Tsvetaeva had already treated with great sympathy in the somewhat mysterious 1917 cycle 'St John' ('Ioann'), where the love of a man for a younger male companion is

likened to the relationship between Christ and the Beloved Disciple
and where the poet voices her envy for the situation of the younger
man in this couple. The first poem of this four-poem cycle remains
unpublished to this day and the identities of the protagonists to
whom 'St John' was addressed remain unknown.

Despite the unconcealed nature of the relationship between
Antokolsky and Zavadsky, both Sonechka Holliday and Marina
Tsvetaeva became smitten by the seraphic Zavadsky. He, for his
part, basked in their adulation, but was unwilling or unable to
respond in a more concrete way. Tsvetaeva's infatuation with
Zavadsky was different from her other involvements in that in his
case she was attracted solely by the actor's outward appearance:

> You are as forgetful as you are unforgettable.
> Ah, but you do resemble your own smile.
> Shall I say more? Fairer than golden morning!
> Shall I say more? Only you in the entire universe!
> Love's own young prisoner-of-war!
> A chalice sculpted by Cellini's hand.

These lines come from one of twenty-three poems addressed to
Zavadsky which form the cycle 'The Comedian' (the Russian word,
'komediant,' has, like the French *comédien*, the implication of 'one
who is putting on an act'). Tsvetaeva felt guilty about pursuing the
indifferent Zavadsky with her attentions. The episode left her
puzzled about the power which physically attractive people can
exert over those who are more complex and creative than themselves, depriving them of their independence and will power. Her
meditations on this subject eventually found their way into such
later works as 'My Pushkin' and 'Natalia Goncharova.' Her verse
play *Fortuna* is a portrait of Zavadsky (in the guise of the Duc de
Lauzun) as a glamorous nonentity. Her later feelings about this
actor were recorded in a section from *Omens of the Earth* called 'On
Love.'

Tsvetaeva's situation with Vladimir Alexeiev could not have
been more different. She described it as an all-male friendship: 'In
the Moscow of 1918–19, there was no one with whom I could share
the masculine in me, the direct and steely in me.[. . .] [There were]
the young Reds who would come to Moscow for recuperation
between two battles. They were probably wonderful, but I couldn't
be friends with them because there is no friendship between the
vanquished and their victors. With Volodya I could unburden my

male soul.' Tsvetaeva tried to be a matchmaker between Vladimir and Sonechka, but they did not take to each other. Shortly after Easter 1919, Alexeiev left for the south, telling no one but Tsvetaeva of his intention to join the remnants of White resistance to the Bolsheviks. He was never seen again and was presumed to be missing in action. Tsvetaeva addressed poetry only to those she loved, not to friends, so she wrote no poems to or about Vladimir Alexeiev. But the last section of 'The Tale of Sonechka,' which bears the title 'Volodya,' is one continuous eulogy of him.

Sonechka Holliday was the object of Tsvetaeva's most intense Sapphic passion since her breakup with Sophia Parnok in 1916. But this time there were no dimensions of unbridled sensuality such as had wrecked that earlier affair. Instead, the relationship took the form of a passionate schoolgirl crush. Its vocabulary and emotional range, as recorded in 'The Tale of Sonechka,' suggest a novel by Lydia Charskaya. 'This tale of mine may well be a lump of sugar,' Tsvetaeva admitted in the text, 'but at least it felt *sweet* to write.' The fervor and the intensity also bring to mind Sonechka's favourite novel, *Netochka Nezvanova* by Dostoevsky. Because Tsvetaeva had no interest in Dostoevsky, she paid little attention to Sonechka's involvement with his work. But the whimsical, willfull and occasionally self-destructive heroine of 'The Tale of Sonechka' does at times emerge from its pages as a Dostoevskian infernal woman, junior grade: her irrationality, her possessiveness and her unprovoked hostility to people who meant her well (e.g., her nasty tongue-lashings of Volodya Alexeiev).

Sophia Poliakova in her study of Tsvetaeva and Parnok saw certain portions of 'The Tale of Sonechka' as 'a field of battle against Parnok.' She found in the memoir a series of textual reminiscences and images that refer to poems that Tsvetaeva had once addressed to Parnok. According to Poliakova, Tsvetaeva must have been indulging in 'theater for oneself' – no one else could have grasped her allusions because the poems of the 'Woman Friend' cycle remained unpublished and Sophia Parnok was already dead when 'The Tale of Sonechka' was being written. The aim, Poliakova surmises, was to immortalize Holliday and to condemn Parnok to anonymity and oblivion (since then, Poliakova herself has defeated that aim by bringing out her edition of Sophia Parnok's poetry and asserting its artistic worth). Poliakova's hypothesis finds confirmation in a highly significant detail which she overlooked in her study: the evening dress of golden-brown faille which Tsvetaeva presented as a gift to Sonechka Holliday must be the dress she mentions wearing the first time she met Sophia Parnok (Poem 10 of 'Woman Friend').

The love affair with Sonechka ended even more abruptly than the one with Sophia Parnok. After going on a tour of the provinces, from which she wrote Tsvetaeva the series of amorous letters cited in the memoir, Sonechka never came to see her again and made no attempt to communicate with her after returning to Moscow. But while Tsvetaeva never forgave Parnok her betrayal and never ceased hating her, she wrote pages and pages in her memoir justifying Holliday's behavior, going to the extent of quoting the biblical injunction that woman must abandon her parents and cleave to one man. 'I was more for her than her father and mother and, without doubt, more than a beloved man, but she was bound to prefer him, whoever he turned out to be. Because this is what God decreed when He created the world. The two of us had transgressed only against "people," never against God and never against man.'

In the cycles of poems addressed to Zavadsky and Holliday, Tsvetaeva shows her remarkable versatility, the variety of tones and styles which she by now had at her command. 'The Comedian' employs a refined, worldly diction, the kind that Tsvetaeva strove for in her first two collections, but had only now mastered to perfection. The verbal manner is that of a well-bred gentleman wooing an enchanting actress. It takes a moment of thought to realize just how unprecedented the reversal of the expected gender roles in this cycle really is. Sonechka Holliday, as Tsvetaeva herself informed us, had terrible tastes in the arts. She relished sentimental doggerel, penny-dreadful romances and treacly barrel-organ ditties. In 'Verses to Sonechka,' Tsvetaeva enters her friend's favoured world of lowbrow urban folklore and by dint of sheer genius raises it to the level of high art. In three of these poems she seems to follow the example of Osip Mandelstam's 1913 poem 'Cinema,' where he subjected a melodramatic silent film to an inspired and ultimately serious poetic treatment. Similarly, in poems 3, 4 and 10 of 'Verses to Sonechka' we get typically banal themes and situations with which wandering street singers used to touch the hearts of lower-class audiences but embodied in poetry of great elegance and mastery, without a shade of mockery or parody (Stravinsky put similar materials to similar use in *Petrushka* and

later in *Mavra*). The second poem of the cycle hybridizes a
sentimental street ditty with the folklore genre of a kind of surrealistic nursery rhyme called *nebylitsa*. Here are its first two stanzas:

> A nestling sang in the woods,
> An organ-grinder under the window:
> – He's a cheat, a rat,
> He's a rat, a cheat!
>
> Devils from a barrel
> Chimed in in chorus:
> – He's sold you out, girlie,
> All of you, for a penny!

Much of Tsvetaeva's poetry from the time of War Communism
dealt with the age in which she lived and her own situation at that
time. But she also reached out to earlier epochs for parallels and
precedents for what was happening to her country, citing the time of
nomadic invasions which ravaged Russia during the Middle Ages
(and which were evoked in the medieval epic *The Igor Tale*, often
alluded to in the poems of *The Demesne of the Swans* and *Craft*) and
the French Revolution, which many others also recalled in what she
termed 'the Soviet Jacobin Moscow of Marat.' Equally important
was her turning to the past as a form of escape from the drabness
and terror of the present. Tsvetaeva's favoured periods for escape
were the ones that were rediscovered and popularized at the very
start of the twentieth century by Sergei Diaghilev's journal *The
World of Art* and by the artists associated with that journal: the
eighteenth century and the Romantic Age.

These periods are present in the themes and imagery of many of
her short poems from this time (the impact of actual Russian
eighteenth-century poetry on Tsvetaeva did not begin to manifest
itself until the 1920s). The eighteenth century is also the time of
action in the majority of the six verse plays she wrote in 1918 and
1919. All these plays were written to be performed by the Third
Studio, though none of them ever was. Four of them contained
showy parts tailor-made for Sonechka Holliday and at least three
contained roles intended for Yury Zavadsky. Unlike her later verse
tragedies on themes from classical antiquity, these plays are not
first-rate Tsvetaeva. Despite passages of considerable beauty here
and there, they are handicapped by the ghost of Edmond Rostand,

which hovers in the wings and from time to time makes an embarrassing entrance.

The Snowstorm (Metel'), the earliest of these plays, is a variation on Alexander Blok's poetic drama *The Incognita (Neznakomka)*, in which a poet's encounter with a woman who is an astral being is shown against a background of vulgarity and incomprehension. Tsvetaeva, characteristically, reverses the genders of the protagonists, so that in her play the man is an astral being and the woman is a mortal. Even so, her debt to Blok is very marked in both the situation and the language of the play. The derivative quality of *The Snowstorm* is further enhanced by the long soliloquy of a character called the Old Woman, which is all too obviously patterned on the monologue of the Countess in Modest Tchaikovsky's libretto for his brother's opera *The Queen of Spades*. *The Stone Angel (Kamennyi angel)*, an idiosyncratic treatment of the Psyche and Eros myth, with a central part for Zavadsky and dedicated to 'Sonechka Holliday, the Woman, the Actress, the Flower, the Heroine' and *The Jack of Hearts (Chervonnyi valet)* have been so far published only from defective, incomplete manuscripts. Neither of them seems to have the makings of a major work.

Somewhat more successful are the three plays from the same cycle which are set at the time of the French Revolution and were based on historical sources. In *An Adventure (Prikliuchenie)* and *The Phoenix (Feniks)*, Tsvetaeva drew on the memoirs of Casanova. She made her initial acquaintance with these memoirs at the age of eighteen, when Voloshin offered them to her as a present. The young Tsvetaeva, who suffered from a certain prudery, refused to read the book and indignantly sent it back to Voloshin. After the revolution, however, Casanova became one of her favourite authors. His memoirs, which captured the sweep, the gaiety and the flavour of the eighteenth century, were written shortly after the French Revolution, which aimed to discredit everything about that century that Tsvetaeva admired. Casanova succeeded in passing on to subsequent generations a seductive image of his century, which his revolutionary contemporaries were doing their best to besmirch. For Tsvetaeva, the parallels with the Moscow of 1918–19 were unmistakable.

In *The Phoenix*, the aged Casanova is shown at the end of his life, in retirement at the castle of Dux in Bohemia. He is mistreated and misunderstood by the boorish local aristocrats and by the plebeians.

But he is valued and appreciated by the celebrated warrior and writer Prince de Ligne (on whose memoirs Tsvetaeva also drew) and by the young peasant girl Francesca, who is both a child and the voice of the future. This play has obvious allegorical significance. It is on the one hand Tsvetaeva's answer to the young post-revolutionary Proletarian poets who were clamoring for the over-throw of older Symbolists such as Balmont, Briusov and Blok; on the other hand, it was her defense of courtly older men she admired, Alexei Stakhovich and, later, Prince Sergei Volkonsky, men who had a great cultural tradition to pass on to the younger generation and did not deserve the contempt in which the newly evolving Soviet culture held them.

An Adventure is a romantic escapist comedy which embodies Tsvetaeva's indistinct dream of an androgynous world where love and intimacy would be based on personal worth rather than looks and where the limitations of the usual division into the two sexes would be overcome. From the vast panorama of Casanova's book, Tsvetaeva selected what is probably its most appealing episode, his brief love affair with the mysterious cello-playing Frenchwoman known only as Henriette. In Casanova's description, she was a sweet, modest person, who wore male attire in order to escape from the custody of her repressive family. In Tsvetaeva's play, she is turned into an ambiguous being called Henri-Henriette, who can function as either man or woman and be alternately a brawling hussar, a seductive and erudite beauty or a virtuoso musician. It is not clear whether this part was intended to be played by an actor or an actress.

By far the best of these plays is *Fortuna*, a dramatization in verse of the memoirs of Armand Louis de Gontaud Biron, Duc de Lauzun (1747–93). Lauzun was an aristocrat who lent his support to the French Revolution and died by the guillotine during the Jacobin terror. While awaiting execution, Lauzun composed his memoirs in which he described primarily his sexual exploits. Among the famous women who in one way or another found Lauzun irresistible were supposedly Queen Marie Antoinette and Princess Izabela Czarto-ryska, the mother of the famed Polish nineteenth-century states-man Adam Czartoryski. The play begins with Lauzun's encounter in childhood with the goddess of fortune, Fortuna, who bestows on him 'the most fearful of gifts, seductiveness.' He is then shown in encounters with three of the women in his life. The scene with Marie

Antoinette is a reflection of Tsvetaeva's involvement with Yury Zavadsky, where she casts herself as the queen and Zavadsky as Lauzun and where passages from 'The Comedian' addressed by the poet to the actor are incorporated into the dialogue.

The final scene of *Fortuna* shows Lauzun awaiting execution at the hands of the revolutionaries whose cause he had supported and for whom he had fought against the peasant insurgents of the Vendée (for Tsvetaeva, the Vendée was always the equivalent of the White Army). Lauzun's long soliloquy in this scene is clearly meant as topical commentary on the plight of many Russian liberals and Socialists who were then being put to death by the revolution they had helped to bring about:

> And I, Lauzun, with my hand whiter than snow,
> Used to raise the goblet to the health of the mob.
> And I, Lauzun, used to proclaim that a nobleman
> And a wood cutter have full rights under the sun!
>
> What was I born? Delight of queens, support
> Of kings. I played with the *fleur de lys*
> As a child. Well then, my young lion,
> For what will you die today? For the Vendée?
> No, I shall have my place in the Louvre Gallery,
> A *général-en-chef* who fought against the Vendée.
>
> Yes, my old world, we rushed into the abyss
> On the same steed, and they will bind our hands
> With the same rope, and on yonder wall
> There is the same verdict on you and on me:
> Weighed and found wanting ... [lit.: too light]

In her memoir 'My Jobs,' Tsvetaeva described a public reading of *Fortuna* which she gave on July 7, 1919. She appeared on the same program with the People's Commissar of Education, Anatoly Lunacharsky, who was also an amateur playwright. 'Never did I read more distinctly,' Tsvetaeva wrote. 'Never did I breathe with such a sense of responsibility. [...] A nobleman's soliloquy right into the commissar's face – now this is what I call life! Too bad it was only to Lunacharsky and not to ... I was about to write "Lenin," but Lenin wouldn't have understood a word of it – well then, not to the entire staff of the Lubianka [i.e., the Cheka Headquarters].'

5

Maturity, emigration, fame

Marina Tsvetaeva made her literary debut in what, as we now know, was the greatest age Russian poetry has so far seen. Her first two books, published in the midst of all that splendour and diversity, could not but appear as a minor, peripheral phenomenon. The highly favourable reviews of *The Evening Album* by Voloshin, Gumiliov and Shaginian, cited earlier, were matched by other reviews, such as Briusov's, which were condescending or hostile. Among the very few people who realized quite early what a unique figure she was we find Ilya Ehrenburg, who in a 1913 article claimed for Tsvetaeva a place in Russian poetry equal to that of Akhmatova. Known mainly for his later activities as novelist, propagandistic journalist and, at the end of his life, memoirist, Ehrenburg was prior to the 1920s a modernist poet with a strong bent for Roman Catholic mysticism. Ehrenburg and Tsvetaeva got to be friends during the years of War Communism and he was a major champion of her poetry in the period that immediately followed her emigration.

Between 1912 and 1922 her reputation slowly grew. Her poetry occasionally appeared in anthologies and literary miscellanies. Now and then, she participated in group poetry readings. Until about 1913, Tsvetaeva had the odd habit of bringing along her younger sister and reciting her poems in unison with her. According to the recollections of Anastasia Tsvetaeva, their voices sounded identical. The effect of such joint reading must have been stereophonic. These duets gave the sisters a sense of closeness, but this mode of recitation was apparently thought distracting by audiences. The publication of the more mature poems from *Juvenilia* and *Mileposts I* in Sophia Chatskina's *Northern Annals* in 1916 and early 1917 and Tsvetaeva's appearance at the Kannegisers' literary soirée brought her, as we have seen, to the attention of St Petersburg poets.

The poetic breakthrough achieved in 1916 in *Mileposts I* and further deepened and enhanced in *Mileposts II* and *The Demesne of the Swans* should have placed Tsvetaeva in the front rank of Russian post-Symbolist poets. It should have – but it didn't, because it was six more years before two of these three collections were published. But if the critics and the reading public were not yet aware of Tsvetaeva's new magnitude, several of her fellow poets were. The much older Konstantin Balmont, one of the founders of Russian Symbolism, became Tsvetaeva's friend and champion late in 1917 or early in 1918. At the end of January 1918, both Balmont and Tsvetaeva took part in the memorable gathering of poets at the apartment of Mikhail and Maria Tsetlin (Mikhail Tsetlin dedicated all his poems to his wife, which was spelled out in his pen name, Amari, i.e. 'à Marie'). Among those present were Viacheslav Ivanov, Andrei Bely, Boris Pasternak and Ilya Ehrenburg. The evening, vividly described by the last two in their memoirs, went down in literary history because it was then that Vladimir Mayakovsky read his epic poem 'Man' and heard himself acclaimed as a genius by the other poets.

On May 14, 1920, Tsvetaeva participated in a festive gathering in honor of the thirtieth anniversary of Balmont's literary debut. She appeared on terms of parity with two distinguished older poets, Viacheslav Ivanov and Feodor Sologub. Balmont made a speech denouncing the injustice of economic inequality, after which Sologub defended the importance of an individual approach to poetry and, to the indignation of many in the audience, proclaimed: 'True equality doesn't exist and thank God it doesn't.' Tsvetaeva found nothing to disagree with in either poet's stand and remembered 'applauding furiously' for both. Also present were two Communist guests from England, a fat, mannish woman wearing 'a kepi with ear flaps' and a man who looked like a prize fighter. (Before the revolution, Balmont had frequently visited England and lectured on Russian poetry at the Taylorian Institution in Oxford.) The woman made a speech in English of which Tsvetaeva understood only the words 'proletariat' and 'the Internationale.' Tsvetaeva mused on the incongruity of the combination 'Communist' and 'guest,' since in her experience 'Communists don't come as guests – they arrive with a search warrant.'

Tsvetaeva's friendship with Prince Sergei Volkonsky, whom she met through Vera Zviagintseva, dated from 1921. Volkonsky was a writer, lecturer, theoretician of the dance and former director of the imperial theaters. Tsvetaeva was charmed that his grandfather was

a famed Decembrist rebel and his grandmother was Maria
Raevskaya, a friend of Pushkin, who supposedly portrayed her as
the young girl on the seacoast in the first chapter of *Eugene Onegin*
(a hypothesis which Vladimir Nabokov took great pains to demolish
in his edition of the novel). Tsvetaeva's motives for seeking out the
elderly Volkonsky were the same ones that drew her to Alexei
Stakhovich. Here, again, was a man of great knowledge and
sophistication, trying to preserve and spread cultural values in a
world growing steadily more ignorant, dogmatic and impersonal.

Their friendship lasted until Volkonsky's death in Paris in 1939.
Writing to Alexander Bakhrakh in 1924, Tsvetaeva likened her
devotion to Volkonsky to the purest form of love: 'This was how I
loved the sixty-year old Prince Volkonsky, who couldn't stand
women. I loved him with all my meekness [*bezotvetnost'*], all my
selflessness [*bezzavetnost'*], and finally I got him – to possess
forever! I conquered him with the stubbornness of my love. He
didn't learn to love women, but he did learn to love love.' Tsvetaeva
addressed to Volkonsky the seven-poem cycle 'The Disciple'
('Uchenik') and described him in the poem 'To Prince Sergei
Volkonsky,' which appear in her collection *Craft*. 'The Disciple'
takes up the theme of her earlier cycle 'St John' – the poet's desire to
be the male lover-disciple of a wise older mentor. But here, this
theme is taken a step further than in 'St John.' The younger
disciple's devotion and self-sacrifice are to be rewarded with solitude and independence after she/he has left the master behind.

During the difficult years of War Communism, Tsvetaeva showed
great concern for her older male friends. She shared her meager
food supply with Balmont and even did household chores for him.
While hating the drudgery of office work for pay, she did not mind
performing secretarial duties for Volkonsky and she personally
copied his manuscripts. In the fall of 1921, when she heard of the
desperate material situation of Voloshin and other writers who
lived in the Crimea, she arranged to be received by Anatoly
Lunacharsky in the Kremlin to secure help for them. As we learn
from her letter to Voloshin of November 7, 1921, there was one
starving writer in the Crimea whom she did not wish to rescue:
Sophia Parnok. Tsvetaeva was accompanied to the Kremlin by the
playwright Vladimir Wolkenstein, who was once briefly married to
Parnok in what was apparently a marriage of convenience. In her
letter, Tsvetaeva reports the following amazing dialogue between

Wolkenstein and herself, which took place as she was writing for Lunacharsky the names of writers in need of help: 'But Sonia! What about Sonia?' 'The hell with her! Max is more important to me.' 'But Sophia is a woman and my former wife!' 'But Max, too, is a woman and my present (*indicatif présent*) friend.'

The People's Commissar Lunacharsky had already impressed Tsvetaeva when he favourably received her reading of *Fortuna* in July 1919. She had other encounters with him, after one of which she wrote to Voloshin: 'Lunacharsky – you may tell this to everyone – is marvellous. A real knight and a real man.' Always attracted to this kind of across-the-barbed-wire friendliness, Tsvetaeva addressed to Lunacharsky an epistle in verse in which she wrote, among other things:

> Your victories are not mine,
> I've dreamt of different ones.
> We're not on two ends of the earth,
> We're on two constellations.
>
> We're votaries of two different stars.
> So what am I doing
> Building [this] bridge
> With an audacious hand?

What she offered Lunacharsky was something higher than any human law: an open heart and an outstretched hand. This, the poet felt, makes ideological opponents equal before God:

> And we shall be judged, I want you to know,
> By the same standard.
> And both of us will go to Heaven
> In which I do believe.

The meter of this poem is ordinary Russian iambic tetrameter alternating with trimeter. But Tsvetaeva subtly displaced the expected stresses and accents, making the lines leap and dance in ways that no translation could hope to convey. We do not know whether Lunacharsky perceived the deep humanity of this epistle or dismissed it as so much mystical twaddle.

There was another member of the Bolshevik Party with whom Tsvetaeva found it much harder to deal and that was Valery Briusov. As a young girl, Tsvetaeva had a great admiration for Briusov's poetry. Her brief 1910 essay on him, the earliest piece of

Tsvetaeva's prose that has survived, shows her affinity for many –
though by no means all – aspects of Briusov the poet. But after the
contacts described in Chapter 2 (pp. 29–34) and Briusov's less-than-
favourable review of *The Evening Album*, Tsvetaeva attacked him
in two poems, one included in *The Magic Lantern* and the other in
From Two Books, the only poem in that collection that was not
culled from the two earlier ones.

In pre-revolutionary times, Briusov was opposed to social or
political involvement in literature. He was, in fact, the only major
Symbolist poet who espoused an art-for-art's-sake stance. Konstantin Balmont and Zinaida Gippius were the political activists among
the senior Symbolists, with Balmont having to go into exile abroad
in 1905 for publishing his collection *Songs of the Avenger* which
urged the overthrow of the Romanov dynasty. Yet, after the
October Revolution, Balmont and Gippius, like thousands of other
revolutionaries, saw in Lenin's course a betrayal of the revolution
for which they had worked for decades, while Valery Briusov soon
joined the Bolshevik Party. He did it, as both Tsvetaeva and
Khodasevich have written, because he had always aspired to a
position of absolute leadership in literature and saw in his support of
Lenin's dictatorship a chance of establishing a dictatorship of his
own in the literary sphere. Mark Vishniak and Feodor Stepun
reported in their respective memoirs the general consternation
occasioned by the fact that the Bolshevik directive which banned
several Socialist Revolutionary publications was signed by Valery
Briusov, only recently known as the leading ideologue of art-for-
art's-sake decadence. Briusov was also put in charge of various
publishing ventures organized by the Soviet Government and in this
capacity he systematically opposed, from 1918 to 1922, the acceptance of any Tsvetaeva manuscripts by the state publishers.

In 'A Hero of Labor,' Tsvetaeva described how she was
approached in the summer of 1920 by Briusov's mistress, the poet
Adalis (pen name of Adelina Efron, apparently no relation), with
an invitation to appear in a reading of women poets, to be chaired
by Briusov. Tsvetaeva wrote that she was reluctant to appear on a
program restricted to women only and mentioned that she had
earlier withdrawn from one such group reading. She meant the
poetry recital in Moscow on January 22, 1916, where, according to
press announcements she was to appear alongside Sophia Parnok,
several other women poets and two actresses who were to recite

Akhmatova's poems. The painful breakup of her relationship with Parnok which was just then taking place may well have been the reason for Tsvetaeva's failure to appear on that occasion.

But in her memoir, Tsvetaeva motivated her withdrawal from the 1916 recital differently: 'I considered that there are more important classifications in poetry than belonging to the male or the female sex. Ever since I was born I have disdained anything that bears the brand of female mass separatism, such as women's colleges, suffragettism, feminism, the Salvation Army, that whole tired woman question, except for its military solutions: the fabulous realms of Penthesilea, Brünhilde or Maria Morevna [a warrior maiden of Russian fairy tales] and the no less fabulous Petrograd Women's Battalion [during World War I].' 'In art, there is no woman question,' Tsvetaeva continued in the same passage in 'A Hero of Labor.' 'There are only women's responses to the human question.' The poet, who was to be exploited by her own family in Prague and Paris precisely because she was a woman, was able to conceive of feminism not in terms of rights or equality, but only of excluding women from the rest of humanity. However, if we consider that 'A Hero of Labor' was written in 1925, Tsvetaeva may have wanted to disassociate herself from any kind of feminism in response to the trend in the Soviet Union in the early 1920s, exemplified by Leon Trotsky's *Literature and Revolution* (see the next chapter, pp. 129–30), toward segregating women poets into a separate, somewhat inferior critical category. Even so, we see Tsvetaeva asserting her admiration for the militant Amazons even in this uncongenial context – the Amazons to whose role she so often aspired but whose company she never allowed herself to join.

Be that as it may, Marina Tsvetaeva did appear on the stage of the Polytechnic Museum in Moscow on December 11, 1920, amidst eight frilly and overdressed versifying ladies. She wore a garment that resembled a priest's cassock ('a rephrasing of an overcoat that had seen better days'), with her usual leather belt and officer's field pouch and a pair of grey felt boots. Following Briusov's introductory lecture, where he asserted that women are capable of writing only about love and passion and are unable to handle any other themes, Tsvetaeva mounted the podium to deliver ('feeling as if I were falling off a mountain') several of her poems from *The Demesne of the Swans*, eulogizing the White Army. She concluded the reading with a remarkable poem not found in any of her

collections and known only from being cited in 'A Hero of Labour.'
It begins with an epigraph from Alexander Griboedov's great neo-
classical verse comedy *The Misfortune of Being Clever*: 'Women
shouted hurrah / And tossed their bonnets in the air.' Tsvetaeva
then points out her lack of aristocratic or conservative roots:

> With my hand on my heart [I affirm]:
> I am no distinguished lady,
> I'm a rebel in my mind and my guts.

To an audience of Red Army soldiers and revolutionary students,
she nevertheless proclaimed her right to shout 'Hurrah!' for the tsar
'the way street urchins shout in all the squares in the world.'
Developing the imagery of the Griboedov epigraph, the poem
concludes:

> The bonnet flies up higher than the towers,
> But passing the crown on the head of the idol,
> It flies upward to the stars!

After this assertion of total independence, Tsvetaeva was
stopped by Briusov, while the audience cheered. 'This was obvious
insanity,' she later commented, 'but I was guided by two, no three,
four aims: (1) seven poems by a woman without the word "love"
and without the pronoun "I"; (2) proof that poetry makes no sense
to the audience; (3) a dialogue with some one particular person who
understood (perhaps a student); (4) and the principal one: fulfilling
here, in the Moscow of 1921, an obligation of honor. And beyond
any aims, aimlessly, stronger than aims, a simple and extreme
feeling of: what if I do?' Had there been a single person in the
audience willing to denounce her to the Cheka, she would have
been arrested that very day. But this was before the days of Stalin,
when non-reporting was made a state crime. Tsvetaeva's unmistakable pride in recounting this episode in such great detail is significant for understanding the image she had of herself in those years.

During the last two years before her departure from Russia,
1920–1922, Tsvetaeva undertook three long epic poems based on
Russian folklore sources, of which she completed two, and she
wrote a long lyrical poem, 'On a Red Steed' ('Na krasnom kone'),
which fused the confessional and the folkloric modes. The earliest
of these long works was 'The Tsar-Maiden' ('Tsar'-devitsa'),

written between July and September 1920 and published in Berlin in 1922 as a separate book. Like its two successors, 'Sidestreets' ('Pereulochki') finished in Moscow in April 1922 and included in the collection *Craft*, and 'The Swain' ('Mólodets') completed in Prague in December 1924, 'The Tsar-Maiden' is nominally a folk tale in verse. This is a genre that was prevalent in the Romantic Age when Zhukovsky and Pushkin popularized quasi-folk tales in verse which often borrowed both their subjects and their versification from foreign sources. Despite this, the results (e.g., Pushkin's 'The Golden Cockerel,' with a plot taken from Washington Irving, or Piotr Ershov's perennially popular 'The Little Hump-Backed Horse,' 1834, extended version 1856) were accepted by generations of parents, children and schoolmasters as genuine Russian folklore.

As Vladislav Khodasevich pointed out in his review of Tsvetaeva's 'The Swain,' real Russian folk tales and magic tales were always narrated in prose. Couching them in verse arose through Russian nineteenth-century poets' imitation of Western models – Ariosto, Evariste Parny and the German romantics. Furthermore, while the pseudo-folk tales in verse by Zhukovsky, Pushkin and Ershov may be enjoyed by adults, they have survived in the culture primarily as reading for children. Tsvetaeva's folklore-based long poems treat philosophical and erotic themes that no child could hope to understand. Drawing on the command of colloquial, peasant and substandard speech which she had developed and perfected in *Mileposts I*, the poet tells complex and highly sophisticated stories using the diction now of a pre-Petrine folk singer, now of an unlettered peasant narrator.

'The Tsar-Maiden' grafts two stories from Alexander Afanasiev's collection of Russian folk tales onto the classical myth to which Tsvetaeva would return again and again in her writings of the 1920s, that of Phaedra's incestuous love for her stepson Hippolytus. The poem tells of a drunken, corrupt old Tsar, his frail musician-son and the Tsar's young, beautiful second wife who resorts to witchcraft to seduce her stepson. The heroine of the title is a curious character who occurs in Russian folk tales and epic poems (*byliny*), the warrior-maiden, a huge and powerful Amazon who is traditionally shown falling in love with a weak, delicate man. She courts the musician prince with the aid of white magic, while the desperate stepmother resorts to the black arts to win his love, or, failing that, at least his body. The stepmother is abetted by the prince's evil, lecherous old tutor, to whom she has to submit sexually in order to secure his help. The Tsar-Maiden is aided by a sexless, non-human character, Wind, who helps her defeat the stepmother.

Two fine studies published in recent years help us understand this poem in greater depth. Sophia Poliakova's essay on the sources of 'The Tsar-Maiden' points out that the two good characters, the Tsar-Maiden and the musician prince, have been made far more androgynous than they were in Afanasiev. And indeed, the reversal or scrambling of gender roles here has a bearing not only on the instances from Tsvetaeva's poetry cited by Poliakova, but also on a number of other works, among them 'Woman Friend,' 'The Comedian' and *An Adventure*. At the risk of sounding simplistic, one can venture to say that in the two lovers of 'The Tsar-Maiden' the poet projected two alternate images of herself: in the Tsar-Maiden, the strong and independent Amazon she would have liked to be and in the prince, the vulnerable artist she knew she was. As G. S. Smith has shown in his essay 'Characters and Narrative Modes in Marina Tsvetaeva's *Tsar'-Devitsa*,' the two lovers' characters evolve and converge in the course of the narrative, so that they come to resemble each other more and more.

The final section of 'The Tsar-Maiden,' an epilogue that takes place after the fate of the principal characters has been settled, depicts a popular revolution during which a mob skins the corrupt old Tsar alive and proclaims the triumph of Red Russia. In her essays 'A Poet on Criticism' and 'The Poet and Time,' Tsvetaeva wrote that occasionally themes select their poets rather than the other way around. This was apparently what had happened with the finale of 'The Tsar-Maiden.' The poet who disagreed with the October Revolution and denounced it in so much of her work seems to assert its truth in textbook Bolshevik terms at the end of her folk tale set in legendary ancient Russia.

'Sidestreets' is the most spectacular manifestation of Tsvetaeva's interest in the folk poetry of magic chants and incantations, an interest also evident in certain poems of *Mileposts I* and *Craft*. On first reading, it seems a puzzle. A work of great verbal virtuosity, it strikes the reader as one vast incantation, with some narrative elements which are, however, hard to perceive as a coherent whole. When Tsvetaeva sent to Boris Pasternak a copy of *Craft*, which contains this poem, she asked particularly for his comments on 'Sidestreets.' In her letter to him of March 10, 1923 she wrote: 'No one seems to grasp the plot (the connection) [. . .] For me this work is as clear as day, *everything* has been said. Others hear only the noises and I find this insulting.'

Fortunately, a decade later, this poem perplexed Tsvetaeva's correspondent George Ivask and he questioned her about its contents. On October 11, 1935, she wrote: ' "Sidestreets" (didn't you know it?) is the story of the ultimate seduction.' Apparently, Ivask was still not satisfied with the explanation, for in Tsvetaeva's letter of January 24, 1937, we find a long commentary on 'Sidestreets': ' . . . you have simply understood nothing in "Sidestreets." Open your *byliny* and find the *bylina* about Marinka who lives in the Ignatiev sidestreets and practices magic behind the bed-curtain, turning young swains into aurochs, getting them drugged. [. . .] She is *deceit* and she is playing with something frightening.'

Byliny are oral folk poems whose themes are thought to go back to the early Middle Ages. Tsvetaeva's letter to Ivask directs us to the proper literary address for the plot of 'Sidestreets.' If ever a poem needed a synopsis, this one does. The heroine, never once identified in the text, turns out to be the sorceress Marina Ignatievna who appears in one of the *byliny* about the epic hero Dobrynia Nikitich. This mythic sorceress was one of the several avatars in the Russian folklore tradition of Marina Mnishek, the Polish wife of the False Dmitry and always one of Tsvetaeva's favourite historical personages. With the narrative canvas provided by the *bylina*, we can follow the action, which is narrated alternately from the vantage point of the sorceress and that of her victim. Many details were taken verbatim from the *bylina*, but much has been added by Tsvetaeva: the role of the victim's horse as the symbol of his masculine integrity destroyed by a conniving woman and the ecstatic apotheosis he thinks he is experiencing at the very moment he is being turned into a beast.

In the cited letter to Ivask, Tsvetaeva assured him that back in Russia everyone could understand this poem with no difficulty, 'every half-educated technical school student.' This was clearly a reflection of Tsvetaeva's idealization of the audience she had left behind in Russia and not of the real situation. As we have seen, fifteen years earlier she was not sure Boris Pasternak – let alone a half-educated student – could understand 'Sidestreets.' Without the *bylina* as a guide, the work is a colorful spray of verbal pyrotechnics; with it, it becomes a haunting and profound poem. We all owe

George Ivask a debt of gratitude for having persisted with his questions.

A third folklore-derived long poem which Tsvetaeva began at that time was 'Egorushka' (the name is an affectionate diminutive of one of the three Russian versions of the name George; the stress is on the second syllable, *Ee-GO-rooshka*). It was based on Russian folk legends about St George the Dragon Slayer which depicted him as a combination of a peasant Superman (the comic-strip one, not the Nietzschean) and Robin Hood. 'St George' is the title of a verse cycle in *Craft*, dedicated to Sergei Efron. In it the dragon-slaying saint, whose traditional Russian sobriquet was 'Bringer of Victories' (*Pobedonosets*), is the symbol of the counter-revolutionary White forces and of the victory which Tsvetaeva had hoped would be theirs. 'Egorushka' was to be a treatment of the same theme expressed in peasant language and imagery. Tsvetaeva completed three sections of this poem before emigrating and worked on a fourth one while living abroad. By then it had become clear that the widespread peasant revolts against the Soviet regime were unsuccessful and that the peasant St George had failed to slay the Bolshevik dragon. The poem remained uncompleted. When Ariadna Efron published fragments from it in *Novyi mir* in 1971, she described it as a celebration of a peasant folk hero, saying nothing about its counter-revolutionary central idea.

'On a Red Steed' was written between January 13 and 17, 1921. It belongs among Tsvetaeva's lyrical-autobiographical *poèmy*, such as 'The Enchanter' which preceded it and 'Poem of the End' and 'From the Seacoast' which were to follow. Yet, it is the only poem of this group which has features of epic poetry and folk tradition. The violent and turbulent poem falls into three segments, with an introduction and an epilogue. Against the background of some calamity – a burning house, a snowstorm or a military battle – the protagonist is exposed to three temptations. Each time she is about to perish unless she renounces what tempts her and each time she is rescued by the symbolic figure of a winged knight on a red steed, who, as the epilogue first makes clear, is her poetic genius. The three temptations have a complex, multi-faceted meaning, but on their basic level they stand for the renunciation of love, religion and pride for the sake of one's artistic calling. After the heroine overcomes the last temptation, her guardian genius finds her on a battlefield (which also represents erotic love) and offers himself as the replacement for all the things he has made her give up:

> And the whisper: 'Now you are as I desired you!'
> And the murmur: 'Now you are as I elected you,
> Child of my passion, my sister, my brother,
> My bride in the ice of armor.
>
> Mine and no one's till the end of years.'
> I, with arms raised: 'My light!'
> 'You will remain so? You won't be anyone's?'
> I, clutching my wound: 'No one's.'

The poem is an allegory about the terrible and demanding nature of art. At its initial publication, 'On a Red Steed' was dedicated to Anna Akhmatova. Akhmatova several times described her Muse as a young foreigner who visited her and enabled her to create poetry. 'On a Red Steed' begins and ends with the assertion that Tsvetaeva never had a Muse as either a nursemaid or a companion. Instead, the personification of her poetic inspiration, Tsvetaeva insists, is masculine: the Knight of the Red Steed (the color of his horse is derived from the purifying fire that in the first segment of the poem destroys the edifice of traditional poetry in which the poet was brought up). The dedication to Akhmatova and the rejection of a female Muse must have been Tsvetaeva's way of pointing out the essential difference between her own poetry and that of a contemporary whom she loved and admired but also perceived as a constant hindrance and rival, as several of her poems addressed to Akhmatova make clear.

Ariadna Efron has asserted in her memoirs that the dedication to Akhmatova was camouflage and that 'On a Red Steed' was actually Tsvetaeva's portrait of Alexander Blok, 'the creator of "The Twelve," the St George the Victory Bringer of the Revolution, the purest and most fearless Genius of poetry.' This statement lacks factual support and makes no sense at all textually since the poem in no way describes Tsvetaeva's relationship with Blok. Commentators, both in and out of the Soviet Union, have quoted it in good faith. By claiming that Tsvetaeva worshipped Blok for his revolutionary commitment, her daughter pursued her usual aim of minimizing her mother's counter-revolutionary views in order to make her poetry more acceptable to the Soviet censors of the 1970s.

By connecting the image of St George with Blok, Ariadna Efron hoped to disguise the meaning which this symbol had in Tsvetaeva's poetry of 1920–22.

At the end of 1920, the White Armies in the south of Russia were defeated. In November, British and French ships evacuated from the Crimea 100,000 military and civilian opponents of the Soviet regime. Sergei Efron was on one of these ships. There remained pockets of opposition in various areas, led by Socialist Revolution-aries, anarchists and anti-Leninist Marxists, such as the Menshe-viks. They were to be exterminated by the Red Army forces in the course of the next two years. In March 1921 came the revolt of Communist sailors at the Kronstadt naval base near Petrograd, the only one of the dozens of such phenomena usually mentioned by non-Russian historians. The sailors demanded that Lenin adhere to the principles in the name of which the February government was overthrown: free Soviets (workers' and soldiers' councils) and the calling of a constituent assembly at which the population could choose the form of government it wanted. The Kronstadt rebels were ruthlessly massacred. Soviet historians to this day describe them as anarchists rather than the Bolsheviks they really were.

After the drought of the summer of 1920, food shortages became calamitous. To save the country from an irreparable catastrophe, Lenin decided on a tactical retreat. The New Economic Policy (NEP) was introduced. It allowed a certain amount of private enterprise in commerce and this instantly improved food distri-bution. Instead of having all of their crops confiscated, the peasants were allowed to pay the government an exorbitant tax in produce and then sell what remained on the open market. This gave them, for the first time in years, an incentive to increase their production. Although the NEP saved millions from starvation, it was an ugly phenomenon. It did not bring back the humble capitalist institu-tions which people in Marxist-Leninist societies so desperately miss: the well-stocked grocery store, the neighborhood bakery and the cozy little provincial restaurant with decent food and service, the kind to which characters in Dostoevsky and Chekhov could so easily repair. Instead, the NEP generated a new class of profiteers, known as Nepmen and Nepwomen, and the stores and restaurants where they could enjoy luxuries in the midst of indigence. Whatever economic inequalities pre-revolutionary Russia may have been guilty of, they were nothing compared to the ostentatious vulgarity of the NEP period.

'Now about Moscow,' Marina Tsvetaeva wrote to Max Voloshin on November 7, 1921. 'It is monstrous. A fatty tumor, a purulent sore. On Arbat [Street], there are fifty four luxury food stores. Buildings disgorge foodstuffs. [. . .] On Tverskaya [Street] there is a gastronomic store called L'Estomac, I swear to you! People are just like the stores: everything is to be had for money. The general law is ruthlessness. No one cares for anyone else. Dear Max, believe me, this isn't envy. If I had millions, I still wouldn't buy whole hams. All this smells too much of blood. Many are starving, but they are somewhere in burrows and slums. The appearances are dazzling.'

Tsvetaeva's own food situation had improved considerably late in 1920 due to the kindness of one man. Piotr Kogan, a Marxist critic and professor of literature at Moscow State University, was described by Tsvetaeva as a man who 'understood neither poets nor poetry but loved and respected both.' Kogan and his wife Nadezhda Nolle were so shocked by the death of Tsvetaeva's daughter Irina that they arranged for the poet and her surviving daughter to receive special food parcels, *paiok*, which the Soviet Government issued to important cultural figures. Tsvetaeva's exceptional productivity in 1921 could not have been entirely divorced from the fact that during that year she was freed from standing in food lines and from the never-ending struggle to survive.

In spring of 1921, Ilya Ehrenburg, who was going abroad, promised Tsvetaeva to locate her husband. On July 1 she received a letter from Sergei, the first communication after years of not knowing where he was. She immediately began making plans to join him in Prague where Efron, the perennial student, had enrolled at the university. She felt that she'd had enough of the 'four-year-long waking nightmare' which life in her country had become. Things were to get even more grim before she left. With a second summer of drought in a row, famine spread to an area that was ten times the size of the one that was affected by the famine of 1892. In desperation, Lenin allowed a group of non-party intellectuals, including some with a Constitutional Democratic Party background, to organize an independent All-Russian Committee on Famine Relief. One of the members of this committee, Maxim Gorky, with the encouragement of the Soviet Government, appealed to America for help. Lenin had serious doubts that the 'Western bourgeoisie,' which he had repeatedly promised to destroy, would ever come to the Soviet Union's aid. But in the West, the issue was seen not as the question of propping up the Bolshevik regime, but of saving human beings from starvation.

In response, the American Relief Administration, under the leadership of the future president Herbert Hoover, came in with massive shipments of foodstuffs. In the meantime, the All-Russian Committee on Famine Relief did its work so successfully and brought forth such an enthusiastic response from the rest of the society that the Soviet Government became alarmed and accused the committee of trying to subvert its authority. The organizers of the committee were arrested and threatened with firing squads. They were eventually expelled from the country in the summer of 1922 as part of a group of some two hundred leading educators, scientists, writers and philosophers. The group included every prominent non-Marxist philosopher in Russia, among them Feodor Stepun, Tsvetaeva's acquaintance from her Musaget days, and also Nikolai Berdiaev, Fr Sergius Bulgakov and Lev Karsavin, with whom she was to associate in her Prague and Paris days. In an interview with the American journalist Louise Bryant, Trotsky called the mass expulsion a humanitarian act. For him, all these people were potential foreign agents and therefore deserved to be shot. Their actual fault was that they were all intelligent, articulate and unconvertible to Bolshevism.

The year 1921 was also devastating to the literary community. On August 2, Nikolai Gumiliov, aged thirty-five, was arrested by the Cheka on charges of belonging to an anti-government conspiracy, charges which were never substantiated. He was shot a short time later. On August 7, Alexander Blok, aged forty-one, died in a state of despondency bordering on insanity. At the end of August, Tsvetaeva heard rumors that Anna Akhmatova, who was the former wife of Gumiliov and a warm admirer of Blok, had killed herself. Vladimir Mayakovsky used his contacts to reach Petrograd and to determine that the rumors were without foundation. In gratitude, Tsvetaeva addressed to him a poem in which she described him as a 'heavy-footed archangel.' In November, Feodor Sologub's wife, the critic Anastasia Chebotarevskaya, was driven to suicide by the inhuman cat-and-mouse game the Soviet Government was playing with her and her husband, granting them an exit visa and then withdrawing it. Early in 1922, the great Futurist poet

Velimir Khlebnikov died at thirty-seven because of the privations he suffered during the civil war. All these events and personalities form the background for the writing of Tsvetaeva's astounding poetic diary of the year 1921, her collection *Craft*.

'And what kind of "Craft" is it?' Tsvetaeva wrote to Bakhrakh in 1923. 'Why, the singing kind, of course. The meaning, the care and the joy of my days.' She then quoted a quatrain from a poem by Karolina Pavlova, where this poet called her 'sacred craft' her misfortune and her wealth. Karolina Pavlova (1807–1893) was a German (née Jaenisch) who happened to be Russia's greatest woman poet of the nineteenth century. Mocked by the Romantics in the 1830s and '40s for being a bluestocking, Pavlova was expelled from Russian literature by the radical utilitarians of the 1860s who were blind to the fire and brilliance of her verse and could not forgive her the inheritance which she had received from a wealthy uncle. Critical attacks were so brutal that Pavlova had to leave Russia for good. Her poetry was rediscovered and rehabilitated in 1915 by Valery Briusov, who restored it to the position it merits. But Tsvetaeva discovered Pavlova through Sophia Parnok one year before Briusov's edition appeared. Sophia Poliakova has shown several hidden quotations from Pavlova in the poems Tsvetaeva and Parnok addressed to each other. The title *Craft*, which does not really fit the collection, may have been chosen by Tsvetaeva as a half-hearted conciliatory gesture toward the woman she once loved and now professed to hate. The gesture could not have been intended to be overt, for Tsvetaeva deleted the epigraph drawn from Pavlova's poem with which she had planned to open her book, 'not wishing,' as she wrote to Bakhrakh, 'to facilitate anything for the reader out of respect for the reader.'

Mileposts I, Tsvetaeva's most comprehensive previous collection, was an uninterrupted poetic diary for one year, 1916. *Craft* follows this precedent, but this time the year encompassed does not coincide with the calendar year, for it covers the period from April 1921 to April 1922. Tsvetaeva had separated the poetry she wrote during the years 1917–21 into two categories, the political (*The Demesne of the Swans*) and the personal and escapist (*Mileposts II*). But the collection *Craft* combines the personal, the political and the philosophical into one alloy, thus marking a new step in Tsvetaeva's evolution. In *Mileposts I*, the central theme was the poet's relationship to the city of Moscow. *Craft* treats many different themes, but two central ones can be discerned: post-revolutionary Russia and the poet's love for her absent husband.

During the five years when Tsvetaeva was separated from Sergei Efron, she lived through a number of more or less transient amorous involvements. There were Yury Zavadsky and Sonechka Holliday of the Third Studio; an unreciprocated infatuation with the poet Yevgeny Lann, of which we know from her published letters to him; the dalliances with the stage director Valery Bebutov and the soldier Boris Bessarabov, to whom she addressed the poem 'The Bolshevik'; and who knows how many others. Most of these romances did not lead to physical consummations, but some undoubtedly did. Yet, through it all, Sergei Efron remained at the center of her consciousness. 'I think of him day and night, I love only you and him,' Tsvetaeva wrote to her sister Anastasia on December 17, 1920.

In June and July 1921, Tsvetaeva composed, one after another, three cycles of poems addressed to her husband: 'Separation' ('Razluka'), 'St George' ('Georgii') and 'Good Tidings' ('Blagaia vest'). The man once described in *Juvenilia* as a jewel and an aquatic plant, is now an epic hero, a shining swan and a radiant knight defending honor and decency from brutal usurpers. At the same time the poet's love for him is something enormously vulnerable and threatened. In the melodious seventh poem of 'Separation,' this love is depicted as Ganymede and as a defenseless little lamb:

> In aquiline thunder
> – Oh, the beak! Oh, the blood!
> A tiny lamb hangs suspended:
> Our love . . .
>
> With disheveled hair
> Prostrate yourself on the ground . . .
> Pray that Zeus
> May not abduct him!

The cycle 'Good Tidings' expresses the poet's joy at the renewed contact with her husband and her assurance to him that his battles have not been in vain. The final poem of this cycle compares the ships that evacuated the White Army soldiers from the Crimea with the Homeric ships in *The Iliad* and prophesies that divine retribution will fall from heaven on the White Army's foes.

Classical and biblical allusions are frequent in *Craft*. The ironically titled cycle 'In Praise of Aphrodite' ('Khvala Afrodite') de-
nounces the goddess of sensual love (who was the villainess in
Tsvetaeva's play *The Stone Angel*) for allocating too much sugges-
tive power to the sexual drive:

> Every cloud in a bad moment
> Curves like [a woman's] breast.
> In every guiltless flower [appears]
> Your visage, you She-Devil!
>
> Perishable foam, salt of the sea,
> In froth and in torment
> For how long are we to obey you,
> You armless stone?

The odic, neoclassical diction of such cycles as 'In Praise of Aphrodite' and 'The Disciple' (addressed, as mentioned, to Volkonsky)
forms one stylistic pole of *Craft*. At the opposite pole is the burst of
incantations and magic chants found in other cycles, such as 'Captured by the Khan' ('Khanskii polon') and 'Snowdrifts' ('Sugroby').
These incantatory poems exploit to the full Tsvetaeva's gift for
verbal creativity and colloquial language. Their culmination is the
already discussed narrative poem 'Sidestreets,' which closes the
collection. Somewhere between these two poles is the diction of
several poems in the collection that describe the devastation caused
by the revolution and the civil war. Tsvetaeva was not only appalled
by the wreckage and the suffering, she was apprehensive that they
would now spread to other countries through the coming world-
wide revolution, which was confidently predicted by many at that
time:

> Migrating
> To what kind of New York?
> With universal enmity
> Loaded on our backs,
> What bears we are!
> What Tatars we are!
> Devoured by lice,
> We bring conflagrations.
> . . . . . .
> In the name of the Lord!
> In the name of reason!
> What a fester we are,

What a leprosy we are!
With a wolfish sparkle
Through the snowstorms' fur,
The Star of Russia
Against the world!

[Whither,] parricides,
Into what absurdity?
Careful you're not mistaken,
You scourge of the universe!

In his sensitive appreciation of *Craft* in the essay 'The Path to Russia,' Efim Etkind has postulated an inner layer in this collection. 'The reader moves from poems which are understandable and quite transparent toward enigmatic and obscure ones,' Etkind wrote. 'And the further he moves, the more obscure they become, until he runs into an impasse with the poem "Sidestreets," which is altogether impossible to understand. [. . .] The reader travels from light to the ever-gathering darkness which at the end becomes impenetrable indeed. And this journey turns out to be a metaphor for Russian life.' Etkind's observations suggest a possible reason why 'Sidestreets' was included at the very end of *Craft*. The poet Georgy Ivanov wrote of Sergei Esenin that he was representative of millions of other men and women who hailed the October Revolution and were soon victimized by it. 'They were caught in its whirlwind and blinded by it,' Ivanov wrote. 'Thinking that they were flying to the stars, they landed face down in the mud.' This is precisely the situation of the male protagonist in 'Sidestreets,' who sees rubies and rainbows and thinks he is flying into the azure while a sorceress is changing him into an aurochs. Promised liberation, he finds himself in brutal captivity – Tsvetaeva's final image of the October Revolution before she left for the West.

Many fine twentieth-century poets, after finding their own individual voices, chose to stay with the same style for decades. Such was the case with Gippius, Akhmatova and Khodasevich. Others underwent a gradual stylistic evolution. Mikhail Kuzmin and Osip Mandelstam moved from simplicity to ever greater complexity, while the development of Boris Pasternak was in the opposite direction. Marina Tsvetaeva, alone, could manage within the same year and the same book of verse, such as *Craft*, a whole gamut of diverse voices, dictions and styles, while remaining her own self throughout. She described this aspect of her talent in a letter to Ivask better than any critic could: 'When you speak of [my] loudness, you must also mention my quiet aspects. I have poems which are *quieter* than anyone's. I can be grasped *only* in terms of contrasts, i.e., of the simultaneous presence of *everything*. [...] I am *many* poets; as to how I've managed to harmonize all of them, that is my secret.'

The real glory of *Craft* lies in its varied and pulsating rhythms, which Andrei Bely qualified as Tsvetaeva's 'invincible rhythms.' Ariadna Efron has likened Tsvetaeva's early poetry and her romantic verse plays to Chopin. *Craft* is comparable to *The Rite of Spring*. Like that epochal work, *Craft* contains slow and reflective passages. But the more striking poems pound and throb in a way found in no other poet, not even in Mayakovsky or Pasternak, who were both masters of percussive verse. The most extreme example in *Craft* is 'The Leader's Return' ('Vozvrashchenie vozhdia'), written entirely in spondees, i.e., lines consisting of two stressed monosyllabic words. More effective are the numerous poems in this collection where the unexpectedly placed stresses lend the verse lines a distinctive rhythm: a march, a dance, a dirge and, quite often, something resembling jungle tom-toms. Nothing like it has been heard in Russian poetry before or, for that matter, since. With this collection of profound and explosive poetry, Marina Tsvetaeva became the equal of any poet, Russian or foreign, who was writing at that time. It took most of her compatriots half a century to realize this. Another paradox about *Craft* is that with this book, the poet who was a romantic conservative in her politics, became a full-fledged radical innovator in her art.

There was no way, during the years of War Communism, for Marina Tsvetaeva to publish any of the vast output of poetry, prose and drama she was producing. Apart from a few poems in transient, obscure periodicals, her work did not appear in print from 1917 to 1921. Occasional public readings brought a pittance: for reading her play *Fortuna* in 1919, she was paid sixty rubles, which at that time was the price of three pounds of potatoes or six boxes of matches. She returned the fee, she wrote in 'My Jobs,' to the Bolshevik organizers of the reading as a protest against the regime that assigned so little value to her labor.

With the authorization of private commerce under the New

Economic Policy, there arose the possibility of literary earnings. In 1921 in Moscow, the so-called Writers' Store opened, where unpublished authors would leave their handwritten books on consignment, to be sold for money or bartered for food or tobacco. This method was called 'Dispensing with Gutenberg.' Tsvetaeva prepared several copies of her books for this store, but they found no buyers. Today, these copies are considered bibliographical treasures. Far more important were the private publishing houses that sprang up both in the Soviet Union and in foreign countries. The latter were organized by Russians who had fled from the revolution. (Between one and two million persons emigrated from Russia between 1918 and 1922, including, in addition to refugees, those who left with the Soviet Government's permission like Tsvetaeva, those who were urged to depart like Maxim Gorky and those who were forcibly expelled like the group of two hundred educators and writers already mentioned.)

Another encouraging development was the appearance in Western Europe of several Russian literary journals of high quality. In 1921–2, writers who lived in the Soviet Union could still sell their work to such publications with impunity. The most respected and durable of these journals, *The Contemporary Annals* (*Sovremennye zapiski*), was started in Paris in 1920 by a group of Socialist Revolutionary politicians. It carried in its very first issue a group of poems by Tsvetaeva. One year later, in 1921, it published another, much larger selection of her poems, accompanied by a brief article by Balmont which claimed for her a place among the most significant contemporary poets.

Finally, the State Publishing House (Gosizdat), which the Soviet Government inaugurated in 1919 for the purpose of inundating the country with huge printings of Marx, Engels and Plekhanov, complete collected works of Lenin and the propagandistic doggerel of the Bolshevik bard Demian Bedny, decided to branch out into *belles lettres* in 1921. Nikolai Meshcheriakov, a long-time Communist revolutionary and member of the editorial boards of both *Pravda* and Gosizdat, disregarded Briusov's injunctions against Tsvetaeva and accepted for publication early in 1922 not only her 'Tsar-Maiden' (understandable in view of its revolutionary finale), but *Mileposts I* as well. A private publishing firm in Moscow, Kostry, had brought out *Mileposts II* in 1921. It thus came about that at the very time when Marina Tsvetaeva was preparing to leave her country, her mature work began to be revealed to Russian readers, both inside and outside the Soviet Union, for the first time and in substantial quantities.

Early in May 1922, after many months of waiting and uncertainty, Tsvetaeva was granted an exit visa by the Soviet authorities. Within a few days, she and her daughter Ariadna left for Berlin. When mentioning the fact of her emigration, Tsvetaeva's sister and daughter in their respective memoirs and the authors of introductory essays to Soviet editions of her writings invariably describe it as the greatest misfortune and the worst mistake of her life. This is, of course, compulsory Soviet cant. Efim Etkind showed a more secure grasp of the situation when he wrote: 'But all things considered, how fortunate that she left! Can anyone doubt that what awaited her was the GULag or simply a bullet in the head?' And indeed, a brief glance at the historical background confirms that Tsvetaeva escaped in the nick of time.

When the Bolshevik Party assumed total control over the political and economic spheres at the time of the October Revolution, it did not occur to its leaders at first that they could also abolish the freedoms of speech, press and expression that had been gained during the pre-revolutionary decade and codified after the February Revolution. In the period of War Communism, a great deal could be said and published that would result in arrests or reprisals by the late 1920s. In 1920, independent poets such as Khodasevich and the soon-to-be-shot Gumiliov, could teach Proletcult courses for Red Army soldiers and factory workers. Idealist philosophers, such as Lev Karsavin, lectured at universities. The anti-Soviet writer Boris Zaitsev headed the Writers' Association. With the introduction of the NEP, publishers in the Soviet Union brought out texts on Freudian theory; Kuzmin and Kliuev could still be explicit about their homosexuality in their published poetry; and the People's Commissar Alexandra Kollontai, after silencing the leaders of the Russian feminist movement and banning their publications as bourgeois, appropriated their goals and rhetoric for a few years, until Lenin and his wife Krupskaya made her drop them. All this was gradually discontinued after 1922.

On June 2, 1922, less than a month after Tsvetaeva's departure, an editorial in *Pravda* bearing the melodramatic title 'Dictatorship, Where Is Thy Whip?' demanded to know why writers were still being published who were not demonstrably loyal to the Soviet

system. Early in 1923, Nadezhda Krupskaya, with the encouragement of her husband Lenin, sent a circular to all public libraries in
the country, directing them to remove from their shelves a number
of 'obsolete, anti-artistic and counter-revolutionary authors,'
among whom were the names of Plato, Kant, Nietzsche, Leo
Tolstoy and Vladimir Soloviov. From that point on, the noose
around free literary expression began tightening. For another
decade or so, enough leeway remained for the innovative Soviet
prose writers of the 1920s and for the Formalist school of criticism to
make their mark. Still, already by about 1925, such poets as
Kuzmin, Akhmatova and Mandelstam had a hard time publishing
anything and if they were mentioned in Soviet criticism, it was in
terms of censure.

Yet, none of them was guilty of what Tsvetaeva had done. None
of them had written anything as counter-revolutionary as *The
Demesne of the Swans* or *Craft*. Nor were Kuzmin or Akhmatova or
Mandelstam as intransigent or as outspoken as Tsvetaeva. In
February 1921, in what amounted to a political denunciation of
Tsvetaeva, Vsevolod Meyerhold, in a letter to the editor of a
theatrical journal, qualified her as a poet 'hostile to everything that
is sanctified by the idea of the Great October [Revolution].' This
was the first of many similar attacks on Tsvetaeva that were to
appear in the Soviet press in the 1920s. She could ignore them only
because by then she was abroad. If her sister Anastasia, a docile and
dutiful Soviet citizen, was sentenced to years of hard labor in 1937,
isn't it obvious that a similar fate would have overtaken Marina
much earlier? A possible model of what could have befallen her
had she stayed is provided by the life of Anna Barkova (1900–76), a
poet of working-class background whose first book, published in
1922, was reviewed with enthusiasm by Briusov and Lunacharsky.
Arrested in 1934, 1947 and 1957, always for writing the kind of
poetry of which the prosecutors didn't approve, Barkova spent a
total of twenty-six years in hard-labor camps until she was par-
doned in 1965 and allowed to return to Moscow. Her once-admired
writings have disappeared from Soviet literary history for good.

Marina Tsvetaeva stepped off the Riga–Berlin train at the Berlin-
Charlottenburg station on May 15, 1922. She went there, rather
than to Prague where her husband lived, because she had more
books to publish and Berlin was at that time the publishing capital

for Russian literature. This strange situation has been thoroughly described in two detailed studies, *Culture in Exile. Russian Émigrés in Germany, 1881–1941* by Robert C. Williams and *Russian Berlin, 1921–1923*, edited by Lazar Fleishman, Robert P. Hughes and Olga Raevsky Hughes. According to the first of these studies, the population of Russians in Berlin in 1922 numbered 100,000. The inflation of the German mark in the early days of the Weimar Republic made life there affordable for foreigners with meager resources. But many of the refugees from the Soviet Union, especially the ones who happened to be abroad during the October Revolution, possessed considerable funds. There had been a hiatus in publishing during the years of War Communism. Now, with the civil war finished, there was a great hunger for new Russian books and periodicals. A large number of publishing houses arose in Berlin in response to this demand. Much of what they printed could still be sent to the Soviet Union and reviewed, at times favourably, in the Soviet press.

With all these publishing opportunities, Berlin became a magnet for temporary visits by writers who lived in the Soviet Union and did not intend to emigrate (tourist visas were then issued with greater liberality than they would be a few years later). Russian émigré literature as a phenomenon distinct from Soviet literature had not yet come into existence. The offices of Berlin publishers and the literary cafés frequented by Russians provided a meeting ground for writers who had aligned themselves with the Soviet regime, those who were opposed to it, and a very large group of those who were still undecided. *The New Russian Book*, the most respected of Russian literary journals in Berlin, made a point of publishing and reviewing the work of all writers of note, regardless of their political affiliation or place of residence. The chapter 'Tobias and the Angel' in Nina Berberova's autobiography *The Italics Are Mine* is one of many vivid reflections in memoir literature of that unique moment just before Russian literature of the twentieth century divided into its two branches.

The atmosphere Tsvetaeva found in Berlin was congenial. Her closest associates were at first Ilya Ehrenburg and his wife, the artist Liubov Kozintseva. Prior to Tsvetaeva's departure from Moscow, Ehrenburg had seen to the publication in Berlin of two slim volumes of her poetry; *Separation*, which consisted of the cycle of that name from *Craft* and the long poem 'On a Red Steed'; and *Verses to Blok*, her poems addressed to this poet, including a few previously unpublished ones. During her stay in Berlin, she arranged for the publication of *Craft* and a second edition of 'The Tsar-Maiden,' and also compiled the volume called *Psyche*, subtitled 'Romanticism' and composed of fifty-two poems on "romantic" subjects culled from her other collections, plus twenty-four hitherto unpublished poems. She had hoped to recast her Moscow diaries and meditations as a book of prose, *Omens of the Earth*, but this book found no publisher. Also in 1922, there appeared two popular anthologies of new Russian poetry, *The Poetry of Revolutionary Moscow* and *Portraits of Russian Poets*, both of them edited by Ehrenburg, which included her work; the second of these anthologies contained the editor's enthusiastic essay on Tsvetaeva.

From the moment she arrived in Berlin, Tsvetaeva emerged as a major literary celebrity. Editors of journals sought her contributions. She was lionized by publishers and fellow writers. At Ehrenburg's table at the café Pragerdiele, she observed and participated in what she later called 'a general exchange of fees and manuscripts.' With her literary earnings, she could afford to stay at a decent hotel and to buy, for the first time in years, some good new clothes for herself and her daughter. The time in Berlin was also a time of intense contact with two great writers: with Andrei Bely in person and with Boris Pasternak through the discovery of his poetry.

Tsvetaeva and Bely had only casual encounters in Moscow between 1910 and the time of her emigration. When he unexpectedly ran into her in a Berlin café, Bely was at a particularly desperate juncture in his life. Abandoned by Asya Turgeneva, disillusioned with the teachings of anthroposophy, to which he had devoted many years of his life and much of his creative energy, and torn by doubt about whether or not to return to the Soviet Union, he rather unexpectedly turned to Tsvetaeva for solace and understanding: 'You are the daughter of Professor Tsvetaev. And I am the son of Professor Bugaev. You're a daughter, I'm a son.' 'Overwhelmed by the irrefutability of this,' Tsvetaeva added, 'I remained silent.'

Apart from the academic standing of their respective fathers, Bely was enormously impressed with Tsvetaeva's new and mature poetic manner. After reading her *Separation*, he published a scholarly essay on its versification and, in subtle homage to Tsvetaeva,

called his own next volume of verse *After the Separation*. The title
was meant to acknowledge that the much older, established poet
Bely was changing the style of his own poetry under the influence of
Tsvetaeva's. It was Bely who helped her arrange the Berlin edition
of 'The Tsar-Maiden.' Their Berlin encounters were later lovingly
described by Tsvetaeva in her memoir of Bely, 'A Captive Spirit,'
written after she learned of his death in 1934.

Tsvetaeva had also met Boris Pasternak on a few occasions prior
to her departure from Moscow. In her letter to him of June 29, 1922,
she recalled some of them: the gathering at the Tsetlins' when
Mayakovsky read his 'Man'; Tsvetaeva's reading of 'The Tsar-
Maiden' at which Pasternak was present; a letter from Ehrenburg
which Pasternak delivered to her apartment in the fall of 1921; and
the funeral of Tatiana Scriabina, the widow of the composer and a
friend of both poets. During those encounters, neither poet realized
the importance of the other's work. Shortly after she came to
Berlin, Ehrenburg gave her a copy of Pasternak's volume *My Sister,
Life*. Reading it came as an unforgettable experience. At the same
time, Pasternak in Moscow was reading *Mileposts II* and for his
part discovering Tsvetaeva. Their correspondence, which Pasternak initiated while she was still in Berlin, was to be her joy and
consolation in the years to come. Tsvetaeva's enthusiasm for *My
Sister, Life* found its expression in her first published critical essay,
'A Cloudburst of Light' ('Svetovoi liven''), which appeared in
Bely's journal *Epopeia* in 1922. Her avowed intention in writing the
essay was to vouch for Pasternak's quality before the Western
world: 'And not because you need it. This is pure selfishness: it is a
precious thing to participate in such a destiny.'

The initial impression that Russian Berlin made on Tsvetaeva
was so pleasant that she briefly considered making this city her
permanent home. But a painful emotional entanglement was to
spoil this impression. Within days after her arrival she met Abram
Vishniak, the proprietor of the small publishing house called
Helicon, which was also the name by which Vishniak himself was
usually known. He was twenty-seven years old and happily married
to a lovely young woman with whom he had a four-year-old son. He
had published Tsvetaeva's *Separation* and was planning to publish
Craft. Tsvetaeva impressed Vishniak both as a poet and as a
woman. Her precocious, not-quite ten-year-old daughter noted in
her diary: 'Marina talks to Helicon like a Titan, and she is as

incomprehensible to him as the North Pole is to an inhabitant of the Near East and just as enticing. [...] I saw that he turns toward her like a plant to the sun, with the whole of his rumpled stem. But the sun is distant because Marina's essence is reticence and clenched teeth, while he is pliant and soft like a pea sprout.'

It is hard to tell how much of this imagery came from the little girl's conversation with her mother, but we do know that Tsvetaeva was amazingly frank with the child about her romantic involvements. There were two types of men that Tsvetaeva found irresistible: athletic, blond Russians (Nilender, Vladimir Alexeiev, the Bolshevik soldier in 'Free Passage,' Boris Bessarabov) and frail, vulnerable Jews. Abram Vishniak epitomized this second type. Tsvetaeva mistook his admiration and his professional interest in her work for something far more personal and intimate. She wrote him a series of love letters, which are a curious mix of passion, condescension and maternal concern. She later reworked them into a prose text, 'Florentine Nights' (1933), an epistolary meditation on the love of a strong woman for a weak man, written in French. The same sentiments were also reflected in a group of poems dated June and July 1922, in which Tsvetaeva's verbal and expressive virtuosity reached astounding heights. Here are three stanzas from one of these missives to Vishniak, cited in Russian to show the coruscating internal rhymes, the stumbling logaoedic meter and the crackling and buzzing sound patterns of the *k*s and *r*s on the one hand and the *zh*s and *shch*s on the other:

> Moi nezhenka! Sedinoi ottsov:
> Sei bezhenki ne beri pod krov.
> Da zdravstvuet levogrudyi kov
> Nemudrstvuiushchikh kontsov!
>
> No mozhet, v shchebetakh i v shchetakh
> Ot vechnykh zhenstvennostei ustav –
> I vspomnish ruku moiu bez prav
> I muzhestvennyi rukav.
>
> Usta, ne trebuiushchie smet,
> Prava, ne sleduiushchie vsled,
> Glaza, ne vedaiushchie vek,
> Issleduiushchie: svet.
>
> My delicate boy! By the grey hair of your ancestors:
> Don't take this refugee girl [that I am] under your roof.

Long live the Amazonian conspiracy
Of uncomplicated goals!

But perhaps, amidst twitterings and [household] bills,
Tired of eternal femininities,
You will still recall my hand, with its lack of rights,
And the masculine [cut of my] sleeve.

Lips that do not demand estimates,
Rights that do not follow you,
Eyes that know no lids
[And which] investigate: light.

Tsvetaeva's one-sided infatuation with Abram Vishniak lasted only
a few weeks. When it was over, she thought of him with revulsion.
In a comical passage at the end of 'Florentine Nights' she tells of
how she met him a few years later and failed to recognize him: she
remembered Vishniak with a moustache and glasses, neither of
which, everyone assured her, he ever wore. Memoirs of her friends
and essays by Tsvetaeva scholars have often mentioned those
misguided infatuations of hers, sources of misery for the woman and
of blazing inspiration for the poet. The most vivid description of this
entire phenomenon was written by a person who, as we can now
learn, was affected by it as painfully as Tsvetaeva herself: her
husband.

In an unpublished letter to Maximilian Voloshin, dating from the
fall of 1923, Sergei Efron wrote: 'Marina is a creature of passions.
To a much greater degree than previously – prior to my departure.
To plunge headlong into a self-created hurricane has become a
necessity for her, the air of her life. Who the instigator of this
hurricane is today doesn't matter. Almost always [. . .] everything is
built on self-deception. A person is invented and the hurricane is
on. If the insignificance and the limitations of the instigator are soon
revealed, Marina is plunged into an equally hurricane-like despair.
This is a condition under which the appearance of a new instigator is
facilitated. It doesn't matter *what*, what matters is *how*. Not the
essence, not the source, but the rhythm, the frenzied rhythm.
Today it's despair, tomorrow it's ecstasy, love, total surrender of
self and tomorrow it's despair again.

'And all this despite her sharp-eyed, cold (possibly even Voltairean-cynical) intelligence. Yesterday's instigator will today be wittily and maliciously (almost always justly) ridiculed. It will all end up in her book. It will all be calmly, mathematically cast into a formula. A huge furnace, to stoke which there's need for wood, wood and more wood. Useless ashes are discarded and the quality of the firewood is not so important. So long as the draught is good, it will all be turned into flames. Poor firewood burns faster, the good – longer. Needless to say, I have long been useless for stoking the furnace. When I went to Berlin to meet M. I sensed at once that there was nothing I could give her. A few days before my arrival, the furnace had been kindled – not by me.' This letter makes a shambles out of Ariadna Efron's portrayal in her memoirs of her parents' joyous reunion in Berlin, but it does help us make sense out of the passage she cites from Sergei's first letter from Prague to Moscow, which Tsvetaeva received on July 1, 1922. The passage reads: 'Without you, there's no life for me. Just go on living! I will make no demands on you, I need nothing from you except that you stay alive.'

In her periodic obsessive involvements with unsuitable or unwilling love-objects, Tsvetaeva's goal was not the person but the need to be in love. She formulated this need in a 1921 poem:

> Love! Love! Even in my death throes, in my coffin
> I'll harken, I'll be tempted, I'll be perturbed, I'll respond.

As Serena Vitale has commented, Tsvetaeva transgressed not against the commandment 'Thou shalt not commit adultery,' but against the one that prohibited the making of graven images. Her intense hero-worship in the cultural and artistic spheres had its counterpart in idolatry of poets and lovers in the personal realm. Non-existent qualities were ascribed to a person of her choice, the person was saddled with desires or expectations he or she never had, hopes were vested in the incipient relationship that could not possibly come true. Tsvetaeva knew what was involved, but she could not stop because these emotional defeats were the raw material of her poetry. After the breakup of one friendship in 1920, she wrote:

> I will not promote you to villain,
> It's not your fault, it's my sin:
> I force feed my insatiability
> To everyone.

But she could be merciless to the discarded objects of her infatuation:

> The birdie still strains for the grove
> No matter what grain it is offered.
> I took you out of the slime.
> To your native slime I now return you.

The impossible demands she made on the unwilling and unresponsive Yury Zavadsky and Abram Vishniak placed these men in untenable situations. But the result was splendid poetry. These relationships set a pattern which was to be repeated again and again in the future.

6

In Czechoslovakia

The young Dmitry Shakhovskoy, soon to be Marina Tsvetaeva's editor and correspondent, had had his first taste of the intellectual climate of Western Europe when he emigrated from the Soviet Union. In 1924, he made a penetrating entry in his journal. 'Other nations,' he wrote, 'perceive Russia the way they perceive [Albert] Einstein's theory [of relativity] – only in versions simplified for the general reader.' And indeed, the complex reality of pre-revolutionary Russia is all too often reduced in the Western imagination to a fairy-tale feudal realm, ruled by implacable tsars and sadistic nobles, surrounded by hordes of destitute slaves. Edmund Wilson, the foremost American literary critic of the first half of the twentieth century, who spent decades studying Russian history and culture, was quite sure during his visit to Leningrad in 1935 that people there looked shabby and glum because they still remembered their lives as serfs in pre-revolutionary days.

Not only are Lenin and the Bolsheviks routinely credited in the West with liberating the Russian serfs (serfdom was abolished by Tsar Alexander II a decade before Lenin was born). They are also said to have dethroned Nicholas II, even though Lenin was in Switzerland at the time of the February Revolution and neither he nor any of his followers had much to do with the events that overthrew the monarchy. The combined effect of the three Russian revolutions of the twentieth century, so vastly different from one another in impulse and results, is invariably attributed to the Bolshevik one alone, the only one most people in the West are likely to have heard about.

Nor were such perceptions altered by the presence of many thousands of refugees from the Bolshevik revolution, who by the early 1920s were making their home in every major city in Europe. Soon enough, a stereotype of a White Russian refugee was created in the West: a former aristocrat who had lost vast property holdings and whose opposition to the Soviet system was easily explicable by

reactionary politics and monarchist sympathies. Thus Sergei Diaghilev, who had actually hailed the 1905 revolution and was over-
joyed when the February Revolution occurred, was portrayed in
the American musical of the 1930s, *On Your Toes*, revived in the
1980s, as an ultra-conservative snob who could be won over by a
display of the tsar's portrait. This was the same Diaghilev who
commissioned Stravinsky to compose a new national anthem based
on the 'Song of the Volga Boatmen,' and had Prince Ivan carry a red
flag in *The Firebird* when the tsar was deposed.

The actual spectrum of political orientations among the Russian
émigrés in the 1920s and '30s, i.e., during Marina Tsvetaeva's stay
in Western Europe, can be established by taking a look at their
periodical press. In the most populous centers of the Russian
diaspora – Berlin during the 1920s and Paris in the 1930s – the
émigré newspapers with the largest circulation were published by
either the Constitutional Democrats or the Socialist Revolutionaries. The SRs were also responsible for the best and the most
durable literary journals of the emigration, the Paris *Contemporary
Annals* and the Prague *Freedom of Russia*. There did exist monarchist, pro-Soviet and, in the 1930s, Fascist émigré periodicals, but
they trailed behind the democratic and socialist ones in both their
quality and circulation. Contrary to the popular stereotype, monarchists who longed to restore the tsar were in the minority among the
refugee Russians. The majority were people who fled partly to
escape economic misery, but most of all to avoid punishment for
failure to convert to a fundamentalist religion – Marxism-Leninism
– in which they could not honestly believe.

When Marina Tsvetaeva left the Soviet Union for the West she
apparently thought that she was going as a kind of ambassador to
the Court of Western Conscience, or at least as a witness capable of
testifying to the world about the nature of Russian post-
revolutionary experience. This can be seen in her remark to Vladimir Mayakovsky, whom she met by chance on the eve of her
departure from Russia: 'Well, Mayakovsky, what message do you
have for Europe?' (His message was: 'That truth is over here.') As
mentioned in Chapter 5, Tsvetaeva's avowed reason for writing the
essay 'A Cloudburst of Light' was her desire to vouch for the quality
of Pasternak's poetry before the West.

A similar attitude underlies another Tsvetaeva statement dating
from the first months of her emigration. This was her open letter

which appeared on June 7, 1922 in the Berlin newspaper *The Voice of Russia (Golos Rossii)* and was addressed to the novelist and playwright A. N. Tolstoy (1882–1945), whom Tsvetaeva had met earlier in Koktebel and at whose Moscow home she had been a guest. Tolstoy had been a vocally anti-Soviet émigré since 1918, but in the spring of 1922 he stunned the émigré community by announcing his support of the Bolshevik government and assuming the editorship of a pro-Soviet newspaper that was subsidized by the Soviet embassy in Berlin. In his editorial capacity, Tolstoy had published a private letter, written to him by the critic and children's poet Kornei Chukovsky, where the latter listed an array of literary figures who lived in Petrograd and were, in his opinion, hostile to the Soviet system. Chukovsky had never intended this letter for publication and was horrified to see it in print.

Tsvetaeva was outraged not by the change in Tolstoy's political outlook, but by his betrayal of his fellow writers through his publication of Chukovsky's letter, which exposed them to reprisals by Soviet authorities, such as refusal of permission to emigrate. The concluding portion of her letter reads: 'The New Economic Policy, which you seem to regard as the Promised Land, is least of all concerned with questions of ethics: fairness to the enemy, mercy for the enemy, nobility toward the enemy. Alexei Nikolaevich, beyond personal friendships, private letters and literary vanity there exists the mutual guarantee of [our] craft, the mutual guarantee of being humane. Five minutes before my departure from Russia (on May 11 of this year), I was approached by a man, a Communist whom I had once briefly met and who knew me only through my verse: "There is someone from the Cheka traveling in the same car. Don't say anything you oughtn't." I shake his hand and refuse to shake yours. Marina Tsvetaeva.'

Within a few months, however, Tsvetaeva had to realize that there was no mutual guarantee between Russian writers who supported the Soviet system and those who were opposed to it and that the Western world in which she now lived had little interest in what she had to tell it about Mayakovsky or Pasternak or, for that matter, about her own experiences. The governments and the people of Western countries may have been initially shocked by the senseless assassination of Nicholas and Alexandra, their children and their servants and entourage. As a result, there was considerable sympathy abroad for the dispossessed Russian royalty and aristocracy.

The exiled musicians, dancers and people in the visual arts were also welcomed. But literary figures, with the exception of those few who had acquired big reputations abroad before 1917, such as Merezhkovsky or Gorky, could not count on any interest abroad once they chose emigration. Neither could the thousands of democratic and socialist political figures, who were ignored because the West could not fit them into its image of pre-revolutionary Russia.

There was only one head of state in the whole of the Western world, it seems, who realized just what had happened in Russia, what was involved and what it meant for the rest of the world. That was Tomáš Garrigue Masaryk, the first president of Czechoslovakia, which had regained its independence in the aftermath of World War I. He had frequently visited Russia and happened to be there during both the February regime and the October Revolution. Through his knowledge of Russian language and culture, Masaryk had acquired a clearer picture of Russian social and political realities than most foreigners. He understood that the triumph of Bolshevism did not spell a victory for democracy and that the people fleeing from Russia were, for the most part, not tsarist reactionaries. His partly American background (his wife was an American and he had lived in America and taught at American universities) had instilled in Masaryk a healthily pluralist outlook. While Masaryk's personal sympathies were undoubtedly with the more democratic Russian circles, his government welcomed refugees of every ilk. At the university which the Czech government had organized in Prague for exiled Russians, former officers of the monarchist White armies, such as Sergei Efron, found themselves in the same classes with those who had served in anarchist or SR counter-revolutionary units and who during the civil war had disliked the Whites almost as much as they hated the Bolsheviks.

Masaryk's government was also the only one in the outside world to perceive that Soviet Russia was forcing into exile some of its best minds and talent. Jobs, stipends and other forms of assistance were made available by the Czechs to Russian scholars, scientists and writers, again without regard to their political outlook. (The far more conservative government of Yugoslavia, then a monarchy ruled by King Alexander I, extended help primarily to Russian cultural figures who were certifiably loyal to the tsar.) Czech generosity paid off in such significant cultural phenomena as the linguistic Circle of Prague, which influenced the study of linguistics and semantics throughout the world; the Seminarium Kondakovia-num (named after the teacher of its founders, Professor Nikodim Kondakov, a one-time friend and correspondent of Chekhov), whose alumni became the leading experts on Byzantine studies in most Western countries; and the already mentioned international literary journal *Freedom of Russia*, published in Prague and later in Paris by the exiled SRs.

Marina Tsvetaeva followed her husband to Prague on August 1, 1922. She stayed in Czechoslovakia for the next three years. During that period, she resided in Prague only in the fall and winter of 1923–4. Before and after that time, she and her daughter shared a succession of rented huts in small villages outside Prague, while Sergei Efron commuted to them several times a week by suburban trains from his dormitory at the university in Prague. The villages had names that to a Russian ear had either a grotesque or depressing sound: Všenory ('All Burrows'), Horní Mokropsy ('Upper Wet Dogs') and Dolní Mokropsy ('Lower Wet Dogs'). Tsvetaeva described Horní Mokropsy in one of her letters to Bakhrakh: 'A tiny mountain village. We live on its very edge, in a simple peasant hut. The *dramatis personae* of our life: a church-shaped well to which I run to fetch water, mostly at night or early in the morning; a chained dog; a squeaky garden gate. Directly beyond us is a forest. To the right, a high rocky crest. There are brooks all over the village. Two grocery stores, like in our provinces. A Catholic church with a flowery churchyard. A school. Two restaurants. Music every Sunday. [...] And in every house one is sure to see a lighted window at night: a Russian [university] student!'

In addition to offering Efron a scholarship, the Czech authorities provided Tsvetaeva with a small stipend, which they went on paying her even after she had moved from Czechoslovakia to France. Living outside Prague cut Tsvetaeva off from some aspects of cultural life in the Czech capital, which had also become a major Russian cultural center precisely during those years. But the rustic surroundings and the constant contact with nature which they afforded her proved stimulating to her creative work. She went on writing and publishing with the same intensity that marked her last year in Moscow and her brief stay in Berlin. It was during her Czech years that her verse collections *Craft* and *Psyche* appeared. Four of the verse plays from her romantic cycle – *The Snowstorm,*

Fortuna, *An Adventure*, and *The Phoenix* – were published in émigré journals between 1922 and 1924.

In the first few years after her emigration, Tsvetaeva was regarded as a valued contributor by most émigré publications, from the most prominent, such as *Contemporary Annals* and *Freedom of Russia*, to some rather obscure ones published in the Baltic states and in the Far East. Mark Slonim, one of the founding editors of *Freedom of Russia*, who soon became Tsvetaeva's friend and champion, recalls in his memoir on Tsvetaeva how he told her that the editorial offices of his journal were located in the building where Mozart was reputed to have composed *Don Giovanni*. He also warned her, when inviting her to become a contributor, that *Freedom of Russia* was an organ of the Socialist Revolutionary Party. Tsvetaeva's reply to this was: 'I am not interested in politics, I do not understand it and, in any case, it is outweighed by Mozart.'

Yet, though Tsvetaeva's writings were in demand, not all of them could find a publisher. Her collection *The Demesne of the Swans* was fated to remain unpublished in her lifetime because the originality of its manner was far too advanced for the taste of the conservative émigré publishing houses, while its glorification of the White Army and its sympathy for Nicholas II were distasteful for the middle-of-the-road and left-leaning ones. A similar lot befell her book *Omens of the Earth*, a volume of memoirs and selections from her diaries dating from 1917–20, which recorded her impressions and experiences during the first four years of Soviet rule. Abram Vishniak read some of those diaries during his encounters with Tsvetaeva in Berlin and at first, he was most anxious to have his publishing firm, Helicon, bring out *Omens of the Earth*. But because Helicon exported books to the Soviet Union, Vishniak asked Tsvetaeva to delete all passages that could be interpreted as 'politics.' Outraged at this attempt at censorship, Tsvetaeva withdrew her manuscript.

Some time later, one of Tsvetaeva's Berlin correspondents, the novelist and biographer Roman Goul, tried offering the book to another publishing house. 'This is a book of living life and truth,' she wrote to Goul upon learning of his negotiations, 'which politically (i.e., from the angle of lies!) is a failure in advance. In it, there are charming Communists and irreproachable White Guards. The first will see only the latter, the latter – only the first.' To another Berlin correspondent, Bakhrakh, Tsvetaeva wrote:

'The danger shoals of this book are: counter-revolution, hatred of
the Jews, love of the Jews, glorification of the rich, vilification of the
rich; despite an undoubted White Guard attitude, certain irreproachable living Communists are given their full due of admiration.
Yes, and also a fierce love for Germany and ridicule of the bovine
patriotism of the Russians during the first year of the war.

'In a word, the publisher, like my own ribcage, should be able to
encompass EVERYTHING. Here, everyone is involved, everyone
stands accused, everyone is acquitted. This is a book of TRUTH.
There.

'Everyone will tear this book to pieces (with their teeth!), everyone ... except for a few genuine unprejudiced persons who know
that TRUTH IS A TURNCOAT.'

But no publisher with such a broad outlook could be found and
Tsvetaeva, realizing this, broke *Omens of the Earth* into separate
prose fragments and memoirs which she began publishing in émigré
periodicals from 1924 on.

Lev Mnukhin's bibliographical guide to publications about
Tsvetaeva's life and activities (it excludes publications of her own
writings) registers between one and twelve items per year during the
period 1910–21. For 1922, the figure jumps to forty-seven. For the
next five years there are between forty and sixty items per year
(reviews of Tsvetaeva's work, discussions of it or news items about
her) to be found in the Soviet and the Russian émigré press. Russian
publications abroad treated her for the most part as a famous and
admired poet, though we find some censorious items occasioned by
the unconventionality of her style. But in the Soviet Union, where
Tsvetaeva's work went on appearing in anthologies and literary
miscellanies and her books were on sale until about 1926, the more
prominent critical voices were invariably hostile. The hostility was
prompted less by the fact of Tsvetaeva's emigration (poets who
remained in Russia, such as Akhmatova, were often treated even
worse in the Soviet press) than by undisguised misogyny.

A few months before Tsvetaeva's departure from Moscow, Osip
Mandelstam published in a Moscow journal a survey of that city's
literary life. In it he wrote: 'The sorriest thing in Moscow is Marina
Tsvetaeva's amateurish embroidery in praise of the Mother of God
[*bogorodichnoe rukodelie*] [...]. The worst thing in the literary life
of Moscow is poetry written by women,' One paragraph later, we

read: 'Adalis and Marina Tsvetaeva are prophetesses and Sophia Parnok is headed the same way. Their prophecy is a cottage industry. At the same time when the elated tone and the raucous rhetoric of male poetry have given way to a more normal utilization of vocal means, women's poetry continues to vibrate on the highest notes, offending both the ear and the historical and poetic sense. The tastelessness and the historical falseness of Marina Tsvetaeva's poems about Russia – pseudo-popular and pseudo-Muscovite – is immeasurably below the poems of Adalis, whose voice at times attains masculine power and truth.' Mandelstam's misogyny reached its peak later on in the same essay when he warned Mayakovsky against trying to simplify his style in order to make it more generally accessible: 'Mayakovsky is wrong to try to impoverish himself. He is in danger of becoming a poetess, which has already half-way happened.'

Mandelstam's ugly attack against Tsvetaeva, whom he had once admired as a poet and loved as a woman, may have been caused by her high-handed treatment of his young wife during the encounter Nadezhda Mandelstam described decades later in her memoirs. But the two spurious ideas about Tsvetaeva's poetry which his essay launched – its limited scope and its supposedly central preoccupation with religion – were taken up one year later by a man whose opinions carried a far greater resonance than Mandelstam's. Leon Trotsky's book *Literature and Revolution (Literatura i revoliutsiia)*, published in 1923, was translated into many languages and had a wide-ranging impact abroad. It is a book from which several generations of foreign intellectuals obtained their notions of such Russian literary figures as Vasily Rozanov, Zinaida Gippius, Andrei Bely, Nikolai Kliuev and Anna Akhmatova – all of them slandered and ridiculed by the author, who assured his readers that these were bourgeois writers, fated to be forgotten once socialism is achieved.

Trotsky's particular contempt was reserved for women who wrote poetry because, in his opinion, all they were capable of perceiving was a man they desired and God, who was for them a combination of errand boy and gynecologist. 'The lyrical purview of Akhmatova, Tsvetaeva, Radlova and other poetesses, real or presumed, is extremely narrow,' Trotsky wrote. 'It encompasses the poetess herself, a certain gentleman in a derby hat or military spurs, and, inevitably, God, shown rather indistinctly. He is a very conve-

nient, portable third person, housebroken, a friend of the family
who performs from time to time the duties of a doctor specializing in
female complaints. How this individual, no longer young and
burdened by the personal, often bothersome errands of Akhmatova, Tsvetaeva and others, manages in his spare time to direct the
destinies of the universe is simply incomprehensible.' Tsvetaeva's
name is invariably linked in Trotsky's book with that of Akhmatova
and occasionally also with the names of Anna Radlova and Maria
Shkapskaya. None of these four poets had as narrow a purview as
Trotsky claimed, nor were they especially preoccupied with God or
religion (in the sense that Zinaida Gippius, for example, was). But
they were not hailing the October Revolution in their poetry or
predicting the imminent advent of the socialist utopia like Demian
Bedny, the only poet to whom Trotsky gave his unreserved and
loving endorsement in *Literature and Revolution*. This was suffi-
cient reason for Trotsky to want to discredit these women poets and
he used their gender and its supposed propensity for religiosity to
achieve this.

Also in 1923, there appeared an attack on Tsvetaeva in *On Guard
(Na postu)*, a journal run by the Bolshevik literary vigilantes, which
made a speciality of reviling as counter-revolutionary and bourgeois
any writer who showed some independence in thought or style.
Although not an official organ of the Soviet government, *On Guard*
initiated and developed the method of literary criticism by vilification which became standard for the whole Soviet press during the
reign of Stalin. In an article that berated the State Publishing House
(Gosizdat) for 'printing and circulating works which are alien to our
ideals, construction and praxis,' Semion Rodov, one of the editors
and founders of *On Guard*, singled out Tsvetaeva's collection
Mileposts I as an example of the works he had in mind. Citing all the
references to churches and the Virgin Mary that he could find in
Tsvetaeva's poems about Moscow's history and traditions, Rodov
came to a conclusion similar to Trotsky's: 'The cult of the virgin and
of the church is central to M. Tsvetaeva's book.'

In 1926, Vladimir Mayakovsky joined the misogynous anti-
Tsvetaeva chorus in the USSR. In an article about the shortcomings
of the Soviet book distribution system, he drew a hypothetical scene
in which a young Communist Youth girl enters a book store
intending to buy a book by Tsvetaeva. Mayakovsky recommended
that the salesman address her as follows: 'Comrade, if you are

interested in Gypsy lyrics, I will venture to offer you [Ilya] Selvinsky. The same theme, but look what he's done with it! He's a
man, after all.' The salesman is then to urge the girl to buy neither
Tsvetaeva nor Selvinsky, but something more revolutionary, such
as a collection by [Mayakovsky's protégé] Nikolai Aseyev, 'all the
more so because the cover matches the color of your kerchief so
nicely.'

Tsvetaeva was deeply hurt by Mayakovsky's sally, since it came
from a poet she admired and with whom she had had cordial
personal encounters. She wrote to Boris Pasternak that it was
unworthy of Mayakovsky. It is indeed striking that in their desire to
discredit Tsvetaeva's poetry for personal (Mandelstam) or political
(Trotsky and Mayakovsky) reasons, these three famous men chose
to attack it not as poetry but as something written by a woman and
for that reason inferior. We can only speculate whether this
approach, unlikely in either pre-revolutionary or émigré criticism,
was connected in any way with the 1922–3 campaign in the Soviet
press to discredit feminist concerns as irrelevant to the new communist society. The campaign, aimed at the theories of Alexandra
Kollontai and Anna Akhmatova's poetry, was instigated by Lenin's
wife, Nadezhda Krupskaya, with her husband's full approval.

After Tsvetaeva's marriage was disrupted in the fall of 1914 by her
relationship with Sophia Parnok, she and Sergei Efron did not get to
live together for more than a few weeks at a time because of his
enlistment as a male nurse and his training at the military school
during World War I. The Russian Civil War separated them for five
years. It thus came that their conjugal life was resumed in Czechoslovakia after a break of almost eight years. As can be seen from her
daughter's memoirs and from her own correspondence, Tsvetaeva
assumed once more that attitude of maternal concern for Sergei
which had marked the earliest stage of their marriage. She worried
about the state of his health (both in Czechoslovakia and later in
France, Sergei had a series of brief relapses of his tubercular
process); provided him with special nourishing foods while she
herself and their daughter had to make do with more modest fare;
and prevented Sergei from helping her with any of the household
chores, such as stoking the stove with coal or taking out the garbage
(things that neither of them had ever had to do before the revolution). As Tsvetaeva wrote somewhat later to Rainer Maria Rilke:

'After all, a man cannot do woman's work, it looks ugly (to a woman, that is).'

In Prague, Sergei Efron studied Byzantine art with Nikodim Kondakov and other exiled Russian luminaries. But he never took his final examinations or obtained a degree. He tried to revive his literary career by publishing a few short stories and memoirs about the civil war in émigré journals. He dabbled in acting, appearing in a semi-amateur production of Ostrovsky's melodrama *The Thunderstorm* opposite Nina Kovalenskaya, a leading lady in several of Meyerhold's productions in pre-revolutionary times (and a resident of California at this writing). He also spent a great deal of time and energy editing the literary journal of the Russian students in Prague, *One's Own Way (Svoimi putiami)*. The one thing that apparently never occurred to him was to pursue any kind of occupation or project that would enable him to contribute significantly to the family budget.

Tsvetaeva loyally backed her husband's various undertakings. She took care of all of his material needs to facilitate his studies, praised him as a writer when she was interviewed by the press and lent the prestige of her name to *One's Own Way* by letting it publish her memoir on Konstantin Balmont and several of her important poems, including 'Eulogy of the Rich.' When this student journal was criticized by the monarchist Paris newspaper *Renascence (Vozrozhdenie)* for its alleged insufficiently anti-Bolshevik stance, Tsvetaeva wrote a spirited rebuttal, defending the right of the students to have their own views and outlook without being bullied by the larger émigré publications. In this brief essay, Tsvetaeva showed herself as intolerant of the political regimentation of literature that some émigré groups would occasionally attempt as she was of the Soviet variety of regimentation.

In September 1923, Tsvetaeva placed her daughter Ariadna in a boarding school for Russian children in a small town in Moravia, Moravská Třebová. The separation from Ariadna was not as painful as it would have been a few years earlier. The child, who had been a precocious intellectual and her mother's closest confidante, had suddenly become an ordinary little girl. 'Alya, who from the age of two to nine was my "echo in the mountains," now plays with dolls and treats me with profound indifference,' wrote Tsvetaeva to Bakhrakh. 'O, God must indeed want to make me a major poet, otherwise He would not thus deprive me of everything!' At about the same time, Sergei was advised by doctors to stay for a while in a tuberculosis sanatorium located not far from his daughter's school. Left on her own, Tsvetaeva rented a small apartment in the section of Prague called Smíchov ('Place of Laughter'). The apartment was on the top of a hill (immortalized later in her 'Poem of the Hill'), with a large window and a view of the city. It has become a place of pilgrimage for Tsvetaeva's admirers in recent years.

She made few Czech literary contacts during her stay in the capital, but she did make some highly interesting Russian ones. She got to be friendly with the innovative and influential prose stylist Alexei Remizov, whom she later called 'a living treasury of Russian soul and Russian speech.' In November 1923 she saw quite a lot of Vladislav Khodasevich and his then companion Nina Berberova. That spring, Vladimir Nabokov, who had not yet published his first novel, came to visit his mother in Prague. In the Russian version of his autobiography, he recalled accompanying Tsvetaeva on a 'strange lyrical hike,' 'in strong springtime wind, over some hills of Prague.' None of these contacts proved durable: Remizov and Tsvetaeva lost interest in each other in a few years; Khodasevich and she went through a period of mutual hostility before they came to appreciate each other as friends and poets in the 1930s; and Nabokov did not come to value Tsvetaeva's poetry until after her death.

Of greater significance in Tsvetaeva's life were the friendships she formed in Prague with several older women. Her neighbor in Smíchov was Olga Kolbasina, the wife of Victor Chernov, from whom she was by then separated. Chernov, whom the Soviet government could not forgive getting the majority of the votes in the Constituent Assembly, had managed to escape abroad, evading a massive, nation-wide manhunt. Kolbasina and her daughters survived their various incarcerations by the Cheka and were expelled from Russia when their ordeal, especially the imprisonment of teenaged daughters as hostages, got to be an international embarrassment. Tsvetaeva found Kolbasina, her daughters and their fate fascinating. Their friendship, which began when Tsvetaeva dropped by to borrow some cutlery, was described in Kolbasina's posthumously published memoir as an intellectual *roman*, i.e., romance or love affair. It continued for many years after everyone involved had moved to Paris.

Also living in Prague was the family of the old revolutionary

writer Yevgeny Chirikov (1864–1932). Repeatedly arrested and
sent to Siberia for anti-government activities in the 1880s and '90s,
Chirikov was a member of Maxim Gorky's neo-realist group Znanie
at the turn of the century. Like the majority of that radical literary
association, Chirikov emigrated after the October Revolution. In
Berlin, Tsvetaeva had met and started a correspondence with
Chirikov's daughter Liudmila, an artist who had designed the cover
for her poem, 'The Tsar-Maiden.' Tsvetaeva described her relationship with Liudmila Chirikova as 'a masculine friendship with a
woman – what could be better?' Now, in Prague she met Liudmila's
family. Possibly through them, she also met Anna Andreyeva, the
widow of the most famous of Znanie writers, Leonid Andreyev, and
her children. All these families – the Chernovs, the Chirikovs and
the Andreyevs – came from a background that was both more
radical and more democratic than Tsvetaeva's own. She was not
interested in the writings of Chirikov or Andreyev. But the people
themselves and especially the women of this group understood and
admired her poetry and she felt at home in their company. The same
can be said of the SR editors of *Freedom of Russia*, at whose offices
Tsvetaeva was always welcome both personally and as a contributor.

But all these new friendships did not satisfy Tsvetaeva
emotionally. Nor, apparently, did her epistolary friendship with
Boris Pasternak. Pasternak came to Berlin shortly after Tsvetaeva
had departed for Prague. She made plans to visit him in Berlin and
was disappointed when she learned that he had decided in March of
1923 to return to Moscow. Her disappointment was vented in a
passionately expressive cycle of ten poems 'Telegraphic Wires'
('Provoda') in which the poet lamented her separation from the
man she later called 'my brother in the fifth season, the sixth sense
and the fourth dimension.' The fires of her smouldering love for
Pasternak were banked for the time being, though many of her
poems from that period were unmistakably addressed to him.

In June 1923, Tsvetaeva wrote to the young critic and journalist
Alexander Bakhrakh (later known in France as Alexandre Bach-
erac), who resided in Berlin, to thank him for his review of her
books *Craft* and *Separation*. As a rule, she disliked critics. But in
this review she believed she sensed an affinity for the content of her
poetry such as she had never encountered. Her letters written to
Bakhrakh that summer soon reached a considerable emotional

intensity. Reading these letters, which Bakhrakh published in the journal *Bridges (Mosty)* in 1960–1, it is hard to keep in mind that she is writing to a man she had never met: 'I want from you a miracle. A miracle of trust, a miracle of understanding, a miracle of unselfishness. [. . .] I do not know who you are, I know nothing of your life, with you I am utterly free, I converse with a ghost.' We do not know to what extent Bakhrakh's letters responded to her need. But the depth of understanding she expected and demanded was certainly beyond what he or any other mortal man was able to give.

When Bakhrakh stopped replying to her letters in August 1923, Tsvetaeva was plunged into despair. 'The Bulletin of Illness' which she attached to one of her letters traces the suffering caused by her realization that Bakhrakh did not need her romantic friendship and was altogether not the man she took him to be: 'Pain has ceased being an event, it has become a state. I no longer believe you ever existed, you are my pain.' In a subsequent letter she described her emotional vulnerability: 'I am not made for [this] life. With me, everything is a conflagration. I can be engaged in ten relationships at a time (fine "relationships," these!), and assure each one from the deepest depth that he is the only one. But I cannot tolerate the slightest turning of the head away from me. I HURT, do you understand? I am a person skinned alive, while all the rest of you have armor. You all have art, social issues, friendships, diversions, families, duty, while I, in the depth, have NOTHING. It all falls off like the skin and under the skin there is living flesh or fire – I'm Psyche. I do not fit into any form, not even the simplest form of my poems.'

In Tsvetaeva's letters to Bakhrakh it is particularly clear that she was writing not to the real young man of that name, who actually lived in Berlin, but to her own poetic creation – an ideal dream correspondent who saw the world and responded to it in exactly the same way as she and was capable of communicating on her emotional and poetic level. These letters are not only a record of her self-delusion and her pain but works of literary art as well. In them she recorded for us her unique outlook, her poetic self, her literary projects and preferences and her relationships with Ehrenburg, Bely, Mandelstam and Pasternak. They are messages to posterity rather than to their putative addressee. A further result of the correspondence with Bakhrakh are the ten remarkable poems he inspired. They were written in July and August 1923 and included in the collection *After Russia*.

That fall, while still conducting her exchange of letters with
Bakhrakh, Tsvetaeva became involved with another man. This time
it was not an imaginary relationship, but a genuine love affair,
comparable in seriousness and intensity to the 1914–16 one with
Sophia Parnok. 'I am in love with another – there is no simpler,
cruder and more honest way of saying it,' she wrote to Bakhrakh on
September 20, 1923. 'How did it happen? O, my friend, how do
these things happen? I turned to someone, he responded, I heard
great words, the simplest in the world, which I have now heard for
perhaps the first time in my life.' The man who spoke those words
was Konstantin Boleslavovich Rodzevich. He was born in 1895 and,
as his patronymic and family name indicate, must have been of
Polish origin. He had served in the White forces during the civil war
together with Sergei Efron and together with him was evacuated to
Constantinople. When Tsvetaeva met him, he was her husband's
fellow student at the university.

Because Rodzevich is connected with the origin of her most
popular long poem, 'Poem of the End,' his identity has been
revealed in the more recent publications of writings by or about
Tsvetaeva. In the Soviet Union, Tsvetaeva's editor and annotator
Anna Saakiants as well as Ariadna Efron in her memoirs have
applied to Rodzevich such adjectives as 'knightly,' 'chivalrous' and
'gallant.' Tsvetaeva's daughter told her readers that the man her
mother fell in love with was a Communist and a hero of the Spanish
Civil War and the French Résistance during World War II. She was,
of course, referring to his situation and beliefs in the late 1930s,
many years after he and Tsvetaeva had parted ways. Rodzevich's
membership in the French Communist Party and activities in Spain
are brought up to create a heroic halo for him and to exculpate
Tsvetaeva retroactively of loving an exiled White officer back in
1923 and of having committed adultery, which is usually an unmen-
tionable subject in Soviet literary studies of admired writers.

The testimony of persons who knew Rodzevich at the time of his
relationship with Tsvetaeva is far less flattering. Sergei Efron, in a
letter to Max Voloshin, called Rodzevich 'a small-time Casanova.'
Nikolai Elenev, who knew Rodzevich well in Prague, described him
in his memoir on Tsvetaeva as 'sly and congenitally false.' And the
woman whom Rodzevich married some time after the end of his
relationship with Tsvetaeva told Véronique Lossky he was 'a total
nonentity' and 'a seductive swine' (she and Rodzevich were divor-

ced shortly after their marriage). Tsvetaeva, it would seem, also at first took a negative view of Konstantin Rodzevich, greeting him with mockery and finding that she had nothing in common with him. Then, after the departure of Sergei for the tuberculosis sanatorium, their affair began. Its doomed, hopeless quality is conveyed in the poem 'Nocturnal Places' ('Nochnye mesta'), dated October 4, 1923:

> The darkest of nocturnal places
> Is the bridge. Lips to lips.
> Well, why should we drag our cross
> To places of ill repute?
>
> There, to the laughing gas
> Of gaslight, of eyes? To a Sodom for rent?
> To a cot where all have slept,
> To a cot where no one's alone.
> . . . . . .
> If we could only arise
> In the ages of faith, holding hands!
> (The river feels light to the body
> And it's better to sleep than to live.)
>
> Love: chills to the bone.
> Love: burns to white heat.
> Water loves ends.
> River loves bodies.

Other extramarital relationships were conducted by Tsvetaeva without concealment. This one, to spare Sergei's feelings, was carried out clandestinely. Sergei was hurt to learn of the affair from mutual friends. He described the subsequent events to Voloshin: 'My decision was to part. I informed Marina. For two weeks she went out of her mind. She kept rushing from one to the other (during that time she had moved in with friends), couldn't sleep, lost weight. It was the first time I saw her in such despair. And finally, she declared that she couldn't leave me because the realization that I am somewhere out there all alone will not give her a moment's peace, let alone happiness. (I knew, alas, that this is how it would happen.) I could have been strong in this matter if I knew that Marina were going to a man in whom she could have confidence. But I knew that the other (a small-time Casanova) is sure to leave her in a week, which in Marina's state would mean death.'

As the rest of Sergei's letter shows, he would have welcomed the opportunity to terminate the marriage, except that he felt Marina could not survive without him. On January 26, 1925, Marina wrote to Olga Kolbasina that life with Sergei and the household chores it involved were destroying her soul. But she couldn't leave: 'After all, I came abroad to join Sergei. Without me he would perish – from the simple inability to manage his life.' Each one sought an honorable escape from the marriage that had become, in Sergei's words to Voloshin, an oppressive shared solitude (*tiagostnoe odinochestvo vdvoem*). They both sacrificed themselves for the sake of the other and their marriage was saved. It was further consolidated when Marina became pregnant early in 1924. In his letter to Voloshin, Sergei Efron described his function in Marina Tsvetaeva's life as a combination of lifebelt and millstone. During the next fifteen years, the millstone aspect came to predominate more and more.

Tsvetaeva's affair with Rodzevich lasted from September to December 1923. She devoted the month of January 1924 to writing 'Poem of the Hill,' the first of her two poetic epitaphs to that relationship. The second and much longer epitaph, 'Poem of the End,' took from February to June. As we by now know, emotional reverses invariably awoke Tsvetaeva's creative powers. But even without the added stimulation, the productivity of her Czech period is astounding. Early in 1923 she completed the long, folklore-based epic poem 'The Swain,' which was brought out as a separate book by a Prague publisher in 1924. *Ariadne*, the first play of her projected trilogy of verse tragedies derived from the myth of Theseus, was begun in October 1923. The writing of this tragedy was interrupted by work on the two long poems about Tsvetaeva's love for Rodzevich and then resumed in the summer of 1924. The tragedy was finished that fall and eventually published in 1927.

Also in 1924, for the one and only time in her life, Tsvetaeva made a stab at working as an editor. Together with Valentin Bulgakov (he was the last secretary of Leo Tolstoy, about whom he wrote important memoirs) and another co-editor, Tsvetaeva prepared and later published *The Ark* (*Kovcheg*), a not particularly interesting collection of émigré writing, in which the only noteworthy contribution was her own 'Poem of the End.' In 1925, she wrote the longest of her narrative poems, 'The Pied Piper' ('Krysolov'). Most of this poem was written in Czechoslovakia, but the last of its six cantos had to be finished after the poet's removal to Paris.

It appeared in serialized form, one chapter at a time, in *Freedom of Russia*. The plans made by Tsvetaeva's friends to publish 'The Pied Piper' as a separate book never materialized. The poem appeared in the Soviet Union in 1965 in a severely censored form (265 lines were deleted for political reasons). An annotated academic edition, prepared by Marie-Luise Bott, with the full Russian text and a translation into German printed *en face*, came out in Vienna in 1982. Also written during Tsvetaeva's Czech period was the first and longest of her prose portraits of other writers, 'A Hero of Labor,' and practically all the lyrics that made up her collection *After Russia*. The prose book *Omens of the Earth*, although written earlier in Russia, was prepared for publication in Czechoslovakia.

The winter of 1924–5 was spent by Tsvetaeva in near-seclusion in the village of Všenory. Her son was born there on February 1, 1925. As recalled in the memoirs of Ariadna Efron, Tsvetaeva was attended at the time of delivery by six loyal women friends, among them Anna Andreyeva, Maria ('Mouna') Bulgakova (the daughter of the noted theologian, she later married Konstantin Rodzevich) and Alexandra Turzhanskaya, the estranged wife of the well-known film director Victor Turzhansky. A few days later Tsvetaeva was visited by her Czech friend, Anna Tesková. 'Grey-haired, majestic, inwardly regal,' was how Tsvetaeva described Tesková after that visit. 'An aquiline nose, like a mountain crest between the sky-blue lakes of her genuinely calm eyes, her grey hair arranged in a crown. A high neck, a high bosom – everything about her is high.' Tesková was a journalist, a translator of Russian writers and the president of the cultural section of the Prague Czech–Russian Society, where she had occasionally invited Tsvetaeva to give readings of her poetry and prose. In later years she was to prove a loyal friend who unfailingly came to Tsvetaeva's help with prolonging the Czech stipend and in other financial and administrative matters. Tsvetaeva dedicated her verse cycle 'Trees' ('Derev'ia') to Anna Tesková; their correspondence, which continued until Tsvetaeva's return to the Soviet Union, is an important biographical and literary source.

Tsvetaeva had originally wished to name her son Boris, 'in honor of my favourite contemporary, Boris Pasternak.' But the name finally selected was, at Sergei Efron's insistence, Georgy – the title of Tsvetaeva's poetic cycle about St George which she addressed to her husband during the civil war. She later wrote to Rilke that her son was named in honor of the White Army. In daily usage,

however, the boy was known to his family and friends as Mur, after
the wise tomcat in E. T. A. Hoffmann's fantastic novel *Lebensan-
sichten des Katers Murr*. The birth of the son coincided with the
worsening of the family's financial situation, a worsening occasioned by the running out of Sergei's university scholarship.
Tsvetaeva was tired of living in small villages and she hated the idea
of raising her new baby in such primitive surroundings. An invitation from Olga Kolbasina and her daughters to visit them in Paris,
accompanied by an offer to arrange a poetry reading there, was
accepted with gratitude. At first there was only talk of a brief stay.
By the time the final plans were formulated in October 1925, the
move was seen as permanent.

In 'Poem of the Hill' ('Poèma gory') and 'Poem of the End' ('Poèma
kontsa'), Tsvetaeva takes up the confessional, autobiographical
mode she had initiated with 'The Enchanter' in 1914. But to
compare this earlier poem to them is to realize what a wide-ranging
stylistic and structural evolution Tsvetaeva's poetic manner had
undergone in the intervening decade. 'Poem of the Hill' is actually
not a narrative poem, but rather a sequence of ten interconnected
lyric poems, preceded by a dedication and followed by an epilogue,
about the hill in Prague on which the poet and her lover used to
meet during the brief period of their happiness. The hill itself is the
protagonist of the poem, rather than either one of the lovers. The
hill is anthropomorphized and endowed with knowledge, desires
and emotions. The Czech commentator Vladimir Smetáček has
pointed out in his essay on the semantic and spatial relationships in
'Poem of the Hill' the systematic opposition between the summit of
the hill, where love and suffering are possible and where the poet
feels at home, and the city below, associated with 'rabble, market
place, barracks,' which is inimical to strong emotions and where she
feels alienated. In the ninth and tenth sections of the poem, the
persona imagines the hill becoming a part of the city of Prague, built
over with cottages and shops. She lays a curse on the complacent
philistines she expects to reside in the future on her hill for she
assumes that they will be indifferent to the happiness and misery she
had once experienced there:

> Your daughters shall be harlots
> And your sons grow up to be poets!
> . . . . . .

May you not have earthly happiness,
O you ants, on my hill!

At an unknown hour, at an unexpected time
Your entire family shall recognize
The immeasurable and immense
Hill of the seventh commandment.

'Poem of the Hill' is a poem of great pain. Its indiscriminately vengeful tone and the destructive urge of its final sections are sure to repel many readers. Tsvetaeva herself may not have been entirely satisfied by such a bitter memorial to her love, because immediately after completing this poem she embarked on its companion piece, 'Poem of the End.' This poem is genuinely narrative and highly dramatic. It describes in great detail the evening on which the lovers decide that their relationship must end. The reader follows them on their strolls through the streets and suburbs of Prague, a walk by the river, a visit to a café and their conversations during which the need to separate is articulated. In the last two sections, the man is unable to hold back his tears, making the woman realize that he loves and needs her and causing some merriment on the part of three prostitutes who happen to witness the final farewell. Every word, glance and action of her departing lover is analyzed by the desperate woman, with a constant conflict between her imagination and what her reason and senses tell her to be facts. The method is that of a stream of consciousness, conveyed in a choppy, telegraphic diction, with insight and expressivity that make 'Poem of the End' one of the great psychological poems in the Russian language.

'Poem of the Hill' and 'Poem of the End' deal with powerful and often confused emotions. Yet, these emotions are couched in verbal structures of harmony and logic which are often of considerable complexity. 'Tsvetaeva constructs her apparently unbalanced and excessively emotional poems like a logician and an architect,' wrote Vladimir Smetáček. This is attained in 'Poem of the End' by a system of recurrent refrains and by sequences of stanzas which are sets of variations on a syntactic or semantic theme. Individual words are often broken up by dashes which create stresses where they do not occur in normal Russian prosody. This is one of the devices that enabled Tsvetaeva to create new, unprecedented meters (she was also using them in shorter poems written at that time). All this, combined with a frequently elliptical style, gives 'Poem of the End' a kind of cubistic verbal texture that is highly original and that has defied, so far, the best efforts of translators to render this poem into other languages. Because of its theatrical quality, 'Poem of the End' has been given dramatized stage presentations in Moscow and in Prague in recent decades. Since its first publication in the Soviet Union in 1961 it has won an appreciative new audience and become one of the best loved narrative poems of the twentieth century.

'The Swain' ('Mólodets'), dedicated to Boris Pasternak, is the last of Tsvetaeva's trilogy of pseudo-folk poems on subjects derived from folklore collections. Like 'The Tsar-Maiden,' it is based on a tale from Alexander Afanasiev's book. Unlike it, 'The Swain,' except for its ending, follows its source with utmost fidelity, to the point of incorporating quotations from Afanasiev's version into its text. The poem tells the story of the village maiden Marusia who goes to a dance and meets a handsome young swain with whom she falls in love. He turns out to be a vampire. Instead of denouncing him to the authorities and saving herself, Marusia keeps silent while her mother, her brother and finally herself, in a scene of mixed horror and tenderness, are killed by the vampire. Marusia is buried in accordance with certain magic rites specified by the vampire (in Afanasiev, by her grandmother) and is incarnated in a flower that grows on her grave and can periodically turn into a woman.

In this new guise, Marusia marries a local nobleman who puts a sign of the cross on her to prevent her from turning back into a flower. Listless and apathetic, she remains with the nobleman for five years during which time she bears him a son. Then her husband forces her to attend a church service, where she senses the presence of her first love, the vampire. At this point, Tsvetaeva's plot and denouement become radically different from her source in Afanasiev. In the original folk tale, Marusia threw some holy water on the vampire, destroying him forever, and lived happily ever after with her husband. In 'The Swain,' she forsakes her husband and son, yields once more to the vampire and, against the background of solemnly intoned fragments from the Church Slavic liturgy and quotations from the Book of Psalms, flies with him toward heaven in a burst of scarlet light.

'By some miracle,' wrote Dmitry Shakhovskoy of this poem, 'a plume of the fabled Firebird of Russian folk song has been stolen and this plume is being used to write "civilized" – in terms of plot and form – poems. Instead of congratulating civilization (or at least being offended on behalf of epos), some of our critics merely shrug their shoulders.' And indeed, apart from Vladislav Khodasevich's sympathetic essay on 'The Swain,' Russian critics did not quite know what to make of this poem with its unexpected and morally ambiguous finale. In her 1926 essay 'A Poet on Criticism,' Tsvetaeva outlined her reasons for writing 'The Swain.' 'I read "The Vampire" [in Afanasiev's collection] and was puzzled. Why is it that Marusia, who fears the vampire, so persistently refused to admit what she had seen while knowing that to name it is to be rescued? Why no instead of yes? Fear? But fear can make us not only bury ourselves in a bed, it can make us jump out the window. No, not fear. Granted, fear, but something else as well. Fear and what else? When I am told: do this and you are free and I do not do it, that means that I do not want freedom, that my non-freedom is more precious to me. And what is this precious non-freedom that exists between people? Love. Marusia loved the vampire. This is why she would not name him and kept losing, one after another, her mother, her brother, her life. Passion and crime, passion and sacrifice. Such was my task when I started working on "The Swain." To uncover the essence of the folk tale already implicit in its skeleton. To release it from its spell [raskoldovat' veshch']. And not at all to create a "new form" or "folkloric form".'

The metrical texture of 'The Swain' is once again a new departure when compared with Tsvetaeva's earlier folklore-based poems. This texture is permeated with Russian folk dance rhythms which begin throbbing from the very first lines:

> Sin' da sgin' – krai sela,
> Rukhnul dub, trost' tsela.
> U vdovy u toi u trudnoi
> Doch' Marusia vesela.

> The azure. And begone! At the village edge,
> The oak has toppled, the reed is standing.
> That hard-working widow yonder
> Has a merry daughter, Marusia.

These dance rhythms keep recurring throughout the length of the poem. The bouncy trochaic meter, typical of Russian dance tunes, blends organically with Tsvetaeva's special logaoedic and choriambic meters into patterns reminiscent now of the coachmen's and nursemaids' dances in Stravinsky's *Petrushka* and now of the orgiastic choruses of the last section of the same composer's ballet-cantata about a village wedding, *Les Noces* (*Svadebka*).

In 'The Pied Piper' ('Krysolov'), Tsvetaeva turned to the German medieval legend of the Pied Piper of Hamelin (*Der Rattenfänger von Hameln*). As Marie-Luise Bott pointed out in the annotations to her edition of this poem, Tsvetaeva must have been familiar with various treatments of this legend in the German literary tradition, including those by the Brothers Grimm, Goethe and Karl Simrock's ballad 'Der Rattenfänger.' An essential source for her version was Heinrich Heine's satire on power-hungry radicals, 'Die Wanderratten.' Heine and his poetry were very much on Tsvetaeva's mind while she was writing 'The Pied Piper' and she was at one point thinking of dedicating the poem to him. Another important source for this poem, which Marie-Luise Bott uncovered in a separate study, was Vladimir Belsky's libretto for Nikolai Rimsky-Korsakov's opera *The Legend of the Invisible City of Kitezh*, on which Tsvetaeva drew for a number of situations and reminiscences. A German source not mentioned by Dr Bott is the thirteenth chapter of *Der Trompeter von Säkkingen* by Victor von Scheffel, the long poem which Tsvetaeva had known and loved since her childhood, and on which she based the situation and argument of Canto Five of 'The Pied Piper.'

The subtitle of 'The Pied Piper' is 'A Lyrical Satire.' The targets of Tsvetaeva's satire are both social and political. From her romantic literary roots, especially from Pushkin and Heine, Tsvetaeva inherited the nineteenth-century notion that the enemy of the poet and the artist is the faceless philistine, preoccupied with materialistic values only and hostile to the life of the spirit. This concept is conveyed in German by the noun *Spiessbürger* and the adjective *borniert*; Russian has a whole array of terms for conveying philistinism and narrow-minded vulgarity: *meshchanstvo*, *obyvatel'-shchina*, and the more abstract one, made popular in Western languages by Nabokov, *poshlost'*. Tsvetaeva knew this phenomenon not only through denunciations by her favourite poets but from personal experience as well: the profiteering Bolsheviks described in 'Free Passage,' the shady dealers in rare commodities of the NEP period, and, in emigration, families who arranged their material well-being with no thought of creative or spiritual realms. In her letter to Olga Kolbasina of November 6, 1924, Tsvetaeva wrote with fury of a placid émigré family in Prague who spent their days in leisure and fed their children choice cold cuts and pastries, while her own eleven-year-old daughter Ariadna had to 'rush all day from the broom to the garbage can.' But the ultimate image of smug philistinism was found by Tsvetaeva in the small Czech town where her daughter attended a boarding school, Moravská Třebová. It was situated near the German border and its German name was Mährisch-Trübau. Tsvetaeva felt alienated by the patriarchal and prosperous way of life in this town. It was a town, as she told her daughter, which 'deserved a Pied Piper because of its practical, soulless way of life, its adherence to *meshchanstvo* as the only possible, the only rational form of existence.'

'The Pied Piper' is in six cantos. The German locale is asserted not only in proper names, but in occasional macaronic passages of Russian and German which occur throughout the poem. The first two cantos describe, in sparkling and humorous verse, the prosaic and materialistic way of life enjoyed by the burghers of Hamelin. 'A Digression about a Button,' incorporated into the first canto, asserts the similarities between the creative artist, the pauper and the criminal. The third canto opens with a sarcastic description of the food market. The monstrous abundance of food in Hamelin is equated in the poem with moral decay, which is seen as the direct cause of the rat plague. The rats, like 'Die Wanderratten' of Heine, organize a revolutionary movement and take over the city. Their language is a parody of Communist jargon and contains Soviet-style abbreviations transposed into a murine key: *glavkhvost* ('Central Administration of Tails'), *narkomchort* ('People's Commissariat of Devils'), *narkomshish* ('People's Commissariat of Insults') and the like. The main weapon of the rats is their irreverence and lack of respect for the conventions which the burghers assume to be eternal and sacrosanct. But once the rats are victorious they become victims of overfeeding and of creeping *embourgeoisement*.

In 'Pushkin and Pugachov,' Tsvetaeva wrote of 'every poet's attraction to rebellion,' but to a rebellion 'personified in one person.' 'He who is not attracted to the transgressor is not a poet,' she went on. 'It is only natural that under a revolutionary system this attraction for the transgressor becomes counter-revolutionary in the poet, inasmuch as the rebels themselves have become the authorities.' The poet's sympathy in 'The Pied Piper' is neither with the capitalist burghers nor with the revolutionary rats – both are equally philistine and devoid of spirituality. The real protagonist of the poem is the Pied Piper, a flutist garbed in green, whose 'only Mistress is Music,' and who first appears in the fourth canto. For the promise that he will be given in marriage the hand of Greta, the adolescent daughter of the mayor of Hamelin, he delivers the city from the rats by luring them into a swamp where they drown. The rats follow his flute in the mistaken belief that they are on their way to India, where they intend to start a world revolution. In the fifth canto, the flutist tries to claim his prize, but the entire city council lectures him on the impossibility of marriage between the mayor's daughter and an impoverished artist (this is the section of the poem where Tsvetaeva relied on *Der Trompeter von Säkkingen*). In the contemptuous speeches of the city officials about the impracticality and uselessness of artistic creation Tsvetaeva's satirical war on philistinism achieves its most vivid expression. In the sixth canto, the musician has his revenge by luring all the children and ado-lescents in town, including the fair Greta, into a lake where they drown.

The death of the children at the end of 'The Pied Piper' is not a simple murder, any more than Marusia's flight with the vampire at the end of 'The Swain' was a simple case of desertion of husband and child. The real revenge of the Pied Piper is to lure the children into an anarchy of freedom and to open to them the world of spirit and imagination, which their parents are unable to perceive. The poem ends in an apotheosis, comparable to other apotheoses that we find in Tsvetaeva's long poems, such as 'On a Red Steed' and 'The Swain' – an ultimate deliverance from everything transient and petty:

> In my kingdom there is no mumps, no measles,
> No higher matters, no medieval histories,
> No racial strife, no execution of [John] Hus,
> No children's illnesses, no children's fears.
> The azure. Fair summer [eternally].
> And – time – for everything.

When the serialization of 'The Pied Piper' was completed, D. S. Mirsky wrote in his review of this poem: 'Undoubtedly, "The Pied Piper" is not only what it appears to be at first glance. It is not only a verbal structure that is astounding in its richness and harmony, it is also a serious "political" (in the broadest sense of this term) and ethical satire which is perhaps destined to play a role in the growth of consciousness of all of us.' But this dazzlingly brilliant poem found a very limited circle of readers at the time of its publication. It had to wait until the 1970s and '80s to be appreciated and studied as it deserves.

It has been said that Tsvetaeva came to idealize Czechoslovakia, that she longed for it only after she had left it and that she cared little for it when she lived there. But it is quite understandable why her Czech period looked so attractive to her in retrospect. Despite emotional turmoil and occasional physical discomfort, she was better off personally and professionally during that time than she would ever be again. Her books were published and they found appreciative audiences both in the Soviet Union and abroad. She earned money with her writings and did not experience the kind of indigence that she lived with during the time of War Communism in Moscow and would know again a decade later in Paris. The years 1922–5 were for Marina Tsvetaeva a time of achievement and hope and, as we can now see, one of the happiest periods of her life.

7
Splendours and miseries of 1926

When the refugees from the October Revolution fled from their country by the hundreds of thousands they expected to stay away for a few years at most. The reversal of the economic prosperity and of the personal and artistic freedoms that had been won after the 1905 and February 1917 revolutions was too sudden, brutal and illogical, they reasoned. Surely the Russian people would not endure indefinitely this new tyranny, which Marina Tsvetaeva in her poetry and Yevgeny Zamiatin in his fiction were quick to liken to the Mongol invasions of the Middle Ages. Surely the Western democracies whose pluralist systems Lenin and Trotsky had vowed to subvert and destroy would oppose the Bolsheviks out of self-preservation. But with the crushing of the last internal resistance in 1922 such hopes began to dwindle. To Lenin's disbelief and astonishment, the 'bourgeois' countries kept coming to the aid of the Soviet Union: with food to combat the famine in 1921, then with loans and technical experts to help with the reconstruction in the next few years. By 1924, France, Great Britain and numerous other countries extended their diplomatic recognition to the Bolshevik regime as Russia's only legitimate government.

The years Marina Tsvetaeva had spent in Czechoslovakia – 1922–1925 – were more bearable and hopeful for her people than the preceding period of War Communism. True, the concentration camps, inaugurated in 1920, were in operation (on a more modest scale, however, than they would be later). The show trial of a large group of Socialist Revolutionaries, which shocked the international Socialist movement in 1922, launched the new Leninist form of criminal justice, under which the defendants were convicted in advance of the trial, not for anything they did but for who they were. Priests, nuns, monks – anyone, in fact, who was connected with the Russian Orthodox church – were persecuted as savagely as the former members of the now-outlawed non-Leninist revolutionary parties.

But during Lenin's long final illness and for about two years after his death in 1924, his heirs were so engrossed in their rivalries that they relaxed temporarily their economic and artistic controls. The New Economic Policy and the introduction of a stable new unit of currency, the *chervonets*, enabled the farming population to free the country from the specter of famine that had haunted it in the years of War Communism. The great age of innovation in literature and the arts which the culture had inherited from the pre-revolutionary decade was maintaining its momentum in the 1920s in the work of already established poets, such as Kuzmin, Mandelstam and Mayakovsky; in a galaxy of brilliant new prose writers, among them Babel, Zoshchenko, Platonov and Olesha; in the exciting new theater and cinema of the period; and in abstract and modernist painting which was allowed to continue undisturbed until about the middle of the decade.

All these developments in the Soviet Union were avidly followed by Russians in exile. Along with the factions which persisted in their rejection of Bolshevism, whether from monarchist, moderate-democratic or libertarian-socialist positions, there were others who sought to come to terms with it or to rationalize in some way its continuing success. In the early 1920s there came the trend known as 'Changing Landmarks' (*Smena vekh*). Inspired in part by Boris Pilniak's popular novels about the October Revolution and the civil war, this view held that the Bolsheviks were merely an instrument of a genuine revolution, whom the Russian people had used to rid themselves of the decadent Western institutions that the moderates and socialist parties had threatened to impose. The adherents of 'Changing Landmarks' hoped that Bolshevism would eventually lead to an autocratic Russian peasant empire, impervious to Western rot. The same idea that Bolshevism was only an unwitting tool of some higher design was basic to another movement among the émigrés in the 1920s, Eurasianism, which however was on a much higher intellectual plane than 'Changing Landmarks.' The Eurasians, among whom we find some of the most important philosophers, historians and theologians of the Russian emigration, held that because of her geopolitical position and past history (centuries of domination by Mongol nomads), Russia's revolution could have taken no other form but the Bolshevik. The democratic institutions generated in Western Europe were by their very nature unsuitable to Russia, since Russia was not only a European but also an Asian country.

The ideas of such groups had their impact, leading thousands of exiled Russians to re-examine their views of the Soviet regime and to opt for repatriation. But the majority of the exiles had realized, by about 1925, that they were in for a long, perhaps indefinite stay abroad. The realization was reinforced by the gradual ban on importation into the Soviet Union of émigré books and periodicals and by the increasing restrictions on travel abroad by Soviet citizens. By 1925, Russian literature of the twentieth century had divided into its two distinct, somewhat artificial branches, Soviet and émigré. The center for émigré literature was now Paris, and that was where most of the working Russian writers abroad were headed.

Paris did not offer the advantage of a favourable currency exchange as Berlin had in 1921–2, nor were there any stipends or scholarships to be had there as in Masaryk's Prague. The French government was anything but welcoming. Residence permits were hard to obtain. Foreigners were not allowed to hold any jobs with regularly paid salaries, being restricted to occasional work only (exceptions were made for a few large factories, such as Citroën). But Paris now had the highest concentration of Russian newspapers, journals and publishing houses. There was a large and active Russian literary community there, which must have figured in Marina Tsvetaeva's plans when she came to Paris with her two children on November 1, 1925.

Olga Kolbasina-Chernova and her three daughters had a three-room apartment in a bleak, working-class section of Paris. She let Tsvetaeva and her family have one of these rooms. At first, the poet spent all her time writing the last canto of 'The Pied Piper.' A week after her arrival she wrote to Anna Tesková: 'The quarter where we live is horrible, something out of a cheap novel called *The Slums of London*. A rotting canal, the sky cannot be seen because of the chimneys, endless soot and endless clatter (of trucks). There is nowhere to take a stroll, not a shrub. The nearest park is forty minutes by foot and it's too cold to walk. So we stroll along the rotting canal.' And later in the same letter: 'I go nowhere because I have nothing to wear and no money with which to buy anything. [. . .] I get numerous invitations, but I cannot show myself because there is no silk dress, no stockings, no patent leather shoes, which is the local uniform. So I stay at home, accused from all sides of being too proud.' The kindly Tesková responded by sending an elegant black dress.

When Sergei Efron joined his family at the end of December, Tsvetaeva wrote to Tesková: 'My situation is very bad. There are four of us crammed into one room and I cannot write at all. I think with bitterness that even the most mediocre newspaper columnist who doesn't even bother to re-read what he has written has a writing desk and two hours of quiet. I do not have it, not for a moment. I'm always with other people, in the midst of conversations, continually torn away from my notebook.' It was during those months that she wrote the poem that begins: 'Praise, be quiet! Fame, don't slam doors.' Other portions of this poem read:

> Youth is for love,
> Old age, for keeping warm.
> There's no time *to be*,
> Nowhere to hide.
>
> If only a sty
> But without other people!
> Faucets leak,
> Chairs clatter,
>
> Mouths talk:
> Filled with porridge
> They thank me
> 'For beauty.'
> . . . . . .
> My God shall be he
> Who will grant me
> (Tarry not!
> The days are numbered!)
> Four walls
> For peace and quiet.

Asked by one of the Russian newspapers about her wishes for 1926, Tsvetaeva responded: 'For myself – a separate room and a writing desk, for Russia – whatever she herself wants.'

Marina Tsvetaeva's arrival in Paris aroused great interest in the Russian émigré press there. In November and December 1925, the two leading newspapers, *Days* (*Dni*), the SR paper which had moved from Berlin to Paris and was now being edited by Alexander Kerensky and *The Latest News* (*Poslednie novosti*), the organ of the Constitutional Democrats, edited by Pavel Miliukov, printed a great deal of Tsvetaeva's verse and prose (excerpts from *Omens of the Earth*). *Contemporary Annals*, the most prominent Russian literary journal in Paris, published three new poems and the memoir 'My

Jobs' in 1925, while the Prague *Freedom of Russia*, which was widely read in Paris, featured 'A Hero of Labor' and the serialized 'Pied Piper.' Even the right-wing, monarchist newspaper *Renascence (Vozrozhdenie)*, which Tsvetaeva had recently attacked in *Days*, when she defended her husband's journal *One's Own Way*, solicited her replies for a round-table style questionnaire on literary topics which it addressed to prominent literary figures. It would not be an exaggeration to say that in late 1925 and early 1926 Tsvetaeva was the most frequently published writer of the Russian emigration. With the aid of the dress provided by Tesková, she was able to attend receptions and New Year's balls (the Russian literary community in exile still celebrated holidays according to the pre-revolutionary Julian Calendar, so that the New Year's Eve fell on January 13). In a report in *Days* on the charity ball organized by a committee to aid indigent Russian scientists and writers, we find Tsvetaeva listed along with other literary celebrities who were present, among them Ivan Bunin, Alexander Kuprin, Vladislav Khodasevich, Nina Berberova and the popular humorist Nadezhda Teffi.

The main object of Tsvetaeva's trip to Paris was to hold a poetry reading. This proved far more difficult to organize than she had expected. A hall had to be rented, tickets distributed, invitations sent. There were several prominent patronesses in Paris, such as Maria Tsetlina and her cousin Amalia Fondaminskaya, the wife of Ilya Fondaminsky, the one-time Socialist Revolutionary Commissar of the Black Sea Fleet and now one of the editors and publishers of *Contemporary Annals*. The family of Tsetlina and Fondaminskaya owned tea plantations in Ceylon from which the two cousins still received considerable incomes, which they used to support Russian journals and other literary projects in Paris. Tsvetaeva had been friendly with Tsetlina in Moscow (it was at her home that she first heard Mayakovsky read his poetry) and had earlier corresponded with her. But in Paris she did something to antagonize Tsetlina, who then withdrew her promised help with finding the hall for Tsvetaeva's reading. As Tsvetaeva wrote to Valentin Bulgakov in Prague: 'I do not know how to plead poverty and to fawn. On the contrary, irony is blooming in me now more richly than ever. And the "benefactors" clench the hand (more exactly the wallet) which was about to open.' In the same letter, she informed Bulgakov: 'I've met Lev Shestov, Ivan Bunin and Teffi.

The first is nobility personified, the second pomposity personified, the third *poshlost'* personified. The first likes me, the second tolerates me, the third ... well, the third one and I are not on speaking terms.'

The reading, initially scheduled for January, had to be postponed several times. It finally took place on February 6, 1926. An entry in the diary of Vera Sudeikina, later the wife of Igor Stravinsky, shows that Tsvetaeva came to her apartment on that day and that Stravinsky was not present. This may have had to do with the adjustment of Tsvetaeva's costume for her public appearance, since Mme Sudeikina was known at the time as a dress designer and a *couturière*. Tsvetaeva shared the program with two supporting artists, a soprano and a violinist. The recital was treated by the Russian community in Paris as the literary event of the year. Announcements kept appearing in all the Russian daily papers during the two weeks that preceded it. *The Latest News* ran a long essay on Tsvetaeva by Mikhail Osorgin, a journalist and novelist whom Tsvetaeva had known in Moscow in the post-revolutionary years, when, as she wrote to Shakhovskoy, 'he came to my rescue many times.' (Osorgin was a principal organizer of the All-Russian Committee for Famine Relief, for which he was expelled from the Soviet Union on Trotsky's orders in 1922.) Other newspapers also ran feature stories about Tsvetaeva and her writings in connection with her poetry recital. A detailed account of the event appeared a few days later in the Berlin newspaper *The Rudder* (*Rul'*), a Constitutional Democrat publication founded by Vladimir Nabokov's father. The author of this account was the noted Pushkin scholar Modest Gofman.

'Only recently considered among the lesser-known names in contemporary poetry, Marina Tsvetaeva has lately become not merely one of its biggest names, but indubitably *the* biggest name. Her recital is a new confirmation of her instantly grown popularity, of her vogue. During my four years in Paris I had no occasion to see such a multitude of people, such a crowd come to listen to a contemporary poet. Long before the recital began, not only were the large auditorium and the balconies filled to overflowing, but even the aisles were so crowded that it was impossible to move. The recital was a success and the audience applauded generously after the performances of the singer Cunelli and the violinist A. Mogilevsky. But the main attraction of the evening, Marina Tsvetaeva, had the greatest success of all. She recited both her old poems from *The Demesne of the Swans* [...] and her recent poems.' Also present at that reading was the young poet Irina Knorring. In a poem written the next day, she described herself as wandering aimlessly about in the rain, being stopped by a policeman, and barely escaping being hit by passing automobiles, all because 'that woman's voice yesterday / Had taken too much out of me.'

A week or two before the recital, the anthology *The Ark*, which Tsvetaeva had co-edited in Czechoslovakia and which contained 'Poem of the End,' reached Paris. There was a volley of enthusiastic articles in periodicals, especially by younger critics such as Gleb Struve and Daniil Reznikov, acclaiming the poem as a major masterpiece. The abundant publications in periodicals at the end of 1925, the publicity given Tsvetaeva in the first two months of 1926, the favourable reception of 'Poem of the End' and the triumphant recital of February 6 constituted the high point of Tsvetaeva's welcome by the Russian literary community of Paris. But she had already embarked on the collision course that would isolate her from important segments of that community and deplete much of the credit which her success had won for her. As Irma Kudrova has pointed out in her detailed study of Tsvetaeva's first six months in Paris (part of a biography in progress), it was at precisely that time that the seeds of Tsvetaeva's subsequent conflicts were planted.

Among the numerous new acquaintances that Tsvetaeva had made during her first months in Paris were two young noblemen, both bearing the title of prince and the first name of Dmitry. Prince Dmitry Shakhovskoy was twenty-three. A novice poet and a student at the University of Louvain in Belgium, he had conceived the idea of publishing a Russian literary journal, named after a Sentimentalist journal of the early nineteenth century, *Blago-namerennyi* (something like *The Well-Intentioned One* or *The Loyal One*). With persistence and charm, the young student managed to line up some of the biggest names in Russian émigré literature for his venture. In the fall of 1925, he wrote to Tsvetaeva, asking her to contribute. For his first issue, she let him have a fragment from *Omens of the Earth* and a poem. After meeting Shakhovskoy in person in Paris, Tsvetaeva offered him for the second issue of his journal a major new essay she was writing during January 1926, 'A Poet on Criticism' ('Poèt o kritike').

Prince Dmitry Sviatopolk-Mirsky, known in the English-speaking countries as the historian of Russian literature D. S. Mirsky, met Tsvetaeva early in 1926. A former officer in the Imperial Guards and a minor poet, he was now a prominent literary critic. He published in British, French and Russian émigré journals and taught Russian literature at the School of Slavonic Studies, London University. In 1926–7, he would publish his two-volume history of Russian literature, written in English, which remains to this day the best such survey available in any language. At first, Mirsky did not appreciate Tsvetaeva's poetry. In 1923, he excluded her from an anthology of Russian poetry he edited, describing her in his preface as 'a talented, but hopelessly undisciplined Muscovite.'

But after meeting Tsvetaeva in person and reading her most recent work, such as 'The Swain' and 'The Pied Piper,' Mirsky concluded that Tsvetaeva was next to Pasternak the most important poet of the age. He wrote about her with great enthusiasm throughout 1926, in Russian and in English, and devoted to her a highly favourable section in his history of Russian literature. Mirsky was a friend of one of the founders of Eurasianism, Piotr Suvchinsky, later known as Pierre Souvchinsky, the musicologist and intellectual mentor of Igor Stravinsky (it was apparently through Suvchinsky that Mirsky met Tsvetaeva). Since Sergei Efron found himself also strongly drawn to Eurasianism at the time of his move to Paris, he, Mirsky and Suvchinsky conceived the idea of publishing a journal of their own. They called it *Mileposts*, after the title of two of Tsvetaeva's collections. The three editors intended the journal to be a showcase for the work of the writers they considered to be the most important poet, the most important prose writer and the most important philosopher of the Russian emigration. These were Marina Tsvetaeva, Alexei Remizov and Lev Shestov (the Russian precursor of French existentialism and a great favourite of Tsvetaeva's, both as a writer and as a person). Mirsky and Efron (and, to some extent, Tsvetaeva) also intended their journal as an assault on what they saw as the Russian literary establishment in Paris.

Now, the literary community that Tsvetaeva found in Paris was by no means unified either aesthetically or politically. The one point on which Russian Parisians tended to agree was their negative view of literature that came from the Soviet Union. Unlike Prague journals, such as *Freedom of Russia* and *One's Own Way*, which tried to separate the wheat from the chaff in what was written under Communism, the Paris journals tended to berate it or to ignore it *in toto*. For Tsvetaeva, as for Mirsky, a writer's place of residence or political affiliation was not a criterion. It was decided that each issue of *Mileposts* would feature reprints of interesting new works by writers who lived in the Soviet Union.

Tsvetaeva sent the manuscript of 'A Poet on Criticism' to Shakhovskoy on March 3. A week later, on the 10th, she left with Mirsky for London, where he had arranged two poetry readings for her and where she stayed for two weeks. In London, she corrected the galleys of 'A Poet on Criticism,' and, her pugnacious mood continuing, wrote an angry essay about Osip Mandelstam's book *The Noise of Time* (she later withheld the publication of this essay on her husband's advice and it remains unpublished to this day). She was taken by Mirsky to the British Museum, which she loved, and to some elegant restaurants which bored her. From London, she wrote Anna Tesková that she was delighted to have two weeks of freedom 'for the first time in eight years – four Soviet and four émigré' and that London was wonderful. Some years later she wrote to Khodasevich that London had failed to coincide with the London of her imagination 'where the Thames would flow in both directions, Hyde Park would be next to Westminster Abbey and Queen Elizabeth [I] would appear arm in arm with Lord Byron.'

When 'A Poet on Criticism' appeared in the second (and last) issue of Shakhovskoy's *Blagonamerennyi* in April, many of the literati in Paris felt that the poet they had admired and welcomed had unexpectedly kicked them in the face. The essay is a searching examination of the relationship between the art of poetry and its public evaluation. The central theses are unarguable: new art can be evaluated and criticized only by people who understand it or who at least approach it with an open mind. The opinion of critics who do not trouble to find out what the artist has set out to do or who have failed to understand it is of no value. The essay also offers important insights into the creative laboratory of a particular poet, Tsvetaeva. Stylistically, it is a dazzling piece of writing, the work in which Tsvetaeva found herself as an innovative prose writer and inaugurated the manner that would serve her so well in her prose of the 1930s.

But in her negative examples, meant to serve as instances of incompetent or wrong-headed criticism, Tsvetaeva went after the scalp of a wide variety of practicing critics of the day: the venerable Yuly Eichenwald, whose reputation dated from the turn of the century; the reactionary critical hack Alexander Yablonovsky, who denounced modern trends in the monarchist paper *Renascence*; and the subtle post-Acmeist poet Georgy Adamovich, who was emerging as the most admired younger critic of Russian Paris. The Formalist school of criticism was taken to task by Tsvetaeva as too technical and specialized. Two of the biggest literary names in the emigration were also attacked: Zinaida Gippius for failing to appreciate Pasternak, and Ivan Bunin for his hostility to Blok and Esenin (at Shakhovskoy's request, Tsvetaeva changed her reference to Bunin's 'disgraceful article' to read 'deplorable article'). Appended to 'A Poet on Criticism' was a section with the heading 'A Flowerbed' ('Tsvetnik'), which consisted of excerpts from the critical writings of Georgy Adamovich, interspersed with withering comments by Tsvetaeva intended to show up Adamovich as inconsistent, irresponsible and superficial.

Small wonder that the essay elicited a critical storm. It made an enemy of the previously friendly Mikhail Osorgin, who condemned the essay in a long article in *The Latest News* and who for the rest of 1926 repeatedly wrote of Tsvetaeva with hostility. Vladimir Pozner (who in the 1930s joined the French Communist Party and became a Stalinist French writer) came to Adamovich's defense in *Days*. Peter Struve, once a leading figure in Russian Marxism and an associate of Lenin, but now an anti-Bolshevik exile, was plainly baffled by the style and syntax of 'A Poet on Criticism.' In an article in *Renascence* which chastised both Tsvetaeva and her victim Adamovich, Struve qualified her prose and poetry as pointless, unnecessary and incomprehensible. A few days before Struve's piece, *Renascence* published Alexander Yablonovsky's rebuttal to Tsvetaeva's accusations against him. Bearing the title 'In a Bathrobe' ('V khalate'), his article qualified Tsvetaeva as an ill-mannered person, lacking all sense of decorum: 'She enters literature wearing curlers and a bathrobe, as though she were headed for the bathroom.'

Irma Kudrova has pointed out a circumstance that needs to be taken into account when considering the passions aroused by 'A Poet on Criticism.' She reminds us how new Tsvetaeva's reputation as a major literary figure was (even her greatest booster, Mirsky, became aware of her importance only at the beginning of 1926).

'From a Dostoevsky or a Tolstoy,' wrote Kudrova, 'or at the very least from Merezhkovsky or Zinaida Gippius, such a personal tone would of course have been accepted and forgiven. But Tsvetaeva as a poet and authority, from the viewpoint of her contemporaries in May of 1926, had barely emerged from the shadows.' So an open season on Tsvetaeva was proclaimed in the émigré press. With the appearance of the first issue of *Mileposts* only a few weeks after her essay she found herself facing some heavy artillery indeed. Ironically, this was happening at the very same time when the publication of her memoir 'My Jobs,' with its angry denunciations of the Soviet system, brought down on Tsvetaeva the wrath of the Soviet ideologues and cut off the further possibility of the appearance of her work or any favourable mention of it in her native country. From being the most praised of Russian poets at the beginning of 1926, she was moving by spring of that year to the position of one of the most berated, both in the Soviet Union and abroad.

The first issue of *Mileposts* was preceded by Mirsky's public lecture on April 5. Invitations were sent to the leading literary figures in Paris to come to the lecture and to debate the positions of the forthcoming journal with the speaker. Mark Vishniak, one of the editors of *Contemporary Annals*, later described the stupefaction caused by Mirsky's sudden condemnation of that liberal journal (to which Mirsky had been a regular contributor) and of numerous authors associated with it. In his lecture, as in his essays in *Mileposts*, Mirsky branded a whole array of writers living abroad, including Bunin, Merezhkovsky, Gippius, Khodasevich, Mark Aldanov and Boris Zaitsev, as belonging to the past, outmoded and 'dead.' Living Russian literature for him consisted of Tsvetaeva, Remizov, Shestov and a number of people who lived in the Soviet Union, among them Pasternak, Andrei Bely (who had returned to Russia in 1923 despite Tsvetaeva's efforts to keep him abroad) and the new prose writers of the 1920s.

Considered from the vantage point of the 1980s, *Mileposts* (of which only three issues appeared) seems a fascinating if quirky document of the literary life of its time. But for many Russians abroad its publication seemed an outrage. What rankled was not only the high praise for Soviet literature, but the Eurasian outlook of the journal, with its contempt for democratic institutions, which the liberal-minded émigrés found offensive. Vladislav Khodasevich published in *Contemporary Annals* an article in which he denounced the three editors and called one of the contributors, the composer Arthur Lourié, a Soviet agent. The article later necessitated apologies and retractions. Peter Struve called *Mileposts* a 'repellent superfluity' and qualified the reprints of the Soviet authors (Pasternak, Esenin, Babel, Tynianov and others) as 'carrion.' Tsvetaeva's contribution to the first issue was 'Poem of the Hill.' She offered no opinions on other writers, nor did she attack anyone in *Mileposts*. But it was generally regarded as 'her' journal as well as Mirsky's, and some of the people she had offended in 'A Poet on Criticism' took the opportunity to get back at her while writing about *Mileposts*.

Ivan Bunin, who enjoyed an almost Olympian status in the émigré community, was one of Mirsky's principal targets (it is curious that while assaulting Bunin, Merezhkovsky, Gippius *et al.* in *Mileposts*, Mirsky was writing of them simultaneously with fairness and objectivity in English in his history of Russian literature). In his criticism of the journal published in *Renascence* in August, Bunin called it 'boring and irritating' and wrote that the mere presence of the names of Shestov and Tsvetaeva on the same masthead was 'nonsense and irresponsibility.' His comment on 'Poem of the Hill' consisted of citing the fifth and sixth lines of the poem which, taken out of their context, emerged as an obscene pun (Tsvetaeva later changed the wording of these lines so as to avoid the implication suggested by Bunin).

The status of Zinaida Gippius, one of the principal founders of Russian symbolism, was if anything even more august than Bunin's. Gippius detested Tsvetaeva's poetry as she detested the work of all post-symbolist Russian poets, with the exception of Khodasevich, with whom she was friendly, and Mandelstam whom she was one of the first to discover. Both Gippius and Bunin had been in their day pioneers of writing frankly on sexual matters, including, in the case of Gippius, the less common forms of sexuality. But 'Poem of the Hill' and 'Poem of the End' depicted Tsvetaeva's extramarital affair, which in these poems was displayed for the whole world to see. This went beyond what the older writers' sense of propriety could tolerate. In the letters of Gippius to Khodasevich, we see that she actually regarded Tsvetaeva as a shameless harlot who used her sexual favours for purposes of political subversion. Gippius was especially concerned that Tsvetaeva might use her seductive wiles on Alexander Kerensky and thus prevent his paper from exposing

Mileposts as a Bolshevik plot, which Gippius had no doubt it was. (Tsvetaeva had indeed met Kerensky in Prague and presented him with a copy of *Craft* on which she had inscribed her poem from *The Demesne of the Swans* where Kerensky was likened to Napoleon and a copy of 'The Tsar-Maiden' with a dedication in which she wrote: 'To Dear Alexander Kerensky, a Russian folk tale in which nothing goes right.')

In her letters of summer 1926 to Khodasevich, we see Gippius trying to organize a press campaign against Tsvetaeva, Mirsky and their journal and also against those émigré commentators, such as Feodor Stepun and Mark Slonim, who had written favourably on *Mileposts* or on the issue of *Blagonamerennyi* that contained 'A Poet on Criticism.' Gippius saw the editors of both these journals as a 'gang,' with Tsvetaeva as a sort of gangsters' moll. Soon Gippius convinced herself, as was her wont, that the Devil himself was behind it all. For Gippius, Tsvetaeva and Mirsky were despicable and at the same time endowed with almost supernatural powers. They were protected from her wrath by liberal editors, such as Fondaminsky (he refused to publish her denunciation of *Blagonamerennyi* in *Contemporary Annals*), Kerensky and Miliukov, who insisted on fair play and would not print unsubstantiated allegations. Gippius finally managed to place a savage article on *Mileposts* in *The Latest News*, where it was published over the protest of one of the editors and led to the resignation of a staff member. The article, called 'On *Mileposts* and Other Things' ('O "Verstakh" i o prochem') appeared on August 15. Tsvetaeva and her poetry are treated in it in a tone of utter contempt. The publication of this article and of her earlier attack on Shakhovskoy and his *Blagonamerennyi* led several old friends of Gippius to break off contact with her, among them Remizov's wife, Serafima Dovgello, whose friendship and correspondence with Gippius went back to 1905 (they resumed writing to each other in 1930). The philosopher Nikolai Berdiaev wrote to Gippius, accusing her of hounding Mirsky and other participants in *Mileposts* and of resorting to methods worthy of the Cheka. His letter and her reply marked the end of a friendship that had begun at the turn of the century.

Tsvetaeva left Paris just as the press hurricane occasioned by 'A Poet on Criticism' and *Mileposts* began to gather momentum. With her literary earnings and the proceeds of the February reading, she was able to fulfil a long-standing dream: a summer on the Atlantic coast in the Vendée, the home of the royalist uprising of 1793–95, the area she regarded as the homeland of her soul. Early in April, she went there in search of lodgings and rented a fisherman's hut in a village called Saint-Gilles-sur-Vie. She and her children moved there on April 24. Sergei joined them a month later. It was in Saint-Gilles that Tsvetaeva was to have her most satisfying experiences of mutual love and understanding, experiences which involved the men who were for her the two greatest poets of the age. Most fortunately for Tsvetaeva, this took place on a disembodied, non-physical level, which made it all the more real for her. As she had written to Boris Pasternak on November 19, 1922: 'My favourite form of communication is in the beyond: in dreams. To dream of someone. The second choice is correspondence. Letters are a form of communicating in the beyond, less perfect than dreams, but subject to the same laws.'

In March 1926, Pasternak happened to see a privately-circulated, typewritten copy of 'Poem of the End' in Moscow. Unappreciated and perhaps not even understood by its protagonist, Konstantin Rodzevich, the poem ricocheted to Pasternak, causing an emotional explosion. In her earlier cycles of poems addressed to him, such as 'Telegraph Wires,' 1923, and 'The Two' ('Dvoe'), 1924, Tsvetaeva wrote of Pasternak as her ideal soul-mate, the only person in the world who was fully attuned to her wavelength. Now, in the wake of reading 'Poem of the End,' there came a torrent of letters from Pasternak, in which he offered himself to Tsvetaeva as her ideal reader, ideal critic and as a man desperately in love: 'You were sent to me straight from Heaven, you fit the ultimate extremes of my soul. You are mine, you were always mine and my whole life is for you.' And later: 'What a huge, devilishly huge artist you are, Marina!' By April 20, Pasternak's passionate outpourings culminated in an offer either to abandon his wife and child at once and come to join Tsvetaeva or to postpone this for one year: 'There is nothing else left to be said. I have a goal in life and this goal is you.' Tsvetaeva recommended postponement. As she was to write to Anna Tesková five years later: 'In the summer of 1926, after reading somewhere my "Poem of the End," Boris conceived a mad yearning for me and wanted to come, but I declined. I did not want a catastrophe for *everyone*.' On May 8 Pasternak wrote that he accepted her decision: 'You have indicated the boundaries.'

In the meantime, during the same month of March, when
Tsvetaeva was in London with Mirsky and Pasternak was discovering 'Poem of the End' in Moscow, Pasternak's father, the painter
Leonid Pasternak, who lived in Germany with his wife and two
daughters, had resumed contact with the poet Rainer Maria Rilke.
The Pasternak family had met Rilke when he visited Russia with
Lou Andreas-Salomé in 1899 and 1900. In 1925, Rilke turned fifty
and spent some months in Paris, where he had heard from Russian
friends of the spreading fame of Boris Pasternak (whom he had last
seen as a little boy in Moscow) and where he read some of his poetry
in French translation. In a letter of March 14 to Leonid Pasternak,
Rilke expressed pleasure that Boris Pasternak, whom he saw as 'the
acknowledged leader of the new generation' of Russian poets,
appreciated his work and made clear his own enthusiasm for
Pasternak's poetry. For both Boris Pasternak and Marina
Tsvetaeva, Rilke had long been a loved and revered figure: for him,
along with Scriabin and Mayakovsky, one of the greatest formative
models; for her, the living equal of her favourite German poets of
the past, such as Goethe, Heine and Hölderlin.

On April 12 Boris Pasternak sent Rilke an ecstatic letter, filled
with exclamations, superlatives and assurances of devotion. At the
end of that letter, he informed Rilke that on the day he learned of
the latter's interest he also read a new poem by a woman poet, a
poem the likes of which 'no one in the USSR could now write,' 'a
poet of great talent akin to that of a Desbordes-Valmore.' (That
Pasternak could think of no one more important than the minor
elegiac poet of the French romantic age, Marceline Desbordes-
Valmore, to compare to Tsvetaeva at the peak of her powers
suggests that for him, too, as for Trotsky or Mayakovsky, women
poets were a category apart, not to be compared to any male poets.)
Pasternak pleaded with Rilke ('oh, please, please forgive my bold-
ness and the apparent importuning of you') to send Tsvetaeva an
inscribed copy of his latest book, because it would give her joy and
mean a great deal to her.

Rilke responded by sending Tsvetaeva inscribed copies of his last
two books, *Duino Elegies* and *Sonnets to Orpheus* ('they are for
you, they are your property'), accompanied by a friendly letter
inviting her to start a correspondence and requesting her help with
forwarding his books to Pasternak (there were no postal connections between the USSR and Switzerland, where Rilke then lived,

and he was afraid that his books might be confiscated by the Soviet censor). On May 9, Tsvetaeva began the first of her letters to Rilke from Saint-Gilles: 'Rainer Maria Rilke! May I thus address you? You, poetry incarnate, must surely know that your very name is a poem. [. . .] You are not my favourite poet – "favourite" implies a degree. You are a natural phenomenon which cannot be mine and which one doesn't love but rather experiences, or (more than that!) you are the incarnated fifth element: poetry itself, or (still more than that) you are that which generates poetry and which is greater than it (than you).' The letter was continued on the next day, maintaining the same hyperbolic level and shifting, in its middle part, to the intimate *du* from the formal *Sie* with which it began and ended, thus implying an utter lack of barriers between the two poets. For Rilke, Russia was always a magical, fairy-tale realm. Tsvetaeva's tone charmed him. It corresponded to his rather simple-minded notion of Russian culture as the last refuge of spontaneity and untrammelled emotions, the very opposite of Western inhibitions and conventionality. He replied to Tsvetaeva on the same level and in the same tone.

Tsvetaeva's correspondence of that summer with Pasternak and Rilke took place in a world of spiritual essences, not of gross realities. Konstantin Azadovsky, who prepared that correspondence for publication, described it as a 'conversation between conspirators or accomplices.' 'This is a conversation,' he wrote, 'between people who understood each other's slightest hints, who seem to be initiates of a mystery which they have no need to interpret to each other. An outsider is obliged to pore attentively over these letters and poems.' In response to Rilke's books, Tsvetaeva sent him copies of her collections *Verses to Blok* and *Psyche*, to which she added glossaries and marginal explanations. To her intense disappointment, although Rilke's Russian had once been good enough to translate Lermontov and *The Igor Tale* into German, it was not up to understanding her complex poetry.

Pasternak, who as Tsvetaeva later put it, 'made her a present of Rilke,' was most anxious to hear about the progress of her correspondence with the German poet. Instead, he received a wholly unexpected request to contact Sophia Parnok and to help her in some way. In March 1926, Parnok published her collection *Music (Muzyka)*, the earlier of her last two collections, in which her talent fully unfolded. Several of the poets who were Tsvetaeva's friends, such as Vera Zviagintseva and Maximilian Voloshin, greatly valued Parnok's newly matured poetry of the mid-1920s. But her *Music* was totally ignored in the Soviet press. After its publication, Parnok was no longer able to place her poems in Soviet journals, possibly because of her occasional lesbian themes. Appended to Tsvetaeva's letter to Pasternak was a love poem addressed to Parnok from her then unpublished 1915 cycle 'Woman Friend.'

Tsvetaeva's letter about Parnok was not included in the volume of her correspondence with Rilke and Pasternak. But Pasternak's hurt reply to it was. The letter produced on him the effect, he wrote, of 'touching an electrical condenser, charged with pain, jealousy, bellowing and suffering.' He happened to read the letter and the enclosed poem while on his way to the editorial offices of the newspaper *Izvestia*, where he was going on business. Pasternak wrote that he immediately understood 'the music and the entire hell and the entire secret they [i.e., the letter and the poem] contained.' In his anger, he made a nasty scene at the *Izvestia*, causing the employees there to say that 'a poet behaved like a bull in a china shop.'

Pasternak refused to take an interest in Sophia Parnok: 'There is nothing I can do for her because she and I have never gotten along. Besides, your letter reached me during a new falling out with her. It was partly on her account that I recently quit "The Juncture" [*Uzel*, a cooperative poets' publishing venture, which in 1926 brought out a volume of Pasternak's *Selected Poems*]. In such a context and on top of the information which you have crashed over my head, only a St Sebastian could write to her about the twenty-year-old Marina.' The matter was not pursued any further in their correspondence. Tsvetaeva's sudden interest in the fate of the woman she was willing to let starve during the Civil War was to revive at least two more times during the 1930s, when she wrote her two most overtly lesbian prose pieces, 'Letter to an Amazon' and 'The Tale of Sonechka.' Apparently, the loss of Parnok was a wound that never did quite heal.

As could have been expected, the correspondence between Tsvetaeva, Pasternak and Rilke was generating not only letters but also poems. Pasternak was as impressed by 'The Pied Piper' as he had been by 'Poem of the End.' He read it at the very end of May and on June 4 he sent Tsvetaeva a long, detailed and wildly enthusiastic analysis of this poem, which he saw as a literary equivalent of a Wagner opera because of its virtuosic use and development of leitmotifs. Pasternak kept discussing 'The Pied Piper' in several of his following letters. Under the impact of these two long poems, Pasternak decided to try his hand at narrative poetry, something he had not written before. Casting about for a subject, he found it in Tsvetaeva's replies to the questionnaire for the projected bibliographical dictionary of twentieth-century writers which she had filled out at his request in April of that year (see Chapter 1, p. 21). In her response, Tsvetaeva stressed her youthful involvement with the revolution of 1905 and its martyr Lieutenant Piotr Schmidt, and her rejection of the subsequent February and October revolutions. That spring, Pasternak embarked on his two long historical poems, 'The Year 1905' and 'Lieutenant Schmidt,' which were published piecemeal throughout 1926 in various Soviet journals. The first part of 'Lieutenant Schmidt' appeared that fall in the Moscow journal *The New World* (*Novyi mir*) with a prefatory poem about a hunted stag, which was actually an acrostic. Read downward, the first letters of each line of the poem spelled 'To Marina Tsvetaeva.' This cryptic dedication of an ostensibly revolutionary poem to an exiled, openly anti-Soviet poet was soon deciphered. The disclosure caused difficulties for both Pasternak and the journal's editor. Pasternak's penitent letter about this incident to the editor Viacheslav Polonsky is reproduced in Lazar Fleishman's book *Boris Pasternak in the Twenties*. The dedicatory acrostic was deleted from the later editions of the poem. As Olga Raevsky Hughes has shown, Tsvetaeva also served as a model for one of the principal female characters in Pasternak's novel in verse *Spektorsky*, on which he worked from 1924 to 1930.

During four days from May 23 to 26, Tsvetaeva wrote Pasternak a long, lyrical letter about her yearning for a dream encounter with him that would take them back to their respective childhoods and about her inability to appreciate the ocean as Pushkin had in his poem 'To the Sea,' which she had loved as a child, the ocean which Pasternak had described in his 'The Year 1905,' which she had recently read. The themes of this letter were simultaneously incorporated into the long, semi-humorous poem 'From the Seacoast' ('S moria'), which she completed before the end of May. Although the poem is about a dream encounter, its mode is realistic and also strongly satirical, the barbs being aimed at Soviet censorship of literature and the journal *On Guard*, which was denouncing both

Pasternak and Tsvetaeva. In June, Tsvetaeva wrote another long poem about a dream encounter with another poet, 'Essay of a Room' (literally, 'An Attempt to Construct a Room,' 'Popytka komnaty'). This poem, far more abstract and surrealistic than 'From the Seacoast,' is addressed to both Pasternak and Rilke, but its central theme is identical with that of its predecessor: the spiritual and erotic interpenetration of two poets' innermost beings, a fusion which is achieved in the absence of any physical contact between them.

On June 8, two days after Tsvetaeva completed 'Essay of a Room,' Rilke sent her his long and very beautiful 'Elegie an Marina Zwetajewa-Efron.' It came at a time when she had temporarily stopped writing to him. She had feared being a burden to Rilke. His greatness overwhelmed her. 'How to manage this looming *Nibelungenhort* [the treasure of the Nibelungs in Wagner's operatic tetralogy]?' she asked Pasternak. On June 14, she wrote Rilke a penitent letter about how she had tried to exclude Pasternak from their tripartite relationship because she wanted Rilke's friendship all to herself (as Ariadna Efron later commented, 'in the realm of non-material values, [Tsvetaeva's] proprietary instincts were insatiable'). At the end of June, Rilke sent Tsvetaeva the collection of poems he wrote in French, *Vergers*, on which he inscribed a French poem addressed to her:

> Marina: voici galets et coquillages
> ramassés récemment à la française plage
> de mon étrange cœur ... (J'aimerais que tu conusses
> toutes les étendues de son divers paysage
> depuis sa côte bleue jusqu'à ses plaines russes).

Tsvetaeva's correspondence with the two poets continued in July and August. On July 1, she sent Pasternak a rather severe critique of the completed portions of 'Lieutenant Schmidt.' She admitted the use of historical sources in poetry only if they were transformed by the alchemy of the poet's personal vision. Pasternak, she felt, had used the record of Schmidt's trial too slavishly and furthermore, his revolutionary hero emerged in the poem as an average intellectual out of Chekhov, a writer she had always detested. Pasternak agreed with her strictures. For later editions, he reworked and abridged this poem. Despite her rejection of the poem he wrote especially for her, his love and need for her flared anew. In his July letters he clearly oversteps 'the boundaries' to which he had agreed in May. On July 10, Tsvetaeva outlined for him a series of reasons, some of them highly metaphysical, why they would never be able to live together as lovers or spouses. On July 31, he replied: 'You are my torment, you are my delight, you are my fate.' Pasternak made an effort to bring Tsvetaeva's latest work to the attention of the poets who were associated with Mayakovsky and Lilia and Osip Brik. He managed to get Nikolai Aseyev, Nikolai Tikhonov and Semion Kirsanov to admire 'Poem of the End' and 'The Pied Piper.' He even discussed with them the possibility of publishing 'Poem of the End' in Mayakovsky's journal *Lef* (an acronym for 'The Left Front'), but they all knew that neither the Soviet authorities nor Mayakovsky would allow this.

In the correspondence of that summer, the possibility of a tripartite reunion in the spring of 1927 was mentioned several times. Then in her letter to Rilke of August 2, 1926, Tsvetaeva took a direct approach. 'Rainer, I want to come to you,' she wrote. 'Don't be angry, after all it's *me*, but I want to sleep with you. Simply to fall asleep and to sleep. [. . .] And nothing further. No, there is something: to bury my head in your left shoulder, my arm on your right one – and nothing else. No, something else: to know in the deepest sleep that you are there. And also to hear the sound of your heart. And to kiss the heart.' In Moscow, back in 1920, Tsvetaeva had explained to Vera Zviagintseva that her main passion was contact with people and that physical touch was essential because 'that was the only way of penetrating into a person's soul.' It was this kind of closeness that she now hoped to establish with Rilke. In the same letter to him, she also wrote: 'You are always traveling, you live nowhere, and you keep seeing Russians who are not me. Listen and get this straight: in Rainerland I alone represent Russia.'

At the time of this correspondence, Rilke was already mortally ill with what was later diagnosed as leukemia. But even apart from his physical state, the tone of Tsvetaeva's letter of August 2 was not the right one to adopt with this poet. As his friend and biographer J. R. von Salis wrote: 'Whenever he sensed a danger of being enchained by a woman he took fright and on these occasions he would be painfully torn between his desire for bondage and for freedom.' And further: 'Friendship with a woman, if it was to continue bearable and free from misunderstanding, was only possible for Rilke when no element of compulsion entered it, when the relation-

ship did not confront him with claims and pretensions.' From being
the Swan Princess out of a Russian fairy tale that Tsvetaeva had
seemed to him at the beginning, she was now turning into the kind
of woman from whom Rilke had fled many times in his life. On
August 14, she repeated her request for a meeting, perhaps in a
small town in the French Savoy, where Rilke could come to see her
from Switzerland. She also informed him that she no longer wanted
to write to Pasternak who was torn between his love for her and for
his wife and son, who were in France at the time. Tsvetaeva did not
want him writing to two loved beings abroad, herself and his wife: '*I
am his abroad. I am and I will not share this.*'

On August 19, Rilke wrote Tsvetaeva an affectionate letter:
'Yes, yes and yes, Marina, yes to everything you want and are [. . .],
but there are also ten thousand unforeseen noes.' He approved of
and agreed to her desire for shared intimacy, but he also expressed
at some length his doubts that a meeting would be feasible. He also
told her that she was being too strict, even harsh, in her refusal to
have anyone else represent abroad for Boris or Russia for himself: 'I
reject any kind of exclusion (which takes root in love and then turns
to wood).' She replied with a letter full of passion and desperation,
describing her life of privation and hard work, pleading with Rilke
to plan and finance her trip to him, to select a meeting place and to
pay for her train ticket and hotel. She obviously had no idea what a
burden this would inflict on Rilke in his deteriorating physical
condition. This letter was not answered. Tsvetaeva waited for more
than two months and then, from her new home in the Parisian
suburb of Bellevue, she sent Rilke a plaintive postcard: 'Dear
Rainer! Here is where I live. Do you still love me? Marina.'

Marina Tsvetaeva learned of Rilke's death (December 29) on
New Year's Eve. She had lost him through her letters of that
August, but now, in death, she felt that she had regained him for
eternity. At 10 o'clock on the night of the 31st she wrote him an
affectionate posthumous letter in German (the language of all their
correspondence), a letter she was to develop into a long poem
addressed to him, 'New Year's Greetings' ('Novogodnee'), which
she completed on February 7, 1927. The poem is a combination of
personal letter, epitaph and elegy. Like the 'Essay of a Room' that
preceded it and 'Poem of the Air' that was to follow in 1927, 'New
Year's Greetings' is also a metaphysical meditation on the nature of
life, death and time. It was fitting that Joseph Brodsky, the most

metaphysical of this century's Russian poets, wrote a splendid and highly personal line-by-line exegesis of 'New Year's Greetings,' an essay that is also a prose poem about the nature of Tsvetaeva's art and thought. Another epitaph to Rilke was the meditation in prose 'Your Death' ('Tvoia smert''), written at the end of February 1927. Tsvetaeva's attitude to Rilke after his death was best expressed in a letter to Anna Tesková: 'He was the German Orpheus, that is Orpheus who *this time* happened to appear in Germany.'

Tsvetaeva's correspondence of that summer with Rilke and Pasternak and the poems they addressed or dedicated to each other represented the highest level of *bytie*, the subjective elevated level of existence which she so valued. But there was also the lowly *byt* to be lived through that spring, summer and fall. A large part of every day was taken up by pushing her little son in his baby carriage through the streets and on the beach of Saint-Gilles-sur-Vie. There was the task of keeping the hut they rented warm enough during what turned out to be an exceptionally cold summer. There was socializing with Russian friends who were staying at Saint-Gilles or neighboring villages, among them the families of Konstantin Balmont, with whom Tsvetaeva continued her old friendship, and of Anna Andreyeva. There were also worries about the future: the Czech stipend could be cut off unless Tsvetaeva returned to Prague. For a while she did plan to return there, but concern for the editorial and journalistic career of her husband impelled her to stay in France. The Czech subsidy was, however, prolonged through the efforts of her Prague friends despite her failure to return.

In her letter to Pasternak of June 21, she wrote about the press response to *Mileposts* and to her essay in *Blagonamerennyi*. In her view, she was being unfairly persecuted by all the people she had attacked in 'A Poet on Criticism.' She saw the press campaign as a conspiracy of ill-wishers to have her and her children thrown out into the street. As the summer waned, the two princely Dmitrys, who had precipitated her conflict with the Paris writers and in whose journals she had hoped to find the main outlet for her future work, began to move out of her life. Dmitry Shakhovskoy, after the publication of the second issue of his journal, departed for Mount Athos in Greece to take monastic vows. He later rose to the top of the hierarchy in the Russian Orthodox Church, eventually becoming the Archbishop of San Francisco and the Western United

States. Dmitry Sviatopolk-Mirsky remained in contact with
Tsvetaeva for the next five years, contributing to her financial
support and visiting her occasionally when he was in Paris. But they
drifted apart. He never again wrote of her work as much or with
such enthusiasm as he had in 1926. His life followed a trajectory that
was the very opposite of Shakhovskoy's. From Eurasianism, Mirsky
was later converted to Communism. He joined the British Communist Party and in 1932 returned to the Soviet Union. After a few
years of activity there as a fanatical, ultra-Stalinist critic and
journalist, in 1937 Mirsky was sent to a labor camp in the far north,
where he died two years later at the age of forty-eight. *Mileposts*
published two more ever-thinner issues in 1927 and 1928. Instead of
a journal, it ended up as an annual miscellany, a state of affairs
attributable to Sergei Efron's inept management of its financial and
editorial affairs.

The period from November 1925 to the end of September 1926
was the most eventful time in Tsvetaeva's life, both publicly and
privately. Never before or after was she so successful, so publicized,
so extolled and so berated. In her correspondence of that summer
with Rilke and Pasternak she was for once dealing with two beings
whom she felt to be her equals in combined poetic and human
strength. With the move from Saint-Gilles to Bellevue in the
outskirts of Paris at the end of September, Tsvetaeva entered a new
phase of her life. It was a phase marked by privation, isolation and
dwindling poetic output. She had known a life of poverty before – in
Moscow after the Revolution and later in Czechoslovakia. The
ugliness of life in the working-class suburbs of Paris struck her when
she first experienced it immediately after her arrival. In January
1926, she began writing a long poem about life in the slums which
she completed in Saint-Gilles in July, after writing her two dream
poems, 'From the Seacoast' and 'Essay of a Room.'

'Poem of the Staircase' ('Poèma lestnitsy') belongs, together with
'Poem of the End' and 'The Pied Piper,' at the very summit of
Tsvetaeva's achievement in the realm of lyrical-narrative poetry. It
is a philosophical and satirical poem with a verbal texture that
corresponds to the techniques of Synthetic Cubism in painting and
to the use of jazz in serious compositions of George Gershwin and
Darius Milhaud. The poem falls into three contrasting sections. The
first part is a brisk, syncopated depiction of the staircase of the title,
the back stairs of a large apartment house inhabited by the poor.

The sights, sounds and smells of this dingy setting are portrayed through kaleidoscopic shuffling of bits and pieces of metonymic images which convey the atmosphere of cynicism and social oppression. As Tsvetaeva herself characterized this section in the text of the poem, it is

> A Marxist sermon
> In Stravinskian manner
> By means of a multitude of patches.

The middle section of 'Poem of the Staircase' is an adagio that follows the boisterous allegro of the beginning. In the stillness of the night, the objects and substances which make up the paraphernalia of urban civilization attempt to regain and to reassert their original nature and purpose. The antecedents of this section are the philosophy of Jean Jacques Rousseau and the poetry of Feodor Tiutchev, one of whose main themes was that the primeval chaos that underlies the veneer of civilized life can be best perceived at night. Its contemporary parallels were the works that depicted the revolt of objects against people: Velimir Khlebnikov's poem 'The Crane' and his play *Marquise Desaix*, for example, or Colette's libretto for Maurice Ravel's opera *L'enfant et les sortilèges*. This middle section begins:

> Night: how to express it?
> Night: the object's confession.
> Night begs for sincerity.
> The object wants to unburden itself –
>
> Totally! They are all humiliated,
> Every single one, the immovable
> Included. An access of eloquence:
> The object wants to straighten up.
>
> The spiral of the back stairs –
> Do you really think it cleaves to the wall?
> Night: the time of prayerfulness.
> The spiral wants to stretch out.

The objects and substances refuse to serve the humiliating uses to which they are put by man. For several pages Tsvetaeva develops her romantic and Rousseauist conception of material civilization. She condemns mankind ('that visible spirit, that ailing god') for leaving its smudge on the original paradise of nature by inventing 'the inanimate object, that most false of all slanders.' The filthy, evil-smelling staircase of the beginning is seen as the summit achievement of this civilization, its most typical, most basic symbol. There follows a shattering digression on belongings of the poor, objects which are humanized by the poet and take on the properties of their owners' miserable existence. The final section of the poem proposes the ideal solution to the squalor described: the magnificence and nobility of the destruction of material civilization by fire. But the poet realizes that arson and violence are not her province, and that a better way of dealing with the ugly conditions just described and discussed would be to write a poem about them. In the final lines, as the staircase resumes its morning activities, the poet puts the just-completed poem to rest.

'Poem of the Staircase' is a powerful indictment of artificial ugliness and of the conditions that force human beings to live in the midst of it. The circumstances of Tsvetaeva's own life forced her to take a closer look at the basic premises of industrial civilization, as she tells the reader in several brief asides. Despite its central social theme, the poem draws for some of its ideas and images on the poetry of Rilke, as Patricia Pollock Brodsky has discovered – a not unlikely connection, since the poem was completed at the height of the Tsvetaeva–Rilke correspondence. The central theme of this poem has perhaps the most universal application of all of Tsvetaeva's long poems. Unlike Mayakovsky, who was then preaching the virtues of urbanization, industrialization and technological growth as a panacea for all social and human problems, Tsvetaeva clearly saw that an unchecked proliferation of technology not only breeds ugliness but may also lead to the destruction of mankind in an out-of-control conflagration. A flight of poetic fancy in 1926, this aspect of 'Poem of the Staircase' has now acquired an uncanny prophetic ring.

Poetry trapped between kitchen and politics

In the Western imagination, Paris of the 1920s is the city of Colette and Jean Cocteau, of Pablo Picasso and Georges Braque, of Maurice Ravel, Erik Satie and *les Six*, of bohemian cafés and jazz. For literary scholars of English-speaking countries, it is the Paris of James Joyce and Gertrude Stein, of Ernest Hemingway, F. Scott Fitzgerald and of so many other American, English and Irish literary expatriates. Few people think of Paris in the 1920s as a major center of Russian literature. Yet, as Gleb Struve has shown in his survey *Russian Literature in Exile*, Paris was the place where some of the best Russian writing of that period was produced and published. The senior exiled writers, among them Bunin, Kuprin and Remizov, were doing some of their most important work in the later 1920s. So were the exiled philosophers, such as Berdiaev, Shestov, Lev Karsavin and a number of others. After 1925 or so, a younger literary generation began making its mark: prose writers such as V. S. Yanovsky and Vladimir Nabokov (then known as Sirin, he lived in Berlin, but published much of his work in Paris) and interesting new poets such as Boris Poplavsky, Anna Prismanova and Anatoly Steiger.

A few émigré writers were affluent: Ivan Bunin, whose work was translated into many languages, and Nadezhda Teffi, whose humorous stories and sketches were enjoyed equally by intellectuals and lowbrow readers and were in constant demand. Others were able to make a modest living with their writing. But the majority of Russian writers in Paris lived in poverty that ranged from genteel to dire. One of the worst examples of the latter was the situation of Marina Tsvetaeva from 1927 on. A productive poet, memoirist and essayist, she realized that she could not subsist on her literary earnings alone. In the late 1920s and early 1930s, she still had her small Czech stipend. There were friends and admirers who contributed to her support. Anna Tesková regularly sent from Prague money, clothes and other gifts. D. S. Mirsky between 1926 and 1931 contributed toward Tsvetaeva's rent on a quarterly basis. During Tsvetaeva's first year in Paris, she met Salomea Halpern, who was born a Georgian princess and had been a friend of Mandelstam and Akhmatova before the Revolution. During the years 1926 to 1934, Mrs Halpern (she was married to an émigré lawyer resident in London and was herself gainfully employed in Paris) gave one-third of her monthly salary to Tsvetaeva and also arranged for monthly contributions from her friends, so that for a time she was able to provide the poet with 1000 francs a month, a respectable amount in those days.

Another benefactress entered into Tsvetaeva's life in the spring of 1928 through the good offices of Boris Pasternak. Raisa Lomonosova, the wife of an affluent Russian-born railroad expert based in England, corresponded with Pasternak, Kornei Chukovsky and other Soviet writers. In his letter to Lomonosova of April 5, 1928, Pasternak asked her to help transfer a small amount of money from him to Tsvetaeva. This led to a correspondence between the two women and to Lomonosova's offer of financial aid. Tsvetaeva's letters to the three women who helped her survive – Tesková, Halpern and Lomonosova – are somewhat different in tone and content from the rest of her correspondence. Besides literary matters, they address the details of her everyday living, its hardships and rewards. In these letters we see Tsvetaeva coping on a day-to-day basis, sometimes resourcefully, sometimes humorously and often despairingly.

Had Tsvetaeva lived by herself, the financial resources described above – the Czech stipend, the contributions of friends and the modest income provided by her writings – would have been more than adequate. But she had to support three other people: her daughter, her son and, most expensive of all, her husband. In Paris, Sergei Efron occasionally worked as an extra in film studios, appearing, *inter alia*, in Carl Dreyer's *La Passion de Jeanne d'Arc*. But this brought a mere pittance. With the demise of *Mileposts*, he started publishing a newspaper, *Eurasia*, which lasted from 1928 to 1929. In 1930, he enrolled as a student in a film school operated by the Pathé studios. Tsvetaeva raised the money for his tuition, expecting him to become a cameraman or an expert on Soviet film. But as usual with Efron, he found no application for this training after graduation. His recurrent episodes of tuberculosis necessitated repeated stays at sanatoria, which his wife also had to finance.

But Sergei's heart during those Paris years was not in jobs or studies: it was in politics. In the late 1920s, his politics were Eurasian. 'Sergei is entirely immersed in Eurasianism,' Tsvetaeva wrote to Tesková on February 15, 1927. She herself was vaguely attracted to this ideology, but she felt that ideological commitment of any kind was not for her: 'The idea of a state, the state of Russia has no need of me. I am needed by a series of other things which I serve.'

The need to support Sergei and the children, combined with the patriarchal notion that men must never be allowed to help with housework (as Tsvetaeva once wrote to Rilke), forced the unique and brilliant poet that was Tsvetaeva into the roles of scullery maid, charwoman, laundress, cook, nursemaid, – roles which many women have traditionally accepted as their lot in life, but which meant a slow death to Tsvetaeva. While still in Czechoslovakia, before her son was born and before Sergei became a full-time dependent, she wrote to Olga Kolbasina-Chernova: 'I'm writing this in the morning, glancing in distaste at the garbage that needs to be taken out, at coal that needs to be brought in, at the unswept floor and the unlighted stove.' In Paris, with three dependents to look after, things got grimmer. On September 12, 1929, Tsvetaeva wrote to Lomonosova: 'I am up at seven, I go to bed at two or three and what's in between? My daily life [*byt*] is laundry, cooking, taking my boy for a walk [...], dishes, dishes, dishes, mending, mending, mending and on top of it sewing new things for which I have no talent. Often there is not even a half an hour per day for myself (for my writing).'

Tsvetaeva eventually came to see that life was extracting too exorbitant a price from her for the right to be a wife and a mother: the sacrifice of her art. 'Marriage and love are destructive to one's personality, they are a trial,' she wrote to Tesková on May 26, 1934. 'This was what both Goethe and Tolstoy thought. And an early marriage, such as mine, is a total catastrophe, a blow from which you can't recover for the rest of your life.' Surveying her Paris years toward the end of her stay there, she wrote to Tesková on January 26, 1937: 'Now, taking stock, I can say: I've lived my life in captivity. And, strange as it may seem, a freely chosen captivity, because, after all, no one forced me to take everything so seriously. It was in my blood, in its German component.' But seven years earlier, on October 17, 1930, she already realized the injustice of her situation:

'Sometimes I think that, considering my ceaseless work, such a life is undeserved. [. . .] If I were like all the other women of my circle (but do I have a circle?) or like all the other writers (of my circle, which most definitely does not exist!), others would do everything for me and I'd watch them. The woman would watch and the writer would write. If I get to live another time, I'll know what to do.'

The kitchen martyrdom described in these passages and numerous similar ones in Tsvetaeva's correspondence was real. But it was also a myth, which she deliberately fostered. During those same years she did not only clean and mend. She also wrote; attended lectures and literary gatherings; gave one or two public readings a year and participated in a number of group readings; went to parties at homes of famous writers and received them as her guests. Every summer she took her family on vacations at the seaside or in the mountains, vacations which were financed by the proceeds of her poetry recitals. The same ambivalence characterizes the other two personal myths which Tsvetaeva devised in her poetry and correspondence: the myth of her living as an outcast in Paris and the myth of her banishment from the émigré press after 1926. Both of these myths have roots in concrete reality, but they reflect only one side of the multi-faceted truth. Yet they have become accepted both in the Soviet Union and in the West as reflecting the total picture of Tsvetaeva's situation in Paris.

'Tsvetaeva thought in myths,' said George Ivask. Another of the poet's correspondents, Roman Goul, in a letter to me, took this idea somewhat further: 'She was a difficult person because she was, clinically speaking, certainly a *mythomaniac*. This helped her literature. But in her life, this was a catastrophe.' One can indeed cite many situations in this poet's life when she almost willfully confused fact with fiction, such as her conviction that her sisters-in-law Vera and Lilia Efron were somehow responsible for the death of her daughter Irina (with which they had nothing to do) or that the son of Nadezhda Nolle and Piotr Kogan was actually fathered by Alexander Blok, something that was maintained in several of her poems and letters. One of Tsvetaeva's most frequently anthologized poems, 'Roland's Horn' ('Rolandov rog'), has occasionally been read (by myself, among others) as a reflection of the exiled poet's solitude and her rejection by the émigré community:

Like a poor jester in his misshapen state
I recount to you my orphanhood.

. . . .

Met with the derisive whistles of fools and laughter
      of philistines,
I'm alone amidst all – for all – against all!

I stand and I send, petrified from soaring,
This loud call into the heavenly voids.

And this flame in my breast is a gage
That some Charlemagne will hear you, o horn!

Actually, 'Roland's Horn' was written before her emigration, in
Moscow in March 1921. Tsvetaeva inherited from her romantic
models the notion that a poet is under all circumstances an outcast
and a pariah. While it is true that she often found herself rejected
during her Paris years – by critics, by editors, by other writers – it is
also true that she deliberately sought and courted such rejection.

In 1933, Tsvetaeva wrote to Ivask that she was 'alone all my life,
without books, without readers, without friends, without a circle,
without a milieu, with no defense, belonging nowhere, worse than a
dog, but on the other hand . . . But on the other hand [I have]
everything.' This statement may correctly reflect the subjective
feeling that must have frequently overcome her. 'But on the other
hand,' when we study her biography we see that she had family and
children, that she published numerous books, that even in her
lifetime she had many loyal readers and friends and that until the
last year of her stay in Paris, she remained one of the most
prominent members of the Russian literary community there.
Similarly, she wrote the same year to the same correspondent: 'In
the emigration they at first (hotheadedly!) publish me, then, having
come to their senses, withdraw me from circulation, realizing that it
is something that is not theirs: it is from over there! The content, it
would seem, is "ours" but the voice is "theirs".' This statement is
invariably cited in recent publications about Tsvetaeva in the Soviet
Union as evidence that she was a Soviet sympathizer all along
whether she knew it or not and that her fellow-exiles persecuted her
for it.

Again, the statement may accurately reflect Tsvetaeva's feelings, which does not qualify it as factual. Her work was published in the emigration in ever increasing volume for six years, from 1920 to 1926, which can hardly be described by the terms 'at first' and 'hotheadedly.' After the assault by *Mileposts*, generally regarded as Tsvetaeva's journal as well as Mirsky's and Efron's, on all liberal and conservative émigré periodicals, there was a two-year hiatus in her publishing in journals other than *Mileposts* and the SR *Freedom of Russia*. But by 1928 we see her resume publication in some of the very journals that the editorials in *Mileposts* had singled out for particularly contemptuous treatment, such as *Contemporary Annals* and the newspaper *The Latest News*. The comment about the 'voice' which is 'theirs' is absolutely on target, but it has nothing to do with Tsvetaeva's political sympathies. Many émigré commentators sensed quite correctly that Tsvetaeva was a poet of the same stylistic origins and orientation as Pasternak and Mayakovsky, poets whom they persisted in seeing as only 'Soviet' rather than the major Russian poets of our century which they were. Tsvetaeva's affinity with these two poets and her defense of them in her writings, her association (through her husband) with Eurasianism, combined with her continued eulogizing of the monarchist White Army in her poetry confused and irritated the moderate and liberal Russians in Paris. She was somehow too far left and too far right at the same time. As Tsvetaeva wrote to Vera Bunina in 1933: 'Some consider me a Bolshevik, others a monarchist, still others think I'm both, and all of them miss the point,' the point being that her outlook was above and beyond politics. She agreed with and praised Anna Tesková for translating Russian literature of every variety: prerevolutionary, Soviet and émigré. 'You are so profoundly right,' she wrote, 'in loving Russia thus! The old, the new, the Red, the White – all of it!'

In the spring of 1927, Anastasia Tsvetaeva in Moscow read several recent books by Maxim Gorky and wrote the famed writer (with whose children she had once played as a little girl) an enthusiastic fan letter. Although Gorky had gone into exile in Mussolini's Italy with Lenin's blessings, he remained on good terms with the Soviet government and was not regarded as an émigré writer. Touched by Anastasia's letter, Gorky invited her to visit him in Sorrento. His invitation enabled her to obtain an exit visa and gave Marina Tsvetaeva an opportunity to see her sister after a five year separation. In Paris, Anastasia also renewed her childhood friendship with Galia Diakonova who was then married to Paul Eluard. In her memoirs, written in the 1970s, Anastasia described Marina's hard life in Paris and quoted her as denouncing the 'banality of capitalist life,' terminology that Tsvetaeva is not likely to have used even if the sentiment is plausible. It is instructive to juxtapose Anastasia's account of her visit with the following sentence from Marina's letter to Salomea Halpern, written during that visit: 'Asya has a lot to tell about Russia; morale is much worse than it was in 1922.'

Striving to achieve for her sister a retroactive, Soviet-style respectability, Anastasia maintained in her memoirs that Gorky spoke to her with great admiration about Tsvetaeva's poetry. He was either being hypocritical or Anastasia made it up. We know Gorky's real view of Tsvetaeva from his correspondence with Pasternak that dates from that same year, 1927. Pasternak had expressed to Gorky his concern for the 'huge talent of Marina Tsvetaeva and for her unhappy, unbearably twisted fate' and sought his aid in 'restoring to Russia this tremendous person, who perhaps was not able to align her gift with destiny or, more correctly, vice versa.' Gorky replied: 'I cannot agree with your high estimate of Marina Tsvetaeva's gift. Her talent strikes me as flashy, even hysterical. She has a poor command of speech, speech commands her, as is the case with Andrei Bely. She knows Russian poorly and treats it brutally, distorting it in every way. Phonetics does not constitute music, but she thinks it's music.' Gorky's reply, which was supported by citations from some of Tsvetaeva's latest poems, showed a considerable familiarity with her work. He was no more interested in her fate than he was in her poetry. 'M. Tsvetaeva, of course, ought to return to Russia,' he wrote to Pasternak, 'but this is hardly possible.' Pasternak's hasty response to this, for which he later offered Gorky his apologies, is not reproduced in their published correspondence. But we know that it led to a temporary break of his contact with Gorky.

The rejection of Tsvetaeva's poetry of the 1920s by Maxim Gorky was, as we have seen, for aesthetic and stylistic rather than for political reasons. This was also the case with a number of other writers and critics who were not able to keep up with the continuous evolution of her poetic art. Tsvetaeva's growth as a poet between 1916 (the collection *Mileposts I*) and 1926 ('Poem of the Staircase') was so rapid that many readers found it bewildering. She herself compared the process to new bends of a river. As usually happens with rapidly evolving artists of great originality, Tsvetaeva kept losing a part of her audience with each new 'river bend.' Thus, Mikhail Osorgin, in his highly favourable article written on the occasion of her first Paris recital of February 1926 (this was before Osorgin was angered by 'A Poet on Criticism' and turned against her), called Tsvetaeva 'the best Russian poet now writing' and had some perceptive things to say about her stylistic affinities with the prose of Alexei Remizov. Yet Osorgin's admiration extended only as far as Tsvetaeva's treatment of eighteenth-century themes in her plays *Fortuna* and *The Phoenix* and her collection *Psyche*, i.e., only to her writings prior to 1920. He described her subsequent poetry as incoherent and he dismissed her *magnum opus*, 'The Pied Piper,' which at the time of his writing (January 1926) was still being serialized, as a piece of 'extremely melodious nonsense.' When Tsvetaeva tried offering her poetry to *The Latest News* for their Sunday literary supplement, the editors usually asked for her earlier work. 'In *The Latest News*, they very much like the old (i.e., the young) me,' she wrote to Tesková on November 18, 1928.

The name of Igor Stravinsky has already been mentioned on these pages. It is to this composer's thematic and stylistic evolution that the progress of Tsvetaeva's art is most clearly comparable, more so than to the evolution of any of her contemporary poets, Russian or foreign. For all the difference between their chosen media, the parallels in their responses to developments in their native culture of the pre-revolutionary and post-revolutionary periods are striking and, indeed, inescapable. Tsvetaeva's first two collections have their counterpart in the Stravinsky of the Symphony in E flat and *The Faun and the Shepherdess*: good schooling, technical assurance, a personal tone, but little that is truly unique or original. Tsvetaeva found her full stature in *Mileposts I*, 1916, a collection deeply rooted in the native traditions of Moscow, just as Stravinsky found his in the score of *Petrushka*, 1911, with its roots in the old St Petersburg. The blend of savage rhythms and muted lyricism in Tsvetaeva's collection *Craft* has, as already stated, analogies with *The Rite of Spring*. 'Poem of the Staircase,' with its *style dépouillé* and its jazzy syncopation, is an equivalent of Stravinsky's *Histoire du soldat*. Both the poet and the composer plunged into Russian peasant folklore and subjected it to highly modernist

treatment, she in 'Sidestreets' and 'The Swain' and he in *Les Noces*
and *Renard*. Tsvetaeva's rococo treatment of the eighteenth
century in *Fortuna*, 1918, was followed one year later by Stravinsky's similar treatment in *Pulcinella*.

Neo-classicism was an important trend in the art and music of the
1920s in Western countries. Stravinsky pioneered this trend and was
one of its main practitioners. Neo-classicism shaped such monu-
mental Stravinsky scores of the 1920s as the Concerto for Piano and
Wind Instruments, 1924, and *Oedipus Rex*, 1927. It was not a
question of imitating the work of eighteenth-century composers but
of appropriating some of their vocabulary and blending it with
Stravinsky's own language so as to express highly modern meanings
in eternal, universalist terms. A similar procedure was followed,
though in linguistic rather than musical terms, in Tsvetaeva's major
works published in 1927 and 1928: the two neo-classical verse
tragedies based on the myth of Theseus, *Ariadne* and *Phaedra*, and
the last verse collection she was able to publish in her lifetime, *After
Russia* (*Posle Rossii*). The two plays were written in 1924 and 1927
and published in periodicals in 1927 and 1928, respectively.

The genre of neo-classical tragedy was imported into Russia in
the middle of the eighteenth century. It flourished for some decades
and reached its culmination in the mellifluous plays of Vladislav
Ozerov (1769–1816), which were greatly appreciated by Osip Mandelstam. Verse tragedy on subjects taken from Greek myths was
prominently revived by the poets of the Symbolist generation, most
notably by two poets much admired by Tsvetaeva, Innokenty
Annensky and Viacheslav Ivanov. These poets were two of the
most erudite Greek scholars in the entire history of Russian culture.
Their attempts to revive classical Greek tragedy and to rethink it in
modern terms were supported by knowledge of its origins and
development. Tsvetaeva was not a scholar. Her use of sources,
when compared to these two predecessors, appears naive to the
point of absurdity. 'The sources of my *Phaedra* and of my mythics in
general,' Tsvetaeva wrote to Ivask, 'are the juvenile adaptations of
the myths by Gustav Schwab. More correctly (since I myself am my
sources, the sources are within me), these are my materials in the
same way as the materials for "The Tsar-Maiden" and "The Swain"
were the corresponding tales in Afanasiev.' The didactic, moraliz-
ing and frequently bowdlerized adaptation of Greek myths by
Gustav Schwab, *Die schönsten Sagen des klassischen Altertums*,

intended for German children of the Victorian age, was first
published in 1837–9. It is reprinted to this day in German-speaking
countries. This was Tsvetaeva's sole source for her planned Theseus
trilogy, and it accounts for some of her more startling departures
from the traditional version of that myth.

'My *Theseus* is planned as a trilogy: *Ariadne*, *Phaedra* and *Helen*,'
Tsvetaeva wrote to Tesková on November 28, 1927. 'But out of
super-(is it?)-stition I did not announce this until completing at least
two parts. Did you know that all women, once and for all, were the
destiny of Theseus? Ariadne (the soul), Antiope (the Amazon),
Phaedra (passion), Helen (beauty). That's the Trojan Helen. The
seventy-year-old Theseus abducted her when she was a seven-year-
old girl and because of her he perished. So many loves and *all of
them* unhappy. The last was the worst because he loved a doll.'

Tsvetaeva's *Ariadne* is a modern retelling of the Cretan adventure of Theseus. It is a dramatic poem that mingles an acutely
twentieth-century sensibility with the structure and narrative techniques of seventeenth-century French and eighteenth-century
Russian neo-classical tragedy. There are heralds that announce
offstage events, long soliloquies by the protagonists and choruses
that comment on the action. It is not a modern adaptation of the
baroque tragedy of Corneille and Racine, however, no more than
the heavy-limbed Greek-Italian goddesses that Picasso was painting
at the same time were an adaptation of Ingres or the music of
Stravinsky's *Oedipus Rex* was an adaptation of Handel. Tsvetaeva
put the simplistic reduction of the Theseus and Ariadne story that
she found in Schwab to her own use, which was consistent with her
outlook and philosophy. After Ariadne has rescued Theseus from
the Labyrinth and agreed to follow him to Athens, he abandons her
on the isle of Naxos not for the reasons usually cited, but because
Bacchus told him that this was the only way Ariadne could attain the
higher fate for which she was destined.

What is usually represented as an act of betrayal is shown here as
an act of heroism. Ariadne, who believes herself to be cheated and
abandoned, is instead moving to a superior level of existence. Her
humiliation and suffering are the price of the already familiar
Tsvetaevan apotheosis, more universal in this case, but not different in kind from the ones experienced by the heroines of 'On a Red
Steed' and 'The Swain.' The final suicide of his grandfather
Aegaeus is the punishment visited on Theseus by the vengeful

Aphrodite for allowing ideal considerations to triumph over the carnal and materialistic ones. To convey this conception, Tsvetaeva resorted to strongly archaized language. It had been traditional since Pushkin's time to draw on the vocabulary, grammar and syntax of the Russian Bible and Church Slavic prayers in order to suggest antiquity, whether Greek, Roman or biblical. This is what Tsvetaeva did in both *Ariadne* and *Phaedra* with considerable virtuosity. The archaic diction, combined with a remarkably fresh and sonorous versification, is fused organically with the philosophic and dramatic aspects of *Ariadne* to produce one of the most memorable examples of neo-classical art of the 1920s.

Phaedra, the only other play of the planned trilogy that Tsvetaeva was able to complete, begins in a similarly neo-classical vein, but in its middle sections its language shifts to that of Russian peasant laments, incantations and folk dances, which Tsvetaeva had already exploited in her folklore-derived narrative poems. This shift happened partly because Tsvetaeva had already treated the situation of the lascivious stepmother bent on seducing her resisting stepson in the folk tale milieu of 'The Tsar-Maiden' and was perhaps unable to break out of that pattern, and partly because she relied on Schwab for her reinterpretation of the myth. In Schwab's version, Phaedra was not to blame because her lust for her stepson was forced on her by the influence of her depraved and permissive nurse. In Tsvetaeva, the figure of the nurse, derived from Schwab, becomes a powerful and amoral Mother Nature figure, who forces the child she loves – Phaedra – to seek carnal pleasure without regard for the consequences to herself and to others.

The figure of the nurse gradually becomes the principal character of the play (the last act is centered entirely on her). Her speech is that of a nineteenth-century peasant from a Russian village, as is the speech of lesser female characters (Phaedra's friends and her servants) and, occasionally, of Phaedra herself. But the male characters, Hippolytus and Theseus, have an archaized diction that suggests the Bible and *The Iliad*. The stylistic heterogeneity of the play reaches a new level in the fourth act, where the death of Phaedra is told in terms that recall Ophelia's death in Shakespeare's *Hamlet*. In February and March of 1923, Tsvetaeva wrote a set of poems about Hamlet and another one about Phaedra in which she partly merged these two myths. In the light of these poems and of the description of the heroine's death in the fourth act of the play,

we can see that the character of Phaedra was meant by Tsvetaeva as
a fusion of Shakespeare's rejected Ophelia and his rejected Queen.
The character of Hippolytus, regarded from this angle, acquires
certain features of a virginal and cerebral Hamlet.

Phaedra thus lacks the unified stylistic conception and structural
ingenuity of *Ariadne*. The various lexical strata clash with each
other. The character of the nurse is not convincing enough dramati-
cally to justify her paramount role. Her prominence in comparison
with the protagonists throws the entire play off balance. It is sad, yet
somehow typical of Tsvetaeva's fate, that the émigré critics passed
over in silence the publication of the beautifully realized *Ariadne*,
but pounced on Tsvetaeva like a wolf pack after the appearance of
Phaedra. Vladislav Khodasevich and Georgy Adamovich, who
rarely agreed with each other about anything, were unanimous in
their condemnation of this tragedy. Khodasevich wrote of an
'inexcusable and tasteless mixture of styles,' while Adamovich
commented that *Phaedra* was 'howled and screamed rather than
written.' Vladimir Weidlé complained of a 'total absence of feeling
for words as responsible and meaningful *logos*.' Vladimir Nabokov,
writing in Berlin, accused Tsvetaeva of 'amusing herself with
unintelligible rhyme-weaving' and stated that *Phaedra* can only
cause 'astonishment and a severe headache.' Faced with this wall of
critical hostility, Tsvetaeva abandoned her plan of completing the
trilogy. The projected third play of the series, *Helen*, was never
written.

The shorter lyric poems which Tsvetaeva wrote in Berlin and
Czechoslovakia between 1922 and 1925 are among her most profound and best-structured. She believed that her poetry of those
years formed a continuum and planned to publish it in a volume to
which she gave the provisional (and highly appropriate) title *Secret
Intentions* (*Umysly*). In the spring of 1927, Salomea Halpern
brought Tsvetaeva together with a man named Iosif Pouterman
who was connected to a publishing house. Pouterman was an
admirer of Tsvetaeva's poetry. From her letters to Halpern and Lev
Shestov it can be seen that she expected her connection with
Pouterman to result in several publications of her work in Russian
and in French. With his encouragement, Tsvetaeva began preparing a volume of her poetry, to which she eventually gave the title
After Russia, a title that may be programmatic but which does not

really correspond to the contents. Instead of bringing the volume out through his publishing house, Pouterman chose to issue it privately and on a subscription basis. This involved the poet in the time-consuming and humiliating business of mailing out the subscription forms, since the size of the printing was not decided until the number of subscribers was ascertained. In turn, this delayed the publication of the collection until the spring of 1928.

In the poems of *After Russia* Tsvetaeva launched a new style. It was based in part on the ripe romanticism of *Mileposts II* and on the colloquial diction of *Mileposts I*, but the most important component was the new kind of twentieth-century neo-classicism. It had already been tried out in several of her earlier collections but it really came into its own in this one. This style, which she also applied in *Ariadne*, is appropriate to the universalist themes this poetry treats. The mature poet of *After Russia* had come a long way from the naive myths of Napoleon, the Duke of Reichstadt and Maria Bashkirtseva which had once preoccupied her. Now her points of reference are Homer, Ovid, the Nibelungenlied, Shakespeare, Racine and Goethe. She remains in this collection her own passionate and rebellious self, but she is now also capable of a detachment that is almost Olympian. And, while using her personal experience and literature as her point of departure as she had always done, she now writes philosophical poetry that probes the nature of time, of space, of human speech and of communication.

Already in 1922, Andrei Bely, in his brief review of Tsvetaeva's collection *Separation*, pointed out the central importance of the choriamb for the haunting effect of her metrical patterns: 'The impulsion is astounding in the plasticity of its gestures [. . .]; and the choriamb (– ◡ ◡ –), which Tsvetaeva wields magnificently, is the obedient expression of this impulsion. Just as in Beethoven's Fifth Symphony the heart beats in choriambic measures, so here a choriambic leitmotif arises, which becomes a palpable melodic gesture, integrated into various rhythms.' A choriamb is a four-syllable metrical unit in which the first and fourth syllables are stressed and the second and third are not. In traditional Russian versification, this sequence occurred on the infrequent occasions of trochaic substitution in iambic lines and vice versa. It never had an independent existence. In *After Russia* and *Ariadne*, Tsvetaeva made the choriamb her basic metrical building block, using it either unadulterated or in various logaoedic mixtures with iambic or trochaic patterns. She had used such combinations before, to be sure (in 'On a Red Steed,' for example, and in *Craft*), but the sheer prevalence of such meters in *After Russia* is what gives the poems of this collection an unprecedented sonority. Here is the beginning of one of these poems, in which the first two stanzas are choriambic, while the third and the subsequent ones are in lines in which an iambic foot is added to the initial choriamb:

> Pomni zakon:
> Zdes' ne vladei!
> Chtoby potom –
> V Grade Druzei:
>
> V ètom pustom,
> V ètom krutom
> Nebe muzhskom
> – Splosh' zolotom –
>
> V mire, gde reki vspiat'
> Na beregu – reki,
> V mnimuiu ruku vziat'
> Mnimost' drugoi ruki . . .
>
> Remember the law:
> Own nothing here!
> So that you later,
> In the City of Friends:
>
> In that empty,
> In that steep
> Masculine heaven
> – Totally golden –
>
> In a world where rivers flow backward,
> On a river's bank,
> [May] take into an imaginary hand
> The illusory hand of another . . .

These choriamb-based logaoedic metrical patterns may lend the poem an energetic lilt, as in the example just cited. But in longer, more complex lines they can also produce the effect of slowness and lassitude. Here is one such instance, cited only in a two-stanza excerpt:

Lety slepotekushchii vskhlip.
Dolg tvoi tebe otpushchen; slit
S Letoiu, – ele-ele zhiv
V lepete srebrotekushchikh iv.

Ivovyi srebroleteiskii plesk
Plachushchii . . . V slepotekushchii sklep
Pamiatei – peretomilas' – spriach'
V ivovyi srebroleteiskii plach.

The blindly-flowing sob of Lethe.
Your debt is forgiven you: merged
With Lethe – barely, barely alive
In the murmuring of silvery-flowing willows.

Willowy, silvery-Lethean splashes,
Weeping . . . Hide it in the blindly-flowing tomb
Of memories (– you are exhausted –),
In willowy, silvery-Lethean weeping.

The neologistic compound adjectives (*slepotekushchii*, 'blindly flowing' and *srebroleteiskii*, 'silvery-Lethean') go back to the practice of Russian eighteenth-century poets, such as Trediakovsky, and they lend the text a quality of timeless universality.

The poems of *After Russia* are rich and rewarding when read on their own, without commentary. But the publication of Tsvetaeva's correspondence in recent years has revealed the hidden themes and addressees of this volume. Much of the book is about the poet's feelings about the four men to whom she was drawn during the years when these poems were written and about the impossibility of a desired, lasting union with any of them. The main protagonist of *After Russia* (how much better the original title *Secret Intentions* would have described this aspect of the book!) is Boris Pasternak, by virtue of both the sheer number of poems addressed to him and the intensity of the emotions he aroused in the poet. His three supporting players are Abram Vishniak, Alexander Bakhrakh and Konstantin Rodzevich, who all proved in one way or another unworthy of the expectations vested in them, but who inspired magnificent poems during their span in Tsvetaeva's orbit.

After Russia is a book in which Tsvetaeva found a new way of

looking at life and art, evolved a successful personal idiom in which
to express this view, and did so in a poetry of unique metrical
freshness and verbal beauty. It is now getting to be more and more
generally recognized that this is the most mature and perfect of her
collections. Yet, at the time of its publication it was noticed by very
few critics. Mark Slonim was the only émigré commentator to give
the collection his unreserved praise. Vladislav Khodasevich, who
had earlier written of Tsvetaeva's poetry with understanding and
sympathy (and would do so again in the future), this time chided
Tsvetaeva for constantly changing her style and wrote that much of
the volume consisted of raw, unformed poetic material that
required further work. Vladimir Mayakovsky, to whom Tsvetaeva
presented a copy of this volume during his 1928 Paris visit (of which
more presently), thought so little of it that he left it at the apartment
of his hostess, Elsa Triolet. *After Russia* had some fervent admirers
in the émigré community, among them the noted Dostoevsky
scholar Alfred Bem and the writer of humorous and topical verse
Don Aminado (the pen name of Aminad Shpoliansky). But the
antagonizing of the liberal press through Sergei Efron's Eurasianist
activities; the publication in *Freedom of Russia* of a series of
Tsvetaeva's long poems ('From the Seacoast,' 'Essay of a Room,'
'New Year's Greetings'), which readers, unaware of Tsvetaeva's
relationships with Pasternak and Rilke reflected in these poems,
found incomprehensible; and the appearance of *Phaedra* the same
year as *After Russia* all conspired to create the impression that
Tsvetaeva the poet had entered a period of decline. The book that
by rights should have secured her her greatest triumph sank with
very few ripples. One could still see copies of the original edition of
After Russia gathering dust on the shelves of back rooms of Russian
bookstores in Paris and New York as late as the 1950s.

The year 1928 was to bring Tsvetaeva several other major dis-
appointments, though there were also consolations. In March, she
entered into correspondence with the wife of Ivan Bunin, Vera. The
two women soon realized that they had had encounters earlier in
life, when Tsvetaeva was a little girl and the teenaged Bunina,
whose maiden name was Muromtseva, was a classmate of Valeria
Tsvetaeva, Marina's estranged half-sister. Bunina had also known
Nadia Ilovaiskaya, with whom the young Marina had been infatuated in Italy during her family's stay in Nervi. The warm and

intimate correspondence between Tsvetaeva and Bunina continued for the rest of Tsvetaeva's emigration. Their shared reminiscences brought into existence several of Tsvetaeva's memoirs of the 1930s: 'The House Near Old St Pimen's Church' and 'Inauguration of the Museum.' Tsvetaeva had difficulties getting these two memoirs published in Paris, the first one because its protagonist, the reactionary historian Ilovaisky, was seen as an odious figure by most émigrés, and the second because its admiring portrayal of Nicholas II and his daughters was distasteful to Tsvetaeva's CD and SR editors. Mindful of her famous husband's abiding dislike for Tsvetaeva, Vera Bunina corresponded with her behind his back and received her mostly when he was not home. Tsvetaeva wrote to Bunina that she especially valued their relationship because it was a friendship 'above and beyond all sorts of Eurasianism and monarchism, beyond old or new poetry – all this nonsensical and superficial strife.'

In the spring of 1928, Tsvetaeva acquired a poetic disciple. In a letter to Tesková of April 10, 1928, she described a long hike to Versailles: 'My hiking companion is a thoroughbred eighteen-year-old puppy. He teaches me everything he learned at the *gimnasia* (which is a lot!), while I teach him everything that goes into my notebook.' This was Nikolai Gronsky, a budding poet. His father was a well-known political figure and a member of the editorial board of *The Latest News*, his mother a sculptress. Much to the indignation of her daughter (who was only two years younger than Gronsky), Tsvetaeva formed what she later called a 'military friendship in the royal forest' with the young poet. That summer, while she was at the seaside resort Pontaillac (near Royan), they carried on an intensive correspondence. In August she wrote to Gronsky: 'About your verse. You still nourish yourself with the external world (a tribute to your sex: men are in general more external than women), whereas a poet's nourishment is: (1) the internal world; (2) the external world filtered through the internal. You still do not dip the visible into yourself, you record it as it is. This is why your verse is superficial. *Your verse is younger than you.* To grow to your own size and then to outgrow it – such is the poet's gambit.'

Gronsky was to join Tsvetaeva in Pontaillac in September. But just as he was about to leave Paris he learned that the marriage of his parents was breaking up. He cancelled the trip, hoping to help salvage their relationship. Tsvetaeva's despairing letter to Tesková of September 9, 1928 about his failure to arrive indicates that she had a deeper attachment for Gronsky than that of a poetic master to a pupil. As she had foreseen, he soon drifted away from her – to his studies of law and Russian literature, to mountain climbing, to a young woman his own age to whom he re-dedicated several love poems that he had originally addressed to Tsvetaeva. But during their brief association, the young student became a true poet. His earliest poetry shows the impact of Tsvetaeva's most clearly. He later blended that early style in an organic way with other influences, the odic manner of Lomonosov and the mystical manner of Blok, to form a fresh amalgam. Nikolai Gronsky was killed in a subway accident in 1934, at the age of twenty-five. Early death prevented him from becoming the major figure he might have been. Tsvetaeva did not see him in the last years of his life. After his death, she dedicated a five-poem cycle 'The Epitaph' ('Nadgrobie') to his memory and wrote two essays about his life and poetry.

In Paris, in the spring of 1928, Tsvetaeva witnessed the death of a young Russian who had been a soldier in the White Army during the civil war. He died of intestinal tuberculosis at the age of twenty-eight and just before his death he had a dream of being chased by a red bull-calf. This incident gave rise to Tsvetaeva's poem 'The Red Bull-Calf' ('Krasnyi bychok'), in which the image in the title grows into a symbol of the October Revolution as the unleashing of blind, unthinking animal violence. That summer in Pontaillac, Tsvetaeva remembered her self-appointed role as 'the chronicler of the White Army' and began writing a narrative poem about the civil war. She called it 'Perekop,' the name of the isthmus that connects the Crimea to the mainland. This was the last area held by the White Army and the crossing of Perekop by the Red Army marked the end of the civil war in the south of Russia. The poem was based on Sergei Efron's wartime diaries, which however were no longer available to her by the early part of 1929 because by then Sergei's views had evolved to the point where he no longer wanted his part in the civil war commemorated in his wife's poetry.

Deprived of her source, Tsvetaeva sought out other witnesses of the battle at Perekop, but they were not interested in talking to her. The poem thus does not show the crossing of the isthmus by Soviet troops. The completed portion was summarized by Tsvetaeva in a newspaper interview of 1931: 'The *poèma* is about the hundred-day siege of Perekop. Life at the fort, fortification work, an air raid, a visit by Wrangel [General Peter Wrangel, the commander of the southern White Army], and finally, the celebrated breakthrough, when at night they said the mass, turned out the lights and entered Russia. Some Latvians were drowned. At this point I ended, but what I wanted to show was the very end of Perekop, the last two or three days, the end of everything.' Tsvetaeva had neither the temperament, nor the knowledge to be a military historian in verse. Compared to 'Poem of the End' and 'Poem of the Staircase,' her civil war epic makes turgid reading. She kept for years trying to place it in various émigré publications, even going to the extent of offering it to a monarchist, right-wing journal, but it was turned down. 'No one will take "Perekop",' she wrote to Tesková. 'Its form is too radical for the right wing and its content is too rightist for the left.' And to Lomonosova: 'For the monarchists, "Perekop" is incomprehensible verbally, for the SRs it is unacceptable inwardly.' She recited this poem at several of her public readings, but its publication had to wait until after her death.

But if 'Perekop' was universally rejected, Tsvetaeva had slightly better luck with another work that dealt with the civil war, the then-unpublished collection *The Demesne of the Swans*. After featuring her poetry regularly and prominently that summer and fall, the largest Russian daily in Paris, the moderate-liberal *The Latest News*, began in October 1928 what looked like a serialization of *The Demesne of the Swans*. The paper did not print, it is true, any of the poems which eulogize the tsar or glorify the monarchist White Army. But Tsvetaeva had read such poems at her recitals and the political orientation of this particular collection was no secret in the literary community. It must, therefore, have been a gesture of singular good will toward Tsvetaeva on the part of the editor-in-chief Pavel Miliukov to run in three consecutive weekend issues poems from this avowedly monarchist volume in his resolutely anti-monarchist paper.

Then, at the end of October, Vladimir Mayakovsky, the staunchest supporter of the Soviet regime among the major Russian poets, came to Paris. Tsvetaeva knew that Mayakovsky had repeatedly denounced her in the Soviet press. This apparently did not diminish her admiration for him as a poet. She inscribed a copy of *After Russia* with a paraphrase from one of his own poems, 'City,'

('To one as fleetfooted as myself'), and presented it to him, possibly at his public reading at Café Voltaire on November 7. (As
already mentioned, Mayakovsky left this book in Paris.) About
two weeks later, Tsvetaeva published in her husband's newspaper
Eurasia an open letter to Mayakovsky. In it she recalled their
meeting on the eve of her departure from Russia, when he told her
that his message for the West was: 'That truth is over here.' She
went on to say that when someone asked her about her reaction to
Mayakovsky's recital, her reply was: 'That strength is over there.'
Strength of the new Soviet state was, of course, precisely what the
Eurasians, in whose organ this statement appeared, admired most
of all. But for Tsvetaeva, we can safely assume, strength meant the
strength of the new poetry then being written in the Soviet Union
by Mayakovsky, Pasternak, and several of the younger poets she
liked, the kind of strength that she badly missed in the work of both
the older and the younger Russian poets resident abroad.

A part of the Russian press in Paris chose to read her open letter
to Mayakovsky as an endorsement of the entire Soviet system. No
further poems from *The Demesne of the Swans* appeared in *The
Latest News* and for the next two years Tsvetaeva's work was
barred from that newspaper. On December 3, she wrote to Mayakovsky an indignant letter, expressing her outrage that Miliukov
refused to publish any more of her poetry because of her declara-
tion in *Eurasia*. The letter makes ironic reading when one realizes
that Tsvetaeva is complaining about the discontinuance of further
printings of her poems to Mayakovsky, who would have immediately censured and denounced them as treasonable. The end of the
letter reads: 'You can now appreciate the explosive power of your
name and communicate the above episode to Pasternak and to
anyone else you see fit. You may also publish it. Goodbye! I love
you. Marina Tsvetaeva.' But her love was not reciprocated. Less
than a year after the Paris encounter, Mayakovsky took part in the
polemics at the Congress of the Russian Association of Proletarian
Writers. When a Marxist critic stated that Tsvetaeva's artistic
achievement was of considerable value and could be used for
teaching, Mayakovsky responded by lumping Tsvetaeva with
Gumiliov (shot in 1921) as being equally counter-revolutionary.
He then summed up his attitude to her poetry with the statement:
'And I consider that a work directed against the Soviet Union,
against us, has no right to exist and it is our task to show it up as

maximally repulsive and not make use of it for teaching anything to anyone.'

The social circle of Marina Tsvetaeva at the end of the 1920s consisted primarily of people connected to the Eurasian movement: Sergei's fellow editors of *Mileposts*, Mirsky and Suvchinsky; the philosophers and theologians who published their work in that journal, such as Karsavin, Berdiaev and Georgy Fedotov (who left the Soviet Union in 1925 and became a contributor to Eurasian publications) and their wives; and people who were friends of Eurasians, among them the composer Sergei Prokofiev and his Spanish-born wife Lina. What had attracted so many acute minds to Eurasianism was its claim that under Bolshevik rule Russia was moving toward a harmonious co-existence between the European and Asian peoples which inhabit its territory, united by a strong, autocratic government similar to that of the medieval Mongol rulers (whom the Eurasians tended to view through rose-tinted glasses). Their insistence on nationalism and on rule by an autocratic elite and their idealization of the Middle Ages left the Eurasians in an isolated position in the mostly liberal community of Russian exiles. Assuming that many of their beliefs and goals coincided with those of the Soviet government, the Eurasians sought a rapprochement with it, hoping to influence its policies and to spread their teachings in the home country. On July 31, 1927, Marina Tsvetaeva wrote to Lev Shestov: 'There has been a series of Eurasian (secret) departures for Russia. Recently, we saw off a wonderful young man for whom I felt both sorry and happy.' What Tsvetaeva and many of the Eurasians did not know was that those 'secret departures' took place with full knowledge of the Soviet security agencies. The latter had infiltrated Eurasianism, as they did several other émigré organizations, going to the extent of staging a supposedly clandestine congress in the Soviet Union to which exiled Eurasians traveled, as they thought, 'illegally,' so as to meet their Soviet counterparts – who were in reality agents of the GPU (the acronym for 'State Political Administration,' the name that was given to the former Cheka in 1922).

With Eurasian publications sounding more and more like Soviet propaganda, most of its leaders abandoned the movement by the end of the 1920s. Piotr Suvchinsky moved on to musicology. Georgy Fedotov and Fr Georgy Florovsky became prominent theologians.

Prince Nikolai Trubetskoy, the famed linguist, founded the Linguistic Circle of Prague and Georgy (or George) Vernadsky went on to his career as a noted American historian who fruitfully applied Eurasianist concepts to the study of the Russian Middle Ages. The alarm about the Soviet infiltration of Eurasianism was sounded in Paris by Professor Nikolai Alexeiev, one of the movement's founders, about whose lectures Tsvetaeva had written with approval to Salomea Halpern and with whom she had associated during her stay at Pontaillac in 1928. 'The Eurasians are having a schism,' Tsvetaeva wrote to Tesková on January 22, 1929. 'Professor Alexeiev and others are asserting that Sergei is an agent of the Cheka and a communist. Should I run into him I am afraid of what I might do. Professor Alexeiev [...] is a scoundrel, please believe me, I wouldn't say this for nothing. I am personally glad that he is leaving, but I suffer on account of Sergei, with his purity and his ardent heart. Apart from two or three others, he is the only *moral strength of Eurasianism*. Please believe me. This is what they call him, "the Conscience of Eurasianism," and Professor Karsavin has called him "the golden child of Eurasianism." '

The reiteration of the phrase 'please believe me' suggests that it took Tsvetaeva some effort to maintain her idealized view of her 'golden child's' chivalrous character. It was early in 1929 that he took away from her his diaries so as to prevent her from completing 'Perekop.' With the departure from the Eurasian movement of its founders and of its most distinguished adherents, those who remained rapidly moved to unreservedly pro-Soviet positions. This was the case with Mirsky, Sergei Efron and also with Konstantin Rodzevich. In his autobiographical *roman à clef*, *Expectation* (*Ozhidanie*), Vladimir Varshavsky outlined the process of this political evolution in an episodic character who is unmistakably a portrait of Sergei Efron: 'I became a Eurasian. I was converted by a former White officer who was later a student. Tall, with huge Byzantine eyes, this uncommon man was of half-Jewish origin. His whole life was selfless service to the cause of Russia and Truth. With the same readiness for heroism and death with which he had once enlisted in the White Army he now served Eurasianism. I did not quite understand the Eurasian teachings, but when he told me that the Eurasians wanted to build everything on Christianity, I believed him at once. I believed that Eurasianism stands for that highest Truth to which Russia has always aspired. Later on, this man was converted to Bolshevism. When someone asked him what had happened to his Christianity, he replied that communism was also a religion. Having accepted this faith, he stopped reasoning and in the name of the one true teaching was ready to sacrifice his life and the lives of others.'

Varshavsky's portrait can be enhanced by the following brief sketch written by Salomea Halpern: 'Sergei was a very good, unintelligent and kind man, an enthusiast, an idealist (whether Eurasianist or communist), utterly sincere and extremely naive. This, it seems to me, exhausts the subject.' Various published writings of Sergei Efron indicate that the growth of his pro-Soviet sympathies was gradual, paralleling roughly the rise of Joseph Stalin and his assumption of total control over the country. The decisive year for Efron, as for Mirsky and thousands of intellectuals in Western countries, was 1929. That was the year of the Great Depression, which made millions believe that the days of capitalism were numbered and that Western societies were about to disintegrate. Like Tsvetaeva, Efron got to observe and to experience in the West the kind of conditions to which neither of them had ever been exposed before the Revolution: the oppressive poverty of the industrial suburbs of Prague and Paris (of which Tsvetaeva wrote in 'Poem of the Staircase' and in several telling poems in *After Russia*) and the humiliating treatment of stateless Russians by the French bureaucracy. Much was written in the Western press in 1929 about the misery and unemployment brought about by the depression. Very little was said about the fundamental alteration in Soviet society which Stalin felt secure enough to initiate at the end of that year. This was the collectivization of agriculture, which some recent historians see as a cataclysm of even greater magnitude than the October Revolution itself.

When the Bolshevik leaders seized power in October of 1917, they were confident that within a few short years they would achieve a utopia: a classless society enjoying the greatest prosperity in human history. But the first four years of their rule resulted in terror, a prolonged fratricidal war and an appalling famine. The tactical withdrawal to the New Economic Policy and the permission for the farming population to sell their produce on the free market and to make profits was felt by some Bolshevik leaders, such as Alexandra Kollontai, to be a humiliating defeat. A few days after his fiftieth birthday (December 21, 1929), Stalin proclaimed that the

NEP was over, that all agriculture would be collectivized and that there was a class of people in the country called the 'kulaks' who were to be liquidated as the last obstacle on the road to the Socialist utopia. In old Russia, a kulak was a village profiteer, a peasant who enriched himself by grabbing the land and cattle of his neighbours by any means, fair or foul. Now, during the collectivization, any moderately prosperous farmer who so much as employed one or two hired hands or owned a few head of cattle was branded a kulak – an enemy of the people – and sentenced to extermination together with his family and homestead.

From the very beginning, Soviet leaders formed the habit of blaming the failure of their policies on a series of scapegoats, whom the country was incited to hate and to punish. The illegal sellers of bread and grain during the civil war (*meshochniki*), who had actually saved the urban population from the famine, were blamed for causing it. Socialist Revolutionaries, clergymen, foreign and Russian technical experts, bacteriologists, food distribution administrators and a few others were periodically convicted at show trials and shot or sentenced to hard labor throughout the 1920s in order to explain to the population why things were not getting better. With the expropriation of the kulaks, millions of innocent people were stigmatized, deprived of their homes and either resettled forcibly in uninhabitable regions of the frozen north or sent to labor camps. It was one of the great holocausts of this century. Between five and nine million people lost their lives in the deportations and the unprecedented famine of 1929 to 1933.

Yet it was that year 1929, the year that plunged Russia into the worst nightmare it had ever experienced, that marked the turning of uncounted European and American intellectuals toward the Soviet Union as mankind's best hope of achieving a just and prosperous society. Many simply succumbed to the optimism of Marxian rhetoric, without trying to understand what was actually happening in Russia. But it was surely no accident that some of the most vocal boosters of the Soviet system in the West, such as Lincoln Steffens (one of the first to proclaim that Soviet Russia was 'the future' which 'worked'), George Bernard Shaw and Theodore Dreiser, were also most enthusiastic about Mussolini and Hitler during the 1920s. Their rationale was that *anything* was bound to be better than the hated bourgeoisie with its capitalism. Ignoring the post-collectivization famine of the early 1930s and the proliferating concentration camps in Stalin's Russia assumed the proportions of a mass hypnosis in the West, to which even a few exiled Russians succumbed. People who had fled from the Soviet Union when it was ruled by Lenin and Trotsky were now unaccountably drawn to the even more brutal Russia of Stalin. Marina Tsvetaeva provided a shrewd analysis of how this worked when she wrote of her husband in her letter to Tesková of October 16, 1932: 'Sergei is entirely immersed in the Soviet Russia, he sees nothing except it and in it he sees only what he wants to see.'

Early in 1929, Mark Slonim introduced Tsvetaeva to the famed painter and stage designer Natalia Goncharova, with whom he was on friendly terms. As had been the case with Vera Bunina, Tsvetaeva discovered that she had common roots with Goncharova, since the two had once attended the same school in Moscow (the painter a few grades higher than the poet) and their families had been neighbours. Always anxious for new contributions by Tsvetaeva for *Freedom of Russia*, Slonim suggested that she write a study of Goncharova and her art. The result was Tsvetaeva's longest prose piece, a rambling essay of some 60 pages that had to be serialized in three issues of the journal. It was a rare effort to break out of the poetic universe in which she was at home and which consisted of life as *she* saw it, of people she knew, and of literature, history and philosophy filtered through her personal vision. As she remembered in 'Story of a Dedication,' she was challenged in 1917 by a soldier to try writing not from her own point of view but from that of a soldier or a peasant. Tsvetaeva later conceded that the soldier's suggestion was a valid one, but at the time of her conversation with him she rejected it, seeing it as a form of social command. 'There is nothing wrong with social,' she went on, 'and nothing wrong with command. What *is* wrong with social command is that it is always a *direct order*.'

The essay 'Natalia Goncharova,' like the poem 'Perekop,' is Tsvetaeva's attempt at writing about things she knew little about and did not really love. In the poem she stuck grimly with the subject, but in the essay she provided herself with escape hatches. While she was writing this essay, she also read Vikenty Veresaev's compilation of biographical materials about Pushkin, whose wife was also named Natalia Goncharova and was remotely related to the painter. The near-sighted poet did not really care for the visual arts, but she loved and understood Pushkin. So, writing about the painter Goncharova, whom she personally liked and admired and of the importance of whose work she was aware, Tsvetaeva could not sustain her main subject for more than a few pages at a time. On the slightest pretext and sometimes without one, she launches into digressions on every imaginable subject: Paris and its buildings, her own childhood, the nature of the creative process, the importance of the machine in modern life, the origins of her poem 'The Pied Piper,' her acquaintance with the poet Tikhon Churilin, but most of all Pushkin and his marriage and death. The painter of the title is repeatedly upstaged by her long-dead namesake because a poet's life (and wife) interested Tsvetaeva far more than any painter, even the one she undertook to portray. 'Natalia Goncharova' is full of Tsvetaeva's fascinating pronouncements, but regarded as a monograph on a painter it is without any doubt a failure. But it must have served the poet as some kind of an object lesson, because in her subsequent prose essays Tsvetaeva wrote only of people and things she knew and understood and she organized her material into coherent patterns – something that she had always done masterfully in her poetry, but learned to do in prose only in the early 1930s.

The last ten years in Paris

In some of her poetry written during the civil war (e.g., 'On a Red Steed'), Marina Tsvetaeva had already begun to reject this world, the conditions of human existence on earth, in favour of a more perfect reality which she was sure must exist elsewhere and which could be glimpsed in dreams and intuited in poetry. The strife and misery she had witnessed during War Communism, the life cluttered with endless petty and distasteful chores that she had to endure in emigration intensified this attitude. In the summer of 1926, at the height of her triple correspondence with Pasternak and Rilke, Tsvetaeva wrote to the young writer Bronislav Sosinsky: 'Indignation – that's what's growing in me year by year, day by day, hour by hour. Indignation. Contempt. An avalanche of hurt that began in childhood. It's unjust. It's unreasonable. It's ungodly. This is the intonation of Blok's line: "Is this how it was fated to be between people?"'

Here is the source of the persistent theme of escape into other, better realities that we find in such long poems as 'The Swain' and 'The Pied Piper.' On January 1, 1927, writing to Pasternak about Rilke's death, Tsvetaeva expressed her doubts about their earlier plans to meet Rilke, because it would have to be in 'this world' rather than in another one which she knew and loved 'through dreams, through the air of those dreams, through that sense of liberation and basic need.' This outlook formed the background for the series of long poems about dream encounters and fusion with another person inspired by her correspondence during the summer of 1926 with Rilke and Pasternak ('From the Seacoast,' 'Essay of a Room' and 'New Year's Greetings'). The culmination of this series was 'Poem of the Air' ('Poèma vozdukha'), written 'in the days of Lindbergh,' i.e., in May 1927, and published in *Freedom of Russia* early in 1930. In her perceptive dissertation about the significance of the four elements in Tsvetaeva's poetry, Ieva Vitins wrote that air, as the 'most dynamic and least physical of the elements,' was

Tsvetaeva's preferred substance, for in it her poetry could 'transcend the limits of ordinary space and time in order to communicate with her addressee.'

Just as the back staircase in 'Poem of the Staircase' was made to represent the worst aspects of civilization, the historic solo flight of Charles Lindbergh represents in 'Poem of the Air' all that is best and purest in the human condition. The poem is a set of variations, with the physical and acoustical properties of air as its basic metaphor, on the themes of the ideal conditions of freedom for the poet and of the unity and harmony with another human being for which all persons yearn. The subject, to quote Ieva Vitins again, is Tsvetaeva's 'dislike of physicality, immobility, the horizontal axis, confines and limits,' with the air providing an upward escape, analogous to the escapes afforded in other long poems by Tsvetaeva by water ('The Pied Piper,' 'Essay of a Room') and, especially, fire ('On a Red Steed,' 'The Swain,' and 'Poem of the Staircase'). Together with 'Sidestreets,' 'Poem of the Air' is Tsvetaeva's most arcane and impenetrable long poem, and a key in the folk poem which has enabled us to unlock 'Sidestreets' is in this case missing.

Tsvetaeva greatly admired the motto of the Duc de Rohan 'ne daigne' and frequently cited it as her own. 'Essay of a Room' and 'Poem of the Air,' beautiful poems though they may be, showed her lack of concern for what her émigré readers could be expected to grasp without some notes or commentary. The long poem on which she worked from 1929 to 1936, the subject of which was the assassination of Nicholas II and his family by the Bolsheviks, epitomizes Tsvetaeva's disdain for what was or was not acceptable for the editors of the liberal émigré periodicals which were her only publishing outlets. 'Damn them to hell, all those Miliukovs, Rudnevs and Vishniaks, past, present and future, with their VILE political yardstick!' Tsvetaeva wrote on September 12, 1933 to Vera Bunina about the editors of *The Latest News* and *Contemporary Annals*, for whom her sympathy for the White Army, the tsar and Dmitry Ilovaisky was too reactionary and her involvement with Mayakovsky and the Eurasians appeared pro-Soviet. Her failure to place 'Perekop' with any émigré publication did not discourage Tsvetaeva from embarking on this new project, which she had no real hope of ever publishing. 'It will be an enormous amount of work, a mountain, which gives me joy,' Tsvetaeva wrote to Lomonosova on February 1, 1930. 'No one needs it. Here, they won't get it because of the "leftishness" (of its "form" – I'm using quotation marks because these are vile words), over there they will simply not get it physically, even more – less – so than all of my books. Am I doing this for posterity? No. For clearing my conscience. And also from the awareness of the strength of my love and, if you like, of my gift. Of those who care, I alone am able to do it. Therefore I must.'

The title of this poem is assumed to have been 'Poem of the Tsar's Family.' Only one section from it has been published, a chapter bearing the title 'Siberia' ('Sibir''), which describes the history of the city of Tobolsk, the place where the imperial family was deported. Tsvetaeva prepared for writing this poem by studying historical sources and interviewing some people who knew the victims. She recited completed portions of the poem at homes of friends (Mark Slonim and Elena Izvolskaya recalled two such readings in their memoirs) and discussed it in a newspaper interview and in some of her letters. But she was never able to publish this poem anywhere and its text has apparently been lost. The 1934 edition of the Great Soviet Encyclopedia denounced Tsvetaeva for 'glorifying the Romanov family, while her manner of writing verse had degenerated into naked rhythmic formalism.'

With the onset of the 1930s, there came a quantitative shift in the genres practiced by Tsvetaeva. After the disastrous critical reception of *Phaedra*, she abandoned dramatic form for good. 'Poem of the Tsar's Family' was her last big narrative poem (two other brief narrative poems she undertook in the mid-1930s were left unfinished). There was also a drastic reduction in the number of short lyric poems. Throughout the second and the third decades of the century, Tsvetaeva produced short poems, either individual ones or in cycles, on a steady basis. From the end of the 1920s, their number dwindled. In the 1930s she wrote a cycle of poems only once every few years, usually under the inspiration of a particular event or relationship.

A highly memorable cycle was brought about by the suicide of Vladimir Mayakovsky in the spring of 1930. In the aftermath of that suicide, the Russian artistic community in Paris found itself bitterly divided over an obituary of Mayakovsky, disparaging and contemptuous in tone, written by the Russian critic of literature and ballet Andrei Levinson and published in the French newspaper *Les Nouvelles littéraires*. Almost every well-known Russian writer or painter in Paris signed either the protest that defended Mayakovsky against Levinson's treatment or the 'counter-protest' that heaped further abuse on the late poet.

Tsvetaeva, as might have been expected, did not attach her signature to either of these two declarations. Instead, she expressed her feelings about Mayakovsky and his suicide in a magnificent cycle of seven poems 'To Mayakovsky' ('Maiakovskomu'), written in August of 1930. In it, among the laments and eulogies, Tsvetaeva vented her contempt for both the Soviet and émigré press for viewing the death of a great poet solely from the political and propagandistic angle. The sixth poem of the cycle, which is probably the high point of Tsvetaeva's political poetry, depicts an imaginary conversation in the Kingdom of Heaven between the two suicide poets, Esenin and Mayakovsky. True to Tsvetaeva's vision of poets as perpetual rebels, Esenin and Mayakovsky agree at the end of the poem to blow up paradise with a hand grenade. The cycle marks the appearance of a new, deliberately harsh diction in Tsvetaeva's poetry and ushers in the trend toward political invective, which became prominent in her poetry of the 1930s. Passages from the Mayakovsky cycle have been cited by Soviet commentators, such as Anna Saakiants, but the complete text, because of Tsvetaeva's 'a-plague-on-both-your-houses' attitude, has not yet been published in the Soviet Union.

As if in compensation for the reduced output of her poetry, Tsvetaeva's prose of the 1930s grew both in quantity and quality. She considered the writing of prose to be subsidiary to her principal activity, writing poetry, but practical necessities compelled her to devote more and more time to prose. Many of her prose pieces of the 1930s were initially written to be read at her annual public readings and later published in periodicals, which made them doubly profitable. 'About my prose,' Tsvetaeva wrote to Pasternak in the fall of 1935. 'Please understand that I write it to earn money, for reading aloud in a reinforcedly articulate, elucidatory manner. Verse for myself, prose for everyone else [vsekh], which rhymes with success [uspekh]. My courtesy does not allow me to stand and read to my last faithful few manifestly incomprehensible things – and for their own money.' But all these financial considerations did not prevent Tsvetaeva from writing memorable and highly individual prose which got better and better as the decade progressed.

Various hypotheses have been advanced to account for Tsvetaeva's reduced poetic production during her last decade in Paris. They range from the miseries of emigration and the effect of the oppressive life 'in the capitalist West' (Vsevolod Rozhdestvensky in his preface to the 1980 two-volume Moscow edition of Tsvetaeva) to the absence of firm Christian faith, which would have presumably safeguarded the poet's productivity (Nikita Struve). But surely a major factor must have been the poet's drowning in household chores, so amply documented in her correspondence, and the amount of time and care, excessive by any standard, that she chose to lavish on her growing son Mur (Georgy). As Irma Kudrova has written: 'Mur is a separate theme in Tsvetaeva's life and this theme is a tragic one.' From the beginning, his mother loved him more passionately than his older sister, though Ariadna was clearly the more talented, sensitive and original person of the two. As a baby, Mur was raised on a particularly rich and hard-to-prepare baby formula, which involved scorching flour in fresh butter and mixing the results with milk and water. A new batch of this had to be prepared for every feeding. Because in the pre-revolutionary Russia of Tsvetaeva's youth children of her circle were taken out on strolls by nannies and other retainers, Tsvetaeva spent long hours every afternoon promenading her son in the park. When the boy was four, she described him to Lomonosova as 'a little giant,' 'Siegfried,' 'Mussolini' and 'a future great beauty.' When Boris Pasternak, to please Tsvetaeva, characterized a photograph of Mur as 'your Napoleonid' (i.e., a descendant of Napoleon), this appellation was repeated in Tsvetaeva's letters for years.

Dmitry Sezeman, who knew Mur as a child and was one of the last people to see him alive in the USSR, described Tsvetaeva's love for her son in a conversation with me as irrational: 'the love of a female beast for her cub.' Mur's most casual and even inane remarks were reported in her letters as pearls of wisdom. Even the boy's gluttony (as when he ate eight large pancakes) and the fact that he was overweight and burst out of his clothes were found touching by his mother. She kept him out of school as long as she could so as to have him all to herself. When she yielded to the pressure of friends and enrolled Mur in a French school when he was nine, she insisted on walking him there and picking him up after school every day and doing all his homework together with him. Only very rarely do we see in Tsvetaeva's letters an intimation of what was clear to many others: that her 'exceptional' Mur was growing up to be a sullen, self-centered, and ill-mannered boy. Tsvetaeva's powerful maternal instinct, less manifest with regard to her daughters, had two main focal points in the 1930s: her husband and her son. It was her concern for these two people that eventually determined her fate.

Despite the strain put upon Tsvetaeva's relationship with the Paris Russian community by the *Mileposts* affair of 1926 and the Maya-kovsky incident of 1928, she continued being a prominent figure in that community, contributing to its publications and taking part in its literary activities. Thus, on April 26, 1930, she was one of the participants in 'An Evening of Romanticism,' which also featured Teffi, Georgy Adamovich, Prince Sergei Volkonsky, Vadim Andreyev, Georgy Ivanov, Nikolai Otsup and Boris Poplavsky. In fact, Nadezhda Teffi, whom Tsvetaeva detested when she first met her, calling her the personification of *poshlost'*, turned out to be most kind to her, helping with the subscriptions for *After Russia* and, in 1932, with arranging Tsvetaeva's poetry recital. Georgy Adamovich whom she had mauled badly in 'A Poet on Criticism' and who since that time often wrote of her work with undue harshness (alternating his critical statements with occasional praise), welcomed her as a contributor to a journal he co-edited, *Encounters* (*Vstrechi*), six issues of which were published in 1934. On March 31, 1933, Tsvetaeva wrote Adamovich a warm letter, inviting him to appear as a commentator at her lecture on Maya-kovsky and Pasternak.

Tsvetaeva's contacts with Vladislav Khodasevich, the only exiled poet of a magnitude comparable to hers and in many ways her polar opposite, underwent a complex evolution during her emigration. They both lived in Moscow before the Revolution and made their literary debuts at the same time. Tsvetaeva did not care for Kho-dasevich's poetry during the 1920s, though she recognized its value. Khodasevich's angry denunciation of *Mileposts* in 1926 and his adverse review of *Phaedra* in 1928 led to a period of complete estrangement of the two poets. But in the early 1930s, there came a period of closeness and mutual appreciation. This may have hap-pened in part because with the advent of the new decade both Tsvetaeva and Khodasevich felt themselves isolated from the new currents in émigré literature. At the end of the 1920s, there arose in Paris a younger generation of Russian poets and prose writers whom Vladimir Varshavsky had dubbed the Unnoticed Generation. The poets of this group were disciples of Adamovich and their writings sounded what was later called the Paris Note: metaphysical despair and existential boredom, which went hand in hand with a distrust of technical brilliance and a lack of concern with the verbal aspects of literary art. Tsvetaeva's innovative complexity and the neo-romantic precision of Khodasevich's verse were equally alien to the poets of the Paris Note.

The literary outlet of this younger group was the journal *Numbers (Chisla)*, eight thick volumes of which were published between 1930 and 1934. Tsvetaeva was only a peripheral contributor to *Numbers* and Khodasevich was not represented in it at all. Nonetheless, Tsvetaeva was invited to take part in the public poetry reading organized by *Numbers* in March 1933, where she appeared in the second half of the program, alongside such older poets as Balmont and Gippius; the first half of the program featured younger poets: Boris Poplavsky, Antonin Ladinsky, Lydia Chervinskaya and Dovid Knut. In this new atmosphere of the thirties, Khodasevich became the major critical champion of Tsvetaeva's poetry and, especially, her prose, of which he wrote frequently and with glowing praise in his literary column in the newspaper *Renascence*. Their correspondence of the 1930s reflects the warm friendship that arose between them in the course of that decade.

The friendship with Khodasevich was, however, not typical of Tsvetaeva's relationship with the émigré literary community. As she made clear in her 1932 essay 'The Poet and Time,' for all her disagreements with the October Revolution, she was gradually coming to regard her poetry as revolutionary in essence: 'I know that the proper audience for my White "Perekop" are not White officers – to whom, every time I read the poem, I want to tell it in prose – but Red students, who would have understood – who *will* understand – all of it [...]. Oh, if only politicians wouldn't stand between the poet and the people!' Chafing at the small size of the audience for her poetry in the emigration, Tsvetaeva idealized the mass audience she believed she had left in Russia. In line with this view was her idea that the literary art of the future was possible only in Russia ('If they would only let it have its say'), and that exiled Russian literature was bound to be backward and meaningless for

the new generations. In 'The Poet and Time' and in her letters of the
1930s, Tsvetaeva often returned to this notion, which had, of
course, already been asserted by Mirsky in his essays in *Mileposts*.

The general attitude towards Tsvetaeva of many Russian émigré
commentators in the 1930s was that an extremely gifted poet had
somehow wrecked her talent either by excessive imitation of Pasternak (although her mature style was fully formed before she ever got
involved with Pasternak's poetry) or by becoming incoherent and
incomprehensible. Tsvetaeva, for her part, took less and less interest in what went on in émigré literature. She overlooked the rise of
Vladimir Nabokov, whose novels had become by the early 1930s
one of the central phenomena of that literature. After reading in
1936 one of Nabokov's most brilliant stories, 'Spring in Fialta,'
Tsvetaeva wrote to Anatoly Steiger that it was the sort of thing that
no one needed, not even its author. The historical novels of Mark
Aldanov, hugely popular with émigré readers, were for her the work
of 'a gossipy *raisonneur*' and a 'little grave-digging worm.' She qualified Boris Poplavsky, the most significant and original of the
younger exiled poets, in a letter to Tesková as 'a poet of some talent
but a mixed-up, dissolute man.' When Poplavsky was poisoned by a
deranged friend and died at the age of thirty-three, Tsvetaeva felt
no regret, choosing to believe the rumors that the young poet had
actually died of an overdose of heroin.

In 1933, Ivan Bunin was awarded the Nobel Prize for literature.
This event was felt as a vindication of the entire Russian literature in
exile and caused a great jubilation not only among the Russians in
Paris, but in all the other centers of the Russian diaspora. Tsvetaeva
was prominent enough in the literary community to be invited to sit
on the stage during the ceremony that honored Bunin after he had
returned from Stockholm with his prize. On November 24, 1933,
she wrote to Tesková: 'On the 26th I am to sit on a platform and to
congratulate Bunin. To try to avoid it would be to protest. I make
no protest, I simply disagree.' Tsvetaeva believed that both Gorky
and Merezhkovsky were more important than Bunin and more
deserving of the Nobel Prize. She does not seem to have read
Bunin's *magnum opus*, the autobiographical novel *The Life of
Arseniev* (published in 1930, it must have been the direct pretext for
the Nobel Prize). Her sympathy for Gorky and his family, of whom
she had been fond since her childhood, in this case clouded
Tsvetaeva's artistic judgment. For all the historical importance of

Gorky or Merezhkovsky, as a literary artist Bunin was certainly head and shoulders above either of them.

Uncomfortable in the literary milieu of the exiled Russians, Tsvetaeva made several efforts in the early 1930s to break into the French literary world. While Tsvetaeva was writing her essay on Natalia Goncharova in 1929, the painter did a series of illustrations for Tsvetaeva's poem 'The Swain.' Goncharova later wanted to arrange for a translation of this poem into French with a view to publishing it with her illustrations. Tsvetaeva undertook the translation herself, which necessitated her learning, for the first time, the principles of French versification. Dissatisfied with the results, she decided to write a new French poem, 'Gars,' based on 'The Swain.' Brice Parrain, the editor of the journal *Nouvelle Revue Française* (he was married to a woman who had once been Tsvetaeva's classmate in Moscow), considered publishing 'Gars' but gave up the idea. The poem, which is in the Tsvetaeva archive in Moscow, remains unpublished and so does the English translation of 'The Swain,' which the poet and novelist Alec Brown did at Mirsky's instigation and which Tsvetaeva hoped would be published in England and America.

In 1929 and 1930, Tsvetaeva took part in Franco-Russian literary discussions organized by the journal *Cahiers de la quinzaine*, at which a number of prominent French and Russian figures appeared. In the subsequently published transcripts of those discussions, we can read Tsvetaeva's opinions on Marcel Proust and Paul Valéry, among other topics. 'Florentine Nights' ('Les Nuits florentines'), a French prose piece based on Tsvetaeva's letters to Abram Vishniak, was offered to several French journals in 1933, but no one published it despite the praises lavished on it by some of the editors. Tsvetaeva's French contacts included the prominent critic Charles Du Bos, a friend of Salomea Halpern (primarily a specialist in English literature, Du Bos also wrote brilliantly on Tolstoy and Chekhov); the critic and philosopher Alain (his real name was Émile Auguste Chartier and he was a regular contributor to Parrain's journal); and the poet and playwright Charles Vildrac, who was put in touch with Tsvetaeva by Pasternak after Vildrac visited him in Moscow. Tsvetaeva corresponded with Vildrac, attended parties at his home and was the beneficiary of his advice during her work on 'Gars.'

After the essay 'Letter to an Amazon' became known to Western Tsvetaeva scholars in the late 1970s, there were speculations about which of Tsvetaeva's French friends could have introduced her to Natalie Clifford Barney, to whom this essay is addressed. Serena Vitale, in her splendid introduction to her 1981 bilingual (French and Italian) edition of that essay, 'Retracing the Steps' ('Su tracce a rittroso'), has pursued every possible clue to establish when and how the two women could have met. The riddle was solved in 1985, with the appearance in English of the posthumously published auto-biography of Tsvetaeva's long-time friend and neighbour, Elena Izvolskaya. Daughter of a noted diplomat, Izvolskaya was a journal-ist and translator with wide-ranging contacts in the French and American literary communities of Paris. After World War II, she gained renown in the United States as Helene Iswolsky, a prominent participant in the Catholic-Orthodox ecumenical movement and the editor of the ecumenical journal *The Third Hour*.

It was Izvolskaya who arranged the invitation for Tsvetaeva to read the French version of her poem 'The Swain,' 'Gars,' at Natalie Clifford Barney's literary salon at 20 rue Jacob. The reading ended in a complete fiasco: the listeners had no idea of what it was Tsvetaeva was trying to do. In addition to the complexity of Tsvetaeva's style, the theme of the poem – a woman sacrificing herself, her mother and her child for the sake of a vampire she loves – could not have been very congenial to the predominantly lesbian audience. But the encounter with Barney herself moved Tsvetaeva to write the essay on which she worked for almost two years and which, as Serena Vitale has shown, is a reply to Barney's book *Pensées d'une Amazone*, 1920.

The very juxtaposition of the names of Marina Tsvetaeva and Natalie Clifford Barney is pregnant with endless ironies. A beauti-ful, accomplished heiress from Dayton, Ohio, Barney devoted her considerable fortune, her social graces and her modest writing talent to the promotion of one single cause: spiritual and physical love between women. She spent most of her long life (1876–1972) in Paris, where she could be free from American puritanical pre-judices, and she wrote her poetry and essays in French. She had well-publicized love affairs with some of the most attractive and talented women of her age, among them the famed courtesan Liane de Pougy, the poet Renée Vivien (pen name of the Englishwoman Pauline Tarn) and the painter Romaine Brooks, whose liaison with Barney endured for over half a century. Barney served as a model for lesbian characters in almost every novel of the first three decades of this century that dealt with the subject, including Radclyffe Hall's famous *The Well of Loneliness*, where she appears as Valerie Seymour. Her salon, one of the most elegant in Paris, mingled writers and artists, international aristocracy, and beautiful women of every sexual persuasion. To appear at Barney's Friday afternoon gatherings, duchesses and film stars ordered gowns from the most expensive couturiers of the day. It boggles the mind to imagine Tsvetaeva – impoverished, shabbily dressed and totally unknown except to Russians – at one of those gatherings.

The nickname Amazon was given to Barney by her great admirer, the French writer Remy de Gourmont, who addressed her thus in a series of essays which were eventually published as a book, *Lettres à l'Amazone* (when Tsvetaeva used the same title, she may not have been aware of Gourmont's book). Barney appropriated the nickname, staking a further claim to it in the title of her book *Pensées d'une Amazone*, an eloquent defense of the right of women to love women and of men to love men. This was the book which Tsvetaeva read and to which she responded in her essay written in French. As Serena Vitale has pointed out, the image of an Amazon, perceived as a strong, independent woman, unencumbered by domestic duties, had attracted Tsvetaeva since some of her earliest poems. We do not know of any lesbian involvements during the period of her emigration comparable in importance to her earlier affairs with the two Sophias, Parnok and Holliday. But it is clear that she went on being attracted to women. In *Craft*, there is a brief poem about women's breasts, dated November 22, 1921, which concludes with an evocation of the Amazons:

> A playground of disdained and disdainful
> Pleasures, a woman's breast! A penetrable
> Armor. It's of them I'm thinking,
> Of those single-breasted ones, those women friends.

Nina Berberova's account of Tsvetaeva in her book *The Italics Are Mine* includes a description of an unmistakable lesbian pass which Berberova turned down. A friend of Tsvetaeva's told me of a fling in Prague, which Tsvetaeva supposedly had with a married Russian woman, who much later did a great deal to revive the interest in her poetry. On February 20, 1931, Tsvetaeva wrote to Raisa Lomonosova about her great longing for a loving relationship with a woman friend. The letter to Salomea Halpern of August 12, 1932, published in full in the West and in truncated form in the Soviet Union, records in detail a dream Tsvetaeva had of being passionately in love with Halpern in a vaguely neo-classical Greek setting. This sudden, wild outpouring, after seven years of Halpern's steady friendship and financial aid, may have been prompted by reading Barney or visiting her salon. In their efforts to justify lesbianism, Barney and other women of her circle often reached back to the classical precedents of the Amazons and of Sappho and her followers.

It can thus be seen how an encounter with Barney and her ideas could have touched a raw nerve in Tsvetaeva. The result was 'Letter to an Amazon' ('Lettre à l'Amazone'), written in November and December of 1932 and revised at the end of 1934. Part essay, part story, it sets forth Tsvetaeva's idea of lesbian love on the basis of her own experiences in this area. It begins with a salute to Barney: 'you are close to me like any unique being and, above all, any unique female being.' But this is soon followed by a threat: 'Listen, you don't have to respond, you only have to hear me out. I am going to inflict a wound right in the heart of your cause, of your belief, of your body, of your heart.' The cause of lesbian love will always be defeated, according to Tsvetaeva, by an even more powerful cause: the maternal instinct.

As she sees it, love between two women is enormously beautiful and rewarding. God is not opposed to it. The Church and the State, which are, have no right to oppose any kind of love so long as they send thousands of young men to die in wars. But Nature, which insists on perpetuating the species, says no. The main body of the essay is a fictionalized account of what Tsvetaeva considers a typical lesbian affair. The couple, she believes, invariably consists of an experienced older woman and a younger woman whom she seduces. The two live in harmony and happiness until the maternal instinct awakens within the younger woman. It is not her need for a man that wrecks the lesbian love affair, but her need for a child. She will inevitably leave the older woman and seek out a man to fulfill her destiny. In the light of 'The Tale of Sonechka,' written a few years later, we can see that up to this point, Tsvetaeva was postulating the motivations that would explain why Sophia Holliday had walked out of her life. The narrative pursues the subsequent fate of these lesbian lovers: the younger one's contented life with her husband and child and the older one's search for other young women to replace her lost love. Eventually, many years later, the younger woman hears of the death of her former lover and reacts with indifference to the news. This, as Sophia Poliakova has pointed out in her book on Tsvetaeva and Parnok, must have been an echo of Tsvetaeva's own reaction when she heard of Parnok's death in 1933, one year before writing the final version of 'Letter to an Amazon.'

The relationship outlined in this essay is in no way a depiction of Tsvetaeva's concrete experiences with either Parnok or Holliday. But a great deal of her thinking and feeling about these two women went into what is, curiously, the only piece of totally fictional prose Tsvetaeva ever wrote. Written when Tsvetaeva was in the throes of her possessive and obsessive love for her son, the essay assumes that a woman who 'does not love her child more than her love' is exceptional and pathological. Tsvetaeva enumerates some of these exceptional cases, such as a non-maternal woman, a depraved girl who chooses lesbianism because it's fashionable or a 'grande amoureuse' who looks only for love in love and takes it in whatever form she can get. There is also a portrait of a lesbian couple whose passion lasted till their deaths. Although she does not name them, these two aged lovers whom Tsvetaeva had observed on the savage coast of the Crimea are clearly the sister of Vladimir Soloviov, Polyxena, and her life-long companion Natalia Manaseina. 'There was around them,' writes Tsvetaeva, 'a void more empty than around a "normal" infertile old couple, a void more isolating, more emptying. Only for this and for no other reason are they a race of the damned.'

In this day and age, in the West, where there are clubs for lesbian mothers and where lesbian couples adopt and raise children, the central argument of 'Letter to an Amazon' – which is that the choice is between lesbianism and motherhood – makes no sense whatsoever. But taken on its own terms, this poetic and often moving prose rhapsody about a poet's attraction to a form of love which she could not reconcile with other aspects of her personality is a remarkable piece of writing. Whether Natalie Clifford Barney ever read it and what she thought of it if she did is anyone's guess. From the detailed biographies of Jean Chalon and George Wickes, we can see that the problems which Tsvetaeva postulated as typical of any lesbian relationship simply did not arise for Barney and other women of her circle. If in literary matters Tsvetaeva was, for all her lack of reputation in non-Russian circles in those days, a consummate professional and Barney an amateur, in matters of lesbianism the situation was the reverse. When Barney read Marcel Proust's

Sodome et Gomorrhe, she informed him that his lesbians in that novel were not believable because he did not know them well enough to portray them accurately. This may well have also been her response to the essay by Tsvetaeva which her book inspired.

In 1932, the journal *Freedom of Russia*, which for many years had been Tsvetaeva's principal literary outlet, lost its Czech subsidy and was forced to close. The financial help of friends began to dwindle due to worsening economic conditions. In May 1932, Tsvetaeva's family was forced to give up their apartment in Meudon (2, Avenue Jeanne d'Arc) and to seek cheaper lodgings in the suburb of Clamart. From 1931 to 1933, Tsvetaeva lived in the worst poverty she was ever to experience. In her letters of those years to Halpern, Ivask, and Georgy and Elena Fedotov, we see Tsvetaeva in utter indigence and often on the brink of physical starvation. 'Hunger and cold are in our home,' she wrote to Halpern on March 18, 1932. To Fedotov, in December of that year: 'Because of my total poverty, I go nowhere and see no one.' Even more telling is the explanation offered the Fedotovs of why Tsvetaeva did not visit them as she had promised: just as she was starting out, the soles of her only pair of shoes fell apart. The quarterly payment of rent was a constant source of anguish. In March 1933, her belongings were about to be confiscated. She was also threatened with deportation from France for non-payment of back taxes.

Then, in 1934, just when her Czech stipend was discontinued and Salomea Halpern and Raisa Lomonosova were obliged to halt their financial aid, Tsvetaeva's conditions improved. As Mrs Halpern wrote to Gleb Struve: '... Marina's material situation became easier. She climbed out of hopeless penury.' The source of this relief was Sergei Efron. For the first time in his twenty-two year marriage to Tsvetaeva, he took a full-time paying job in 1934 and became the family breadwinner. Like many an admirer of Stalin's regime, Efron longed to go to the Soviet Union. He applied for a Soviet passport and for permission to be repatriated. 'Sergei is still here,' Tsvetaeva wrote to Salomea Halpern on October 2, 1933, 'there is still no passport, which makes me profoundly happy, for the letters of those who have returned (I myself saw them off and waved goodbye!) are most eloquent. [...] Besides, I am definitely not going, this would mean separation, which, for all our bickering, would be hard after twenty years of togetherness [*sovmestnost'*].

And the reason I am not going is that I already left once. Salomea, did you happen to see the film *I Am a Fugitive from the Chain Gang*, where a convict voluntarily returns to forced labor? Well, there you are!' A year and a half later, the situation was similar: 'Sergei is torn between his country and his family. I *firmly* refuse to go and ending a twenty-year togetherness, even if one has "new ideas" is hard. So he is torn asunder' (Letter of April 6, 1934).

To alleviate his guilt for having participated in the civil war on the White side and for failing to return to Soviet Russia, Efron began working for an organization called 'The Union for Repatriation,' ostensibly devoted to facilitating the return of exiled Russians. Efron was connected with it from 1932, and became its secretary-general in 1934. This organization, which later changed its name to 'Union of Friends of the Soviet Motherland,' was a GPU front, financed by Soviet funds. Its real function was recruiting agents for the Soviet secret police, agents whose tasks eventually entailed acts of terrorism directed against Soviet defectors and the émigrés who were too vocal in their criticism of Stalin. This was the source of the salary on which Sergei Efron was now able to support his family.

Could Tsvetaeva have been ignorant of all this? Kirill Henkin, whose mother was a neighbour and friend of the poet at this time, wrote: 'Did Marina know? She could not have been totally unaware, but she must have somehow explained it all to herself in a way that would not disturb the Rostand-derived view she had of herself and her husband: his selflessness, his chivalry, his sense of honor.' The tinge of doubt that we have seen in Tsvetaeva's response to Professor Alexeiev's accusation that her husband was a communist and a Cheka agent back in 1929 (see Chapter 8, p. 194) must have remained, but she managed to keep the full implications of Sergei's activities from the foreground of her mind until her departure from France.

Very soon, Sergei converted to his new faith first his daughter, then Mur. Ariadna Efron had a gift for art and studied at the 'Arts et Publicité' school for a number of years. She began rebelling against her mother in 1932. By 1934 the relationship between them had become strained. The documentation of Tsvetaeva's conflict with her daughter has been deleted from the published correspondence with Tesková and Vera Bunina out of deference for Ariadna Efron's feelings; but an unpublished passage in the letter to Halpern of April 6, 1934 indicates what things were like. Later, Ariadna took a job with a French communist magazine and began moving only in pro-communist circles. 'Mur is riven between my humanitarianism and the near-fanaticism of his father,' Tsvetaeva wrote to Tesková in 1935.

The possibility of her own return to the Soviet Union was broached as early as 1931, when she wrote to Tesková: 'Everything is pushing me into Russia, where I *cannot go*. Here no one needs me. There I'm *unthinkable*.' In 1932 Tsvetaeva wrote the three-poem cycle 'Verses to My Son,' and in it she advised Mur to forget the crumbling, decadent West and to travel to 'your country, your century, your hour, away from us/To your Russia, the Russia of the masses.' As her subsequent poems and letters show, 'Verses to My Son' reflected a transient mood. Most of the time she understood what went on in the Soviet Union. And yet the idea that her son would have a better future there than in the West took hold. From a letter to Tesková of February 15, 1936: 'Briefly: Sergei and Alya and Mur all yearn to go. All around is the threat of war and revolution, of catastrophic events in general. [...] And finally, Mur has no prospects here. After all, I see those twenty-year-olds – they are all in a blind alley.'

After Hitler assumed power in Germany, the Soviet Union began to look better and better to many Western intellectuals. The brutality of the Nazi regime and the atrocities it committed were publicized more widely than the ones that took place in Stalin's Russia. In the days of the Popular Front, it was often claimed that Nazi Germany had laid bare the ugly essence of capitalist democracy, while the Soviet Union was a beacon of future freedom, equality and cultural flowering. Willi Münzenberg, who had been Lenin's disciple in Zürich on the eve of the February Revolution and who in the 1920s specialized in organizing communist-sponsored cultural congresses, collaborated with Ilya Ehrenburg in preparing a huge 'Congress of Writers in Defense of Culture,' held in Paris in June 1935. Intended as an international protest against Hitler's cultural policies, the congress was manipulated (mostly by German anti-Nazi, pro-Soviet exiles) into becoming a massive outpouring of international sympathy for the Soviet Union. Celebrated writers such as André Gide and André Malraux (both of whom were to change their views a few years later) eulogized Soviet society and Stalin's leadership as the only bulwark of culture in a world being engulfed by imperialism and fascism.

When it appeared that the Soviet delegation of writers at the Paris conference did not have enough internationally recognized names, Stalin personally ordered that Isaak Babel and Boris Pasternak be sent to Paris at the last moment. This enabled Pasternak and Tsvetaeva to meet after years of corresponding and addressing poems to each other. It was not the encounter of which either of them had dreamed. Their passionate letters to each other were ten years in the past. In February 1931, Tsvetaeva had learned from Boris Pilniak, whom she had met at Charles Vildrac's, that Pasternak had left his wife for Zinaida Neuhaus, with whom he had fallen in love and whom he later married. As Tsvetaeva commented in a letter to Lomonosova: 'To lose him without ever having him.' Now, what she mainly hoped for was his advice: should she follow Sergei to Russia? But Pasternak was brought to the congress against his will and on the verge of a nervous breakdown. Tsvetaeva found him incoherent and evasive. Astounded at the pro-Soviet outlook of her husband and daughter, Pasternak responded to her queries about her prospects in the Soviet Union by saying: 'You'll get to love the collective farms.' Tsvetaeva missed the irony of this remark. Citing it in a letter to the Soviet poet Nikolai Tikhonov, whom she met at the congress and with whom she could communicate better than with Pasternak, she complained that Pasternak was casting himself in the part of Turgenev's ideological hero Bazarov and her as Bazarov's aged and incomprehending parents.

Actually, Boris Pasternak had very strong misgivings about Tsvetaeva's return. But he expressed them not to her but in his autobiography, written many years after her death. Recalling their Paris encounter, he wrote: 'I did not know what to advise her and was all too afraid that in our country she and her remarkable family would experience difficulty and insecurity. The total tragedy of the family exceeded by far my fears.' Tsvetaeva wrote to Tesková about their meeting: 'It happened – and what a *non-meeting* it turned out to be!' Not aware of the extent to which people were terrorized in Stalin's Russia, Tsvetaeva wrote to Tesková with disdain that Pasternak came to the Paris congress because he was too frightened to refuse after getting a direct order from Stalin's secretary. She took Pasternak's whispered confession of this as a sign of weakness or cowardice: 'He let them put him on a plane and take him away.'

Nor did she know that Pasternak's experiences at the congress culminated in an actual breakdown, for which he needed to receive psychiatric care after returning home.

One year after her non-meeting with Pasternak, Tsvetaeva had an even more foredoomed non-meeting with a Russian poet of a very different stripe. This one, however, lasted most of the summer and part of the fall of 1936. The poet was Anatoly Steiger. He was descended from a russified Swiss family and was one of the most typical poets of the Unnoticed Generation. Tsvetaeva had met him briefly after one of her public lectures, and she was friendly with his sister, the poet Alla Golovina. Steiger wrote fragile, aphoristic poems many of which were about the hopeless passion of a sensitive, vulnerable man for another man – handsome, brutal and unattainable. In July 1936, he sent Tsvetaeva an inscribed volume of his verse. She replied with a letter that reached Steiger in a tuberculosis sanatorium in Switzerland, where he was about to have an operation. He sent her a confession about his life and loves. She interpreted it as the appeal of a romantic wanderer, a desperately ill poet who needed her love and understanding. A poem addressed to him begins:

> At last I met
> The very one I need:
> The one who has a mortal
> Need of me.

In one of her earliest letters to Steiger, she wrote: 'You with your letter broke through my icy crust, under which I at once fell, head and all. You.'

Many things attracted Tsvetaeva to Steiger: his descent from a historical figure she admired (Nikolaus Friedrich von Steiger, 1729–99, the leader of the conservative Swiss emigration at the time of the French Revolution); his belonging to a hostile literary camp (he was a friend of Adamovich and a devotee of Poplavsky's poetry, which Tsvetaeva disliked); and his self-evident homosexuality, for which she felt an affinity. But her main motivation was the need to be needed: 'Convince me that you *need* me. Good God, why, that's the whole point: convince me once and for all, make me believe it and then everything will be fine, because then I can work miracles' (Letter of August 31, 1936). In August and September, Steiger was recovering from his operation in a Berne hospital, while Tsvetaeva and her son were living in a castle in the Savoy, Château d'Arcine, owned by a Russian family named Strange (pronounced SHTRAN-gay), who were Sergei's confederates at the Union for Repatriation. She wrote Steiger every few days and composed a cycle of poems about him, which was later published under the deliberately mis-leading title 'Verses to an Orphan' ('Stikhi sirote').

In some ways, Tsvetaeva's involvement with Steiger resembles the one with Bakhrakh, because here again she took what she knew of the reality of the man and used it to construct a poetic fiction, with which she then corresponded and for which she yearned. In other ways it is a bit like her correspondence with Rilke, because with Steiger she also wanted to commune in a dream room: 'there is no such room, because it has to be a non-room, its negation, its opposite, namely: a room of dreams which expands and contracts, appears and vanishes depending on need, with a door when it must have one and not when not.' This, of course, is the room already described in verse in the poem 'Essay of a Room.' But unlike the correspondence with Bakhrakh and Rilke, the letters to Steiger, poetic and emotional, are singularly devoid of intellectual content. One of them, bearing the title 'My Geneva,' about her ill-fated trip to that city for the purpose of mailing a parcel to Steiger, is in a comical vein – a genre that does not occur in Tsvetaeva with any frequency.

Anatoly Steiger's need of Tsvetaeva did not prove lasting. He was of a solitary, independent nature. In his contacts with Tsvetaeva he was hoping for friendship, not infatuation and possessiveness. When he recovered sufficiently from his illness, he made Tsvetaeva's mistake clear to her. She was disappointed and hurt, especially when after leaving the hospital Steiger chose to visit not her but Georgy Adamovich and his gay friends in Paris. 'I had believed,' she wrote to Tesková, 'that someone needed me as one needs bread. But it turned out that what he needs is not bread, but an ash tray with cigarette butts. [. . .] It's bitter. It's stupid. It's a pity.' It was over, and what remained were her twenty-six expressive and often witty letters. And a cycle of six poems was added to the Tsvetaeva canon.

The letters Tsvetaeva wrote to Steiger make for an interesting contrast with her correspondence of 1933–7 with another young exiled poet, Yury Ivask, later known as Professor George Ivask

who taught Russian literature at several American universities in
the second half of the century. In 1933, Ivask was living in Estonia
and planning to write a book about Tsvetaeva. The book was never
finished and its manuscript was lost. But for four years, in response
to Ivask's skillful questioning, Tsvetaeva supplied him with important information about herself, her past, her literary preferences
and her current activities. Unlike the letters to Steiger, the letters to
Ivask are highly intellectual and are a storehouse of important
commentary about Tsvetaeva's life and writings. In her correspondence with literary men, especially with Rilke, Bakhrakh and Ivask,
Tsvetaeva was a consummate artist, producing letters which are
also expressive and beautifully written essays. Such letters are as
important an aspect of her achievement as her poems and memoirs.

Tsvetaeva's prose writings of the 1930s have already been cited or
drawn upon in the earlier chapters of this book. Much of her writing
of that decade was of a retrospective character. She looked back at
her own past, studying her early childhood and family background
in a series of memoirs. She commemorated the deaths of people
whom she had once known or admired in literary epitaphs in prose
and verse. Thus, Mayakovsky's suicide in 1930 brought into being,
as mentioned, the cycle 'To Mayakovsky.' Voloshin's death in 1932
occasioned the memoir 'The Living About the Living' and the cycle
of poems 'Ici-haut' (in Russian, despite its French title). Andrei
Bely's death led to his prose portrait in 'A Captive Spirit' (1934),
Mikhail Kuzmin's death to 'An Otherworldly Evening' (1936), and
the belated news of Sophia Holliday's death from cancer engen-
dered an extensive reconstruction of Tsvetaeva's contacts with her
in 'The Tale of Sonechka' (1937). Less personal are the essays about
the nature and uses of poetry which she hoped to include in a book
that never materialized, which was to be called *Art in the Light of
Conscience*. These include 'The Poet and Time,' 'Poets with History
and Poets without History' and the essay that bears the same title as
the projected book. Even more purely literary are such works of
literary criticism as 'The Two Erlkings' ('Dva lesnykh tsaria'), a
textual comparison of Goethe's ballad and its Russian adaptation
by Zhukovsky, published in 1934. The celebration of the centenary
of Pushkin's death in 1937 resulted in the writing of two prose pieces:
'Pushkin and Pugachov' (a juxtaposition of Pushkin's novel *The
Captain's Daughter* with its historical sources) and 'My Pushkin.'
For the centenary, Tsvetaeva also translated a set of Pushkin's

poems into French and published her cycle of poems 'Verses to Pushkin' ('Stikhi k Pushkinu'), written earlier, in 1931.

Whether Tsvetaeva's prose dealt with her mother and family, famous poets or theories about art, it remained at all times the prose of a poet – not necessarily because it was written by a poet, but because in her prose Tsvetaeva consistently employed the lexicon and the stylistic and structural devices which she had developed in her verse. Except for meter and rhyme, the texture of her prose was the same as that of her verse. Here, too, she employed her play on verbal stems (paranomasia), alliteration and anaphora, and used the ellipsis of verbs and nouns, which is typical of Russian colloquial speech, but rare in conventional 'literary' prose. In prose, as in verse, Tsvetaeva created verbal effects that make one think of musical or architectural procedures rather than of literary usage. Vladislav Khodasevich, who commented extensively on these essays and memoirs immediately after the publication of each of them, pointed out the multiplicity of literary levels on which they could be read. Of 'My Mother and Music' Khodasevich wrote: 'In subject matter, this is part of an autobiography, but in execution, in the solution of the tasks which the author had undoubtedly set up for herself, these are not memoirs,' because 'in the foreground we have a psychological pattern which is of interest in itself, without regard to the historical and literary personality of the memoirist.' Khodasevich pointed out that Tsvetaeva's portrait of Bely in 'A Captive Spirit' was 'not a photograph, but a painting in which the personality of the painter is distinctly felt.'

The publication of Tsvetaeva's masterful prose of the 1930s in émigré periodicals caused some of her sharpest conflicts with her liberal editors. After the demise of *Freedom of Russia*, Tsvetaeva was left with only three outlets: *Contemporary Annals, The Latest News* and the Zagreb journal *Russian Archive* (*Ruski arkhiv*), which published some of her writings in Serbo-Croatian translation. Tsvetaeva's frequent complaints that no one wanted to publish her during the 1930s are belied by the large number of works she managed to place in these three publications. With the reduction in the volume of émigré publishing in the 1930s, we find similar complaints about being ignored and neglected in the correspondence of a number of exiled writers, including such established figures as Alexei Remizov and Zinaida Gippius. The younger writers of the Unnoticed Generation, for their part, were convinced that *they* were the ones that the émigré editors were slighting, while giving the writers of Tsvetaeva's standing all the exposure they could possibly wish. But if Tsvetaeva's oft-quoted statement about being 'withdrawn from circulation' was unfounded, her simultaneous outrage about editorial mutilations of her texts, expressed in letters to Bunina, Fedotov and Ivask, was very much justified.

The five Socialist Revolutionary politicians who started *Contemporary Annals* in 1920, and the editors of *The Latest News*, like the majority of pre-revolutionary radicalized intelligentsia, were not affected by the broadening of cultural horizons brought about by Sergei Diaghilev and the Symbolist movement at the turn of the century. Their cultural roots were the same as Lenin's and Trotsky's: the radical utilitarianism of the nineteenth century, as represented by Belinsky and Chernyshevsky. While these men of the February Revolution would not dream of censoring literature like Lenin or being as abusive and dictatorial toward established writers as Trotsky, they were nonetheless raised on some of the same attitudes: art and literature had to be simple, realistic, uplifting and continue narrowly defined 'progressive' traditions. In the 1920s, the editorial board of *Contemporary Annals* understood that their background was not adequate for dealing with the complex writing of the Symbolists and post-Symbolists they wanted to attract to their journal and they employed literary advisers. Tsvetaeva's contributions were then read and accepted by the philosopher Feodor Stepun and the poet Mikhail Tsetlin, who knew better than to tamper with her texts.

But in the 1930s, Tsvetaeva's editor at *Contemporary Annals* was Vadim Rudnev, the mayor of Moscow during the Provisional Government. According to the memoirs of Mark Vishniak, Rudnev was selected to handle Tsvetaeva because they had 'a similar religious outlook' (by which Vishniak must have meant that both Rudnev and Tsvetaeva belonged to the Orthodox Church, whereas the rest of the editors were agnostics or Jews). Like Igor Demidov of *The Latest News* who reduced Tsvetaeva to tears with his editorial mutilation of her memoir 'My Mother's Fairy Tale', Rudnev may have sincerely believed that he was clarifying Tsvetaeva's prose with his heavy-handed abridgements and other tampering. What both of these editors actually tried to do was to make her highly idiosyncratic writing fit their notions of realistic and accessible literature. It has been possible in later editions to reinstate the passages deleted by Rudnev from 'The Devil' and 'The

Living about the Living.' But the essay 'Art in the Light of Conscience' survives only in the version which appeared in *Contemporary Annals*, where, according to Tsvetaeva, Rudnev had cut it to one half of its original length. To deepen the perspective a bit, it should be mentioned that Tsvetaeva was not the only author whose texts were changed or abridged in *Contemporary Annals*. Vladimir Nabokov was obliged to delete a chapter from the most perfect of his Russian novels, *The Gift*, because of its satirical portrayal of Nikolai Chernyshevsky, regarded as a saint by the Russian radical tradition. And in a ground-breaking essay on Gogol by the scholar Dmitry Chizhevsky, published by the journal in 1938, all references to devils were removed, though, as Chizhevsky later complained, these devils were not his but Gogol's. To deepen the perspective even more, *Contemporary Annals* was, when all is said and done, the finest Russian literary journal of the post-revolutionary period; furthermore, it published works by Tsvetaeva in thirty-six of its seventy issues – a body of her prose, poetry and plays that might otherwise not have seen the light of day.

In March 1937, Ariadna Efron returned to the Soviet Union. She left laden with clothes and gifts from her parents and friends, including an elegant record-player given to her by her mother. She obtained a job as an illustrator and wrote her parents glowing letters about her wonderful new life in Moscow. At the time of her arrival, the Soviet Union was in the second year of what is now called the Great Terror. While not as vast numerically as the peasant holocaust of 1929–33, the wave of frameups, arrests and executions that began in 1935 was far more visible because it affected every class and category, including the Red Army, the upper echelons of the Communist Party, and a large number of celebrities in literature and the arts. Among the millions who perished were Osip Mandelstam, who had once loved Tsvetaeva, Vsevolod Meyerhold, who had once denounced her as a traitor, and Boris Pilniak, with whom she had spent a memorable evening at Charles Vildrac's in 1931. Before the year 1937 was over, Anastasia Tsvetaeva was sent to a labor camp. A large archive of Marina's manuscripts and memorabilia which her sister kept at her apartment was confiscated and never recovered.

    Like many phenomena in Marxist-Leninist societies, the Great Terror was not understood in the outside world while it was happening. The purges and show trials in Moscow were written about in the Western press, yet thousands of Russian exiles were returning home during those years from Europe and, especially, the Far East. We now know that after a year or two, they were all accused of espionage or sabotage and sent to labor camps or shot. But there was no worry about her daughter's future in Tsvetaeva's letters to friends about Ariadna's departure, only contentment that Ariadna had realized her long-standing dream. From one of her daughter's first letters from Moscow, Tsvetaeva learned that Sophia Holliday was no more. She spent the summer of 1937 at Lacanau-Océan on the Atlantic coast writing 'The Tale of Sonechka.' The beginning of this work, published in a new literary journal *Russian Annals* (*Russkie zapiski*), was one of Tsvetaeva's last appearances in an émigré periodical ('Verses to an Orphan' in *Contemporary Annals* early in 1938 was the last). This was due to the events that unfolded that fall.

Early in September 1937, the bullet-riddled corpse of an unknown man was found on a road near Lausanne in Switzerland. An investigation by the Swiss authorities revealed that the victim was Ignace Reiss (his real name was Poretsky), an important official of the Soviet secret police. He had been sent to France and Holland on an intelligence assignment, become disillusioned with Stalin's policies and decided to defect. At the end of September, while the Reiss case was still being untangled, Russian exiles everywhere were appalled by the sensational abduction by Soviet agents of General Yevgeny Miller, head of the All-Russian Military Union, an association of pre-revolutionary servicemen in Paris. The Union for Repatriation and Sergei Efron, who was by then its head, were deeply involved in both of these cases. Later investigations established that Efron planned and took part in the assassination of Poretsky and that earlier, in 1936, he had had a hand in the murder of Trotsky's son, Lev Sedov, which was carried out on orders from Moscow. When the Reiss-Poretsky case first broke, the French police picked Efron up for interrogation at the request of Swiss authorities. But this was the time of the Popular Front, when France regarded the Soviet Union as an ally against Hitler and was reluctant to do anything to embarrass it. Efron was released after some questioning. By the time the evidence against Efron became incontrovertible and the French police came to arrest him, he had already fled to Spain, from where he made his way to the Soviet Union.

Unable to find Efron, the police arrested Marina Tsvetaeva. But she insisted that she knew nothing about her husband's activities, could not even understand most of the police officers' questions, and after a while began to respond to the interrogation by reciting her poem 'Gars' (the French version of 'The Swain') and lines from French seventeenth-century tragedies. She was soon allowed to go home. As more and more of Sergei's terrorist activities were disclosed in the press in the following months, Tsvetaeva kept assuring her friends that it was all a misunderstanding, that she knew Sergei better than anyone and was 'ready to swear that [Sergei] could not be involved in the bloody affair.' Her friend Elena Izvolskaya wrote later that Tsvetaeva really did know nothing and that 'her loyalty and absolute confidence in Sergei remained unshaken.' Many people in Paris had known for years that Sergei Efron was a Soviet agent. Tsvetaeva's disbelief and denials were taken for dissembling. She was ostracized by most people in the Russian community.

She remained in France until the summer of 1939. It is to those last eighteen months of her stay that the words of Vladimir Markov, 'Tsvetaeva is on the conscience of Paris' (meaning the Russian Paris), apply in both the literary and the human sense. The recollections of Nina Berberova, Yury Terapiano and V. S. Yanovsky indicate that many of Tsvetaeva's associates and acquaintances shunned her. Other documents that have recently come to light show actual hatred for her. It was during this period that Alexei Remizov noted in his diary: 'I strongly dislike Tsvetaeva for her posturings, her ignoble character and her female irresponsibility [babstvo]. And for her extraordinary vanity.' On March 29, 1939, a few months before Tsvetaeva's departure from France, Ivan Bunin wrote to a correspondent who asked him about Tsvetaeva's poetry: 'I do not remember her "Roland's Horn." I can't stand that psychopath, with her leaden eyes, gifted, but lacking in shame, taste, etc.' Her Russian neighbours forced her to leave her home in the suburb of Vanves and to move to a cheap hotel on Boulevard Pasteur.

But Tsvetaeva also had friends who went out of their way to keep her company and to show their loyalty and support. Among them were Mark Slonim, Elena Izvolskaya, Ilya Fondaminsky (one of the editors of Contemporary Annals), Nikolai Berdiaev and Vladislav Khodasevich. Also, according to the recollections of Aleksis

Rannit, in March of 1938 Tsvetaeva saw quite a lot of the elegant younger poet of the Unnoticed Generation, Vladimir Smolensky, with whom she seems to have become briefly infatuated. In December 1938, Yury Ivask came to Paris and had several memorable visits with Tsvetaeva after years of correspondence. By that time she was already resolved to join Sergei and Ariadna in the Soviet Union. Tsvetaeva was concerned about the fate of her manuscripts and her unpublished writings, many of which she was afraid to take with her. Ivask advised her to deposit them with Professor Else Mahler of the University of Basel. This decision preserved in the West several important works which otherwise might have perished or be still resting in closed Soviet archives: *Demesne of the Swans*, 'Perekop' and 'The Tale of Sonechka.' Another part of Tsvetaeva's archive, which she left in Paris in the care of her friend Margarita Lebedeva, was lost during World War II.

We know from Tsvetaeva's letters to Tesková how reluctant she was to return to the USSR and how she resisted for years the entreaties of her husband, daughter and son to accompany them. On February 15, 1936, she wrote that the main obstacle was her own character: 'I, with my *Furchtlosigkeit* [fearlessness], I who cannot refrain from responding, I who cannot sign a salutary address to the great Stalin, for it was *not* I who called him great, and even if he is great it is not my kind of greatness, and perhaps the most important thing – I hate every triumphant, bureaucratized church.' A few days before the final departure, Tsvetaeva wrote to Tesková: 'God, what anguish! Right now, in the heat of the moment, with everything in a fever – my hands and my head and the weather – I still have not sensed it fully. But I know myself, I know what awaits me! I'll break my neck looking back: at you, at your world, at our world' (June 7, 1939). As she saw it, Sergei was in trouble and needed her: 'I had no choice, one can't abandon a person in trouble, that's how I was born' (same letter).

But her main concern was with Mur. She feared that she might lose him once he got to Moscow: 'Already, I feel a horror of a smug, happy, no longer childlike Mur, with a mouthful of platitudes they'll drum into him' (to Tesková, March 29, 1936). But she convinced herself and, more importantly, Mur convinced her that in Moscow he could be happy and have a future. The testimony of those who saw Tsvetaeva during her last year in Paris – Elena Fedotova, Ivask,

V. S. Yanovsky and Mark Slonim – is unanimous on the subject of Mur: he was puffy, looked older than his age, had atrocious manners and was insufferably rude to his mother in front of visitors. 'He had only one thing on his mind,' wrote Slonim, 'which was to leave for the Soviet Union. With the persistence of one possessed, he demanded this from his mother and he played a major role in her decision.' She could exist without Sergei and Ariadna, but to part from Mur was more than she could bear. Pasternak showed keen perception when he wrote that Tsvetaeva sacrificed both herself and her poetry for the sake of her son.

The intrusion of politics and violence into her life made Tsvetaeva, the poet, take a closer look at the world in which she was living. The civil war in Spain and the menacing stance of Hitler's Germany outraged and repelled her. The German takeover of Czechoslovakia was an unmitigated horror: the country she had loved and honored in her poetry and prose invaded the country that had supported her financially for a decade and in which she had lived some of her happiest years. Throughout the months of the Czech crisis she wrote Tesková impassioned letters about her concern for and her gratitude to the Czechs. In September 1938 and March 1939 she wrote two big cycles of poems 'Verses to Czechoslovakia' ('Stikhi k Chekhii'), which eulogized the victimized country and cursed the invaders. Czechoslovakia was for Tsvetaeva

> The freest and most generous
> Of all the countries in the world.
> Those mountains are the birthplace
> Of my son.
> . . . . . .
> Here I raised my son.
> And there flowed – was it water?
> Days? Or white
> Flocks of geese?
> . . . . . .
> Accursed are those who betrayed
> – Never to be forgiven! –
> The age-old homeland
> Of all those without a country.

But Germany was apostrophized in a passionate invective of the kind that Tsvetaeva had last used in *The Demesne of the Swans*:

You've put half the map in your pocket,
You ethereal soul!
Of old, you spread the fairy tale mists,
Now you send your tanks.

Before the Czech peasant girl
You do not lower your eyes,
As you roll your tanks
Over the rye of her hopes?

Before the immeasurable sorrow
Of that *little* country
What do you feel, Hermanns,
Sons of Germany?

The note of despair that was heard in some of Tsvetaeva's poetry
of the 1930s is sounded most powerfully of all in one of the poems of
the March cycle, with its quotation of the famous Schiller-
Dostoevsky formula about respectfully returning one's entrance
ticket to the Creator. This poem is cited here in its entirety:

Oh, tears in my eyes!
Weeping of anger and love!
Czechoslovakia in tears,
Spain drenched in blood.

Oh, the black mountain
That has eclipsed all light!
It is time, it is time, it is time
To return my ticket to the Creator.

I refuse to exist.
In the Bedlam of non-humans
I refuse to live.
With the wolves of city squares

I refuse to howl.
With the sharks of the plains
I refuse to swim
Downstream over inclined backs.

I don't need the apertures
Of my ears, nor my prophetic eyes.
To Thy insane world
There is only one answer: a refusal.

10

Moscow, Elabuga and after

This is not a *political* book, not for a second. This is a living soul in a hangman's noose, and nevertheless living. The background is morbid. It is not I who invented it.   Marina Tsvetaeva, 1923

In the spring of 1938, there was a great deal of Russian cultural activity in Paris. A newly organized theater, which employed some of the best-known exiled actors and actresses, presented a season of new plays by Mark Aldanov, Nina Berberova and Vladimir Nabokov. In April, a Russian writers' ball was held, attended by all the writers and poets of any repute. In May, there was an 'Evening of Contemporary Poetry,' with readings by all Russian poets resident in France. The name of Marina Tsvetaeva is conspicuously absent from the announcements and press reports of these events. She was now no longer a member of the émigré literary community. Her source of income was the stipend payable to Sergei Efron by the Soviet consulate in Paris which his wife now collected.

That spring she stayed on the seacoast at Dives-sur-Mer in the region of Calvados, sorting out her archive. She prepared fair copies of her unpublished manuscripts, and selected offprints of her published work which she believed would be dangerous to take to the Soviet Union. She intended to store these things at the University of Basel. On June 17, 1938, she happened to re-read 'October Revolution in a Railroad Car,' which was to be a part of her unrealized book *Omens of the Earth*. In it, she cited a diary entry made in November 1917 when she was not sure of Sergei Efron's fate after the October takeover: 'If God performs this miracle and leaves you among the living, I will follow you like a dog.' In the margin next to these words she wrote: 'And here I am following him –

like a dog (21 years later).' Despite her resolve to leave, she stayed
in France for one more year. Perhaps the decision about the time of
her departure rested not with her but with the Soviet authorities.
One of her last public appearances in Paris was described by Yury
Terapiano in a passage that reads like a *mea culpa* of the younger
generation of Russian writers in Paris: 'Now, when one thinks of
Tsvetaeva's fate, of her death, one is perplexed: how could we have
allowed her to leave amidst general indifference? A few days before
Tsvetaeva's departure, Prince Shirinsky-Shikhmatov, who was
later tortured to death in a Nazi concentration camp, gave a literary
soirée. Among those present were Tsvetaeva and her son – aloof,
remote from everyone. She talked to hardly anyone and hardly
anyone talked to her. She's leaving? Let her leave! Who in the
world cares?'

Marina Tsvetaeva and Mur (Georgy Efron) finally left Paris on
June 12, 1939. They traveled by train to Le Havre, by ship to Poland
and from there again by train to Moscow, where they arrived on
June 18. Tsvetaeva's departure was not reported in the French or
émigré press. Nor was it considered a newsworthy event by the
Soviet newspapers. Her return was not one of those symbol-laden
homecomings, such as those of the writer Alexander Kuprin and the
composer Sergei Prokofiev (both also in the 1930s), which Stalin's
government publicized and represented to the world as the penitent
artists' endorsement of the entire Soviet system. As Viktoria Schweitzer has pointed out, for the Soviet authorities in 1939 Tsvetaeva
was not a great or even a noted poet, but the wife of a secret agent
who had bungled his mission, a wife whose continued presence in
the West might prove embarrassing.

On February 15, 1936, Tsvetaeva wrote to Anna Tesková with
some optimism: 'In Moscow I have my sister Asya who loves me
perhaps more than she loves her only son. In Moscow, at least, I
have a circle of genuine writers, not relics.' For all her reluctance
and apprehensions, she was hoping to find the kind of literary milieu
that she had left behind in 1922. Tsvetaeva did not take into
consideration the effects of the Great Terror, which, like most
people abroad, she had underestimated. By 1939, the wave of show
trials and executions that had reached its peak in 1937 had abated.
But something like eight million of those arrested during the purges
were still in prisons or concentration camps. Everyone in the
country had relatives, friends or neighbours who were accused of

having participated in a vast conspiracy against the Communist Party and the people. There was no defense against such accusations: once charged, one was found guilty. The entire population lived in fear. The only concern of everyone was to avoid displeasing the authorities and to survive. Since the evil conspirators were allegedly controlled from abroad (by Trotsky, by foreign socialists, by capitalists, by fascists, by the bourgeoisie), those who had returned from the West were treated like plague carriers. Old friends, with whom Tsvetaeva had hoped for a reunion, stayed away, waiting to see what the authorities would do to her.

She found herself in a villa in Bolshevo, outside Moscow, which was a kind of safe house operated by the NKVD (People's Commissariat of Internal Affairs, formerly Cheka and GPU) for Soviet agents who had to flee from the West after being discovered. Besides Sergei Efron and Ariadna, the house was occupied by Nina Klepinina, a woman who had helped Sergei Efron in his work in Paris, her husband (like Efron, a former White officer) and her son from an earlier marriage, Dmitry Sezeman, who was the same age as Mur. Another person at the villa was Samuil Gurevich, nicknamed Mulia, the man with whom Ariadna Efron was living and by whom she was pregnant at the time of her mother's arrival. Gurevich, it turned out later, was watching the inhabitants of the villa for the NKVD. The Klepinins and Efron lived on a salary paid for their earlier services to the Soviet government. Because of this arrangement, it was no longer possible for Tsvetaeva to deny to herself the nature of her husband's activities of the past years. It was also at this point that she was informed that her sister, Anastasia, whom she had hoped to see in Moscow, was in a concentration camp.

We have a diary entry Tsvetaeva made a little over a year after her return which records her initial impressions: 'Arrival in Moscow on 18 June. To Bolshevo on the 19th. To the villa, a reunion with the unwell S. Discomfort. To fetch kerosene. S. buys apples. Gradually becoming heartsick. The ordeal of telephoning. The enigmatic Ariadna with her forced gaiety. I live without documents, seeing no one. [. . .] There are pastries and pineapple, but that doesn't make it easier. Strolls with Mulia. My *solitude*, dishwater and tears. The overtone and the undertone of everything: horror.' Adding further to her dismay was the constant angry whining of Mur. The boy who had pleaded with his mother for years to take him to the Soviet Union was disgusted with that country once he was there. He

bitterly reproached his parents for having misled him and ruined his
life.

A little over two months after Tsvetaeva's arrival, on the night of
August 27, police came to arrest her daughter. Ariadna reacted
with bravado, treating the whole thing as a joke, refusing to say
goodbye to her family. An elderly arresting officer commented:
'That's better. Protracted farewells mean extra tears.' Tsvetaeva
did not live to learn that her daughter lost her baby from the brutal
beatings to which she was subjected after her arrest. Ariadna Efron,
who was twenty-seven at the time, was to spend the next seventeen
years of her life in concentration camps and remote penal
settlements in the frozen north. After she was taken away, the
inhabitants of the villa in Bolshevo lived in constant expectation of
further arrests. On the eve of the November 7 celebrations of the
anniversary of the October Revolution, police came for Sergei
Efron and the Klepinins. Tsvetaeva, her son and Dmitry Sezeman
were ordered to vacate the villa. As Sezeman later wrote: 'My
further encounters with Marina Ivanovna took place in the reception room of the Butyrki Prison, where she would bring parcels for
her husband (already killed by that time, as it turned out later) and I
for my parents.'

There are two versions of the end of Sergei Efron. When Ariadna
Efron initiated her father's posthumous rehabilitation in the 1950s,
she was shown a file according to which Efron was interrogated
personally by the dreaded Lavrenty Beria. He became rude to Beria
and yelled at him, whereupon Beria ordered him taken out and shot
on the spot. Later, however, this version was withdrawn, and the
date of Efron's death was changed from 1939 to 1941, with a vague
implication that that was when he was either shot or died in a
concentration camp. The revision came in connection with the
overall upgrading of Tsvetaeva's biography after she was accepted
within the Soviet literary canon. Be that as it may, Tsvetaeva
experienced the standing in prison lines with food parcels which
Anna Akhmatova immortalized in her cycle of poems 'Requiem.'
The significance of the parcels was that as long as they were
accepted, the arrested person could still be presumed alive. But
as Efron's case suggests, prison authorities would also on occasion
accept parcels for people who had already been executed.

Evicted from the house in Bolshevo, Tsvetaeva was left without
money or a roof over her head. Her half-sister Valeria, who had a

large house, refused to see her or have anything to do with her. Tsvetaeva and Mur were given temporary shelter by Lilia Efron, who shared a tiny apartment with another woman. Tsvetaeva had to sleep on a trunk in a closet. In search of the income she needed in order to survive, Tsvetaeva tried turning to the Moscow literary community. During the years she had been away, literature in the Soviet Union was thoroughly bureaucratized. Access to publication, literary earnings and the privileges which the government reserved for the more docile and conventional writers were all monopolized by a hierarchy of writers' organizations under the control of the Communist Party. A constant and ostentatious show of political reliability was a writer's only means of survival. Nikolai Aseyev and Nikolai Tikhonov, who had admired 'Poem of the End' and 'The Pied Piper' in the 1920s, avoided Tsvetaeva. Old friends, such as Ilya Ehrenburg and Pavel Antokolsky, when she tried to see them somewhat later on, proved evasive and embarrassed by her presence. Three women poets, whom Tsvetaeva had known during the Civil War – Vera Zviagintseva, Vera Merkurieva and Olga Mochalova – turned out to be more brave and loyal than these men. They saw Tsvetaeva and corresponded with her, but none of them had the power to provide her with work.

It was Boris Pasternak who came to Tsvetaeva's aid in her hour of need. Back in the 1920s, he had lived in Moscow in poverty just as dire as Tsvetaeva was to experience in Paris. But in the 1930s, his second wife Zinaida took over the management of his financial situation. She saw to it that Pasternak was properly integrated into the writers' organizations, and that his translations of foreign classics – the main source of income for major poets under Soviet conditions – were paid for at the highest available rate. When Tsvetaeva first arrived from abroad, several writer friends warned Pasternak to stay away from the woman many of them referred to as a White Guard. But after the arrest of Tsvetaeva's daughter and husband, Pasternak overcame his qualms and drew on his contacts to rescue Tsvetaeva. His bringing her together with his old friend, the critic and editor Viktor Goltsev, was the greatest stroke of good luck of Tsvetaeva's entire period after her return. Goltsev (he was the son of a well-known journalist of the turn of the century, Viktor Goltsev, Sr, who was a friend and correspondent of Anton Chekhov) was in charge of translations into Russian of the poets of non-Russian nationalities who live in the USSR.

Viktor Goltsev arranged for Tsvetaeva to translate (from line-by-line cribs) long epic poems by the nineteenth-century Georgian poet Vazha Pshavela (his real name was Luka Radzikashvili) and also poems by Federico García Lorca, Polish and Yiddish poets and English and German folk ballads. These translations are what enabled Tsvetaeva to live through the months that followed. They kept her from writing any poetry of her own, but they also testify to what extent her poetic ability had survived all her trials. A real gem is her rendition of Charles Baudelaire's poem 'Voyage,' a dazzling piece which not only translates French into Russian but also Baudelaire into Tsvetaeva – an awesome amalgam. But these translations, for all their excellence, are also a monument to the waste of talent in the Stalin years, when some of the best Russian poets (Kuzmin, Akhmatova and Pasternak, in addition to Tsvetaeva) were prevented by the regime from making their own creative contribution and were forced to put their gifts in the service of other literatures.

Goltsev must have also been instrumental in arranging for Tsvetaeva another modest source of income: checking for the journal *Red Virgin Soil* (*Krasnaia nov'*) the quality of unsolicited poetry manuscripts. Finally, he may have been connected with arranging for Tsvetaeva a sojourn at the Writers'-Union-operated club in Golitsyno outside Moscow. This was a privileged residence, reserved for the more established writers. Tsvetaeva's stay there seems almost miraculous. She was not, it is true, allowed to occupy one of the rooms at the residence and had to rent a room in the nearby village. But she and Mur could take their meals at the Golitsyno club, which were of a quality far above what was available to most of the population. And Tsvetaeva found herself in the company of literate people at Golitsyno, people who knew who she was. The mere fact of her presence at such an institution freed other residents of their fear of Tsvetaeva and enabled them to treat her with the respect and admiration they knew was her due. This was where she and Mur spent the winter of 1939–40.

Much of the time she lived in fear. As she wrote to Olga Mochalova on May 29, 1940, she slept poorly, felt lonely and, just as in the years of War Communism, was terrified by the sound of an automobile at night: 'who the devil knows what it's looking for?' But those who saw Tsvetaeva at the Golitsyno club remembered her as friendly, entertaining and courteous in an old-fashioned manner. Among the residents of Golitsyno during her stay were Marietta

Shaginian (who had published reviews of Tsvetaeva thirty years earlier, but now pretended that she had never heard of her before); the humorist Viktor Ardov, whose wife was a close friend of Anna Akhmatova; the minor novelist and short story writer Nikolai Moskvin and Moskvin's very young wife, Tatiana (Tania) Kvanina, who worked as a schoolmistress. To the people who saw Tsvetaeva in Moscow and Golitsyno, her clothes, although foreign, looked cheap and her appearance shabby. But for the naive young Tania Kvanina, the aura of a poet who had returned from Paris and the few modest silver bracelets which Tsvetaeva habitually wore combined to create an image of an almost supernatural being. Many years later, Kvanina described her first impression: 'The door opened and . . . but no, she did not really enter and no one opened the door: there arose in the doorway a shapely woman entirely covered with silver ornaments.' Soon, Moskvin and Kvanina became Tsvetaeva's trusted friends.

Marina Tsvetaeva's stay at Golitsyno epitomized in a way the irrational, haphazard mode of life in Stalin's Russia. After her husband and daughter who had sincerely served the Soviet Union and supported its policies were arrested as enemies of the people, the poet herself, with her long record of counter-revolutionary writings, was moving on the fringe of the privileged elite of Soviet society. As could have been predicted, this did not last. In March 1940, Tsvetaeva was told by the manager of the Golitsyno club that she would have to pay for her meals twice as much as the other residents paid for room and board. The decision was made in Moscow and the amount asked was far above what she made with her translations. She stayed at her rented room in Golitsyno until June, receiving half-rations at the club, which she took home to share with her son. Then she left for Moscow, hoping to find shelter there.

The first year of Tsvetaeva's stay in the Soviet Union, the year of the arrests of her daughter and husband and of her residence at Bolshevo and Golitsyno, was also a year of momentous historical events. Hitler and Stalin, who had been watching each other with tacit admiration for years, signed a mutual non-aggression pact in August 1939. Tsvetaeva's 'Verses to Czechoslovakia' had cursed Hitler for invading that country, denounced the Western powers for betraying it at Munich, and voiced a hope that Stalin's Russia would come to its rescue. Now the two dictators formed an alliance, agreed on their respective spheres of influence, and untied each other's hands for grabbing their neighboring countries. On September 1, 1939, Germany invaded Poland, compelling Great Britain and France to declare war. Following Hitler's example, Stalin attempted invading Finland in November, but met with fierce resistance which claimed the lives of 100,000 Soviet soldiers. In the spring and summer of 1940, while Germany occupied Denmark, Norway, Holland and Belgium and invaded France, the Soviet Union annexed the three independent Baltic countries, Latvia, Lithuania and Estonia, and claimed the eastern areas of Poland and Rumania. If Tsvetaeva thought the Munich capitulation of September 1938 and the invasion of Czechoslovakia of March 1939 meant that the world had turned into a 'Bedlam of non-humans,' what did she think of the world now?

In the summer of 1940, she was thinking mainly of finding a place to live for herself and her son. In a telling letter to Vera Merkurieva of August 31, 1940, Tsvetaeva described her desperate search, both privately and through writers' organizations, for some kind of shelter in the city where she was born and which she had glorified in her verse as no other poet had. She wrote Merkurieva that she couldn't rid herself of the feeling that she had a certain right to be in Moscow. Her father had founded one of the city's important museums. Her mother, father and maternal grandfather had donated their enormously valuable libraries to the Rumiantsev Museum. 'I cannot, without being insincere, put myself in the place of any collective farmer or resident of Odessa who also cannot find a room in Moscow,' she wrote. '*We* lavished Moscow with gifts. Moscow is throwing me out: ejecting me.' Only in the fall of 1940 did she find some kind of housing in Moscow, at Pokrovsky Boulevard No. 14.

That August, Tsvetaeva's luggage, sent from Paris fourteen months earlier, had finally cleared the Soviet customs. By Western standards, her belongings were those 'things of the poor' of which she wrote so eloquently in her 'Poem of the Staircase,' things one could easily discard or burn. But in the commodity-hungry Soviet Union, her luggage turned out to be a godsend. By selling some of her things and using others as gifts to influential people who could help her, Tsvetaeva was able to survive for another year. Her luggage also contained her earlier manuscripts, which she used for a

project that might seem unbelievable were it not so well documented. This was a plan to bring out in the Soviet Union a volume of her
selected poems. Viktoria Schweitzer, who made a special study of
this project, wrote: 'We do not know who insisted that Tsvetaeva
prepare a book for a Soviet publishing house, but it is most likely
that she did not do this on her own initiative.' In a diary entry of
October 24, 1940 she wrote that although she had conscientiously
prepared the manuscript and paid someone to have it typed, she had
no hopes of having it accepted: 'I am almost sure they won't take it,
I would be utterly astounded if they did. Still, I've done my share
and showed my total good will (I obeyed). [. . .] Well, at least I
tried.'

With the imposition of Socialist Realism in the 1930s as the only
possible theory and method for Soviet literature, there came a
near-total ban on all non-realist or modernist trends of the early
twentieth century. Symbolist and post-Symbolist poets either were
treated as nonexistent or were vilified if mentioned (exceptions
were made for Briusov and Blok because of their support for Lenin
at the time of the October Revolution). The surviving Futurists and
other modernist poets had either switched to writing propagandistic
doggerel or were not published. Nikolai Kliuev and Osip Mandelstam had perished in labor camps. Mayakovsky, somewhat neglected after his suicide in 1930, was revived in a big way in the
mid-1930s on Stalin's personal order, but he was now studied as a
realist poet and an enemy of modernism. Even Boris Pasternak, the
most acclaimed and accepted of the innovative poets in the 1920s
and early 1930s, had not published a book since 1934. Through
some fluke, however, a selection of Akhmatova's old poems
appeared in 1940, her first book since the early 1920s. Tsvetaeva
read that volume, wondering why Akhmatova had made no progress in the past two decades and why her poetry had failed to
evolve. Even after a year in the Soviet Union, it did not occur to
Tsvetaeva that Akhmatova might have written a great deal of
poetry in that time that could no longer be printed.

Given this situation and this atmosphere, publication in the
Soviet Union of a book by a poet as unique and unprecedentedly
original as Tsvetaeva was indeed unlikely. Furthermore, while she
did her best to adapt herself to Soviet norms of behavior in her daily
life, she was incapable of adjusting her poetry to the standards of
Socialist Realism, with its requirement of simple-minded clarity and

social relevance. As Viktoria Schweitzer has pointed out, Tsvetaeva could have found in her earlier output a number of poems that would appeal to Soviet editors and censors: the pro-Soviet 'Verses to My Son,' the denunciations of urban poverty and bourgeois hypocrisy in certain poems of *After Russia* and of the mid-1930s, or the poems that express her longing for Russia. But instead of including any of these in the manuscript she offered to the State Publishing House (Gosizdat), Tsvetaeva filled it mostly with complex and original poems on personal and philosophical themes from *Craft* and *After Russia*. Gosizdat invited Kornely Zelinsky, a founder and theoretician of the Constructivist movement in the early 1920s, but by now an 'influential flunky' (to borrow Pasternak's term for conformist literary Stalinists), to write an evaluation of Tsvetaeva's volume. As could have been expected, Zelinsky wrote that Tsvetaeva's poetry was 'anti-humanitarian and devoid of true human content,' that although gifted, 'she has nothing to say to the people,' and does not include herself 'in the great cause which her people now serve.' He qualified her poetic mastery as 'formalism' (Soviet cant that means the writer has nothing to say and hides this under complex effects). 'This is what happens,' Zelinsky concluded, 'when a poet becomes the servant of the purse strings, but not when poetry is the voice of the revolution and of the people.' Tsvetaeva wrote on a copy of Zelinsky's report that has been preserved: 'A man capable of qualifying such verse as formalism has simply no conscience. I am saying this *out of the future*.' Needless to say, her book never appeared.

During that time she frequently thought of killing herself. She told Vera Zviaginsteva that once she had stepped onto the gangplank of the ship that took her from Le Havre to Poland, she understood that everything was over. On September 5, 1940, she wrote in her diary: 'No one can see, no one knows that for a year (approximately) my eyes have been searching for a hook, but there aren't any, because they have electricity everywhere. No chandeliers. For a year I have been trying death on for size. Everything is ugly and terrifying. To swallow is disgusting, to jump is inimical, my inborn revulsion to water. I do not want to frighten anyone (posthumously), it seems that I am already posthumously afraid of myself. I do not want to *die*. I want *not to be*. Nonsense. As long as I'm *needed* ... but, oh God, how insignificant I am, how little I can do! To live my life out is to chew bitter wormwood to the end.' Even in this desperate

moment Tsvetaeva could not resist her favorite device of parono-
masia – she juxtaposed *dozhivat'*, 'to finish living,' with *dozhiovy-
vat'*, 'to chew to the end.' She was visibly aging. 'Mama, you look
like an old village crone,' her son told her early in 1941.

But there were still occasional joys such as her friendships with
the poet-translators Semion Lipkin and, especially, Arseny Tarkovsky. She appreciated Tarkovsky's talent and liked him personally. From a draft of her letter to him found in her diary for 1940,
we learn with some amazement that she had hopes of doing a public
poetry reading in Moscow (it never materialized). Either in 1940 or
in spring of 1941 (sources differ), Anna Akhmatova came to
Moscow to intercede with the authorities on behalf of her son who
was in and out of concentration camps for much of his life. She and
Tsvetaeva met in person on that occasion, spending two days
together. Beginning in 1915, Tsvetaeva had conceived a great
admiration for the woman who was then Russia's most famous
female poet. Akhmatova's attitude to Tsvetaeva was for a long time
critical and guarded. But the two women had corresponded spora-
dically in 1921–5. Now, after Tsvetaeva's return, Akhmatova came
to realize the importance of Tsvetaeva's poetry. But Tsvetaeva's
esteem for Akhmatova's had, unfortunately, declined. Tsvetaeva
failed to appreciate Akhmatova's subsequently famous 'Poem
without a Hero,' thinking it labored and old-fashioned. Despite the
time the two poets spent together, it seems to have been the same
kind of 'non-meeting' as Tsvetaeva's encounter with Pasternak in
Paris in 1935. When Akhmatova learned of the arrest of Tsvetaeva's
daughter and husband, she wrote a moving poem called 'The
Belated Reply,' which she apparently failed to recite to Tsvetaeva
when they met. The reply is to Tsvetaeva's 1916 cycle 'Verses to
Akhmatova' from *Mileposts I*. In Akhmatova's poem, Tsvetaeva
appears as an invisible being, a double, a mockingbird. Then the
echo of her voice calls from a tower:

> 'Today I have returned home.
> Admire, O my native fields,
> What has happened to me for this.
> Abyss has swallowed my loved ones
> And my parents' home has been pillaged.'

The poem concludes with a vision of the encounter of the two poets,
which is more poetic and somehow rings more true than the way
things actually happened:

Tonight, Marina, you and I
Are walking through the midnight capital
And behind us are millions of such as we
And there is no procession more silent.
All around ring the funeral bells
And the savage Muscovite moaning
Of the blizzard that obliterates our traces.

Tsvetaeva's days were taken up by mundane chores: her literary
translations, shopping in the often empty food stores (in a letter to
Olga Mochalova, she described a shopping expedition when all
that was available anywhere was margarine and lingonberry jam),
trips to editorial offices. But she knew that her poetic gift was still
there and that it could be brought to the kindling point if she were
to become infatuated. She was drawn to Arseny Tarkovsky, to
whom she addressed the only new poem she wrote during that
period, and to Yevgeny Tager, the husband of her and Pasternak's
friend, the memoirist Elena Tager. Her most ardent attraction,
however, was once more centered on the person least inclined to
reciprocate: Nikolai Moskvin's young wife Tania Kvanina. The
young woman's offer of help in practical matters ('Should you ever
need me ...') and her ability to feel affection for a particular pine
tree suggested to Tsvetaeva possibilities that were clearly not
there. In her letter to Tania of November 17, 1940 Tsvetaeva
explained that her need is not to be loved, but to love another
person: 'the whole point is for us to love, for our heart to pound
even if it should break to smithereens. I always got broken to
smithereens and all of my poems are those silver smithereens of my
heart.'

Tsvetaeva told Tania that she thought of her always, day and
night, and that what she needed was to love her: 'I need you like one
needs bread – I can't think of a better thing one person can say to
another. Yes, I can: like air.' And a little earlier in the same letter:
'You can give me – boundlessly – much, because the only person
who can give me something is the one who causes my heart to
pound. This pounding heart of mine is what gives me [everything].
When I do not love, I am not I. It's been so long since I've been I.
With you I am I.' To make Tania understand what she meant,
Tsvetaeva told her about Sonechka Holliday and lent her a manuscript of 'The Tale of Sonechka.' A year before leaving France,

Tsvetaeva wrote to Tesková about Holliday: 'She was a female being whom I loved more than anyone else in the world. Perhaps more than *all* beings, male or female' (Letter of July 16, 1937). She went on to tell Tesková that the news of Holliday's death had touched her innermost depths 'and perhaps I descended into that eternal well where everything is always alive.'

Now she hoped that she had found a new version of Sonechka Holliday. She apologized for writing her letter to Tania of November 17 in the old orthography which had not been used in Russia since 1918. 'But I couldn't have written this kind of letter in the new [orthography]. It is the old I – the young I – who is writing to you, the one who was twenty years ago, as though those twenty years never happened! The I who belonged to Sonechka.' But reading 'The Tale of Sonechka' didn't help. Kvanina simply had no idea what it was that Tsvetaeva wanted from her. If the love Tsvetaeva needed was possible in the Russia of 1914 and 1920 or in Natalie Clifford Barney's Paris, in Stalin's time it was not even a love that dared not speak its name. It was a love that had no name. Tatiana Kvanina's memoir about her friendship with Tsvetaeva, published more than forty years later, is a mixture of pride and perplexity. Even in her sixties Tsvetaeva's Tania still had no clue to the kind of emotions she had aroused in the poet whose memory she revered for the rest of her life.

In April of 1941 Ariadna Efron was granted permission to correspond with her relatives and on the 11th of that month Tsvetaeva received the first letter since her daughter's arrest in August 1939. She wrote Ariadna a long, encouraging letter, promising to send her food parcels, a blanket, dresses and jewelry. It is clear from the letter that Samuil Gurevich (Mulia), who considered himself Ariadna's husband, had hopes of coming to visit her at her remote penal settlement. This letter, dated April 12, also tells of Tsvetaeva's translation projects ('I am not writing anything of my own, there's too much work') and of her recent election to a group committee of the writers' trade union of the State Publishing House (Tsvetaeva had to join this government-run trade union so as to be paid for her translations; election to the group committee placed her on the lowest level of union activists, a formality that would provide her with better pay and greater job security). It is possibly as the result of this election that a poem by Tsvetaeva appeared in the journal

Thirty Days (*30 dnei*) that spring, the only such instance prior to her post-Stalinist rehabilitation. It was an old poem, written in 1920 and already published in Prague in 1924. For publication in the Soviet Union, one stanza about the inevitability of death was removed by the censor.

A valued friendship was formed between Tsvetaeva and Alexei Kruchionykh. One of the founders of Russian Futurism, the creator of the abstract 'trans-sense' language (*zaum'*), a close friend of Khlebnikov, Mayakovsky and Pasternak, Kruchionykh was by the 1930s barred from publishing. He survived as a bibliophile and book dealer. Tsvetaeva donated some of her manuscripts to him and annotated some others that were in his possession, earning thereby the gratitude of later scholars. Kruchionykh also made copies of some of Tsvetaeva's letters to Pasternak, preserving them for posterity when most of their correspondence was lost during World War II. On the second anniversary of Tsvetaeva's arrival in Moscow, Kruchionykh invited Tsvetaeva, her son, and the young writer Lydia Libedinskaya on an excursion and a picnic at the Sheremetiev Palace in Kuskovo near Moscow. A photograph taken of the four of them on that occasion shows a trim, friendly Tsvetaeva and a hulking Mur who looks at least fifteen years older than his actual age, which was sixteen. On the reverse of the photograph Tsvetaeva wrote: 'To dear Alexei Kruchionykh with gratitude for my first beauty here. Kuskovo, the lake and the island, porcelain. On the second anniversary of my arrival.' This was written on June 18, 1941. Four days later, on the 22nd, Germany attacked Russia.

Joseph Stalin, Marina Tsvetaeva's employer at the People's Commissariat of Nationalities back in 1918, was the most mistrustful human being who ever lived. As Alexander Solzhenitsyn described it in a memorable passage of his novel *The First Circle*, Stalin had no confidence in anyone, beginning with his own mother and going all the way to the generals who served him and his associates at the Politburo. He sacrificed uncounted millions of human lives to his suspiciousness. There was only one man in his entire life whom he fully trusted and that was Adolf Hitler. Stalin had observed with approval Hitler's invasion of Poland, France, Belgium and other countries and his air blitz against England. Throughout the spring of 1941, Soviet intelligence and Western leaders, including Winston

Churchill, kept warning Stalin that a German attack on the Soviet Union was imminent. He refused to believe that his admired ally might turn against him. The invasion of June 22 found the Soviet armed forces utterly unprepared. The rapid German advance was facilitated by the voluntary surrender of many towns and military units. Whole areas welcomed the Germans, because people felt that anything, any rule at all was bound to be better than the terror and starvation they had experienced under Stalin. It was only later, when the Nazis showed themselves fully as capable of brutality as the communists, that Russian resistance against the occupiers arose.

By July, German planes were dropping incendiary bombs on Moscow and the German army was moving toward the Soviet capital. Tsvetaeva's primary concern was, as always, for the safety of her son. Because of his husky build, Mur was called to work with a civilian squad that defused and extinguished bombs. Tsvetaeva was terrified for him. She decided to join a group of writers that was being evacuated to the Tatar Socialist Republic in the eastern part of European Russia. Boris Pasternak strongly advised her against this. What she had hoped was that Pasternak might offer to shelter her at his country cottage in Peredelkino and thus get Mur away from the air defense work. But, as Olga Ivinskaya reported, Pasternak was reluctant to invite her out of consideration for his wife's comfort. But he did see Tsvetaeva and Mur off when they left Moscow for the Tatar Republic on August 8, 1941.

Elabuga is a small Tatar town situated at the confluence of the rivers Toima and Kama. In the nineteenth century, it was known in the Russian cultural tradition as the residence of two celebrities: the 'cavalry-maiden' Nadezhda Durova (1783–1866), who took part in the Napoleonic wars disguised as a man, had her memoirs published by Pushkin and later retired in Elabuga, still maintaining her male attire; and the realist painter Ivan Shishkin, whose sentimental painting of bear cubs in a pine forest is the all-time favourite art work of Russians of middlebrow taste and who was born in Elabuga. The town has acquired a new fame in the past two decades as the last resting place of Marina Tsvetaeva.

The better-placed writers within the union hierarchy, evacuated in the same group as Tsvetaeva, were settled in the town of Chistopol. There were better facilities there, including a projected communal mess hall. Chistopol was where Boris Pasternak found

himself in the fall of 1941 and so did, for a brief period, Anna
Akhmatova. Tsvetaeva belonged to a less well-regarded group
which was sent to the more provincial Elabuga. She arrived there on
August 21 and rented a room for herself and Mur at a hut belonging
to a retired local couple named Bredelshchikov. She brought along
a supply of rice, semolina and other non-perishable foods, and some
silver spoons she was hoping to sell. But she had very little money
and there was no prospect of any kind of work for her in Elabuga. A
few days after arriving, she traveled to Chistopol, hoping to get a
residence permit there. Her sojourn in Chistopol was shrouded in
mystery until 1982, when Lydia Chukovskaya sent abroad her
memoir about Tsvetaeva, 'At Death's Threshold' ('Predsmertie'),
based on her diaries of August 1941. Lydia Chukovskaya, daughter
of the critic and children's poet Kornei Chukovsky, chronicler of
Anna Akhmatova's works and days, novelist and a heroically
outspoken woman, first learned that Tsvetaeva was in Chistopol
when she heard that a council of evacuated writers had refused to
approve a residence permit (*propiska*) for her. Chukovskaya's
account of the events that followed is a valuable record of Soviet
literary mores during World War II and an unforgettable portrait of
Tsvetaeva at the end of her days.

Chukovskaya had never met Tsvetaeva, but she admired the little
of her poetry that she knew. As she heard it, the senior literary
statesmen in Chistopol, who were trying to prevent Tsvetaeva from
living there, were the poet Nikolai Aseyev and the playwright
Konstantin Treniov (Treniov's best-known play, performed all over
the Soviet Union in the 1920s and 30s, is *Liubov' Yarovaya*; it is
about a schoolmistress who heroically betrays her Socialist Revolutionary husband to the Bolsheviks). Their objection was that
Tsvetaeva's husband and daughter had been arrested as enemies of
the people and that in wartime one had to be particularly vigilant.
Chukovskaya was outraged that writers had arrogated to themselves the functions of the secret police. She prevailed on her
father's friend, the Yiddish poet Lev Kvitko, a Communist Party
member and holder of a Stalin Prize (he was murdered during
Stalin's purge of Jewish writers in 1952), to use his influence to make
Aseyev change his mind. Shortly thereafter, Chukovskaya met
Tsvetaeva. She found her grey-faced, emaciated and in a state of
near-despair. She kept Tsvetaeva company while a committee of
writers debated her fate. 'If they refuse me a residence permit in

Chistopol, I'll die,' Tsvetaeva told Chukovskaya. 'I feel sure they'll refuse. I'll drown myself in the Kama.' Tsvetaeva was subjected to a humiliating cross-examination about her reasons for wanting to move to Chistopol. She replied it was mainly because of the Chistopol trade school, where she wanted to enroll her son. Aseyev pretended illness, but sent in a written vote in Tsvetaeva's favour, which meant that Kvitko's intercession was successful. Treniov was outvoted and the committee ruled to grant her the permit.

At this point, Chukovskaya learned that Tsvetaeva had applied for a job as a dishwasher at the writers' mess hall which was still being built. She was staggered: 'Yes, of course, every kind of labor is honorable. And God grant that she gets it! But won't anyone feel ashamed? Here I am, say, eating broth or carrot patties and my plates, spoons and forks are to be washed not just by anyone, but by Marina Tsvetaeva. If Tsvetaeva can be appointed to wash dishes, why not let Akhmatova wash the floors or hire Alexander Blok, if he were still alive, as the mess hall stoker? That would really make it a writers' mess hall.' But Tsvetaeva was told that there were many other applicants for the job. After the favourable committee decision, Chukovskaya volunteered to help Tsvetaeva find Chistopol lodgings for herself and her son. But Tsvetaeva, dejected, spoke of the world coming to an end. To cheer her up, Chukovskaya took her to the home of her friends, the writer Mikhail Schneider and his wife Tatiana, who was later married to Konstantin Paustovsky. The Schneiders were a well-organized couple who lived in comfortable quarters. It turned out that they were Tsvetaeva's ardent admirers. They begged her to stay for dinner and for the night. The capable and energetic Tatiana Schneider promised to help Tsvetaeva find lodgings the next day. Surrounded by all this kindness and admiration, Tsvetaeva changed right before Chukovskaya's eyes. Color appeared in her face, she looked younger, less despondent. Like most of Tsvetaeva's admirers in the Soviet Union, the Schneiders and Chukovskaya knew only what she had published up to the early 1920s. They were amazed to hear from her of all the lyrics, long poems and prose which she had written since that time.

As described by Lydia Chukovskaya, meeting her and the Schneiders was exactly what Tsvetaeva needed at this point in her life: concerned, sympathetic people, who took an interest in her situation and were in a position to offer concrete help. But apparently the pain and humiliation through which the writers' committee had put her wounded her deeper than her friends knew. After dinner with the Schneiders, she went out saying that she would be back for the night. But she never returned. She went back to Elabuga instead. Her landlords, the Bredelshchikovs, remembered her as arriving in a state of utter depression. Next Sunday, August 31, was a day of compulsory labor duty (officially called 'voluntary'), when one member of each household had to help with the building of a nearby airport. Anastasia Bredelshchikova and Mur elected to go. Mikhail Bredelshchikov took his grandson fishing. Marina Tsvetaeva was left alone at home.

It is hard to evaluate the mood of Tsvetaeva on the last day of her life, because the key is most likely in her relationship with her son and we don't know what went on between them in the last days. Dmitry Sezeman, who was Georgy Efron's friend, describes him as monstrously egotistical, with no concern whatsoever for anyone's feelings. He adds that Mur was only partly responsible for this, because he was brought up to think that he was the center of the universe. The Bredelshchikovs reported hearing violent arguments between mother and son in French, and his constant reproaches and demands for luxuries she could not provide. Tsvetaeva's sister Anastasia devised in the new edition of her memoirs a theory that Tsvetaeva chose death to save her son. The motivation she cites is implausible. As Viktoria Schweitzer has shown, Anastasia was nowhere near her sister during the events in question, and her theory is simply one more manifestation of her ceaseless striving to exculpate Soviet society and its history of ever being wrong in any way. Kirill Henkin's book proposes that Tsvetaeva was driven over the brink when a local NKVD chief, in the misguided belief that he was helping Tsvetaeva to consolidate her position in the eyes of the Soviet authorities, ordered her to report on other evacuated writers. This kind of order could not be easily refused, and if the story were true, it would provide us with the most plausible motive of all. But Henkin's assertion is based on third-hand information which is not corroborated in any way. There is no point in adding further conjectures until some new evidence comes to light. Tsvetaeva's known experiences during the last two years of her life provide enough motivation to account for her step.

When Anastasia Bredelshchikova returned home on the afternoon of August 31, 1941, she found Marina Tsvetaeva hanging from a hook inside the entrance to the hut. The police were called. They

found two letters, one addressed to the authorities and the other to
Nikolai Aseyev, in which he was asked to look after Tsvetaeva's son
(to no avail, as it turned out). The first letter was confiscated and
never seen again. The letter to Aseyev was delivered to him by Mur
a few days later and it, too, disappeared. Neither her son, nor the
Bredelshchikovs attended the poet's funeral. Her death was not
reported in the Soviet press. There was no drawn-out funeral
procession through the streets of Moscow, as she had predicted in a
famous poem from *Mileposts I*, written at Easter of 1916. The
unknown young passerby, addressed in a poem written in 1913, will
never be able to accept her invitation to pause briefly at a tomb-
stone, a bunch of lupine and wild poppies in his hand, to read her
epitaph. Marina Tsvetaeva, one of Russia's greatest poets of this or
any century, was buried in Elabuga in an unmarked common grave
whose location is unknown. In 1960, Anastasia Tsvetaeva, allowed
to return to Moscow after many years of labor camps and exile,
traveled to Elabuga to look for her sister's grave. No one there was
able to tell her the exact place of the burial. An approximate spot
was finally selected and on it Anastasia arranged to have a wooden
cross placed with the inscription: 'On this side of the cemetery is
buried Marina Ivanovna Tsvetaeva. Born September 26, 1892, old
style, in Moscow; died August 31, 1941, new style, in Elabuga.' The
contrast between the two calendars, the old style Julian one and the
post-revolutionary new style Gregorian, subtly yet overwhelmingly
points to the contrast between the two epochs: the old one into
which Tsvetaeva was born and in which she was able to develop into
the poet she was and the new one, in which there was no room either
for her or, for the time being, her poetry.

Georgy Efron was the messenger who spread the news of his
mother's death. After selling her few belongings in Elabuga, he
traveled to Chistopol to deliver her letter to Aseyev and bring the
news to the evacuated writers there; then he went to Moscow to
inform his aunt Lilia Efron of Tsvetaeva's death. She passed the
information on to the literary community. Georgy was later evacuated from Moscow to Tashkent in Uzbekistan, where he attended
school. Dmitry Sezeman, who visited him there, found Mur
unchanged. He felt no regrets about Tsvetaeva's death, only
annoyance at all the fuss and bother it was causing. As Sezeman put
it in a conversation with me: 'Mur was no hypocrite, he owned up to

his disgust.' In December 1942, Tsvetaeva's son was drafted into the
Red Army. He hated military service. His unit consisted for the
most part of criminals who had been released from prisons to
participate in the war and who treated him with contempt. He
begged his relatives in Moscow to send him money and food. All
traces of him disappear in summer 1944. The official version is that
he was killed in action. But at the end of the war there was a
persistent rumor in Moscow that Georgy Efron was shot by the
sergeant of his own unit for rudeness and insubordination.

News of Marina Tsvetaeva's death spread slowly by word of
mouth. On November 10, 1941, Boris Pasternak wrote from
Moscow to his wife Zinaida, who was in Chistopol, that he had
heard of Tsvetaeva's suicide from the writer Konstantin Fedin:
'How guilty I am if this is true! [. . .] I shall never be forgiven for it.'
This letter, and Pasternak's letter of March 20, 1942 to Nina
Tabidze, the widow of his friend, the Georgian poet Titian Tabidze
(shot in the purge of 1937), show that Pasternak did not really
understand Tsvetaeva's situation and the conditions under which
she lived. He thought that she was always surrounded by a circle of
appreciative friends and that Aseyev and Treniov, who he knew
were in Chistopol, were sure to help and support her. In 1942 he
dedicated to Tsvetaeva two remarkable commemorative poems.
Anna Akhmatova was evacuated from Leningrad to Chistopol in
the fall of 1941, but she soon arranged to be transferred elsewhere
because she did not want to live in the place where Tsvetaeva had
been driven to suicide. Akhmatova, too, wrote of Tsvetaeva's death
with warmth and sympathy in several poems that could not be
published until the 1960s. On November 28, 1941, in German-
occupied Pskov, a German-sponsored newspaper *For the
Motherland* (*Za rodinu*) printed a combined appreciation and
obituary by a certain O. Anisimov, which shows a good grasp of
Tsvetaeva's poetry and of her place in the literary pantheon. This
was one of the two obituaries that appeared after her death, the
other being an article by Alexander Bakhrakh, published in a
Russian literary miscellany brought out in Paris in 1946, after its
liberation from the Germans. Along with a few unfair things about
her poetry, commonplaces of unfavourable Paris criticism of the
1930s, Bakhrakh drew a sympathetic portrait of the late poet: '. . . a
unique person and a major Russian poet is gone, leaving in the
memory of people who knew her an image that cannot be erased.'

Anastasia Tsvetaeva, exiled to Siberia, learned of Marina's death only two years later. In the summer of 1943, she received a letter from her half-sister Valeria. At the end of the letter, after various other news, Valeria wrote: 'Musia, the author of *The Magic Lantern*, is no more. Her son is somewhere in the Caucasus with the Writers' Union.' The wording was certainly peculiar. Either Valeria was so estranged from Marina that she remembered her only by her childhood nickname and knew her work only up to her second book; or she was using Aesopian language, current in the Soviet Union, so as not to mention Tsvetaeva's name in case the letter was censored. Anastasia refused to believe Valeria's news. But it was confirmed later that summer by a brief letter from Lilia Efron: 'Marina perished two years ago on August 31. We kiss your heart. Lilia, Zina.' (Zina was Lilia Efron's life-long companion Zinaida Shirkevich.) Asked about the manner of Marina's death, Lilia Efron sent a three-word telegram: 'Like our mother.' Anastasia knew that Sergei and Lilia Efron's mother had committed suicide by hanging herself in 1910, after the suicide of her youngest son. Now Anastasia Tsvetaeva had her answer.

The decade of the 1940s was the time when Marina Tsvetaeva seemed forgotten. Her work was not published anywhere. Among the few meager references one finds to her during that decade in Russian publications abroad, two can be cited. Georgy Fedotov wrote in New York in 1942: 'Without being guilty of partiality, one can call Marina Tsvetaeva the foremost Russian poet of our epoch.' An opposing view appeared in Ivan Tkhorzhevsky's history of Russian literature, published in Paris in 1946 and reissued there in 1950: 'Marina Tsvetaeva is entirely engrossed in trying to astound the reader with her talent [...], giving him nothing in return. Tsvetaeva has nothing to say. Her art resembles a gaping, empty stone quarry.' In the Soviet Union there was total silence, as if Marina Tsvetaeva had never existed. In the atmosphere of the witch hunts that characterized the second half of that decade, this may well have been for the best, because the only terms in which the Soviet press could have written of Tsvetaeva in the postwar years would be vituperation and hatred.

With World War II victoriously concluded, Stalin's government felt free to revert to the practice of selecting particular groups of people to blame for whatever was currently wrong, as had been the

Soviet custom since the October Revolution. This time artists and
intellectuals were the target. The 'Zhdanov period,' named after
Andrei Zhdanov, who orchestrated the hate campaigns, began with
the resolution of the Central Committee of the Communist Party of
August 14, 1946 which branded Akhmatova and the beloved Soviet
humorist Mikhail Zoshchenko as 'ideologically harmful,' guilty of
leading young people astray and 'alien to our people.' There had
already been a press campaign against Akhmatova in the 1920s, but
now it was no longer a matter of a few derogatory articles. This time
the full power of the government, the party and the media was
mobilized to ridicule and revile the poet – not for anything she had
done or written, but, as in all such cases, simply for being what she
was. The next years saw similar attacks on playwrights, stage
directors and literary scholars. In 1948 came the turn of the musicians, with Sergei Prokofiev and Dmitry Shostakovich denounced
and forced to abase themselves and apologize for having written
their music. Andrei Zhdanov seemed to recognize quality, because
it was the most talented and successful people that he usually
selected for savaging. A dense atmosphere of denunciation, sus-
picion and fear blanketed the country. An anti-Semitic campaign
was unleashed under the pretext of eliminating 'rootless cosmopoli-
tans.' Numerous Jewish writers and other intellectuals were
arrested in 1949 and a large group of them shot in 1952. Among the
latter were Lev Kvitko, who had defended Tsvetaeva from Treniov
in Chistopol, and her daughter's lover Samuil Gurevich. It took
Ariadna Efron two years to learn of his fate. On June 3, 1954, she
wrote to Boris Pasternak: '. . . I have learned of S.'s demise. Last
year I had learned of his illness, but had hopes of recovery. Now
there is no hope left.' In the Aesopian language of the period,
'illness' meant arrest and 'recovery' meant release.

After her incarceration in 1939, Ariadna had been subjected to
beatings and starvation. Other forms of physical and psychological
torture were used to extract from her a confession that she was a
spy. She was sentenced to eight years of hard labor, which she
served in full. She was released in 1947 and allowed to live in the
provincial city of Riazan. In 1949, possibly because of her connection with Gurevich, she was denounced by someone and arrested
again. As a repeat offender (though there was no crime), Ariadna
Efron was this time sentenced to exile for life in the penal colony
Turukhansk, on the shore of the river Yenisei in the frozen arctic

wastes of Siberia. Her correspondence with Boris Pasternak during that period, published in Paris in 1982 as *Letters from Exile* (*Pis'ma iz ssylki*), is a fascinating document of her survival under conditions which most people in the West couldn't imagine. To make up for what he had failed to do for her mother, Pasternak remained in constant touch, helping Ariadna in any way he could. She was one of the earliest readers of his famous novel *Doctor Zhivago*, chapters from which he sent her in the late 1940s, when he had no hope in the world of publishing it. Nikolai Aseyev also corresponded with Ariadna and offered to visit her in Siberia. But she doubted his sincerity and refused to take his concern seriously.

Stalin's death on March 5, 1953 ended the era of mass frameups and terror directed against entire categories of people initiated by Lenin and Dzerzhinsky in 1918 and continued, with greater or lesser intensity, up to this point. The Khrushchev years brought on the post-Stalin 'thaw,' as Ilya Ehrenburg dubbed the liberalization of the mid-1950s. Millions were allowed to return from concentration camps and exile, among them Tsvetaeva's sister and daughter. An array of cultural phenomena, banned in the 1930s and '40s, was amnestied and brought back. The thaw coincided in time with a new development in the West: the growth of Russian-language publications in the United States, many of them supported by CIA funds during the Cold War. These two events, occurring more or less simultaneously, made possible the revival of Marina Tsvetaeva's reputation in the 1950s.

The first harbinger came the year Stalin died. Ekaterina Eleneva, Tsvetaeva's friend from her Prague days, prevailed on the Chekhov Publishing House, founded in New York with US government support for the purpose of publishing Russian books banned in the USSR, to bring out a volume of selected Tsvetaeva prose. Eleneva wrote to Vladimir Nabokov, inviting him to provide the collection with an introduction. She received a reply from Nabokov's wife Vera who wrote that while Nabokov had a high regard for Tsvetaeva as a writer and poet, he did not want to do the essay because of Tsvetaeva's connection with Soviet espionage and possibly with the abduction of Kutepov. (General Alexander Kutepov was kidnapped and killed by Soviet agents in 1930. Tsvetaeva wrote of him with some sympathy in a letter to Salomea Halpern.) In another letter to Eleneva, Mrs Nabokov wrote that she and her husband refused to believe that Tsvetaeva could not have been aware of her husband's activities. Eleneva then turned to Feodor Stepun and the collection appeared with his introduction. The year 1953 also brought an anthology of Russian émigré poetry edited by Yury Ivask. It contained thirteen poems by Tsvetaeva, among them her three-poem cycle addressed to Anatoly Lunacharsky during the civil war and published for the first time.

The appearance of the collection of Tsvetaeva's prose was treated as an important literary event by the émigré journals in Paris and New York (which became a major émigré publishing center after World War II). From that time on, Tsvetaeva was a constant presence in the Russian-language journals published abroad. Her earlier supporters, such as Yury Ivask, Gleb Struve and Mark Slonim, wrote about her and published her previously unknown manuscripts. They were joined by commentators such as Vladimir Weidlé and Vladimir Nabokov, who had earlier written of Tsvetaeva with scorn, but had come to a new appreciation of her work in the later years. Gleb Struve's section on Tsvetaeva in his 1955 history of Russian émigré literature, and his publication of the first edition of *The Demesne of the Swans* in 1957 confirmed the reinstatement of Tsvetaeva, after a fifteen-year hiatus, to the position she had enjoyed in émigré letters in the 1920s and early 1930s. Memoirs by her friends, such as Izvolskaya, aroused much interest. But there were also some dissenting voices among the exiled Russian commentators, the most prominent of them being Georgy Adamovich, who throughout the 1950s and '60s kept obsessively repeating in article after article that the new fashion for Tsvetaeva was a transient fad and that she could not possibly be as good as others claimed. But even he ultimately relented, publishing shortly before his death in 1972 a haunting poem which expressed his regret about missing the chance to get to know Tsvetaeva better during her Paris years.

In the sixties and the seventies, reprints of Tsvetaeva's writings, editions of her previously unpublished work, her letters, and scholarly studies of her *œuvre* kept appearing steadily in Russian-language publications of America and Western Europe. The journals *The New Review* (*Novyi zhurnal*), New York, and *Le Messager* (*Vestnik*), Paris (the latter is a Russian-language religious publication, which also features an excellent literary section in each issue), have been particularly generous over the years with space allocated to Tsvetaeva materials. The culmination of this Tsvetaeva renaissance among the exiled Russians was the bringing out by Alexander Sumerkin of the Russica Publishers, New York, of two volumes of Tsvetaeva's prose and four volumes of her poetry (with a fifth volume of plays pending at this writing), in 1979 and 1980–3, respectively. These are the most comprehensive editions of Tsvetaeva's work ever attempted. They are blessedly free of the censorship cuts that plague the recent editions of Tsvetaeva in the Soviet Union, and they have been referred to with gratitude many times during the writing of the preceding pages.

In the Soviet Union, the first post-Stalinist thaw brought about a liberalization in the cultural sphere that took place in 1956, subsequently dubbed 'the Year of Protest' (in a collection of Soviet writing from that year edited by Hugh McLean and Walter Vickery). One of the products of that year was the anthology *Literary Moscow* (*Literaturnaia Moskva*), vol. II, in which a selection of Tsvetaeva's poems appeared, accompanied by an essay about her by Ilya Ehrenburg. Just as Ehrenburg had spearheaded the recognition of Tsvetaeva at the time of her emigration in 1922, he now made up for his failure to do anything for her in 1939–41 by introducing her to a new generation of readers who knew nothing about her. Tsvetaeva's poetry appeared in two more Soviet anthologies in 1956 and 1957, and then the thaw was followed by a temporary freeze. In the meantime, *samizdat*, the private circulation in typescript of literature not officially published in the country, became a major fact of intellectual life in the Soviet Union. Numerous non-approved, non-Socialist-Realist authors were circulated in *samizdat*, of which Tsvetaeva soon emerged as the most popular. Her spiritual independence, her tragic fate and her verbal brilliance all combined to make her the most beloved poet of Soviet youth in the 1960s and '70s.

Ilya Ehrenburg's memoirs about Tsvetaeva, Boris Pasternak's second autobiography (published first in the West and only years later in a Soviet journal), and a new Soviet edition of her poetry all appeared in 1961. These three publications brought the enthusiasm for Tsvetaeva to the point of adulation. The greater portion of the printing of the slim 1961 volume of her verse, and of the far more comprehensive 1965 one which appeared in the prestigious 'Poet's Library' series, were exported abroad to earn foreign currency. The copies of these editions that were made available in Moscow were sold out within one day and later brought astronomical prices on the black market. But there were powerful voices opposing this new tide of Tsvetaeva popularity. Influential Stalinist critics such as Alexei Surkov (a promising poet in the 1920s, he was the party's watchdog in matters of ideological purity from the 1940s on), Alexander Dymshits and Elena Serebrovskaya repeatedly warned their readers that Tsvetaeva was a minor figure who was mired in the past, that her poetry did not belong in socialist society and, above all, that she was not a suitable influence for the younger generation.

But there was no way for the Soviet literary establishment to stop the growth of Tsvetaeva's reputation to towering proportions. Once this was realized, only one course was possible: to take over her work and her outlook, to tailor her views and her biography to the requisite dimensions of a patriotic and progressive poet, who may have made a few mistakes in her day, misunderstood the October Revolution, was alienated from her people, but eventually emerged with a politically correct (pro-Soviet, anti-Western and anti-émigré) ideology. This is the simplistic image that is found in the introductory essays to the recent Soviet editions of Tsvetaeva's work. Tsvetaeva's sister and her daughter, each in her way, have lent their testimony as indispensable witnesses to the consolidation of this image.

Ariadna Efron's sentence was reviewed early in 1955. She was fully rehabilitated 'due to absence of evidence of any crime' – a standard official formula in such instances – and allowed to return to Moscow. Her aunt Anastasia, who was arrested two years earlier than Ariadna, had to wait till 1959 to have her rights reinstated. The ascendant popularity of Marina Tsvetaeva gave the two women a new cause in their lives and a place of honor in Soviet society. Each of them regarded herself as the true keeper of the flame. Their respective memoirs have been frequently cited in the present book. They are enormously valuable as sources of information about Tsvetaeva, but they both need to be used with considerable caution. Whatever reservations one may entertain about the total veracity of Marina Tsvetaeva's own memoirs, one thing about them is beyond doubt: when she wrote them in Paris, she gave no thought to censorship. Nadezhda Mandelstam, in her books about her husband, and Lydia Chukovskaya, writing about Akhmatova, had no hope of publication in the Soviet Union and wrote what they did for export. They were concerned with establishing the unvarnished truth. But Anastasia Tsvetaeva and Ariadna Efron had docility and obedience imprinted on their minds and memories during their long years as prisoners. Their recollections of Tsvetaeva were written with one eye firmly and always on the Soviet censor.

Apart from the public requirement of making Tsvetaeva's life and views more conventional than they actually were (for example, concealing the evidence of her relationship with Sophia Parnok and its significance), her sister and her daughter each had her private agenda. Anastasia was especially eager to discredit Marina's memoirs about the harshness of their mother during the time of her and Anastasia's childhood (the articles by Irma Kudrova and Viktoria Schweitzer, which cast doubt on the veracity of Anastasia Tsvetaeva's memoirs, have been cited in Chapter 1, p. 8). Ariadna Efron's primary concern was with whitewashing the posthumous image of her father. She worshipped the memory of Sergei Efron and saw him as a hero of almost superhuman proportions. In an unpublished letter to Ekaterina Eleneva, she wrote of her father: 'I have seen many wonderful people in my life, but never, never, never anyone who could even remotely be compared with him.' In a letter to Mouna Bulgakova of February 18, 1968, Ariadna paraphrased Tsvetaeva's statement from a letter to Ivask that the only two people she ever encountered who equaled her in poetic and human strength were Pasternak and Rilke. Ariadna replaced Rilke's name with that of her father. Tsvetaeva's daughter took a violent dislike to my 1966 book about the poet, calling it distorted and false in letters to friends abroad – not because of the numerous factual errors the book did contain, but because it included an account of Sergei Efron's activities during the 1930s and documented Tsvetaeva's opposition to the October Revolution. She was furious about Gleb Struve's publication of *The Demesne of the Swans* in 1957. Vadim Morkovin's edition of Tsvetaeva's correspondence with Anna Tesková also angered Ariadna Efron because Morkovin took advantage of the Czech liberalization of 1968 to publish the volume in Prague without the cuts usually required by communist censorship. Ariadna feared that the uncensored letters might jeopardize further Tsvetaeva publications in the Soviet Union.

In the last two decades of her life (she died in 1975), Tsvetaeva's

daughter devoted a heroic amount of work to establishing a
Tsvetaeva archive, deciphering her mother's manuscripts, and
getting her work published in the Soviet Union. She corresponded
with Tsvetaeva's friends abroad and got some of them, such as
Salomea Halpern and Ekaterina Eleneva, to send to the Soviet
Union Tsvetaeva's letters and other archival materials. In April of
1975, Ariadna Efron deposited the entire archive with the Central
State Archive of Literature and Art (TSGALI) in Moscow, with the
proviso that it be closed to researchers until the year 2000. Her
strangest exercise in rewriting history (and there are several others
in her memoirs and in her interviews with Véronique Lossky) was
her collaboration with Stanislav Gribanov, a military historian of
sorts who has specialized in manufacturing a new Georgy Efron. In
two articles, one published under his own name in 1975 and another
under a pen name in 1976, Gribanov drew a glamorous portrait of
Mur as an ardent Soviet patriot who adored Moscow, a fearless
warrior remembered for his heroism by the other soldiers of his unit
and a future literary scholar who was planning to write a book about
his great mother (a book about Tsvetaeva in 1942?). Viktoria
Schweitzer rightly called Gribanov's work a primitive falsification,
done for the purpose of furnishing Tsvetaeva posthumously with a
properly respectable Soviet son. But these articles cite Mur's
letters, supplied by Ariadna Efron, which are also full of official
clichés. The Mur that we know from all the other sources was not
likely to have written them except as a joke.

However, Ariadna Efron was apparently kind and helpful to the
pleiad of Soviet Tsvetaeva scholars which emerged in the 1960s. At
its worst, Soviet scholarship on Tsvetaeva can be insufferably banal,
a morass of half-truths propped up with out-of-context quotations:
Tsvetaeva as a leader of a progressive opposition to the right-wing
émigrés headed by Zinaida Gippius; or a comrade-at-arms of
Gorky and Mayakovsky, her 'attention riveted to the successes of
socialism at home' (examples cited from a 1974 article by a provincial critic). But the work of Irma Kudrova, Viktoria Schweitzer
(who emigrated to the United States in the 1970s), Sophia Poliakova and Lev Mnukhin has been an inspiration to everyone
interested in Tsvetaeva. Their access to sources not available in the
West, their devotion, and their insights have permanently
broadened our knowledge of this poet.

Soviet literary authorities still keep a very tight rein on what can be written about Tsvetaeva and which of her writings may be published. This is understandable. With her explosive individuality and her refusal to be reduced to any literary, political or any other kind of common denominator, Tsvetaeva herself as well as her poetry are the very opposite of the slogans and stereotypes inherent in any compulsory ideology. In 1925, Tsvetaeva wrote that she would return to Russia 'not as a permitted relic of the past, but as a desired, eagerly-awaited guest.' This has, to a large extent, come true. But the day of an uncensored Tsvetaeva in the Soviet Union, a Tsvetaeva entitled to all her loves, all her ideas and all of her prose and poetry – that day is still hidden in a very remote future.

Appendix on sources
(and list of abbreviations)

The sources consulted for the book as a whole are listed below, as are the abbreviations used for major sources repeatedly cited. Additional sources mentioned in each chapter are cited separately chapter by chapter. Autobiographical information supplied in Tsvetaeva's own prose and poetry, found in the principal editions listed below, is not, as a rule, further identified under chapter headings.

Principal Editions of Marina Tsvetaeva's Writings

T-65 Ariadna Efron and Anna Saakiants, eds., *Selected Works* (*Izbrannye proizvedeniia*), Moscow–Leningrad, 1965.

N *Unpublished Works. Poetry, Drama, Prose* (*Neizdannoe. Stikhi, teatr, proza*), Paris, 1976. (Contains *Juvenilia, The Stone Angel*, and 'The Tale of Sonechka'.)

IP 1 and 2 Alexander Sumerkin, ed., *Selected Prose in Two Volumes*, (*Izbrannaia proza v dvukh tomakh*), New York, 1979.

S1 and S2 Anna Saakiants, ed., *Works* (*Sochineniia*), 2 vols., Moscow, 1980.

SiP 1, 2, 3 and 4 Alexander Sumerkin and Viktoria Schweitzer, eds., *Lyric and Narrative Poetry in Five Volumes* (*Stikhotvoreniia i poèmy v piati tomakh*), New York, 1980–83. (The four volumes so far published are the most comprehensive edition of all of Tsvetaeva's poetry. The projected fifth volume is to contain her plays, a chronology of her life and writings and essays on her work.)

Letters of Marina Tsvetaeva

(Listed here are the principal publications of Tsvetaeva's letters, which have been frequently cited in the text. Sources of other letters by Tsvetaeva are identified in this appendix under the individual chapters that quote them.)

L Ariadna Efron and Anna Saakiants, eds., excerpts from letters to various persons, published in *Novyi mir*, Moscow, 1969, No. 4.

NP Gleb and Nikita Struve, eds., *Unpublished Letters* (*Neizdannye pis'ma*), Paris, 1972. (This volume is the largest and most comprehensive collection of Tsvetaeva's letters so far published.)

Letters to George Ivask in *Russian Literary Archive* (*Russkii literaturnyi arkhiv*), Dmitry Chizhevsky and Michael Karpovich, eds., New York, 1956.
Letters to Anatoly Steiger in *Opyty*, New York, 1955–7, NNo. 5, 7 and 8.
Letters to Alexander Bakhrakh in *Mosty*, Munich, 1960, vol. 5 and 1961, vol. 6.
Marina Tsvetaeva, *Letters to Anna Tesková* (*Pis'ma k Anne Teskovoi*), Prague, 1969.
Letters to Maximilian Voloshin edited by V. P. Kupchenko, in *Ezhegodnik rukopisnogo otdela Pushkinskogo doma*, Leningrad, 1975; and edited by Irma Kudrova, in *Novyi mir*, 1977, No. 2.

Biographies

Simon Karlinsky, *Marina Cvetaeva. Her Life and Art*, Berkeley and Los Angeles, 1966.
Russian translation of excerpts from the above in the underground (*samizdat*) journal *Chasy*, 1979, No. 16.
Maria Razumovsky, *Marina Zwetajewa. Mythos und Wahrheit*, Vienna, 1981.
Maria Razumovskaya, *Marina Tsvetaeva. Mif i deistvitel'nost'*, London, 1983. (An augmented translation of the above into Russian, with an important updated bibliography.)

Bibliographies

WSA Lev Mnukhin, 'Marina Tsvetaeva. A Bibliographical Guide to Publications on Her Life and Activities, 1910–1928' ('M. I. Tsvetaeva. Bibliograficheskii ukazatel' literatury o zhizni i deiatel' nosti, 1910–1928'), *Wiener slawistischer Almanach*, Sonderband 3, 1981 (a special Tsvetaeva issue).
Tatiana Gladkova and Lev Mnukhin, *Bibliographie des œuvres de Marina Tsvetaeva*, Paris, 1982.
See under biographies, Maria Razumovskaya, *Marina Tsvetaeva. Mif i deistvitel'nost'*.

Memoirs by Relatives

AT Anastasia Tsvetaeva, *Memoirs* (*Vospominaniia*) Moscow, 1971, 1974 and 1983.
AE Ariadna Efron, *Pages from Memoirs* (*Stranitsy vospominanii*), Paris, 1979.
Lev Mnukhin, ed., 'The Poet's Sacred Craft' ('Sviatoe remeslo poèta'), a montage from Ariadna Efron's statements about her mother, in *Literaturnoe obozrenie*, Moscow, 1981, No. 12.

Collection of Essays and Documents

WSA *Marina Cvetaeva Studien und Materialen, Wiener slawistischer Almanach*, Sonderband 3, Vienna, 1981.

On the origins of Ivan Tsvetaev and his family: Prince B. A. Shchetinin, 'Ivan Tsvetaev in Memoriam' ('Pamiati I. V. Tsvetaeva'), *Istoricheskii vestnik*, CXXXIV, St Petersburg, 1913; AT; Tsvetaeva's letters to Rozanov in L and NP; Anna Saakiants's annotations to the poem 'My First Grandmother' ('U pervoi babki') in S1 and her and Ariadna Efron's notes to poems No. 9 and 155 in T-65.

On the origins of Maria Meyn and her family: letters to Rozanov and Bunina in NP; AT; AE; Saakiants's notes to 'My Mother and Music' ('Mat' i muzyka') in S2.

On the connection between the famine of 1892 and the formation of the dissident parties, Nicholas V. Riasanovsky, *A History of Russia*, Second Edition, New York, London and Toronto, 1969 (the section 'The Background of the Revolution of 1905,' pp. 449–51).

The debate on the veracity of Anastasia Tsvetaeva's memoirs about her sister: Irma Kudrova, 'Leaves and Roots' ('List'ia i korni'), *Zvezda*, Leningrad, 1976, No. 4 and 'Resurrection and Comprehension' ('Voskreshenie i postizhenie'), *Neva*, Leningrad, 1982, No. 12; and Viktoria Schweitzer, 'An Open Letter to Anastasia Tsvetaeva' ('Otkrytoe pis'mo Anastasii Tsvetaevoi'), *Sintaksis*, Paris, 1982, No. 10.

For rebuttals to the two Kudrova essays, see Anastasia Tsvetaeva, 'Roots and Fruit' ('Korni i plody'), *Zvezda*, 1979, No. 4 and Anna Saakiants, 'On the Truth of "Chronicles" and the Poet's Truth' ('O pravde "letopisi" i pravde poèta'), *Voprosy Literatury*, Moscow, 1983, No. 11. The debate was further discussed and summarized by Viktoria Schweitzer in '"The Kernel of the Poet's Germ." The Debate on Marina Tsvetaeva's Childhood' ('"Zerno zerna poèta." Spor o detstve Mariny Tsvetaevoi'), *Russkaia mysl'*, Paris, May 3 and May 10, 1984.

On 'The Devil,' Lily Feiler, 'Marina Tsvetaeva's Childhood,' unpublished; Valeria Shevliagina's reaction to reading 'The Devil,' Véronique Lossky, 'Marina Cvétaeva. Souvenirs de contemporains,' WSA.

Tsvetaeva's letter to Raisa Lomonosova: from the Brotherton Library, University of Leeds, courtesy of Richard Davies.

The memoir of Alexandra Zhernakova-Nikolaeva, 'The Tsvetaev Home' ('Tsvetaevskii dom'), *Russkaia mysl'*, Paris, March 23 and 26, 1963; also, my personal conversation with her in spring 1963.

Information on Tsvetaeva's trip to Paris at sixteen: letters to Bakhrakh and AT.

On the 1910 scandal about the thefts at the Rumiantsev Museum: Shchetinin, AT, and Andrei Bely, the chapter devoted to Ellis in his book *Between Two Revolutions* (*Mezhdu dvukh revoliutsii*), Leningrad, 1934.

On Ellis, see Gleb Struve's introductory note to Tsvetaeva's letters to Ellis in NP.

The history of the publication and critical reception of *The Evening Album* is outlined in great detail in Lev Mnukhin, 'Marina Tsvetaeva's First Book' ('Pervaia kniga Mariny Tsvetaevoi'), *Individual'nost' pisatelia i literaturno-obshchestvennyi protsess*, Voronezh, 1979. The article quotes and summarizes the various reviews mentioned in this chapter.

On Maximilian Voloshin's personality, see, in addition to Tsvetaeva's 'The Living About the Living,' Boris Filippov, 'Maximilian Voloshin, the Poet of Contrasts and Rebellions' ('Maksimilian Voloshin, poèt kontrastov i miatezhei'), *Vestnik* (*Le Messager*), Paris, 1977, No. 120. Filippov's essay was reprinted as an introduction to the first volume of Voloshin's collected poetry in two volumes (*Stikhotvoreniia i poèmy v dvukh tomakh*), Paris, 1982.

On Marina Tsvetaeva's dislike of the stories and plays of Anton Chekhov and her lack of familiarity with his work, see my essay 'Russian Anti-Chekhovians,' *Russian Literature*, Amsterdam, 1984, No. 15.

On Sergei Efron and his family: AE and AT. Also Véronique Lossky, 'Souvenirs de contemporains' and Irma Kudrova's introductory essay to her publication of Tsvetaeva's letters to Voloshin.

On role conflict in Tsvetaeva's poetry: Antonina Filonov Gove, 'The Feminine Stereotype and Beyond: Role Conflict and Resolution in the Poetics of Marina Tsvetaeva,' *Slavic Review*, Urbana-Champaign, 1977, vol. 36, No. 2.

CHAPTER 3: TWO RIVAL SUNS

Marina Tsvetaeva's portrait by Magda Nachmann and a selection of her photographs for the period 1911–16 are reproduced in *Tsvetaeva. A Pictorial Biography*, Ellendea Proffer, ed., Ann Arbor, 1980.

The poem Zinaida Gippius addressed to the Decembrists was called '14 December.' She included it as the last poem in the second volume of her collected poems published in 1910.

'Alya. Notations on My First Daughter' ('Alya. Zapisi o moei pervoi docheri'), in *Vestnik*, (*Le Messager*), 1981, No. 135.

On the relationship between Tsvetaeva and Parnok, with exhaustive archival documentation: Sophia Poliakova, *The Sunset Days of Yore: Tsvetaeva and Parnok* (*Zakatnye ony dni: Tsvetaeva i Parnok*), Ann Arbor, 1983. Also pertinent are the same author's introductory essay and annotations to Sophia Parnok, *Collected Poems* (*Sobranie stikhotvorenii*), Ann Arbor, 1979, and 'Poetry and Truth in Tsvetaeva's Cycle of Poems "Woman Friend"' ('Poèziia i pravda v tsikle stikhotvorenii Tsvetaevoi "Podruga"'), WSA.

On attitudes to lesbianism and male homosexuality in pre-revolutionary

Russia, see my historical survey 'Russia's Gay Literature & History (11th–20th Centuries),' *Gay Sunshine*, San Francisco, 1976, No. 29/30; and my review essay on Nikolai Przhevalsky and Mikhail Kuzmin, 'Revisionism Revised,' *The Advocate*, San Mateo, Issue 339, April 1, 1982.

A sympathetic and informative portrait of Sophia Chatskina ('Aunt Sonia') is to be found in Olga Chernov Andreyev, *Cold Spring in Russia*, Ann Arbor, 1978. A nasty and sarcastic vignette of her is in Georgy Ivanov, *Petersburg Winters (Peterburgskie zimy)*, New York, 1952, in the section devoted to Sergei Esenin. An English translation of this section is in *The Bitter Air of Exile: Russian Writers in the West 1922–1972*, Simon Karlinsky and Alfred Appel, Jr eds., Berkeley, Los Angeles and London, 1977.

Out of the sizeable literature on Tsvetaeva's personal and poetic relationship with Osip Mandelstam I have relied primarily on the second volume of Nadezhda Mandelstam's memoirs (the Russian-language edition, *Vtoraia kniga*, Paris, 1972, rather than the English translation by Max Hayward, *Hope Abandoned*, New York, 1974); Clarence Brown, *Mandelstam*, London and New York, 1973; and Gregory Freidin's book cited in the text (Berkeley, Los Angeles and London, 1986). I am grateful to Professor Freidin for sharing with me an advance copy of his manuscript. Tsvetaeva's letters to Bakhrakh are indispensable for documenting her encounters with Mandelstam. Also important is her letter to Kuzmin published in Poliakova's book. On Tsvetaeva's aversion to Mandelstam's *The Noise of Time*, see her letter from London to Prince Dmitry Shakhovskoy of March 18, 1926 in NP (the year 1917 cited in the letter is apparently a typographical error).

Tsvetaeva's letter to Lilia Efron about Mandelstam's visit to Alexandrov is in Anna Saakiants, 'On the Truth of "Chronicles" ...', cited under Chapter 1.

On Tikhon Churilin, see my essay 'Surrealism in Twentieth Century Russian Poetry: Churilin, Zabolotsky, Poplavsky,' *Slavic Review*, 1969, vol. 26, No. 4.

On the history of the composition of *Mileposts I*, see Viktoria Schweitzer's essay on it in SiP 1. On Nikodim Plutser-Sarna, the same essay and Serena Vitale's note on pp. 186–7 of her edition of Marina Cvetaeva, *Le notti fiorentine*, Milan, 1983. It must be Plutser-Sarna that Saakiants mentions in 'On the Truth of "Chronicles" ...' as 'another man who entered [Tsvetaeva's heart]' in June 1916, leaving no room for Osip Mandelstam in her life.

On Tsvetaeva's logaoedic meters: Yury Ivask (later, George Ivask), 'Tsvetaeva,' *Nov'*, Tallin, 1934, No. 6; and G. S. Smith, 'Logaoedic Metres in the Lyric Poetry of Marina Tsvetaeva,' *The Slavonic and East European Review*, London, vol. LIII, No. 132, July 1975.

CHAPTER 4: THE CHOIR PRACTICE AND THE MASS

The reaction of Vladimir Nabokov, Sr to the February Revolution in Virgil D. Medlin and Steven L. Parsons, eds., *V. D. Nabokov and the*

Russian Provisional Government, New Haven and London, 1976. The reactions of Andrei Bely and Zinaida Gippius, in Gippius, *The Blue Book (Siniaia kniga)*, reprinted in her *Petersburg Diaries (Peterburgskie dnevniki, 1914–1917)*, New York, 1982.

Vladimir Mayakovsky's censure of Tsvetaeva for mentioning 'God's servant Nicholas' appeared in his review 'The Common Grave' ('Bratskaia mogila'), *Gazeta futuristov*, March 15, 1918. The review is reprinted in Volume 12 of his complete collected works published in Moscow in 1959.

On the background of the two 1917 revolutions and of various personalities involved in them, I've cited George Katkov, *Russia 1917. The February Revolution*, New York, 1967; Mark Vishniak, *The Contemporary Annals. An Editor's Memoirs (Sovremennye zapiski, Vospominaniia redaktora)*, Bloomington, 1957; Olga Chernov Andreyev, *Cold Spring in Russia*; and Dimitri von Mohrenschildt, ed., *The Russian Revolution of 1917. Contemporary Accounts*, London and Toronto, 1971. Feodor Stepun, *What Happened and What Didn't (Byvshee i nesbyvsheesia)*, 2 vols., New York, 1956 is also highly useful and informative. These particular sources were selected out of the multitude of available ones for their pertinence to Tsvetaeva's situation and because some of them (e.g., Chernov Andreyev and Stepun) were written by people personally close to her.

Robin Kemball's English translation of *The Demesne of the Swans*, a bilingual edition, Ann Arbor, 1980.

Vladimir Varshavsky, *The Unnoticed Generation (Nazamechennoe pokolenie)*, New York, 1956. The book is a detailed study of various political and literary movements among the younger Russians in Western Europe during the 1920s and 30s. Varshavsky was an émigré writer who knew Tsvetaeva and Sergei Efron in Paris.

On the parallels between the chiliastic sects and the Jacobin terror on the one hand and Russian Bolshevism on the other, Igor Shafarevich, *Socialism as a Phenomenon of World History (Sotsializm kak iavlenie mirovoi istorii)*, Paris, 1977 (I've used the original Russian text rather than the available English translation); and Vladimir Varshavsky, *The Genealogy of Bolshevism (Genealogiia bol'shevizma)*, Paris, 1982. The two authors, who knew nothing of each other's work, found numerous historical precedents for Lenin's and Trotsky's project of achieving a utopia through terror and repression. Varshavsky's posthumously published book debates against the widespread Western view that Marxism turned repressive in Russia only because of the Russian autocratic heritage, supposedly left over from the days of Ivan the Terrible and Peter the Great. As Varshavsky shows, enforced utopias have preached liberation and practiced enslavement throughout human history.

Rosa Luxemburg's and Emma Goldman's views of the October Revolution are embodied in their respective books on it, Luxemburg, *The Russian Revolution and Leninism or Marxism*, Ann Arbor, 1961 and Goldman, *My Disillusionment in Russia*, New York, 1923, reprinted 1970. Goldman's afterword to her book and her 1935 essay 'There Is No Communism in Russia' are included in *Red Emma Speaks: Selected*

Writings & Speeches by Emma Goldman, Alix Kates Shulman, ed., New York, 1972.

For examples of recent Western historiography of the October Revolution which restricts itself only to Bolshevik sources and accounts by poorly informed foreigners, see my review of three biographies of Alexandra Kollontai, 'The Menshevik, Bolshevik, Stalinist Feminist,' *The New York Times Review of Books*, January 4, 1981.

Ivan Bunin, *Accursed Days* (*Okaiannye dni*), reissued London (Canada), 1973; Vladislav Khodasevich, *The White Corridor. Memoirs* (*Belyi koridor. Vospominaniia*), New York, 1982; Alexei Remizov, *Russia in a Whirlwind* (*Vzvikhrennaia Rus'*), Paris, 1927, reissued London, 1979.

On the Cheka and its reign of terror: Lennard D. Gerson, *The Secret Police in Lenin's Russia*, Philadelphia, 1976 (Henryk Sachs is mentioned on p. 138 as the author of an article that denied the Cheka ever used torture); Roman Goul, *Dzerzhinsky*, second revised edition, New York, 1974. On Leonid Kannegiser's assassination of Uritsky, Goul's book and *Leonid Kannegiser*, Paris, 1928 (essays by Georgy Adamovich, Mark Aldanov and Georgy Ivanov, followed by a selection of Kannegiser's poetry). Georgy Ivanov's contribution also forms a chapter in his book *Petersburg Winters*.

Henryk Sachs appears in the role of a good Samaritan in *Biography of My Youth* (*Biografiia iunosti*) by Archbishop John of San Francisco (Arkhiepiskop Ioann Shakhovskoy), where he helped the then young Prince Dmitry Shakhovskoy to obtain his mother's release from the Cheka. In the 1920s, Shakhovskoy was Tsvetaeva's correspondent and the editor of a Brussels journal to which she contributed. *Biography of My Youth* was published in Paris in 1977.

On the circumstances of the death of Tsvetaeva's daughter Irina: Viktoria Schweitzer, 'Pages for the Biography of Marina Tsvetaeva' ('Stranitsy k biografii Mariny Tsvetaevoi'), *Russian Literature*, Amsterdam, 1981, No. 9.

In addition to Tsvetaeva's 'The Tale of Sonechka,' her contacts with the Third Studio were described in Pavel Antokolsky's evasive memoir 'Marina Tsvetaeva' which appears in the fourth volume of his collected works, Moscow, 1973.

An example of recurrent turning to the precedent of Jacobin terror during the French Revolution to explain and elucidate the period of War Communism in Russia is provided by Maximilian Voloshin's two highly popular collections of verse from that period, *The Deaf-Mute Demons* (*Demony glukhonemye*), Kharkov, 1919 and *Verses on Terror* (*Stikhi o terrore*), Berlin, 1923.

The sources for Tsvetaeva's historical verse dramas were: for *An Adventure*, *Mémoires de J. Casanova de Seingalt écrits par lui-même*, Paris, 1880, vol. 3 (Tsvetaeva erroneously cited vol. 4). For *The Phoenix*, the same work, vol. 8 and, possibly, Le Prince de Ligne, *Mémoires et mélanges historiques et littéraires*, Paris, 1828, vol. 4.

For *Fortuna*, Duc de Lauzun, *Mémoires* (uncertain which edition) and Sainte-Beuve's essay on Lauzun in his *Causeries du lundi*, Paris, 1858.

CHAPTER 5: MATURITY, EMIGRATION, FAME

Ilya Ehrenburg's three 1913 articles that mention Tsvetaeva are cited in Lev Mnukhin's bibliographical guide in WSA.

Tsvetaeva's relationship with Konstantin Balmont was reflected in her two essays on him included in IP and in her memoir on Briusov, 'A Hero of Labor,' in the same collection. IP also reprinted the final chapter from Balmont's book *Where Is My Home?* (Prague, 1924) which describes Tsvetaeva's life during the period of War Communism.

Tsvetaeva's presence at Mayakovsky's reading of his poem 'Man' at the Tsetlins' apartment was described by Boris Pasternak in *Safe Conduct* (*Okhrannaia gramota*), Leningrad, 1932, English translations, London, 1945 and 1959 (the latter one, by Lydia Pasternak-Slater, is preferable); and by Ilya Ehrenburg, *People, Years, Life* (*Liudi, gody, zhizn'*), Moscow, 1961.

Tsvetaeva's 1910 essay on Briusov was published by Anna Saakiants in the collection *Den' poèzii*, Moscow, 1979.

Tsvetaeva's participation in the 1916 'Evening of Contemporary Poetesses' was announced in the women's magazine *Zhenskaia zhizn'*, Moscow, 1916, issue of January 22 and in the theatrical journal *Rampa i zhizn'*, Moscow, 1916, No. 3.

The date of the poetry reading at the Polytechnic Museum, chaired by Valery Briusov, which Tsvetaeva described in 'A Hero of Labor' (December 11, 1920), is cited by Vsevolod Rozhdestvensky in his introductory essay to S1.

Vladislav Khodasevich's discussion of Tsvetaeva's 'The Swain' and the relationship of folk epics in verse to genuine folklore appeared in his column 'Notes on Poetry' ('Zametki o stikhakh') in the Paris newspaper *Poslednie novosti*, issue of June 11, 1925.

The folklore sources of 'The Tsar-Maiden' are tales 232 and 233 in A. N. Afanasiev, *Russian Folk Tales* (*Narodnye russkie skazki*), Moscow, 1958, vol. 2.

The cited essays on 'The Tsar-Maiden' are S. Poliakova, 'The Question of the Sources of Tsvetaeva's Poem "The Tsar-Maiden"' ('K voprosu ob istochnikakh poèmy Tsvetaevoi "Tsar'-Devitsa"'), *Russika – 1981*, New York, 1981; and G. S. Smith, 'Characters and Narrative Modes in Marina Tsvetaeva's *Tsar'-Devitsa*,' *Oxford Slavonic Papers*, New Series, Oxford, 1979, vol. 12. See also G. S. Smith's study of 'Sidestreets,' 'Versification and Composition in Marina Cvetaeva's *Pereulochki*,' *International Journal of Slavic Linguistics and Poetics*, The Hague, 1975, No. 20; reprinted as a separate brochure, Lisse (Belgium), 1975.

A remarkably thorough and well-documented brief study of the famine of 1921, the All-Russian Committee on Famine Relief and its fate, the

American ARA help and the forcible expulsion of 200 intellectuals and their families in 1922 is Mikhail Geller's 'The First Warning – a Lash of the Whip' (' "Pervoe predosterezhenie" – udar khlystom),' *Vestnik* (*Le Messager*), Paris, 1978, No. 127.

On Karolina Pavlova, see Barbara Heldt Monter's introductory essay to her translation of Pavlova's novel *A Double Life*, Ann Arbor, 1978.

Tsvetaeva's letters to Yevgeny Lann were published by V. M. Volosov and Irma Kudrova in WSA. Lann's real name was Yevgeny Lozman, 1896–1958. Tsvetaeva corresponded with him in 1920 and 1921, when she mistook him for a potentially great poet and became infatuated with him. He didn't become any kind of poet, making his mark instead as a literary translator and the author of several historical novels. Tsvetaeva's letters to Lann are a thorough record of her day-to-day existence during their time of correspondence. In her letter of January 19, 1921, she described to Lann her brief fling with the eighteen-year old demobilized Red Army soldier Boris Bessarabov. Her night with Bessarabov, restricted to kisses and stroking of each other's hair, may well be typical of a number of her other transient erotic involvements. The one with Valery Bebutov was described by Vera Zviagintseva to Viktoria Schweitzer, who recorded it in the already cited 'Pages for the Biography of Marina Tsvetaeva.'

Efim Etkind's study of *Craft* is his essay 'A Path to Russia' ('Put' k Rossii'), *Vremia i my*, Tel Aviv, 1979, No. 46.

The implications of the *Pravda* editorial 'Dictatorship, Where Is Thy Whip?' are analysed in the already cited essay by Mikhail Geller. On Nadezhda Krupskaya's removal of books from libraries, see Bertram D. Wolfe, 'Krupskaya Purges the People's Libraries,' *Survey*, London, Summer 1969.

Vsevolod Meyerhold's denunciation of Tsvetaeva was in his open letter to Valery Bebutov, *Vestnik teatra*, Moscow, 1921, No. 83–4.

On the fate of Anna Barkova, see Anon., 'An Ordinary Life' ('Obyknovennaia zhizn''), *Vestnik* (*Le Messager*), Paris, 1977, No. 121.

On Berlin as the center of Russian publishing in 1921–3, the sources are Robert C. Williams, *Culture in Exile. Russian Émigrés in Germany, 1881–1941*, Ithaca and London, 1972; and *Russkii Berlin 1921–1923*, L. Fleishman, R. Hughes and O. Raevsky Hughes, eds., Paris, 1983. The latter reproduces the editorial correspondence of Alexander Yashchenko, the founder and editor of the journal *Novaia russkaia kniga*, with a large array of literary figures, both famous and unknown, as well as the previously unpublished letters of Maxim Gorky dating from that period.

Nina Berberova's autobiography, *Kursiv moi*, has been brought out in an augmented, two-volume version in New York in 1983. The not very satisfactory English translation of the earlier edition, *The Italics Are Mine*, was published in New York in 1969.

Tsvetaeva's 'Florentine Nights' was published for the first time in the original French, accompanied by an Italian translation by Serena Vitale, in *Le notti fiorentine*, Milan, 1983.

Unpublished letter from Sergei Efron to Maximilian Voloshin is cited courtesy of Serena Vitale.

Serena Vitale's comment is cited from her essay 'Tatiana's Bench' ('La panchina di Tat'jana'), which serves as the introduction to her edition of *Le notti fiorentine*.

CHAPTER 6: IN CZECHOSLOVAKIA

Dmitry Shakhovskoy's comment is cited from Archbishop John of San Francisco, *Biography of My Youth* (see the sources for Chapter 4).

Edmund Wison's view of Leningrad in 1935 is in his *Travels in Two Democracies*, New York, 1936.

For a fictionalized but factually accurate depiction of the diverse political attitudes in the Russian émigré periodicals of the 1920s, see the beginning of Chapter 5 of Vladimir Nabokov's novel *The Gift*.

Tsvetaeva's open letter to A. N. Tolstoy was reprinted in the collection *Russika – 81*, with historical commentary by Alexander Sumerkin. For the background of the incident that caused the letter, see Fleishman, Hughes and Hughes, *Russkii Berlin, 1921–1923*.

For a comparison between the Czech and the Yugoslav subsidies to exiled Russian literary figures, see Nina Berberova's introductory essay to Zinaida Gippius, *Petersburg Diaries*.

Photographs of Tsvetaeva's dwellings in Prague and in Czech villages are reproduced in the collection *Marina Cvetaevová a Praha*, edited by Tat'jana Koriakinová, Milada Nedvědová and Galina Vaněčková, Prague, 1984. The volume also contains an essay on Tsvetaeva by Galina Vaněčková and a bibliography of her work in Czech translation.

A brief history of the journal *Freedom of Russia*, written by Mark Slonim, appears in *Russian Literature in Emigration (Russkaia literatura v èmigratsii)*, Nikolai Poltoratsky, ed., Pittsburgh, 1972.

Mark Slonim's memoir 'On Marina Tsvetaeva' ('O Marine Tsvetaevoi') appeared in *Novyi zhurnal*, New York, No. 100, 1970, and No. 103, 1971. It was reprinted in SiP 3.

Tsvetaeva's letters to Roman Goul are in *Novyi zhurnal*, No. 58, 1959.

The cited Mandelstam essay is his 'Literaturnaia Moskva' ('The Literary Moscow'), *Rossiia*, Moscow, 1922, No. 2.

Leon Trotsky's *Literature and Revolution* is cited from the Russian edition, Moscow, 1923, in my own translation. The available English and French translations systematically tone down Trotsky's frequently violent and abusive language. Trotsky repeated his denunciation of women poets, including Tsvetaeva, in his article 'The Formalist School of Poetry and Marxism' ('Formal'naia shkola poèzii i marksizm'), *Pravda*, July 26, 1923.

Semion Rodov's attack on Tsvetaeva was in the section 'A Sinful Woman Goes to Confession at Gosizdat' ('Greshnitsa na ispovedi u Gosizdata') in his survey article 'The "Original" Poetry of the Gosizdat' ('"Original'naia" poèziia Gosizdata'), *Na postu*, Moscow, 1923, No. 2–3. On Semion

Rodov's pre-Bolshevik phase, see Vladislav Khodasevich's article 'People Who Are Failures' ('Neudachniki'), reprinted in his collection of memoirs *The White Corridor*.

Mayakovsky's little scene between the bookseller and the Communist Youth girl is from his article 'Let's Wait Before We Accuse Poets' ('Podozhdem obviniat' poètov'), originally in *Krasnaia nov'*, Moscow–Leningrad, 1926, No. 4; reprinted in his collected works, *Polnoe sobranie sochinenii*, vol. 12, Moscow, 1959.

On the Soviet anti-feminist campaign of 1922–3, see Barbara Evans Clements, *Bolshevik Feminist. The Life of Aleksandra Kollontai*, Bloomington and London, 1979, Chapter 10.

Tsvetaeva's defense of *One's Own Way*, 'Vozrozhdenshchina,' was published in the Berlin newspaper *Dni* on October 16, 1925. It is reprinted in IP 2.

On Tsvetaeva's Prague contacts with Remizov, see AE and letters to Bakhrakh; Prague encounters with Khodasevich are documented in Nina Berberova, *The Italics Are Mine*; the hike with Nabokov in his *Drugie berega (Other Shores)*, New York, 1954.

On Tsvetaeva's friendship with Olga Kolbasina-Chernova, see their correspondence in NP; Kolbasina-Chernova's posthumously published memoir 'On Marina Tsvetaeva' ('O Marine Tsvetaevoi'), *Mosty*, 1970, No. 15; and Natalia Reznikova (Kolbasina-Chernova's daughter), 'Marina Tsvetaeva In Memoriam' ('Pamiati Mariny Tsvetaevoi'), *Vestnik*, No. 135.

On her contacts with Yevgeny Chirikov's family, see the introductory pieces by Valentina and Liudmila Chirikov and Tsvetaeva's letters to the latter, all in *Novyi zhurnal*, 1976, No. 124. On contacts with Leonid Andreyev's family, AE and Tsvetaeva's letters to Olga Kolbasina-Chernova.

The cycle 'Telegraph Wires' ('Provoda') is given a detailed analysis in Ieva Vitins' essay 'Marina Tsvetaeva's "Provoda"' (unpublished at this writing).

A glamorized portrait of Konstantin Rodzevich, complete with a 'politically correct' pro-Soviet biography, appears in Anna Saakiants's annotations to 'Poem of the Hill' in S1. In this version, his service in the White Army or his evacuation through Constantinople did not happen. A similarly retouched portrait is drawn in AE.

Sergei Efron's view of Rodzevich and his account of subsequent events are drawn from his unpublished letter to Maximilian Voloshin, already cited in Chapter 5, which was kindly shared with me by Serena Vitale.

Nikolai Elenev's portrait of Rodzevich is found in his memoir 'Who Was Marina Tsvetaeva?' ('Kem byla Marina Tsvetaeva?'), *Grani*, Frankfurt-am-Main, 1958, No. 39. On p. 58 of *Tsvetaeva. A Pictorial Biography* there is a photograph of Marina Tsvetaeva, Sergei Efron, Ekaterina Eleneva, Nikolai Elenev and Konstantin Rodzevich. The little boy held by Rodzevich is Oleg ('Lelik') Turzhansky, the son of Alexandra Turzhanskaya. P. 107 shows Rodzevich and Maria ('Mouna') Bulgakova at the time of their wedding in 1925. Her later opinion of Rodzevich is quoted by Véronique Lossky in 'Marina Cvétaeva. Souvenirs de contemporains,' in WSA.

The circumstances of the birth of Tsvetaeva's son are described in her letters to Olga Kolbasina and in the memoirs of Ariadna Efron on the basis of her mother's diaries.

Vladimir Smetáček's essay on 'Poem of the Hill' is in WSA. There is also a fine and detailed essay on 'Poem of the Hill' by G. S. Smith, 'Marina Cvetaeva's *Poèma gory*: an Analysis,' *Russian Literature*, Amsterdam, October 1978, No. VI-4.

Dmitry Shakhovskoy's comment is from his review of 'The Swain' in *Blagonamerennyi*, Brussels, 1926, No. 1. Tsvetaeva's explication of 'The Swain' is cited from Paul Schmidt's English translation of 'A Poet on Criticism,' *The Bitter Air of Exile: Russian Writers in the West 1922–1972*, Simon Karlinsky and Alfred Appel, Jr., eds., Berkeley, 1977. The original Russian version of the essay was reprinted in IP 1.

Marie-Luise Bott's commentary is cited from her edition of 'The Pied Piper,' *Krysolov. Der Rattenfänger. Herausgegeben, übersetzt und kommentiert von Marie-Luise Bott mit einem Glossar von Günther Wytrzens, Wiener slawistischer Almanach*, 1982, Sonderband 7. On the connections with Belsky's libretto, Marie-Luise Bott, 'Studien zu Marina Cvetaevas Poem "Krysolov." Rattenfänger- und Kitezh-Sage,' in WSA. On the ties with *Der Trompeter von Säkkingen*, see my forthcoming article in the proceedings of the Tsvetaeva 1982 conference in Lausanne, ' "Puteshestvuia v Zhenevu . . ." Ob odnoi neudavsheisia poezdke M. I. Tsvetaevoi' (' "Traveling to Geneva . . ." On an Unsuccessful Trip of Marina Tsvetaeva's').

In addition to the complete Russian texts of 'The Pied Piper' in SiP 4 and Dr Bott's edition and the latter's German translation, there now also exists a scholarly Italian edition, Marina Cvetaeva, *L'accalappiatopi*, translated by and with an essay and annotations by Caterina Graziadei, Rome, 1983.

On Moravská Třebová as the model for Tsvetaeva's Hamelin, AE and the papers read at the 1982 Tsvetaeva conference in Lausanne by Maria Razumovsky and Galina Vaněčková.

D. S. Mirsky's review of 'The Pied Piper': D. Sviatopolk-Mirsky, ' "Krysolov" M. Tsvetaevoi,' *Volia Rossii (Freedom of Russia)*, 1926, vol. 6/7 (double issue).

CHAPTER 7: SPLENDOURS AND MISERIES OF 1926

On post-revolutionary literature in the Soviet Union, Gleb Struve, *Russian Literature under Lenin and Stalin 1917–1953*, Norman, 1971. On Russian literature outside the Soviet Union during the period from 1917 to the end of World War II, Gleb Struve, *Russian Literature in Exile (Russkaia literatura v izgnanii)*, New York, 1956. The same work outlines the history of the 'Changing Landmarks' movement and of Eurasianism in chapters II and III of its Part One. Another good source on these two movements is Mikhail Geller and Alexander Nekrich, *Utopia in Power. History of the Soviet Union from 1917 to Our Days* (*Utopiia u vlasti. Istoriia Sovetskogo Soiuza s 1917 goda do nashikh dnei*), London, 1982, vol. I, Chapter 3. This two-volume work by two recently exiled Soviet historians, who began writing it while they still had access to secret Soviet archives, includes a thorough coverage of the fate of post-revolutionary exiles. Eurasian theory is outlined in Otto Böss, *Die Lehre der Eurasier*, Wiesbaden, 1961.

The circumstances of Marina Tsvetaeva's move to France and the earliest period of her residence there are described in great detail in Irma Kudrova, 'Six Months in Paris. Toward a Biography of Marina Tsvetaeva' ('Polgoda v Parizhe. K biografii Mariny Tsvetaevoi'), WSA.

Newspaper accounts of Tsvetaeva's activities and the reviews of her work in the Russian press in Paris which are mentioned in this chapter are all tabulated under the year 1926 in Mnukhin's bibliographical guide, WSA. Many of them are also discussed in Kudrova, 'Six Months in Paris.'

Tsvetaeva's letters to Valentin Bulgakov were published (in heavily censored form) in the collection *Encounters with the Past* (*Vstrechi s proshlym*), Moscow, 1976, vol. 2.

Information on the diary of Vera Sudeikina was kindly made available to me by Robert Craft.

Irina Knorring's poem about Tsvetaeva's February 6 reading was published in *The Latest News* (*Poslednie novosti*) on March 21, 1926.

On the founding of the journals *Blagonamerennyi* and *Mileposts*: Archbishop John (Dmitry Shakhovskoy), *Biography of My Youth*, already cited under Chapters 4 and 6 (it includes Shakhovskoy's correspondence with Mirsky and Sergei Efron); Tsvetaeva's letters to Shakhovskoy in NP; and the sections on these two journals in Gleb Struve, *Russian Literature in Exile*.

Tsvetaeva's trip to London was described in her letters to Tesková, to Ivask, to Shakhovskoy in NP and to Khodasevich in L. The picture of her imaginary London is cited from the last-named source.

Tsvetaeva's response to Mandelstam's *The Noise of Time* was briefly discussed by Anna Saakiants (who had clearly read it) in her commentary to S2. On the basis of her comment, Omry Ronen has made a plausible surmise of what could have angered Tsvetaeva about this book: Mandelstam's derogatory and mocking depiction of White Army volunteers. (Omry Ronen, *An Approach to Mandelstam*, Jerusalem, 1983, p. 157.) In her letter to Raisa Lomonosova of February 13, 1931, Tsvetaeva wrote about Mirsky: 'Our parting of the ways came because of Mandelstam's stillborn prose work *The Noise of Time*, where only objects are alive and every living being is an object: he [Mirsky] adores it and I hate it.'

The Russian text of 'A Poet on Criticism' was most recently reprinted in IP, vol. I. The English translation of this essay by Paul Schmidt was cited in sources for Chapter 6 in connection with Tsvetaeva's explication of her poem 'The Swain.' For additional information about the essay, see the annotations to that translation.

Among the angry reactions in the Soviet press to the publication of 'My Jobs' were the articles by Nikolai Smirnov in *The New World* (*Novyi mir*) and Dmitry Gorbov in *Red Virgin Soil* (*Krasnaia nov'*), listed under Nos. 293 and 295 in Mnukhin, WSA. Mayakovsky's attack, 'Let's Wait Before We Accuse Poets,' the only one that hurt Tsvetaeva's feelings, appeared at about the same time.

The conflict between *Mileposts* and the rest of the Russian literary community is described in detail in Mark Vishniak, *The Contemporary Annals. An Editor's Memoirs* (see the sources for Chapter 4).

I am grateful to Richard Abraham for providing me with xeroxes of Tsvetaeva's inscriptions on the copies of her two books which she presented to Alexander Kerensky in Prague in February 1924.

The cited letters of Zinaida Gippius are in the volume of her letters to Berberova and Khodasevich, *Pis'ma k Berberovoi i Khodasevichu*, Erika Freiberger Sheikholeslami, ed., Ann Arbor, 1978. Her conflict with Serafima Dovgello-Remizova: Horst Lampl, 'Zinaida Hippius an S. P. Remizova-Dovgello,' *Wiener slawistischer Almanach*, Band 1, Vienna, 1978. On the break between Gippius and Nikolai Berdiaev, see her letter to him of January 8, 1927 in Temira Pachmuss, *Intellect and Ideas in Action. Selected Correspondence of Zinaida Hippius*, Munich, 1972.

Marina Tsvetaeva's correspondence of the summer 1926 with Boris Pasternak and Rainer Maria Rilke is cited from the volume prepared for publication by Konstantin Azadovsky and Elena and Yevgeny Pasternak, *Rainer Mariia Ril'ke, Marina Tsvetaeva, Boris Pasternak. Pis'ma leta 1926 goda*. I am enormously grateful to Serena Vitale and Angela Livingstone for making available to me the Russian typescript of this volume and copies of the original German texts of all the letters written in that language. At this writing Italian, French and German translations of this volume have appeared and an English version by Margaret Wettlin is about to be published. The Russian text has so far appeared only in excerpts in *Problems of Literature* (*Voprosy literatury*), Moscow, 1978, No. 4. The German texts of Tsvetaeva's letters to Rilke were published, with an introductory essay and annotations by Ilma Rakusa and Felix Philipp Ingold in *Zeitschrift für slavische Philologie*, vol. 41, no. 1, Heidelberg, 1980.

The release of Tsvetaeva's letters to Rilke for study and publication in 1977 has generated considerable scholarly interest. Their correspondence is discussed, *inter alia*, in Ilma Rakusa, 'Marina Zwetajewa und Rainer Maria Rilke. Auf Grund unveröffentlicher Briefmaterialen,' *Neue Zürcher Zeitung*, 1/2 September 1979; and Patricia Pollack Brodsky, 'On Daring to Be a Poet: Rilke and Marina Cvetaeva,' *Germano-Slavica*, vol. 3, no. 4, Waterloo (Canada), 1980.

On Rilke's Russian contacts and interests, Felix Philipp Ingold, 'Rilke, Russland und die "russischen Dinge",' in *Zwischen den Kulturen. Festgabe*

270 Appendix on sources

für Georg Thürer, Felix Philipp Ingold, ed., Bern and Stuttgart, 1978.
See especially the extensive bibliography on the subject cited in the
annotations to this essay. Tsvetaeva's glossaries and comments on the
copies of *Verses to Blok* and *Psyche* which she sent to Rilke are cited
and discussed in Ingold's article 'M. I. Cvetaevas Lese- und Verständ-
nishilfen für R. M. Rilke,' *Die Welt der Slaven*, vol. 24, no. 2, Munich,
1979.

Tsvetaeva's letter to Pasternak about Sophia Parnok was not cited in
their published correspondence because it is one of the numerous
Tsvetaeva letters which Ariadna Efron, in her anxiety about her mother's
posthumous image, relegated to a secret archive closed to scholars. Its
content can be inferred in part from Pasternak's reply and the commentary
by the editors of the correspondence. Parnok's situation in 1926 is discussed
in Sophia Poliakova's introductory essay to her edition of Parnok's poetry,
cited in the sources for Chapter 3.

The background of the writing of Pasternak's 'The Year 1905' and
'Lieutenant Schmidt' and the connection of these two poems with
Tsvetaeva is outlined by Lazar Fleishman, *Boris Pasternak in the Twenties*
(*Boris Pasternak v dvadtsatye gody*), Munich, n.d. (ca. 1980). The prefa-
tory acrostic to Tsvetaeva in 'Lieutenant Schmidt' was not mentioned in the
Soviet Union from 1926 to 1965, when it was printed in the annotations to
the poem in an academic edition of Pasternak's poetry, Boris Pasternak,
Stikhotvoreniia i poèmy, with an introductory essay by Andrei Siniavsky,
Moscow and Leningrad, 1965.

The connection between Tsvetaeva and the character of Maria Il'ina in
Pasternak's *Spektorsky* was first made by Olga Raevsky Hughes in her
'Boris Pasternak and Marina Tsvetaeva. History of a Friendship' ('Boris
Pasternak i Marina Tsvetaeva. K istorii druzhby'), *Vestnik (Le Messager)*,
No. 100, 1971.

Tsvetaeva's statement to Vera Zviagintseva about the desirability of
physical contact between friends was cited by Viktoria Schweitzer in 'Pages
for the Biography of Marina Tsvetaeva,' listed among the sources for
Chapter 4.

The statement on Rilke's friendships with women is cited from J. R. von
Salis, *Rainer Maria Rilke. The Years in Switzerland*, London, 1964.

Joseph Brodsky's analysis of Tsvetaeva's 'New Year's Greetings' is
called 'About One Poem. By Way of Introduction' ('Ob odnom stikhotvorenii. Vmesto predisloviia'). It appears in SiP 1.

A good and thorough analysis in English of 'Your Death,' Tsvetaeva's
prose epitaph to Rilke, has been written by Olga Peters Hasty: 'Your
Death. The Living Water of Cvetaeva's Art,' *Russian Literature*,
Amsterdam, 1983, No. 13.

The connection between Tsvetaeva's 'Poem of the Staircase' and the
poetry of Rilke was made by Patricia Pollock Brodsky in her essay 'Objects,
Poverty, and the Poet in Rilke and Cvestaeva,' *Comparative Literature
Studies*, Chicago, 1983, vol. 20, no. 4.

CHAPTER 8: POETRY TRAPPED BETWEEN KITCHEN AND POLITICS

Excerpts from Tsvetaeva's letters to Salomea Andronikova-Halpern and from Mrs Halpern's letters describing her friendship with Tsvetaeva were published by Gleb Struve in *Vestnik* (*Le Messager*), Paris, 1983, No. 138. I have had access to the complete text of these letters through the courtesy of Professor Struve and the late Mrs Halpern.

Tsvetaeva's letters to Raisa Lomonosova, deposited at the Brotherton Library, University of Leeds, have been prepared for publication by Richard Davies and Lydia Shorrocks and will be included in a volume of Tsvetaeva's letters to be issued by Rossica, New York. The editors' annotations document the circumstances of this correspondence. I am most grateful to Mr Davies for an advance copy of this text.

Sergei Efron's activities at the end of the 1920s are outlined in Tsvetaeva's letters to Tesková and Halpern.

Tsvetaeva's letter to Anna Tesková of December 12, 1927, describing the endless household chores which interfere with her writing is reproduced in English translation in *A House of Good Proportion. Images of Women in Literature*, Michele Murray, ed., New York, 1973.

George Ivask's statement about Tsvetaeva and myths is from his lecture 'Tsvetaeva (The Tsar-Maiden),' of which he kindly sent me a copy. Roman Goul's statement on the same subject is from his letter to me of December 15, 1967.

Tsvetaeva's accusations against her sisters-in-law in connection with the death of Irina Efron: Viktoria Schweitzer, 'Pages for the Biography of Marina Tsvetaeva' and Sergei Efron's unpublished letter to Voloshin, cited under Chapters 5 and 6.

On Blok's supposed fatherhood of Nadezhda Nolle-Kogan's son, the dedication to the two-poem cycle 'Bethlehem' ('Vifleem') in *Craft* and Tsvetaeva's letter to Roman Goul of April 11, 1924. She eventually realized that this hypothesis was wrong, as can be seen from her letter to Vadim Rudnev of June 24, 1934 (*Novyi zhurnal*, 1978, No. 133).

Anastasia Tsvetaeva's 1927 trip to Sorrento and Paris: AT and Marina Tsvetaeva's letters to Halpern.

The exchange of letters between Maxim Gorky and Boris Pasternak on the subject of Tsvetaeva is in *Literary Heritage (Literaturnoe nasledstvo)*, Moscow, 1963, vol. 70.

Tsvetaeva mentioned Stravinsky in 'Poem of the Staircase' and in 'A Poet on Criticism' (in the latter, his name is evoked as an example of a creative person who does not understand Tsvetaeva's poetry). In a letter to Tesková she wrote that attending a concert conducted by Stravinsky was one of the greatest impressions of her stay in Prague. In Paris, Tsvetaeva knew a great many people who regularly associated with the composer: Suvchinsky, Goncharova, Prokofiev, etc. Yet, I have not been able to find any evidence of personal encounters between her and him. Robert Craft assumes that they must have met.

The working title of Tsvetaeva's Theseus trilogy was *The Wrath of Aphrodite* (*Gnev Afrodity*). The history of writing *Ariadne* is outlined by Anna Saakiants on the basis of the poet's drafts and diaries in T-65. The genesis and writing of *Phaedra* is recorded by the same commentator in S1.

Khodasevich's criticism of *Phaedra* appeared in *Renascence* (*Vozrozhdenie*), Paris, on September 27, 1928; Vladimir Weidlé's in the same newspaper on January 10, 1929; Georgy Adamovich's review in *The Latest News* on October 4, 1928; and Vladimir Nabokov's in *The Rudder* (*Rul'*), Berlin, January 30, 1929.

On Iosif Pouterman and his involvement in the publication of *After Russia*: Tsvetaeva's letters to Salomea Halpern and to Lev Shestov (the latter are in *Vestnik* (*Le Messager*), Paris, 1979, No. 129). On the method of publishing *After Russia*, her letters to Halpern, Tesková, Lomonosova and Leonid Pasternak (the latter are in NP).

Andrei Bely's essay on Tsvetaeva's versification is called 'The Singer Poet' ('Poètessa–pevitsa'). It appeared in *The Voice of Russia* (*Golos Rossii*), Berlin, March 21, 1922 and was reprinted, with an introductory note by Vadim Morkovin, in *Československá rusistika*, Prague, March 1968.

There is a considerable literature on the language and versification of Tsvetaeva's mature verse. Most of it is enumerated in Robin Kemball's fine study 'Innovatory Features of Tsvetaeva's Lyrical Verse,' originally presented at the Second World Congress for Soviet and East European Studies at Garmisch-Partenkirchen in the fall of 1980 and published, in an expanded form, in a volume of selected papers from that congress, *Russian Literature and Criticism*, Evelyn Bristol, ed., Berkeley, 1982. See also the section 'Technical Aspects' in my 1966 book *Marina Cvetaeva. Her Life and Art*. The structure of two typical poems from *After Russia* is ably analysed in Barbara Heldt, 'Two Poems by Marina Tsvetaeva from *Posle Rossii*, *The Modern Language Review*, London, July 1982, vol. 77, No. 3.

After Russia was reviewed by Khodasevich in *Renascence* on June 19, 1928. On June 21, an adverse review by Georgy Adamovich appeared in *The Latest News*. Alfred Bem wrote that this collection was 'objectively far more significant than we now realize' in *The Rudder*, Berlin, July 16, 1931. Don Aminado called *After Russia* the most remarkable of Tsvetaeva's books in his autobiography *The Train on Track Three* (*Poezd na tret'em puti*), New York, 1954. Tsvetaeva's admiring fan letter to Don Aminado is included among her letters in L.

The letters to Vera Bunina are included in NP.

Tsvetaeva's relationship with Nikolai Gronsky is documented in her letters to Tesková and Ivask. Her essays about him are in IP. The complete correspondence between Tsvetaeva and Gronsky has been deposited by Ariadna Efron at the Central State Archive of Literature and Art, Moscow. Excerpts from a letter to Gronsky are included in L.

Tsvetaeva described her work on 'Perekop' in great detail in the interview she gave to Nadezhda Gorodetskaya, which appeared in *Renascence*

on March 7, 1931 under the title 'A Visit with Marina Tsvetaeva' ('V
gostiakh u Mariny Tsvetaevoi'). Her failure to publish this poem is traced in
her correspondence with Halpern, Tesková and Lomonosova.

Poems from *The Demesne of the Swans* appeared in *The Latest News* on
October 25, November 1 and November 8, 1928.

Tsvetaeva's encounters with Mayakovsky in the fall of 1928 are docu-
mented in Vasily Katanian, *Mayakovsky. A Literary Chronicle* (*Maia-
kovskii. Literaturnaia khronika*), Moscow, 1961; Viktoria Schweitzer,
'Mayakovsky and Tsvetaeva' ('Maiakovskii i Tsvetaeva'), *Prostor*, Alma
Ata, 1966, No. 8; and Anna Saakiants, 'Vladimir Mayakovsky and Marina
Tsvetaeva' ('Vladimir Maiakovskii i Marina Tsvetaeva'), *Moskva*,
Moscow, 1982, No. 10.

Mayakovsky's blast at Tsvetaeva at the Congress of Proletarian Writers
is to be found in vol. 12 of his complete collected works (*Polnoe sobranie
sochinenii*, Moscow, 1959).

On the infiltration of the Eurasian movement by the GPU: Roman Goul,
'I Took Russia with Me' ('Ia unes Rossiiu'), *The New Review* (*Novyi
zhurnal*), New York, 1979, No. 136.

Vladimir Varshavsky, *Expectation* (*Ozhidanie*), Paris, 1972.

Salomea Halpern's sketch of Sergei Efron is from her letter to Gleb
Struve, cited in his publication of Tsvetaeva's letters to her.

Of the sizeable literature on the period of collectivization, the most
detailed and compact source is Geller and Nekrich *Utopia in Power*
(*Utopiia u vlasti*), vol. 1, chapter 5. An unforgettable fictional reflection is
Andrei Platonov's novel *The Foundation Pit*, an excellent English translation of which was published by Mirra Ginsburg in 1975.

A recent account, based on official Soviet figures, of the loss of life during
the collectivization is Steven Rosefielde, 'Excess Collectivization Deaths
1929–1933: New Demographic Evidence,' *Slavic Review*, Stanford, Spring
1984, vol. 43, No. 1.

The wave of uncritical admiration for the Soviet system among the
Western intellectuals which began to gather momentum precisely at the
time of collectivization has been examined most recently by Paul Hollan-
der, *Political Pilgrims*, New York, 1981. The American context of this
phenomenon was ably documented by Daniel Aaron, *Writers on the Left*,
New York, 1969 and 1977.

Vikenty Veresaev's compilation of Pushkin materials which Tsvetaeva
read was *Pushkin in Life* (*Pushkin v zhizni*), Moscow–Leningrad, 1927.

CHAPTER 9: THE LAST TEN YEARS IN PARIS

The cited letter to Bronislav (or Vladimir) Sosinsky is in NP.

The cited dissertation of Ieva Vitins is *Escape from Earth: A Study of the
Four Elements and Their Associations in Marina Tsvetaeva's Work*, University of California, Berkeley, 1974.

On Mark Slonim's memoir of Tsvetaeva, see sources for Chapter 6.

Elena Izvolskaya's two memoirs about Tsvetaeva are 'A Shadow on the Walls' ('Ten' na stenakh') in *Experiments (Opyty)*, New York, 1954, No. 3; and 'The Poet of Doom' ('Poèt obrechennosti') in *Aerial Ways (Vozdushnye puti)*, New York, 1963, No. 3.

Levinson's obituary of Mayakovsky: André Levinson, 'La poésie chez les Soviets: le suicide de Maiakovsky', *Les Nouvelles littéraires*, Paris, May 31, 1930. The protest against this obituary appeared in the same newspaper on June 14 and the counter-protest on July 12. The affair is documented and summarized in Vasily Katanian's chronicle of Mayakovsky's life cited under Chapter 8. The most detailed account and citations of Tsvetaeva's 'To Mayakovsky' to have appeared in the Soviet Union so far are in the essay on Tsvetaeva and Mayakovsky by Anna Saakiants, cited under Chapter 8.

Tsvetaeva's statement to Pasternak about her prose is from a letter in NP.

Vsevolod Rozhdestvensky's preface appears in S1. Nikita Struve has emphasized Tsvetaeva's alleged deficiency in Christian faith as the key to the tragedy of her life in his annotations to her letters to Rozanov in NP; in his essay 'Tragic Disbelief' ('Tragicheskoe neverie'), *Vestnik (Le Messager)*, 1981, No. 135; and in a paper he read at the Tsvetaeva Symposium in Lausanne in June 1982.

Irma Kudrova's statement on Mur is from her essay 'Six Months in Paris,' cited under Chapter 7.

Dmitry Sezeman's statements about Tsvetaeva and her son, here and in the next chapter, were made during a personal interview in Paris on May 15, 1984. Tsvetaeva described her upbringing of Mur in her letters to Kolbasina-Chernova, Tesková, Halpern and Lomonosova.

The participants in 'An Evening of Romanticism' are listed by Vadim Morkovin in the annotations to his edition of the letters to Tesková on the basis of announcements in the press. A portion of Tsvetaeva's grateful letter to Teffi is in L. Her letter to Adamovich is in NP.

On Tsvetaeva's relationship with Khodasevich in the 1920s and 1930s, my introductory note to her letters to Khodasevich, *The New Review (Novyi zhurnal)*, New York, 1967, No. 87; and David M. Bethea, *Khodasevich. His Life and Art*, Princeton, 1983. Tsvetaeva's letters to Khodasevich are to be found in the edition of *The New Review* just mentioned and in L.

Tsvetaeva's appearance at the reading organized by *Numbers (Chisla): The Latest News (Poslednie novosti)*, March 16, 1933 and *Numbers*, Paris, 1933, No. 9.

Tsvetaeva's opinion of Nabokov's story is in her letter to Steiger of July 29, 1936; her view of Aldanov is in her letter to Gronsky in L; her version of Poplavsky's suicide is in an unpublished letter to Steiger.

An English translation of Tsvetaeva's letter to Tesková about Bunin's Nobel Prize is included in the collection *The Bitter Air of Exile*, cited under Chapters 6 and 7 in connection with 'The Swain' and 'A Poet on Criticism,' respectively.

Her French literary contacts are discussed by Tsvetaeva in her letters to Tesková, Halpern and Lomonosova. A letter to Charles Vildrac is included (in Russian translation) in L. The English translation of 'The Swain' and the plans for its publication are mentioned in the letters to Lomonosova.

On Tsvetaeva's participation in the Franco-Russian discussions organized by the *Cahiers de la quinzaine*, the following volumes of that journal: 'Rencontres,' 1930, 'Marcel Proust,' 1930, and 'Paul Valéry,' 1931.

On Natalie Clifford Barney, her entourage and her salon, Jean Chalon, *Portrait d'une séductrice*, Paris, 1976 and George Wickes, *The Amazon of Letters*, London, 1977. On the possible contacts between Barney and Tsvetaeva and the connection of the text of 'Letter to an Amazon' to Barney's book, Serena Vitale, 'Su tracce a rittroso' in Marina Cvetaeva, *Lettera all'Amazzone*, Milan, 1981. The French and Italian texts of 'Letter to an Amazon' are also included in Vitale's edition of 'Florentine Nights' (*Le notti fiorentine*, Milan, 1983).

An earlier French edition of 'Letter to an Amazon' (Paris, 1979), annotated by Ghislaine Limont, is deficient from the scholarly point of view and was saddled by the publisher with a wholly arbitrary title which is not Tsvetaeva's, *Mon frère féminin*. Possible parallels between the text of 'Letter to an Amazon' and Tsvetaeva's concrete experiences with Sophia Parnok have been examined by Sophia Poliakova in her book about Tsvetaeva and Parnok.

On Elena Izvolskaya's role in arranging Tsvetaeva's reading at Natalie Clifford Barney's salon, Helene Iswolsky, *No Time to Grieve ...*, Philadelphia, 1985 (the description of the reading is on p. 199). The book is an edition of Izvolskaya's unfinished autobiography, published by her American friends to commemorate the tenth anniversary of her death. Many of the facts about Russian literary figures in exile and many of the Russian names appear in the book in garbled form (Georgy and Elena Fedotov appear under the name 'Fedorov' throughout). The author's account of the return of Tsvetaeva and of her family to the Soviet Union is based entirely on the erroneous account in my 1966 book. On Izvolskaya's role in the ecumenical movement, see the special memorial edition of *The Third Hour*, New York, 1976, with contributions by, *inter alios*, V. S. Yanovsky, Anne Fremantle, W. H. Auden, Jacques Maritain and Dorothy Day.

The letter to Salomea Halpern of August 12, 1932 was reproduced in its entirety in Gleb Struve's publication of Tsvetaeva's letters to Halpern. In an earlier publication of this letter in *A Day of Poetry (Den' poèzii)*, Moscow, 1980, a passage was omitted in which Tsvetaeva wrote of her desire, after waking up, to bury herself in her addressee's body so as to 'hide from the day, the age, the light, from your eyes and from my own, no less merciless,' after confessing what she had dreamed.

Tsvetaeva's letters to the Fedotovs were published in *The New Review (Novyi zhurnal)*, New York, 1961, No. 63.

Salomea Halpern's statement about Tsvetaeva's financial situation in

1934 is quoted by Gleb Struve in his publication of Tsvetaeva's letters to Halpern.

Kirill Henkin's statement is quoted from his book *The Upside-Down Hunter (Okhotnik vverkh nogami)*, Frankfurt/Main, ca. 1980. Although the book is about the master spy Rudolf Abel, its autobiographical portions contain a great deal about Tsvetaeva, Efron and their children. Kirill Henkin is the son of the well-known popular singer Victor Henkin. His mother, Elizaveta, is mentioned in Tsvetaeva's letters to Lomonosova as one of her dearest friends. The two families were neighbours for many years and in his early youth, Kirill Henkin was a playmate of Ariadna Efron, whom he later saw in Moscow in the 1960s. According to Henkin, Konstantin Rodzevich also became a Soviet agent in the 1930s.

On the 1935 Paris 'Congress of Writers in Defense of Culture,' David Pike, *German Writers in Soviet Exile, 1933–1945*, Chapel Hill, 1982, the chapter 'The Literary United Front.' On Pasternak's activities at the congress and his encounters with Tsvetaeva in Paris, Chapter 7 from Lazar Fleishman's book *Pasternak in the Thirties (Pasternak v tridtsatye gody*, Jerusalem, 1984). I am extremely grateful to Professor Fleishman for providing me with an advance copy of this chapter and the annotations for it which cite a wide array of literature on the subject. Tsvetaeva's letter to Nikolai Tikhonov, with an account of her conversations with Pasternak, was published by Serafima Polianina in WSA.

On Tsvetaeva's correspondence with Anatoly Steiger, the somewhat reticent essay by his friend Kirill Vilchkovsky in *Experiments (Opyty)*, New York, 1955, No. 5. The essay, 'Marina Tsvetaeva's Correspondence with Anatoly Steiger' ('Perepiska Mariny Tsvetaevoi s Anatoliem Shteigerom') is intended as an introduction to Tsvetaeva's letters that follow.

Vladislav Khodasevich's evaluation of 'My Mother and Music' appeared in *Renascence (Vozrozhdenie)* on April 4, 1935 and that of 'A Captive Spirit' in the same paper on May 31, 1934.

On the chronic complaints of émigré writers that they are neglected or excluded by journals and publishers, Mark Vishniak's memoirs, already cited under Chapters 4 and 7. Alexei Remizov, at the end of the bibliography of his works appended to his book *The Circle of Happiness (Krug schast'ia)*, Paris, 1957, claims that no one published him between 1931 and 1949. While it is true that no individual books by Remizov appeared during the period he mentions, his shorter works and sections from longer ones appeared in journals, including the *Contemporary Annals*. Gippius in her letters to Khodasevich, cited under Chapter 7, wrote that she was excluded from most émigré periodicals. The complaints of Vladimir Varshavsky and V. S. Yanovsky are registered in their memoirs, *The Unnoticed Generation* and *The Elysian Fields (Polia Eliseiskie*, New York, 1983), respectively.

Tsvetaeva's letters to Vadim Rudnev, dealing mostly with editorial matters, were published by Ghislaine Limont in *The New Review (Novyi zhurnal)*, 1978, No. 133. The mentioned editorial deletions in Nabokov's novel and Chizhevsky's essay are documented, *inter alia*, in Mark Vishniak's memoirs.

On Ariadna Efron's return to the Soviet Union, Tsvetaeva's letters to Tesková is one of the primary sources, though this departure is also evoked in some other letters, e.g., those to Bunina and Khodasevich. On what went on in the Soviet Union at the time of her return, Robert Conquest, *The Great Terror*, London, 1968.

On Sergei Efron's involvement in the murder of Reiss-Poretsky and other terrorist activities, there is a considerable literature, most of which does not state that he was married to Tsvetaeva. Among the basic sources are Victor Serge, Alfred Rosmer and Maurice Wullens, *L'Assassinat politique et l'U.R.S.S.*, Paris, 1938; Elisabeth K. Poretsky, *Our Own People*, London, 1969; Walter Krivitsky, *In Stalin's Secret Service*, New York, 1939; and Kirill Henkin's book mentioned above. The reporting of the situation in the Russian émigré press is summarized at the end of Chapter 4 of my book *Marina Cvetaeva. Her Life and Art*. The coverage in the Swiss press is traced in Chapter 26 of both the German and the Russian versions of Maria Razumovsky's biography. The phrase 'was ready to swear that [Sergei] could not be involved in the bloody affair' is quoted from Elena Fedotova's introduction to her publication of Tsvetaeva's letters to the Fedotovs.

Vladimir Markov's remark is quoted from his 'Marginal Notes' ('Zametki na poliakh'), *Experiments (Opyty)*, New York, 1956, No. 6.

On ostracism of Tsvetaeva after the exposure in the press of Efron's activities, Nina Berberova, *The Italics Are Mine*; Yury Terapiano, 'Marina Tsvetaeva's Prose' ('Proza Mariny Tsvetaevoi'), *The New Russian Word (Novoe russkoe slovo)*, New York, March 7, 1954; V. S. Yanovsky, *The Elysian Fields*.

Alexei Remizov's words about his dislike of Tsvetaeva are from his unpublished diaries for 1937-9, an excerpt from which was kindly communicated to me by Greta Slobin. Ivan Bunin's words are from his letter to Maria Karamzina of March 29, 1939, which was published in the Bunin issue of *Literary Heritage (Literaturnoe nasledstvo)*, Moscow, 1973, vol. 1. In his later book *Memoirs (Vospominaniia)*, Paris, 1950, Bunin wrote of Tsvetaeva with utter contempt.

Aleksis Rannit's information about Tsvetaeva's closeness with Vladimir Smolensky in March of 1938 (when Rannit spent some time in Paris in the company of both Tsvetaeva and Smolensky): personal conversation in Jerusalem on May 26, 1984 and letter to me of July 7, 1984. Smolensky, like Tsvetaeva, was a rare instance of a poet of stature who made eulogizing the monarchist White Army a major theme in his poetry.

CHAPTER 10: MOSCOW, ELABUGA AND AFTER

The epigraph is from Tsvetaeva's letter to Roman Goul of May 5, 1923. The book she mentions is her unrealized *Omens of the Earth*.

Russian cultural activities in Paris in the spring of 1938 are cited from the reports in *Poslednie novosti*, especially the issues of April 2 and May 10.

Tsvetaeva's stipend from the Soviet consulate in Paris and numerous details about her life after her return to the Soviet Union are found in Viktoria Schweitzer, 'The Homecoming' ('Vozvrashchenie domoi'), *Sintaksis*, Paris, 1983, No. 11. This essay was originally a paper read at the Tsvetaeva Symposium in Lausanne in 1982.

Tsvetaeva's marginal note to 'October Revolution in a Railroad Car' is reproduced in Robin Kemball's translation of *The Demesne of the Swans*, Ann Arbor, 1980.

Yury Terapiano's account is from his article 'Proza Mariny Tsvetaevoi,' cited under Chapter 9. Tsvetaeva's friendship with Prince Yury Shirinsky-Shikhmatov and his wife Yevgenia, the widow of the terrorist Boris Savinkov, is described in V. S. Yanovsky's memoir *The Elysian Fields*.

The figure of eight millions in prisons and concentration camps is from Geller and Nekrich, vol. 2, Chapter 7.

The sources on Tsvetaeva's life in Bolshevo, Golitsyno and Moscow prior to her evacuation are her journal for 1940, printed in a defective transcription in NP and in a corrected version in SiP 3; her letters of 1940 and 1941 in NP; Dmitry Sezeman, 'M. Tsvetaeva in Moscow' ('M. Tsvetaeva v Moskve') and Tsvetaeva's letters to Ivan Moskvin, Tatiana Kvanina and Victor Goltsev, all in *Vestnik*, 1979, No. 128.

Georgy Efron's ceaseless complaints about having been brought to the Soviet Union are reported by Dmitry Sezeman and Kirill Henkin.

The fate of Ariadna Efron: annotations to the fragment from her memoirs in *Vestnik*, 1975, No. 116 and to her book *Letters from Exile* (*Pis'ma iz ssylki, 1948–1957*), Paris, 1982. Also, personal statement by Dmitry Sezeman.

The end of Sergei Efron: Véronique Lossky, 'Souvenirs de contemporains' in WSA and Kirill Henkin's book.

On Tsvetaeva's plans for publishing a volume of verse in the Soviet Union in 1940, Viktoria Schweitzer, 'About the 1940 Collection' ('O sbornike 1940-go goda'), in SiP 3. Kornely Zelinsky's evaluation of Tsvetaeva is cited from this source.

There is a considerable literature on the encounter of Tsvetaeva with Anna Akhmatova in Moscow. Viktor Ardov, 'Anna Akhmatova's Encounter with Marina Tsvetaeva' ('Vstrecha Anny Akhmatovoi s Marinoi Tsvetaevoi'), *Grani*, Frankfurt-am-Main, 1970, No. 76 and Amanda Haight, 'Anna Akhmatova and Marina Tsvetaeva,' *The Slavonic and East European Review*, London, October 1972, vol. 50, say that the meeting took place in 1940 (Amanda Haight cited that year on the basis of her conversations with Akhmatova). But more recent sources state that the year was 1941 and that the meeting took place shortly before Tsvetaeva's evacuation to Elabuga. E.g., Natalia Il'ina's memoir of Akhmatova in *Zvezda*, Leningrad, 1977, No. 2 and Lydia Chukovskaya, *Notes on Anna Akhmatova* (*Zapiski ob Anne Akhmatovoi*), Paris, 1980, vol. 2.

Tatiana Kvanina's memoir about her friendship with Tsvetaeva: 'How It

Was' ('Tak bylo'), *Oktiabr'*, Moscow, 1982, No. 9.

Tsvetaeva's letter to her daughter of April 12, 1941 is in NP.

On Aleksei Kruchionykh and Tsvetaeva's manuscripts, Viktoria Schweitzer's annotations to a letter from Tsvetaeva to Boris Pasternak in *Vestnik*, 1979, No. 128 and her notes to *Juvenilia* in SiP 1.

The photograph of Tsvetaeva, Mur, Kruchionykh and Libedinskaya is reproduced in NP and *Tsvetaeva. A Pictorial Biography*, edited by Ellendea Proffer.

The circumstances of Tsvetaeva's evacuation from Moscow: Olga Ivinskaya, *The Captive of Time* (*V plenu u vremeni*), Paris, 1978.

Tsvetaeva's stay in Elabuga: the 1960 report of the Writers' Union Committee on commemorating Tsvetaeva and Viktoria Schweitzer, 'A Trip to Elabuga' ('Poezdka v Elabugu'), both reprinted in NP.

Lydia Chukovskaya's cited memoir, 'At Death's Threshold' is reprinted in SiP 3. A facsimile of Tsvetaeva's application for the job as a dishwasher is reproduced in the text.

Viktoria Schweitzer's objections to Anastasia Tsvetaeva's version of her sister's death and her debunking of Stanislav Gribanov's articles on Georgy Efron are in her 'An Open Letter to Anastasia Tsvetaeva,' already cited under Chapter 1.

Boris Pasternak's letter to his wife of November 10, 1941 is in *Vestnik*, 1972, No. 106. His letter to Nina Tabidze about Tsvetaeva was published in *Literaturnaia Gruziia*, Tbilisi, 1966, No. 1.

O. Anisimov's essay on Tsvetaeva is reprinted in WSA. Alexander Bakhrakh's obituary was published in *Russkii sbornik*, Paris, 1946. It was called 'A Cloudburst of Sound' ('Zvukovoi liven'') in imitation of Tsvetaeva's essay on Pasternak, 'A Cloudburst of Light.'

The circumstances of Anastasia Tsvetaeva's learning about her sister's death are described in AT, 1983.

Georgy Fedotov's statement is quoted from his essay 'On Parisian Poetry' ('O Parizhskoi poèzii') in *Kovcheg*, New York, 1942. Ivan Tkhorzhevsky's statement is from his *Russian Literature* (*Russkaia literatura*), Paris 1946 and 1950.

On the Zhdanov period, Gleb Struve, *Russian Literature Under Lenin and Stalin, 1917–1953*.

Ariadna Efron's reaction to the death of Samuil Gurevich is in her book *Letters from Exile*.

Ekaterina Eleneva's correspondence with Vladimir and Vera Nabokov and Feodor Stepun, from the archive of the late Mrs Eleneva, was kindly communicated to me by Mark Altshuller. The Nabokov letters are cited with the kind permission of Mrs Nabokov. Ariadna Efron's comments on my 1966 book and on the publication of Tsvetaeva materials by Gleb Struve and Vadim Morkovin are from her letters to Eleneva. Her objections to my book were also expressed in a letter to Mouna Bulgakova, cited in Lev Mnukhin's montage (see item 3 under 'Memoirs by Relatives' at the beginning of this appendix).

In the 1920s, Vladimir Nabokov wrote of Tsvetaeva with a certain condescension. In his *Conclusive Evidence*, New York, 1951, later published as *Speak, Memory*, he called her 'a poet of genius.'

On Ariadna Efron's disposal of Tsvetaeva's archive: E. B. Korkina, 'On Marina Tsvetaeva's Archive' ('Ob arkhive Mariny Tsvetaevoi'), *Vstrechi s proshlym*, Moscow, 1982, vol. 4. Korkina reveals that the articles on Georgy Efron in the journals *Rodina*, 1975, No. 3, signed S. Gribanov, and in *Neman*, 1976, No. 8, signed S. Vikentiev, were both written by Stanislav Gribanov.

Examples of ultra-conventional Tsvetaeva criticism by a Soviet scholar are quoted from K. A. Medvedeva's essay on mythological themes in Tsvetaeva which appears in a volume published by the State University of the Far East, *Certain Problems of Russian and Foreign Literature* (*Nekotorye problemy russkoi i zarubezhnoi literatury*), E. Dement'ev, ed., Vladivostok, 1974. I am grateful to Ieva Vitins for procuring for me a copy of this text.

Index